MW00989390

ALSO BY ROBERT HARTWELL FISKE

The Dictionary of Concise Writing

The Dimwit's Dictionary

The Best Words

Robert Hartwell Fiske's Dictionary of Unendurable English

A COMPENDIUM OF MISTAKES IN GRAMMAR, USAGE, AND SPELLING

WITH COMMENTARY ON LEXICOGRAPHERS AND LINGUISTS

Scribner

NEW YORK LONDON TORONTO SYDNEY NEW DELHI

SCRIBNER
A Division of Simon & Schuster, Inc.
1230 Avenue of the Americas
New York, NY 10020

Robert Hartwell Fiske's Dictionary of Unendurable English was previously published as *The Dictionary of Disagreeable English* (Writer's Digest Books, 2004) and has been updated, revised, enlarged, and redesigned.

First Scribner edition November 2011

Manufactured in the United States of America

1 3 5 7 9 10 8 6 4 2

ISBN 978-1-4516-5131-7
ISBN 978-1-4516-5132-4 (pbk)
ISBN 978-1-4516-5134-8 (ebook)

Contents

First Foreword

by John Simon

There used to be various ways of telling whether a person was of discriminating taste, good breeding, refined sensibility. You could recognize gentility by clothes, hairdos, table manners; by the sports, films, and foods someone preferred. Regrettably, our great democratic society, so worthy and desirable in many ways, has become such a leveler that most of these fine distinctions have been eroded, as if giving your bus seat to someone older, wearing a necktie, covering your mouth when yawning or sneezing, and speaking and writing correctly were signs of snobbish, undemocratic elitism. Being well groomed, well dressed, and well behaved have become obsolete, if not indeed politically incorrect.

Yet do we not want to distinguish ourselves, make good impressions, rise above the lowest common denominator? Is there no form of excellence left untarnished, unridiculed, unremembered—or, conversely, available to any boor who can afford designer clothes, four-star restaurants, or a trophy wife? One sure way remains for fastidiousness to shine forth without undue ostentation in the most ordinary, everyday situations; it is, you may have guessed it, language.

No damsel was ever in more distress, no dray horse more flogged, no defenseless child more drunkenly abused than the English language today. And do not assume that it is attacked only from below, by what used to be called the great unwashed when looking washed was still held to be desirable. Given the sorry state of our education, the catastrophic neglect of book reading on all social levels, and the overwhelming indifference to all but material advancement and worldly success, no wonder that language gets it in the groin from all sides, not least from above. "Above" includes a variety of evils, from individuals who attended the best of schools and, whether through their own or their teachers' fault, learned nothing, to professional linguists of the descriptive or permissive persuasion, who find it more popular and remunerative to accept every change, however dumbing down and obfuscatory, they can lay their tape recorders on. Indeed, by endorsing it, they prove themselves edgy, with it, democratic, rather than courting unpopularity by being thought snobbish, pedantic, or, perish the thought, academic. As if many academics weren't the first to embrace mindless trendiness.

The fallacious but crowd-pleasing argument is that it is the people who use it that make a language, not the wizened fuddy-duddies who desperately cling to antiquated niceties such as holding a door open for a lady, crossing the street on a green light, and knowing the difference between "between you and I" and "between you and me." It is not just a matter of convention and prudence; it is an aesthetic and moral choice. Rules of correctness are not some highbrow conspiracy; they strengthen the social fabric by making social intercourse more gracious, more efficient, and more satisfying.

Dictionaries, usually compiled by permissivists—which is to say copycats, cynics, lickspittles, or opportunists—are, by and large, no longer reliable guides, even when they aren't downright ignorant, as the *Dictionary of Unendurable English* shows them to be. There is no evidence that Robert Hartwell Fiske is against reasonable change, that he hangs on by his fingernails to keep himself from falling into a split infinitive. But he adheres admirably to rules that are practical, that facilitate understanding through logic and lucidity, or even just by a sense of decorum that make speech more communicative and writing more elegant. Most people will understand from the context that you meant "imply" even though you barbarously said "infer." Multitudes, but not Mr. Fiske, will stand by, ignorant and unshuddering, when newscasters and celebrities, preachers and politicians, say "People were laying in the streets," and will comprehend, as Mr. Fiske will, too, that a mass orgy is not what was meant. But isn't there something deeply satisfying, to speaker and hearer alike, when a person uses "prone" or "comprise" correctly, when a judge is said to be "disinterested" rather than "uninterested" when being scrupulously fair. After all, in the world we live in, judges have been known to be bored or even bribed.

Sad to say, some of our very best language authorities make undue concessions. The excellent Geoffrey Nunberg was willing, as long ago as 1983 in the *Atlantic Monthly,* to give up fighting for "disinterested" as a lost cause; the no less excellent Bryan Garner, in his very useful *Garner's Modern American Usage,* grimly concedes that "the battle over [using "hopefully" correctly] is now over." It is not over, should not be over, and I admire—indeed, love—Mr. Fiske for making no such concession but throwing down the gauntlet (not gantlet) to anyone who jumps on this defective bandwagon.

Rules may be there, as some say, to be broken. Sure, if anything is gained thereby. But what if not? The time may be at hand when picking your nose in church, breaking wind at the dinner table, and talking during a concert will be accepted and universally practiced. What enormousness (not enormity) of loss that will be. Even if nobody is there to hear you—let alone correct you—when you say "more preferable," or "flout" for "flaunt," is there no satisfaction to yourself in knowing better? Is it not preferable to be on the side of the angels even if angels do not exist? But unlike angels, people who know better do exist, and would you not want to share their wisdom, partake of their esteem, and, who knows, perhaps even earn a better job on account of it?

John Simon was the theater and film critic at *New York* magazine for thirty-six years. He now reviews theater for Bloomberg News. He is the author of several books on theater, film, language, literature, and poetry.

Second Foreword

by Clark Elder Morrow

The message that Robert Hartwell Fiske brings to us in his *Dictionary of Unendurable English* is needed more now than ever. I say that because I see (among other horrors) that the once mighty *Oxford English Dictionary* continues its slide into stark irrelevancy. The OED just released its addendum of words for the March 2011 *OED Online,* and some of these entries are not even words. Old James Murray's labor of love deems it advisable to continue adding acronyms to its once-fabled wordhoard, and—not content with that (and feeling a little old-fogeyish about limiting its collection to mere words and initialisms)—pops in *symbols* as well. That's right: the once-august and once-respected tsar of all dictionaries has opted to include in its pages the heart symbol, ♥, as one definition under the entry for *love.* The OED mandarins of modernity boast that this may very well be the first time an entry has derived its origin from "T-shirts and bumper stickers." They must be very proud. What do *they* care if they've just helped precipitate the Apocalypse of St. John?

So it is now undeniable that there is no phrase, no adjectival compound, no tattoo symbol, no random smudge on a page or a pair of pants anywhere in the world, that the editors of the OED will not enshrine in its pages—electronic and otherwise. It does not matter how far the term in question may lay from mainstream usage—it doesn't matter how completely unheard-of the word or mark or scrawl may be—it matters not how asinine or silly or childish or contemptible the pictogram or smear may be—it matters only that some sort of consensus emerges among the geeky gurus of the OED as to its inclusion, and the mark or scratching or happy face is hallowed forever in some hidden corner of the estimable tome. This is exactly the sort of thing that Mr. Fiske has been combating throughout his admirable career.

LOL and *OMG* are included now, of course. Not words, you say? Doesn't matter: any burp, any eructation, any sound-producing escape of noxious fumes from a human being, any slathering or dribbling of ink on a surface capable of retaining it, any semidecipherable expression or attempt at communication by any higher primate anywhere in our solar system is legitimate fodder for this blob of a book, which grows with constant feeding on anything in its path. Eventually there will be no beep emitted from a machine or electronic device on the face of the planet, or any human body noise, that will not be transcribed and then inscribed somewhere in the OED, and—when that point is reached—the book will have lost 100 percent of its value as a dictionary. The more illiterate detritus included in a dictionary, the more useless it becomes as a dictionary, just as the more ballast a submarine takes on, the more it sinks under its own bloated and brainless weight, until it becomes useless as a submarine.

For God knows what reason, the cluster *tinfoil-hat-wearing* is now an entry. Slang is always irresistible to the dying-to-be-cool nerdniks at the OED, so we are treated to *muffin top* and *tragic* (Australian slang for a "boring or socially inept person, esp. one with an obsessive interest or hobby") and "*cream-crackered,* adj. (rhyming slang for 'knackered,' that is exhuasted [*sic*])." Nothing, you will notice, is off-limits. You think I'm kidding? Consider this: now carved into the stone of the OED monument, forever and forever, world without end, is the term *fnarr fnarr*. What does it mean, and why is it in the *Oxford English Dictionary* and not on the Urban Dictionary website? Well, apparently *fnarr fnarr* is a "representation of a lecherous snigger popularized in the comic magazine *Viz* and used adjectivally to denote crude sexual innuendo." Well! Chalk up another victory for scholarship against the dim tide of grunting savagery. Wait—*fnarr fnarr* is a sort of grunting, isn't it? A snigger, a grunt, a sneeze, a metric unit of flatulence—it all doesn't matter: some smartphone-toting *homo superbus* was reading a comic book in a coffee dive somewhere, and saw this self-repeating term, and decided it just *had* to be enrolled among the words that made English the lingua franca of the world.

And while the OED is at it, why should it restrict itself (and its endless quest for hipness) to mere two-word phrases? If the Watchdog of the World's Greatest Language is going to include in its pages phrases such as *happy camper* and *bogus caller* and *suicide door,* then why shouldn't it also include popular catchphrases and shibboleths and pop-monologues and trendy comedy routines? Remember: the sky's the limit, nothing's *off-limits,* and any restriction on lexicographical inclusivity would constitute crusty prescriptivism. So why not throw open the doors of the musty old museum and throw in any combination of words that strikes you as indicative of the present linguistic milieu? The goal here, after all, is to depict the blabosphere as completely as possible, and to catch the current gab in all its vibrancy, rules be damned. If that's the case (and I see nothing in the utterances of the OED priests to indicate otherwise), then there is nothing to keep the Grand Old Lady of Lexicons from printing whole sketches from *Seinfeld* (a favorite OED source), and stretches of dialogue from the *Hangover* movies.

Fifty years from now, people will stare at many entries in this dictionary and wonder what the editors were thinking. Why (they will ask themselves) did the presumably educated hierophants of the OED put *wassup* in their book? If the purpose is 100 percent inclusiveness—a desire to write down and publish every possible combination of letters (and now symbols) possessing any shred of meaning for any conceivable human being—then the foolishness of the purpose undermines the entire mission. If the purpose is to create a tony handbook of cool remarks and swank semiotics, together with all the old boring words that have always been in dictionaries, then—once again—the folly of the purpose defeats its own aspirations. How ephemeral do you suppose most of the terms in the online Urban Dictionary will prove to be? Or, to put it another way, how long do you think any of those words and phrases will last? Does the OED really want to produce a fifty-volume set (and it will be fifty volumes if it continues its mad lust for passing verbal hiccups), the vast majority of whose terms will have to be marked *Obs.* in a relatively brief time?

Many of the words added to the March 2011 version of *OED Online* are wholly appropriate for inclusion—which is to say, they are actual words, and not mumblings or sneers or kindergarten ideograms. But it is far from certain that definition-seekers will be thumbing through these venerable pages for an authoritative pronouncement on the meaning of *la-la land.* Who needs one? It's the kind of term that will bear just about any construction put on it, and if you think someone's understanding of it is wrong, the reduplicative word-mutation will elude your (and the OED's) description of it. It's significant that the *American Heritage Dictionary* and Dictionary.com have definitions of this term that are completely at variance with each other (one says it's a place, the other says it's a state of mind). La-la land is some slimy radiation-bombarded hybrid from a 1950s sci-fi film, amorphous and mercurial, and bent on ravaging the foundations of a long-respected title.

If you believe a dictionary should stoop so low as to conquer so ignobly, and with so much loss of authority, then ponder this: any reference work that is so flexible and complaisant that it will take seriously any presumptuous monosyllable, can hardly be trusted when rigor is required for definitions and historical data. Why should the OED set the bar so low for including new words, but set it high for philological scholarship? The inclusion of a heart symbol in the OED renders the entire enterprise suspect, in my view, and *wassup* and *LOL* nestling in its pages mean that I will continue to turn (for all my lexical explanations) to the 1913 edition of Noah Webster's masterpiece. I'm not likely to find T-shirt slogans *there,* thank God. Nor will you be counseled to use bumper-sticker nonsense in the pages of the soon-to-be-classic work you hold in your hands. Now more than ever, Robert Hartwell Fiske's oasis of lexical sanity is a cool and shady place to relax in—especially when the outside world is loud with bellowing, slobbering megalizards of incoherence. The *Dictionary of Unendurable English* will serve as a sort of field guide to a good number of those beasts.

Clark Elder Morrow is a columnist for *The Vocabula Review.*

Robert Hartwell Fiske's Dictionary of Unendurable English

Prologue

Part 1: The Decline of the Dictionary

You're much too much, and just too "very, very"
To ever be in Webster's Dictionary.

Laxicographers All

The slang-filled eleventh edition of "America's Best-Selling Dictionary," *Merriam-Webster's Collegiate Dictionary* (Frederick C. Mish, editor in chief), does as much as, if not more than, the famously derided *Webster's Third International Dictionary* to discourage people from taking lexicographers seriously. "Laxicographers" all, the Merriam-Webster staff reminds us that dictionaries merely record how people use the language, not how it ought to be used. Some dictionaries, and certainly this new Merriam-Webster, actually promote illiteracy.

Some years ago, the editors of the *American Heritage Dictionary* ("America's Favorite Dictionary") caused a stir by deciding to include four-letter words in their product. Since the marketing strategy of including swear words has now been adopted by all dictionary makers, Merriam-Webster, apparently not knowing how else to distinguish its dictionary from competing ones, has decided to include a spate of slang words in its eleventh edition. There's nothing wrong with Merriam-Webster's distinguishing its product, of course, but when doing so means tampering with the English language—by including idiotic slang and apparently omitting more useful words—it's reprehensible.

Merriam-Webster proclaims it has added some ten thousand words to its *Collegiate Dictionary* (though there is some reason to question the staff's ability to count well; see note 7). To do so, as a company spokesman admitted, "some words had to be kicked out" of the earlier edition. More interesting than this new edition would be a book of the words abandoned. Were they sesquipedalian words that few people use or know the meaning of; *disyllabic* words that few people use or know the meaning of? It's quite true: people are increasingly monosyllabic; after all, many people today prefer *dis* (included in the *Collegiate* tenth and eleventh) to *disparage* or *disrespect* or *insult.* And now in the eleventh, there is also the equally preposterous *def,* another word, Merriam-Webster assures us, for *excellent* or *cool* (which among many younger people today is also spelled *kool* and *kewl,* and though both words may have as much—or as little—currency as *def,* neither, curiously, was seen fit by Merriam-Webster to include in their compilation).

What word did Merriam-Webster decide to omit to make room for the all-important *def*? What word did they decide to omit to make room for *funplex* (an entertainment complex that includes facilities for various sports and games and often restaurants)? What word did they omit in order to add *McJob* (a low-paying job that requires little skill and provides little opportunity for advancement)? What words did they omit to add *headbanger* (a musician who performs hard rock), *dead presidents* (U.S. money in the form of bills), *phat* (highly attractive or gratifying), *foodie* (a person having an avid interest in the latest food fads), and *Frankenfood* (genetically engineered food)? Frankly, I rather like the coinage *Frankenfood.* But if people do not enjoy or feel comfortable eating genetically altered foods, which I suspect is likely, the word will be fleeting. Almost all slang, the people at Merriam-Webster should know, is ephemeral. Most of the slang added to the eleventh edition will never see the twelfth—or ought not to. Consider this paragraph from the Merriam-Webster website:

> Many new words pass out of English as quickly as they entered it, the fad of teenagers grown to adulthood, the buzzwords of the business meetings past, the cast-off argot of technologies superceded [*sic*], the catchy phrases from advertisements long forgotten. It is likely

> that many such ephemeral coinages will never be entered in dictionaries, especially abridged dictionaries where space (or time or money or all of the above) are at a premium. That does not mean, however, that the words did not exist, simply that they did not endure.[1]

Odd that Mish and his minions would then agree to the addition of so much slang to the eleventh edition. (Odder still, perhaps, that slang such as *far-out* and *groovy*, even though the popularity of these words has been much reduced over the years, are still entries in the *Collegiate*.[2]) But, as I say, it's a marketing strategy. It's not lexicography. These slang terms are not meant to improve the usefulness of their product; they're meant to help sell "America's Best-Selling Dictionary." Slang, Merriam-Webster believes, sells.

A Catalog of Confusions

Lexicographers are descriptivists, language liberals. The use of *disinterested* to mean *uninterested* does not displease a descriptivist. A prescriptivist, by contrast, is a language conservative, a person interested in maintaining standards and correctness in language use. To prescriptivists, *disinterested* in the sense of *uninterested* is the mark of people who do not know the distinction between the two words. And if there are enough people saying *disinterested* (and I'm afraid there are) when they mean *uninterested* or *indifferent*, lexicographers enter the definition into their dictionaries. Indeed, the distinction between these words has all but vanished owing largely to irresponsible writers, incompetent teachers, and boneless lexicographers.[3]

Words, we are told, with the most citations are included in the Merriam-Webster dictionaries. Are then words with the fewest omitted, or in danger of being omitted? *Merriam-Webster's Collegiate Dictionary*'s eleventh edition includes *alright,*[4] but what word was expelled so that an inanity, an illiteracy like *alright* could be kept in? *Boeotian* is not defined in *Merriam-Webster's*; nor is *diaskeuast*; nor *logogogue*; nor *nyctophobia*; nor *myriadigamous*; nor *ubiety*; nor *womanfully*;[5] nor hundreds of other words that a college student might find infinitely more useful than the entry, the misspelling and definition of, *alright*.

All it takes for a solecism to become standard English is people misusing or misspelling the word. And if enough people do so, lexicographers will enter the originally misused or misspelled word into their dictionaries, and descriptive linguists will embrace it as still another example of the evolution of English.

Merriam-Webster's laxicographers, further disaffecting careful writers and speakers, assign the meaning *reluctant* to the definition of *reticent. Reticent* means "disinclined to speak; taciturn; quiet." *Reluctant* means "disinclined to do something; unwilling; loath." Because some people mistakenly use *reticent* to mean *reluctant,* dictionaries now maintain *reticent* does mean *reluctant.* Dictionaries are complicit with other purveyors and vendors of mangled writing, muddled speech.

There are many other examples of Merriam-Webster's inexcusably shoddy dictionary making. For example, according to the dictionary's editors:

- *accidently* is as valid a spelling as *accidentally*
- *bemuse* means the same as *amuse*
- *enormity* means the same as *enormousness*
- *flaunt* means the same as *flout*
- *fortuitous* means the same as *fortunate*
- *get* is pronounced *GET* or *GIT*
- *hone in* means the same as *home in*
- *impactful* is an adjective of *impact*
- *incent* means *incentivize,* itself ungainly
- *infer* means the same as *imply*
- *less* means the same as *fewer*
- *mischievous* is pronounced *MIS-chi-ves* or *mis-CHEE-vee-es*
- *miniscule* is a variant spelling of *minuscule*
- *nuclear* is pronounced *NU-klee-er* or *NU-kya-ler*
- *peruse* means not only to examine carefully but also to read over in a casual manner
- *predominate,* a verb, is also an adjective meaning *predominant*
- *publically* is a variant spelling of *publicly*
- *replete* means the same as *complete*

- *sherbert* is as valid a spelling as *sherbet*
- *supercede* is a variant spelling of *supersede*
- *tho* is a variant spelling of *though*
- *transpire* means the same as *occur*
- *where* means *that*[6]

Merriam-Webster's Collegiate Dictionary, like other college dictionaries, actually promotes the misuse of the English language. Dictionaries are ever more a catalog of confusions, a list of illiteracies. Dictionaries acknowledge the errors that people make; by acknowledging them they, in effect, endorse them; by endorsing them, they are thought correct by a dull, duped public. Ultimately, all words will mean whatever we think they mean—indeed, whatever we want them to mean.

It's true that *Merriam-Webster's,* like other college dictionaries, does offer some usage notes,[7] but "usage notes" is a misnomer, for *Merriam-Webster's* are largely otiose. In virtually every instance, the editors at Merriam-Webster use these notes to underscore their descriptive bent and to rebut those who believe in maintaining standards of language use:

> **couple** The adjective use of *a couple,* without *of,* has been called nonstandard, but it is not.

> **enormity** *Enormity,* some people insist, is improperly used to denote large size. They insist on *enormousness* for this meaning, and would limit *enormity* to the meaning "great wickedness."

> **me** *Me* is used in many constructions where strict grammarians prescribe *I.* This usage is not so much ungrammatical as indicative of the shrinking range of the nominative form.

> **nuclear** Though disapproved of by many, pronunciations ending in \-kyə-lər\ have been found in widespread use among educated speakers, including scientists, lawyers, professors, congressmen, U.S. cabinet members, and at least two U.S. presidents and one vice president.

> **so** The intensive use of *so* is widely condemned in college handbooks but is nonetheless standard.

Even a usage note that does uphold the differences in meanings between commonly misused words is written begrudgingly:

> **mitigate** *Mitigate* is sometimes used as an intransitive where *militate* might be expected. Even though Faulkner used it and one critic thinks it should be called an American idiom, it is usually considered a mistake.

And here is a definition followed by its usage note, a Merriam-Webster model of helpless confusion:

> **literally** 1: in a literal sense or manner: ACTUALLY <took the remark ~> <was ~ insane> 2: in effect: VIRTUALLY <will ~ turn the world upside down to combat cruelty or injustice—Norman Cousins>

> **usage** Since some people take sense 2 to be the opposite of sense 1, it has been frequently criticized as a misuse. Instead the use is pure hyperbole intended to gain emphasis, but it often appears in contexts where no additional emphasis is necessary.

No Longer Harmless

A few years ago, in *The Vocabula Review,* my online journal about the English language, I offered the following poll and obtained the following results:

Dictionaries should be much more prescriptive, far less descriptive, than they now are.

- Yes! More than that, laxicographers promote the dissolution of the English language (and even society) with their misguided liberality: 19 percent
- Quite so. Dictionary compilers need to maintain, and perhaps even decide, distinctions between words; they need to guide us on matters of usage: 27 percent

- A mix of guidance and license is probably the best course—it's also the commonest course: 22 percent
- Lexicographers are necessarily descriptivists, for their job is simply to record how people use the language: 28 percent
- Obviously, we all must bow to the definitions and spellings found in the dictionary: 4 percent

As you see, 68 percent of the respondents rejected the strong descriptivist idea of dictionary making. Still more heartening to me is that only 4 percent of the people who participated in this poll believe that the definitions and spellings a dictionary offers are those we are necessarily bound to. More than that, though, the Merriam-Webster eleventh edition is a sign that dictionaries, at least as they are now being compiled, have outlived their usefulness. Dictionaries are no longer sacrosanct, no longer sources of unimpeachable information. Dictionaries are, indeed, no longer to be trusted.

That a president can ask *Is our children learning?,* a basketball star can use the word *conversate,* a well-known college professor can say *vociferous* when he means *voracious,* and another can scold a student for using the word *juggernaut* because she believes it means *jigaboo* is disturbing. But these are precisely the sorts of errors, if enough people make them, that the staff at Merriam-Webster will one day include in their dictionaries:

child *n, pl* or *sing* children.

conversate to exchange thoughts or opinions in speech; to converse.

vociferous 1. marked by or given to vehement, insistent outcry. 2. voracious.

juggernaut 1. a massive, inexorable force, campaign, movement, or object that crushes whatever is in its path. 2. *usu offensive* jigaboo; black person.

Over the past forty and more years, linguists and lexicographers have conspired to transform an indispensable reference work into an increasingly useless, increasingly dangerous one. Lexicographers are no longer harmless.

Part 2: Remarks About the "Usage Notes" in the *New Oxford American Dictionary*

Like other dictionaries, the newly published *New Oxford American Dictionary,* Third Edition,[8] in its introduction, discusses how it treats and regards its entries. There are sections on Grammar, Special Vocabulary, Encyclopedic Material, Word Histories, Spelling, Standard English, and the like. There also is a five-paragraph section on Usage Notes, and that will be the focus of my comments in this essay. Here, word for word, is the NOAD section on Usage Notes. (The boldfaced numbers in brackets I added; they identify the preceding phrases or sentences, as they do the comments I make about them that follow.)

> Interest in questions of good usage is widespread among English speakers everywhere, and many issues are hotly debated **[1]**. In the *New Oxford American Dictionary,* traditional issues have been reappraised, and guidance is given on various points, old and new **[2]**. The aim is to help people to use the language more accurately, more clearly, and more elegantly **[3]**, and to give information and offer reassurance in the face of some of the more baffling assertions about "correctness" that are sometimes made **[4]**.
>
> This reappraisal has involved looking carefully at evidence of actual usage (in the Oxford English Corpus **[5]**, the citations collected by the Oxford Reading Programme, and other sources) in order to find out where mistakes are actually being made, and where confusion and ambiguity actually arise. The issues on which journalists and others tend to comment have been reassessed and a judgment made about whether their comments are justified **[6]**.

From the 15th century onward, traditionalists have been objecting to particular senses of certain English words and phrases, for example, "due to" and "hopefully" **[7]**. Certain grammatical structures, too, have been singled out for adverse comment, notably the split infinitive and the use of a preposition at the end of a clause **[8]**. Some of the objections are founded on very dubious arguments, for example, the notion that English grammatical structures should precisely parallel those of Latin **[9]** or that meaning change of any kind is inherently suspect **[10]**.[9]

The usage notes in the *New Oxford American Dictionary* take the view that English is English, not Latin, and that English is, like all living languages, subject to change **[11]**. Good usage is usage that gets the speaker's or writer's meaning across **[12]**, not usage that conforms to some arbitrary rules that fly in the face of historical fact or current evidence **[13]**. The editors of the *New Oxford American Dictionary* are well aware that the prescriptions of pundits in the past have had remarkably little practical effect on the way the language is actually used **[14]**. A good dictionary reports the language as it is, not as the editors (or anyone else) would wish it to be **[15]**, and the usage notes must give guidance that accords with observed facts about present-day usage.

This is not to imply that the issues are straightforward or that there are simple solutions, however. Much of the debate about use of language is highly political, and controversy is, occasionally, inevitable **[16]**. Changing social attitudes have stigmatized long-established uses, such as the word "man" to denote the human race in general, and have highlighted the absence of a gender-neutral singular pronoun meaning both "he" and "she" (for which purpose "they" is now often used) **[17]**. Similarly, words such as "race" and "native" are now associated with particular problems of sensitivity in use **[18]**. The usage notes in the *New Oxford American Dictionary* offer information and practical advice on such issues.

[1] Yes, a great many people, whatever their education, do not shrink from expressing their views on good usage or bad grammar. The English language is not the purview solely of the lexicographers and linguists, the, let us call them, "lexlings"; it concerns all of us who speak and write it. No matter what our station in life, we all need to be heedful of how we express ourselves. Although the NOAD lexlings do not, here, admit this, lexicographers and linguists often disparage people who offer their views on the English language (see my epilogue: "Language Craven: A Definition"). If you do not have an advanced degree in linguistics, these lexlings maintain, you do not have the credentials to offer your views on the language. That lexlings believe, and sometimes admit they believe, people unschooled in linguistics contribute nothing to the debate about usage and grammar is as inane as it is insulting.

[2] Matters of usage and grammar are endlessly being discussed and argued about; lexlings can hardly claim to "reappraise" issues as though no one else ever has or does or is entitled to. What the lexlings maintain is simply their views of the English language. And their views are not any more correct or considerable than others' views. The lexlings themselves would agree with this because their views are not, necessarily, their own; their views are others' views; good little lexlings reflect others' views about language.

[3] Lexlings ought to understand by now that accurate, clear, elegant usage ought not to be "subject to change" quite as readily as these people permit. There is scarcely a better way of stripping a language of its accuracy, clarity, and elegance than by welcoming, as lexlings are wont to do, all manner of change in word definitions, usage, and grammar.

Pay attention to how people speak and write, and you'll not be impressed by the accuracy, clarity, or elegance of their sentences.[10] Consider these popular usages: the childish *way* (and, even, *way way*) instead of, for example, *far* (The Internet is potentially *way* more powerful than television ever dreamed of being); the illiterate *like* instead of *as* (She voted based on the information given to her at the time—just *like* President Bush did, just *like* Senator Edwards did, just *like* all senators did at that time); the grotesque *would have* instead of *had* (If she *would have* done her homework, she would know that); the foolish *friend* instead of *befriend* (Talk to your high school-aged teens about whether they're comfortable letting you *friend* them). There is scant accuracy, clarity, or elegance in these usages that the lexlings applaud and promote.

[4] To "offer reassurance" means merely that the lexlings support people who think as they do—that is, people who don't feel obliged to observe standard English usage and grammar.

[5] The Oxford English Corpus sounds as though it's some unimpeachable source of language, the very best language, but it's simply "a collection of texts or written (or spoken) language presented in electronic form. . . . [It] represents all types of English, from fiction and specialist journals to everyday newspapers and magazines, and from official reports to the language of Internet message boards, chat rooms, and Twitter."

The language used on Twitter, with its 140-character (including punctuation and spaces) limit, chat rooms with their foulmouthed participants, message boards with their slipshod grammar and misspellings, few intelligent people aspire to emulate. But this is precisely the gibberish that other people are writing and speaking, not only in these few arenas, but also, and increasingly, in their email, while texting, on their websites, in their high school and college papers, at their jobs, and elsewhere. Nonsense abounds.

[6] NOAD's lexlings choose to use the passive voice as though trying to absolve themselves from responsibility for what they are saying: "The issues . . . have been reassessed and a judgment made." Is this the sort of writing that lexlings consider accurate, clear, and elegant?

And here, too, the lexlings suggest that they only—with their study of mindless Twitter postings, benumbing commercials and ads, unintelligible official reports, cliché-ridden newspaper and magazine articles, and badly written contemporary fiction—know what usages are "justified."

Lexlings plume themselves on wanting simply to describe, not prescribe, so we have to wonder, with a statement like "a judgment made about whether their comments are justified," if they also are eager to prescribe.

Read some of the usage notes in the NOAD and you'll see that lexlings do, indeed, prescribe:

> The words **discrete** and **discreet** are pronounced in the same way and share the same origin but they do not mean the same thing. **Discrete** means "separate," as in *a finite number of **discrete** categories,* while **discreet** means "careful and circumspect," as in *you can rely on him to be **discreet**.*

Ought not lexlings to allow and welcome each word's having both meanings? They permit this of other words that are often confused. Surely the Oxford English Corpus shows many hundreds of citations for *discrete* being used instead of *discreet,* and *discreet* instead of *discrete*. Could it be that lexlings know not who they are?

At other times, the NOAD's lexlings word their usage notes so that their prescriptions sound like descriptions:

> The spelling **baited breath** instead of **bated breath** is a common mistake. Almost a third of citations for this idiom in the Oxford English Corpus are for the incorrect spelling.

If a third of the citations use *baited breath* is this not, given how the NOAD's lexlings think, reason to allow both spellings?

The way this usage note, like others, is written may make us wonder just exactly what the lexlings are saying, or advising. Again, they may not know who they are.

[7] Yes, *due to* and *hopefully,* misused, are often found in books about good English usage and have been for years, though some prescriptivists—weary of trying to persuade people to use these terms correctly—have abandoned their efforts. But as you'll see in the pages of this book, there are many hundreds of misused, misspelled, and mispronounced words. The lexlings are as responsible for this as anyone and anything.

[8] These two complaints are hopelessly outdated. Lexlings, whenever they want to castigate prescriptivists for their views, admonish them for prescribing that an infinitive ought not to be split and a preposition ought not to end a sentence. But very few prescriptivists have espoused these arguments in years. In *The King's English* (1906), the Fowler brothers called both of these superstitions; it is now more than a century since any critic of standing has condemned using either the split infinitive or the preposition at the end of a sentence. Modern prescriptivists concern themselves with matters that affect our understanding of words, not, as lexlings still maintain, with split infinitives and with prepositions at the end of sentences.

That, in 2011, NOAD's lexlings use such examples to promote the idea that prescriptivists are out of date serves only to reveal that they, the descriptivists, are out of date.

[9] This, too, was the thinking of some early prescriptivists; it is not a concern today. No modern prescriptivist maintains that English grammar should parallel that of Latin. It's remarkable that NOAD's lexlings would mention, and complain about, these few issues. (My complaining about people using *way* and *like, would have* and *friend* are more current issues, as are most, if not all, of the entries in this book.) As I say, no

modern prescriptivist concerns himself with trying to make English grammar obey Latin grammar's rules; no modern prescriptivist insists that infinitives cannot be split; no modern prescriptivist advises that a preposition cannot end a sentence. NOAD's lexlings apparently have little idea of what a modern prescriptivist does believe.

[10] What's more, no prescriptivist believes that all change in the meaning of words is "inherently suspect." The question is whether change contributes to our understanding ourselves and the world around us, or whether it contributes nothing of the sort or even diminishes our understanding.

[11] The meanings of some words do change, but much language change is due to ignorance, confusion, and imitation, among the qualities that define humanity best. Lexicography and linguistics may be the only professions that accept ignorance so readily and reward it so unabashedly.

Other words are coined and created in an attempt to define something for which perhaps there has not been sufficient understanding or something that is newly discovered or recognized. "Lexlings" I believe is a useful contribution: it means both *lex*icographers and *ling*uists, and expresses an opinion of both with the diminutive suffix *-ling*.

[12] Getting "the speaker's or writer's meaning across" means speaking and writing that is most easily and completely understood—that means using grammar that best conveys sense and place and time, and using words that have distinct meanings—not the indistinct, confused meanings that NOAD's lexlings so often prefer, as is clearly illustrated in their entries for *disinterested* and *rein*:

> One of the most contended questions of usage is the difference between **disinterested** and **uninterested**.

According to traditional guidelines, **disinterested** should never be used to mean "not interested" (i.e., it is not a synonym for **uninterested**) but only to mean "impartial," as in *the judgments of **disinterested** outsiders are likely to be more useful.* Ironically, the earliest recorded sense of **disinterested** is for the disputed sense. Today, the "incorrect" use of **disinterested** is widespread; around a quarter of citations in the Oxford English Corpus for **disinterested** are for this sense.

The idiomatic phrase a **free rein**, which derives from the literal meaning of using reins to control a horse, is sometimes misinterpreted and written as a **free reign**. More than a third of the citations for the phrase in the Oxford English Corpus use **reign** instead of **rein**.

[13] By "evidence," NOAD's lexlings can mean only the tiresome descriptive dictum: how people use the language determines all. As for "rules," rules of usage and grammar, of course, are necessary for meaning and understanding. As every society has rules to maintain civility and order, so every language has rules to promote clarity and understanding.

[14] People do, indeed, persist in writing and speaking badly, but because so many do is no reason to suppose that prescriptivism has had little effect. Legions of people are concerned about writing well, about grammar, about usage; books on language are written and bought, websites on language are created and joined, classes on language are offered and attended. But it's the lexlings who compile the dictionaries; they decide what words to include and what to write about those words, so even though they have fewer voices, they have louder ones.

The modern prescriptivist tries to promote good speaking and writing, to make plain what it is to speak and write accurately, clearly, and even elegantly. This is not at all the concern of lexlings; their aim is simply to note how people (Twitterers, chat-roomers, and message-boarders among them) use the language.

[15] Only since the publication of *Webster's Third New International Dictionary of the English Language* in 1961 have lexicographers been *fervently* promoting the idea that a dictionary should record the language as it is used instead of as it ought to be used. People want to know how to speak and write well, clearly, persuasively, compellingly, beautifully. Collecting tripe (already we find LOL and OMG in this book) from Twitter and other dubious sources, NOAD's lexlings help ensure that we—or those people who still, for what reasons we can only wonder, pay any attention to the dictionary—speak and write like every ignoramus.

[16–18] Lexlings are eager to regard prescriptivists as socially and politically conservative, and some prescriptivists certainly are. The modern prescriptivist, however, is as just in his social and political views as he is exacting in his grammar and usage. Upholding the values of accuracy, clarity, and elegance goes beyond speaking and writing the language well; it also means upholding the values of honesty, grace, and justice.

The modern prescriptivist, through his choice of language, has no interest in disparaging women and minorities; no talent for using incendiary or insulting language[11]; no thought of being superior to others who do not speak or write the language as he does. The modern prescriptivist is concerned with speaking and writing well—and with having the language, the usage and grammar, with which to do so.

RHF

A Note on Sentence Examples and Pronunciation

All the sentence examples are real though a few of them have been slightly edited for brevity or clarity. Some 60 percent of them came from Internet sources (newspapers, magazines, blogs, websites) and the other 40 percent from other sources (television and radio and other reading).

As for pronunciation, the syllable shown in all capital letters signifies principal stress; the syllable or syllables shown in italics signify secondary stress; for example, the pronunciation of *anaphylactic* is shown (*an*-ah-fah-LAK-tik), principal stress is on LAK, secondary stress is on *an*.

Imprecation

Liber scriptus proferetur—
dictionaries have had their day
in quo totum continetur—
dictionaries have had their day
unde mundus judicetur—
dictionaries have had their day

Dies irae, dies irae, dies irae

The Dictionary of Unendurable English

Aa

abberation Misspelling of *aberration.* • New employment data Friday will either corroborate recent evidence showing the economy is improving, or indicate that last month's job gain was an *abberation.* USE *aberration.* • Hedman had been a player in search of one, redemptive moment that would grant him forgiveness in the eyes of the fans after his *abberation* in Munich. USE *aberration.*

Abberation is how aberrant users of the English language spell *aberration.* The language has its deviants, its descriptive linguists, its dictionary makers.

abilify The brand name of a drug to treat depression, *Abilify* sounds as though it might be a verb meaning to make able. This is a deliberate corporate strategy to (1) make the drug sound effective, indeed, active and powerful, and, more important, (2) encourage people to use the brand name as a common verb. Although corporations may, to all appearances, try to maintain the integrity of their brand names, they secretly hope these names become part of the vernacular. Tissues are often called *kleenex* after Kleenex brand tissues (that is, let all tissues be considered kleenex or Kleenex brand), bandages are often called *band-aids* after Band-Aid brand bandages (that is, let all bandages be considered band-aids), and photocopies are often called *xeroxes* after Xerox brand photocopiers (that is, let all photocopies be considered Xerox copies). Abilify might one day mean to be powerfully effective or to make able, and the more people use it as such, the more likely, these advertisers (and the linguistic hirelings who work for them) hope, the brand name drug for combating depression will be known and bought. Already people have a sense of this: "*Abilify* sounds like something George W. Bush would say, as in, We need to *abilify* our troops to fight the terrorists"; "We need to *abilify* those kids so they become educationable." SEE ALSO **alleve; realator**.

abominable Misused for *abdominal.* • A valuable isometric exercise, however, is simply tightening and releasing the *abominable* muscles, which is a good way to tone and strengthen them. USE *abdominal.* • But one of the common reasons for *abominable* pain is appendicitis, which can be easily treated by removing the appendix. USE *abdominal.*

Abdominal is also sometimes misspelled *abdominable*: • I went into Mountainside Hospital about 2:30 A.M. on Wednesday morning with unbearable *abdominable* pain. USE *abdominal.* • There is absolutely no point in toning your *abdominable* muscles if they're covered in belly flab. USE *abdominal.*

Abominable (ah-BOM-i-nah-ble) means detestable; hateful. *Abdominal* (ab-DOM-i-nel) means of or relating to the abdomen or belly. *Abdominable,* were there such a word, would likely mean hateful and mawlike.

abrogate Misused for *arrogate.* • Yet, cocooned as they are in their superstitions, the eco-warriors *abrogate* for themselves the right to break the law. USE *arrogate.* • The president might *abrogate* to himself unforeseen power. USE *arrogate.* • Luce also began to *abrogate* for himself some of the paternal rights of the chief executive. USE *arrogate.*

Abrogate means to abolish; to annul. *Arrogate* means to appropriate; to take or claim for oneself without justification; to assign something to another in an unwarranted way. As the examples illustrate, *arrogate,* not *abrogate,* is the correct word if followed by *to* or *for* and a reflexive pronoun.

If we ignore the distinctions between words, we begin to ignore or disapprove of the distinctions between people; individuality, which, even now, is not favorably regarded, will become increasingly frowned upon, eventually unlawful, perhaps.

absolutely Like *definitely, awesome, great,* and similarly tiresome words, *absolutely* is far too often spoken, far too often heard. Yes or completely is all anyone means by *absolutely.* Rather than use this word as an intensive to overstate and overemphasize, let us speak more deliberately and better measure our words. SEE ALSO **awesome; great**.

absorbtion Misspelling of *absorption.* • Total energy *absorbtion* coefficients are used for the calculation of deposited dose by a given energy fluence.

USE *absorption.* • These wheels are used to achieve higher top speed and better shock *absorbtion.* USE *absorption.* • In broccoli for example, cooking increases iron *absorbtion* from 6 percent to 30 percent. USE *absorption.*

Absorption (with a *p*), not *absorbtion* (with a *b*), is the process of absorbing or of being absorbed; the state of being engrossed.

accel (accell) Misspelling of *excel.* • This unique program is recognized nationwide to be an effective and positive way to provide your child with cutting-edge skills to *accell* at home, in school, and in other sports and activities. USE *excel.* • He *accells* at everything he does, from music, to writing, to graphic design. USE *excels.* • In *The Color of My Skin,* she casts Sachse High School as a center of institutional racism, where white students *accell* while minorities go virtually ignored. USE *excel.*

Excel means to surpass others; to be better than. Neither *accel* nor *accell* is a word. SEE ALSO **excell**.

accelerate Misused for *exhilarate.* • For a lot of these Wadsworth seniors, *Grease* will be an *accelerating* experience, but also close to four years of hard work. USE *exhilarating.* • It is an evolving, *accelerating* experience like none other that has come before. USE *exhilarating.* • The old Minerva would have felt sorry for the bickering couple, but she felt *accelerated* by their pain. USE *exhilarated.*

Accelerate means to increase the speed of; to cause to occur sooner than expected. *Exhilarate* means to cause to feel refreshed and energetic; to invigorate. SEE ALSO **exhileration**.

accidently Misspelling of *accidentally.* • Lee admits he may have *accidently* passed secrets to other countries. USE *accidentally.* • Immediately smitten, Guido, who gets a job as a waiter, arranges to *accidently* bump into Dora over the next several days, but eventually realizes that she's engaged—albeit unhappily—to a Fascist official. USE *accidentally.* • If a thrown ball *accidently* touches a base coach, or a pitched or thrown ball touches an umpire, the ball is alive and in play. USE *accidentally.*

At least two well-known dictionaries do recognize the spelling *accidently.* But let this be a further reminder that dictionaries merely record how people use the language, not necessarily how it ought to be used. Some dictionaries, we can reasonably infer, actually promote illiteracy. If we were to rely exclusively on dictionary pronouncements, we'd be altogether undone. SEE ALSO **occasionly**; **publically**.

acclimation Misused for *acclamation.* • "Then, thirty years ago," his voice rose in *acclimation.* USE *acclamation.* • There was applause and *acclimation* in response. USE *acclamation.* • A vote of *acclimation* or a voice vote is appropriate for procedural votes or whenever a record of how individuals voted isn't necessary. USE *acclamation.* • The unanimous decision by the jury, after only 15 minutes of deliberation, is a resounding *acclimation* of support for veterans. USE *acclamation.*

Acclamation, the noun form of *acclaim,* is enthusiastic approval or applause; a vote of affirmation by applause or cheers. *Acclimation,* the noun form of *acclimate,* is adaptation to a new situation or environment.

acrosst Misspelling of *across.* • Do you think of countless sold records and happy fans from *acrosst* the world? USE *across.* • I was not sure what was actually being aborted until I came *acrosst* this website. USE *across.* • These people do not work directly in the Rice Psychology Department, but many of them are *acrosst* the street at UT-Houston Medical School. USE *across.* • The wind is blowing *acrosst.* USE *across.*

Among the ill-bred and ill-read, *across* is spelled *acrosst* and pronounced (ah-KROST).

actionize Misused for *effect* (or similar words). • This course will provide insight and training which can be used to *actionize* communities to organize for change in public policies that will improve community conditions for all. USE *motivate.* • As Muslims have contempt for all other faiths, to answer them, all the rest of us need to band together to exercise and *actionize* our contempt for Islam. USE *show.* • Through such dialogue we see that some senior education leaders are grappling with how to *actionize* their innovation visions. USE *effect.* • The greatest statement you can make about yourself is to *actionize* your thoughts about yourself. USE *realize.*

Actionize, a word that motivational speakers and other swindlers might use, apparently means many things—though the intended meaning in these sentences (and others) is anyone's guess. *Actionize* is a word for people who do not want to be altogether understood.

active Placed before some nouns, *active* diminishes the meaning of the words it modifies. Before words such as *duty* and *lifestyle, active* is indeed informative, but before these other sorts of words, it is useless: • The plot thickens as physicians have recently taken an *active* interest in conducting and being paid for care coordination activities. DELETE *active*. • Like the original Internet, Internet 2 relies on the *active* involvement of research universities to develop, implement, and maintain the network. DELETE *active*. • I am confident his *active* participation as an alumnus of the program will provide ongoing opportunities to make a difference in this arena. DELETE *active*. • It is not fair to deny *active* treatment to these patients. DELETE *active*.

Similarly, *actively* before some verbs is useless. In attempting to strengthen the verb, *actively* succeeds only in weakening it: • OnLive CEO Steve Perlman stated that games are *actively* being adapted for touchscreens. DELETE *actively*. • The Nationals are *actively* pursuing free agent first baseman Derrek Lee. DELETE *actively*.

adaption Misused for *adaptation*. • We also provide a lot of counseling and hand-holding on *adaption* to the community and finding activities for them. USE *adaptation*. • Soldier Ride is outfitting every soldier who's participating with a bike and the prosthetic *adaption* that's needed. USE *adaptation*. • The *adaption* of Stoker's *Dracula,* which is being released as a four-issue miniseries, is, as of issue two, well worth the price of admission. USE *adaptation*.

The noun *adaptation* is preferable to *adaption*; the adjective *adaptive* is preferable to *adaptative*.

> Its publication just happens (oh, yes?) to coincide with the opening on Broadway last month of *Spamalot,* a musical adaption of *Monty Python and the Holy Grail.*
>
> —Ann Geracimos, *The Washington Times*

adieu Misspelling of *ado*. • Without further *adieu,* let us see what they are serving up on this final stretch toward the end of the season. Use *ado.* • With no more *adieu,* I grabbed my submachine gun and sprinted out into the hall. Use *ado.* • And now, without further *adieux,* here is my own personal recipe for absinthe. Use *ado.*

Occasionally, *ado* (or *a duo*) is used in place of *adieu*: • Sometime in early September we bid *ado* to the Green River. Use *adieu.* • The second round of Indian summer is about to wish us *a duo*. Use *adieu.*

Adieu (plural: *adieux*), meaning to God (I commend you), is used largely to mean good-bye or farewell. *Ado* means trouble or bother; fuss. A *duo* is a duet, a pair, or two allied people or things.

adjectify Misused for *describe* (or similar words). • Where the opinion makers and media moguls *adjectify* every political action these days as "vaguely reminiscent of the sixties," I prefer to think of them as "clearly foreshadowing the millennium." Use *describe.* • I think that I'm going to change the name in a totally undefined way: I'm going to use the gjwalberg .com, then *adjectify* it with a nonsensical statement. Use *define.* • It also uses the term "community" to *adjectify* programs in justice as well, so that we have community corrections, community policing, etc. Use *portray.*

As not every phrase can be reduced to a single word, so not every noun should be made into a verb. *Adjectify*—which apparently means to use as an adjective—sounds dreadful, falsely erudite, and its meaning is questionable in nearly every context. If meaning it must have, *adjectify* should mean to modify; to qualify, limit, or specify the meaning of. *Adjectify,* at least in the preceding examples, seems to mean to describe or define. And *adjectify* sounds like it means to dehumanize or objectify. A few words whose meaning is apparent are better than one word whose meaning is not.

In its sense of to use a proper name as an adjective, *adjectify* is irreplaceable; whole sentences need to be reworked: • And academics love to *adjectify* luminaries in their fields. • A search of the Nexus database reveals him to be the most *adjectified* chief executive of recent years.

adjure Misused for *abjure.* • There should also be a commitment on both sides to *adjure* violence against noncombatant civilians and a willingness to pursue the democratic process. USE *abjure.*

And *abjure* is sometimes misused for *adjure:* • In the name of the Lords of the Dead, I command you; with the Three Sigils of the Dreamless Ones, I *abjure* you; by the pleasure of the Dread Majesties of Night, I order you. USE *adjure.*

Adjure (ah-JOOR) means to urge or enjoin solemnly or earnestly; to entreat. *Abjure* (ab-JOOR) means to renounce under oath; to repudiate or abstain from. Both *adjure* and *abjure* derive from the Latin *jurare,* to swear. (The prefix *ad-* in *adjure* means toward or to; the prefix *ab-* in *abjure* means away or from.)

admirous Misused for *admire* (*admirable*). • We *are also admirous of* the fact that Uganda has taken such a leading role in helping to bring peace and stability to the continent. USE *also admire.* • Quick wit, a good laugh, and a sense of humor are *admirous* qualities in both sexes. USE *admirable.* • I *was both admirous of* his character and his cuteness. USE *admired both.* • I doubt Kate will take what Diana took—she seems a little older and more "worldly"; and William is more *admirous* and respectful of her and their relationship than Charles ever was of Diana. USE *admiring.*

No number of people using this distortion, no raving linguists, will persuade those of us with style and sensibility to join them in using it.

adopt Misused for *adapt.* • Maybe you'll need a little time to *adopt* to the Indian English, but that's all. USE *adapt.* • On the basis of this point, there is no reason why Western companies cannot successfully *adopt* to Japanese practices. USE *adapt.* • Universities and other traditional institutions of education must therefore also change and *adopt* to new conditions and societal needs. USE *adapt.*

To *adopt* means to take into one's own family through legal means; to choose and follow a course of action; to take up and use as one's own; to take on or assume. To *adapt* means to make suitable or fit for a specific use.

adultry Misspelling of *adultery.* • Apparently he has said he committed *adultry* and cheated on his wife and now he is being charged with sexual assault. Use *adultery.* • Does chatting and flirting in a chat room count as *adultry*? Use *adultery.*

Those who write *adultry,* like those who commit it, need to know how to spell it. See also **marrage**.

advertize Misspelling of *advertise.* • Be the first to *advertize* and your ad will be right here at the top. Use *advertise.* • There's an *advertizement* at every turn, which gets annoying, but I guess that's the price you pay for free ware. Use *advertisement.*

In both American and British English, *advertise* and *advertisement* are spelled with an *s,* not with a *z,* an exception to the usual rule, whereby *-ise* is the ending used in Britain, and *-ize,* the ending used in the United States. (Other exceptions include *apprise* and *chastise.*)

advice Misused for *advise.* • We will only *advice* them to join those colleges that will be ready to offer quality education. Use *advise.* • If you have a wheelchair please *advice* us at least five days in advance so we can arrange suitable transfers and/or accommodation. Use *advise.*

Advice (ad-VIS)—opinion or counsel—is a noun; *advise* (ad-VIZ)—to offer opinion or counsel—a verb. See also **device**.

aerobic Misused for *Arabic.* • This has a brass dial with silver chapter ring and Roman and *Aerobic* numerals, signed "Lanrie Carlisle." Use *Arabic.* • Notes in a scale are identified using *Aerobic* numbers 1-2-3-4-5-6-7 and the chords in a key use roman numbers I-II-III-IV-V-VI-VII. Use *Arabic.* • The medallions have changed from roman numerals to *aerobic* numerals. Use *Arabic.*

Only people unfamiliar with both fitness and world affairs could possibly confuse *aerobic* with *Arabic,* but flabby xenophobes there are.

aesthetic Misused for *anesthetic.* • Hyaluronic acid is also used for lip enhancement (definition of upper lip) and augmentation (fuller lips); this is carried out under dental block using local *aesthetic.* Use *anesthetic.* • Topical local *aesthetic* preparations such as EMLA cream or Ametop gel are used in reducing the pain of venipuncture and intravenous cannulation in both children and adults. USE *anesthetic.*

An *anesthetic* is a substance that reduces sensitivity to pain during a medical procedure. And *aesthetic,* as an adjective, refers to art or beauty and the appreciation of them. SEE ALSO **ascetic**.

> He said surgical, aesthetic, nursing and physiotherapy staff had all worked together to get him home as soon as possible. . . . He said he had been deeply worried about having a general aesthetic and had been delighted to be offered the epidural in his spine.
>
> —Jane Elliott, BBC News
>
> Ms. Elliott does manage to use the word *anaesthetic* (the British spelling) once in her article but, dulled by her own writing perhaps, not before using *aesthetic* twice.

affect Misused for *effect.* • As for the worldwide *affects* of volcanic eruptions this only happens when there are large explosive eruptions that throw material into the stratosphere. USE *effects.* • Eventually these gases escape and produce a runaway greenhouse *affect.* USE *effect.* • The primary *affect* on property values will come from the aerosols associated with the spray. USE *effect.* • Now breathe deeply for the full *affect.* USE *effect.*

And *effect* is misused for *affect.* • The vice president had become self-conscious about the condition of his teeth, and aides believed it was directly *effecting* his campaign performance. USE *affecting.* • Leslie says she teaches because it gives her a natural high to know she has the power to positively *effect* all who enter her classroom. USE *affect.* • Global warming will *effect* many aspects of daily life in the future. USE *affect.* • How does HIV *effect* me? USE *affect.*

Though both *affect* and *effect* may be either a noun or a verb, it is usually the verb *affect* that is confused with the noun *effect. Affect* as a verb means to influence or have an effect on; as a noun, *affect* means an emotion or emotional response. *Effect* as a verb means to bring about or accomplish ("The company effected many changes that allowed it to begin to compete once again in the same arena it dominated in the past"); as a noun, *effect* means a result or an influence. The word *affect* is much less often used as a noun than it is as a verb. All the same, it is often misused for, or perhaps misspelled, *effect*.

affidavid Misspelling of *affidavit.* • You will be required to sign an *affidavid* stating you paid for a lot but never received it and to file a police report alleging fraud against the seller. USE *affidavit.* • Cindy Shook's *affidavid* was discounted by the court as unbelievable. USE *affidavit.* • Martin Coonce died on March 1, 1909, and Sarah Coonce subsequently filed an *affidavid* for relief under the Widow's Pension Act of 1908. USE *affidavit.*

More than a misspelling, *affidavid* signals that ineptitude and ignorance overwhelm us; today, entertainment is all; learning how to spell correctly or write well interests us no more than do civility and justice, honesty and integrity, yet how we use language is inseparable from how we view and behave in the world.

afflict Misused for *inflict.* • Ripley ultimately ends up committing his own justice against himself in order to escape his predators that threaten his existence, but the greater justice comes from him having to live with his own hollow existence, which is more disturbing than any human *afflicted* punishment. USE *inflicted.* • Other times we choose to *afflict* voluntary suffering on ourselves (as in a fast or long march). USE *inflict.* • She hoped for a different world for her daughters and wanted her sons to understand the issue and not *afflict* any pain on the women in their lives. USE *inflict.* • Jeryl L. Beckett, 28, 208 S. Summitt, died at 2:45 P.M. Monday, March 3, 1997, of a *self-afflicted* gun wound. USE *self-inflicted.*

This distinction is increasingly unobserved, for dictionaries are, not at all helpfully, offering one word as a synonym for the other. Both words mean to mete out or impose pain or suffering, but the object used with *afflict* is most often an animate one, whereas the object used with *inflict* is inanimate. You *afflict* a person with pain, or *inflict* pain on a person. What's more, *inflicted* is usually followed by *on* or *upon; afflicted,* by *by* or *with.*

affluent The pronunciation of *affluent* is (AF-loo-ent), not (ah-FLOO-ent).

affrontery Misspelling of *effrontery.* • Yet, if you ever even hint that racism might somehow be involved, they scream in agony at the sheer *affrontery* of such a charge. USE *effrontery.* • The world is still full of people who don't know how lucky they are, who bemoan the lack of talent around; people who have the *affrontery* to say "There's not that much good music around these days, is there?" USE *effrontery.*

Effrontery, meaning presumptuousness or impertinence, from the French *effronterie,* meaning shameless, is sometimes misspelled *affrontery,* possibly in confusion with the noun *affront* (an insult or deliberate offense). *Affrontery* is not yet a variant spelling of *affront.*

afterwards *Afterward* is the preferred American spelling and (AF-ter-werd), not (AF-ter-werdz), the preferred American pronunciation. SEE ALSO **backwards**; **forwards**; **towards**.

aggravate Misused for *annoy* (or similar words). • What is most needed from us, instead, may be the simple quality of steadfastness—the persistent, openhearted willingness to simply hang in there with the clients who most confuse, *aggravate,* or discourage us. USE *annoy.* • Most of the time, swapping human contacts for electronic ones looks as though it's saving us time, money, and *aggravation.* USE *irritation.* • The first set of people I *aggravated* Tuesday were those of you who get angry when I don't stick to financial topics. USE *irritated.* • Of course, it's a fear that his kid sister, the irrepressibly *aggravating* D.W., is only too happy to bolster. USE *exasperating.* • Skunks stink up campus and *aggravate* students. USE *upset.* • He sincerely regrets all the *aggravation* the school, teachers, and parents have been put through. USE *exasperation.* • Other things have been preset at the factory in odd ways that puzzle, frustrate, and *aggravate* the owner. USE *annoy.* • Every women knows that satisfying a man is easy, but *aggravating* him takes a special talent! USE *exasperating.*

Aside from the added amusement of "Every *women* knows," the online advertisement for *How to Aggravate a Man Every Time,* a book, offers another example; it's too dear: • Learn the best *aggravating* tricks, such as: take over the remote control, make the most of PMS, make friends with his ex-girlfriends. . . .

The modern (as well as, apparently, historical) view is that *aggravate* may mean, along with to make worse or exacerbate, to irritate or annoy.

If people who use *aggravate* to mean annoy also had knowledge of its sense of to make worse and could occasionally use it in that sense, perhaps careful writers and speakers of the English language would be less inclined to carp—while, of course, never agreeing to capitulate.

Let us, if need be, create distinctions between words where, perhaps, there have been none. We have words aplenty that mean to annoy; the only other words that mean to *aggravate* are *worsen* and *exacerbate,* itself often ridiculously confused with *exasperate.* SEE ALSO **exasperate**.

aggress (against) Misused for *be aggressive* (or similar words). • Freudian theory would suggest that the desire to *aggress* would be subconscious, not a product of cognitive processes. USE *be aggressive.* • When we are *aggressed against,* it is our right to face up to the aggression, to confront the aggression. USE *attacked.* • The neighbors were getting nervous because of the crowd of people passing in their hall, and a group of volunteers was *aggressed* by a drunken man. USE *assailed.* • We don't see ourselves as responsible, because it wasn't we who *aggressed* them, but they came and *aggressed* the community. USE *assaulted.*

A wholly useless deconstruction, though certainly embraced by lexlings, *aggress* is inferior to *attack, assault, assail, accost,* and other words. SEE ALSO **elocute**; **enthuse**; **precip**.

agreeance Misused for *agreement.* • In *agreeance* with the Monterrey Consensus, Guinea believes there should be an increase of Foreign Direct Investment (FDI), especially in the continent of Africa. USE *agreement.* • All present members were in *agreeance* that if a problem arises and the bylaws are not adhered to, the current officers might seek legal counsel if necessary to resolve the conflict. USE *agreement.* • Once the two families were in *agreeance* the couple's engagement would be announced. USE *agreement.* • Doctrinal Standards: Contains the text from the Westminster Confession and catechisms; the foundation and standards of the Presbyterian denomination, and the creed our church is in *agreeance* with. USE *agreement.*

Agreeance is obsolete and, when used today, illegitimate.

aide Misused for *aid.* • Support garments used after liposuction can help decrease swelling and *aide* in general comfort. USE *aid.* • As a psychologist with 30 years experience, I will be your personal coach, I will carefully listen, help steer you to healthy sources to *aide* in your growth, guide you in setting up a plan of action and personal goals, and provide support during your voyage of rediscovery. USE *aid.* • ODA names new special assistant to *aide* water quality planning program. USE *aid.* • Polk and Salem housing authorities receive grant to *aide* seniors and the disabled. USE *aid.*

To *aid* is to help, assist, or support someone; to promote or encourage. *Aid,* the noun, is the act of helping or a source of help or assistance. *Aide*—never a verb and invariably a person—is an aide-de-camp; an assistant or helper: • The Syosset Fire Department sent *aide* to Hicksville early Wednesday to help extinguish a large fire in an empty commercial building. USE *aid.* • She urges all countries to keep their promises of financial *aide,* to keep the money coming. USE *aid.* • Did you know we give billions of dollars of *aide* to Mexico? USE *aid.* • A certified nurse's *aid,* or CNA, has most of the contact with a patient. USE *aide.*

The distinction between the nouns *aide* and *aid* has not always been observed, but it is now well established and helpful. Distinctions between words that may otherwise be confused should be celebrated, not, as the lexicographers and linguists claim, deprecated.

a.k.a. An abbreviation for also known as, *a.k.a.* has no place in written language and little in spoken language. Only a writer manqué would use *a.k.a.* • From the data, he saw evidence that computer investments were improving business efficiency, *a.k.a.* productivity. USE *that is.* • According to Wilkinson, enough electricity is generated during simple microbial fermentation to power *a motor—a.k.a.* a gastrobot (a robot with a stomach). DELETE *a motor—a.k.a.* • RUF commander Dennis Mingo, *a.k.a.* Superman, has disappeared from Makeni. USE *also known as.* • "My face is still in Chicago," Oprah announces as she ushers me (*a.k.a.* the poor slob) into the suite. DELETE *a.k.a.* • Sharon Adl-Doost, *aka* the Lunch Lady, may be the most famous cafeteria worker in the country, if not the world. USE *well known as.* SEE ALSO **i.e.**

album The pronunciation of *album* is (AL-bum), not (AL-blum).

alibi Misused for *excuse* (or similar words). • Robert Meacham's toe injury was a pretty good *alibi* early in the season for sluggish play, but lately? Use *excuse*. • Rangel gave a rambling defense of his actions with one *alibi* after another to excuse his behavior all the while declaring that nothing he did was evidence of corruption. Use *explanation*.

An *alibi* is a defense or claim that a person accused of a crime was elsewhere when the crime was committed; in fact, *alibi* means elsewhere in Latin. The word is not a synonym for *excuse* despite the frequency with which it is used as one and despite the allegations of dictionary makers.

aliment Misused for *ailment*. • While well drawn, Altered Beast suffers from an *aliment* known as image breakup. Use *ailment*. • Thumb fatigue is a painful *aliment* that is becoming increasingly common among dental professionals. Use *ailment*.

Though *ailment* (AIL-ment) is far more commonly used than *aliment*, the words are sometimes confused. An *ailment* is a mild illness, whereas *aliment* (AL-ah-ment) is food or something that nourishes.

As some people confuse *ailment* with *aliment*, so they use the nonword *ailmentary* instead of *alimentary*: • Alcohol cannot be called a food for it enters the *ailmentary* canal and is not changed or digested in any way. Use *alimentary*. • With the help of strong muscular walls and the stones and grit, the gizzard grinds the food into a pulp before it passes further along the *ailmentary* canal. Use *alimentary*.

all This informal sense of *all*, meaning very or wholly, is typically used by adolescents and teenagers, but it's best not used at all: • Then she gets *all* rebellious and randomly rips apart a contestant that doesn't deserve it. Delete *all*. • This is the reason why a kid becomes *all* cranky after a few hours of studying. Delete *all*. • Oh, I got *all* silly, I was *all* overcome with the excitement and immediately wanted to buy everything in sight. Delete *all*. See also **or something**; **very**.

alleged *Alleged* means suspected but not proved of having committed, or of being, a crime; supposed: • After receiving reports of *alleged* wrongdoings by one of the 20 participants in the honor program, the state Department of Environmental Management launched an investigation focusing on five boats, four of which were randomly chosen. • Saying it has found no concrete evidence of a crime, the Nevada County Sheriff's Office has forwarded its investigation of an *alleged* rape at Bear River High School to the district attorney's office. • Hononegah High School officials and Rockton Police are investigating two reports of *alleged* criminal sexual abuse.

Often *alleged* is improperly or needlessly used: • Jesse James Miller is being charged with the *alleged* murder of Derek Edward Miller of Peoria. (If Derek Edward was murdered, the murder is not *alleged* though Jesse James may be the *alleged* murderer.)

Alleged is an adjective intended to convey doubt and to protect the principal from false accusation and the writer (or speaker) from libel (or slander).

The pronunciation of *alleged* is (ah-LEJD) or (ah-LEJ-id). SEE ALSO **beloved**.

alleve Misused for *relieve* (or similar words). • She enjoys chewing on these, and they help *alleve* her aching gums. USE *relieve.* • Anytime I do this, I feel an overbearing sense of guilt for being so callous toward other people's sufferings and for doing so little to *alleve* them. USE *alleviate.* • Although some of your current problems may be *alleved,* they would be replaced by newer and bigger problems. USE *eased.* • The car is suffering from "monster truck syndrome," but that will be *alleved* next week when I get my new springs on! USE *fixed.* • We also got a great book, called *The Kissing Hand,* to read before school started, to *alleve* anxiety. USE *relieve.*

A mix of *relieve* and *alleviate,* and a dose of the medication Aleve, the nonword *alleve* is being used by people who have more familiarity with television commercials or drugs than they do written literature. SEE ALSO **abilify**.

> When the organizers were able to alleve her of her concerns, the concert was back on again.
>
> —Lola Ogunnaike, CNN reporter

> The goal of Lakeside Doggie Lounge is to provide your pet a natural, nurturing, and loving environment that will alleve the stress and strain of being away from you and their home.
>
> —Lakeside Doggie Lounge

alliterate Misused for *illiterate.* • An additional 35 million are *alliterate*—they can read a few basics with difficulty, but that is about all. USE *illiterate.* • The *Washington Post* dubbed independent publishing a "bright and vital spot" in "this *alliterate* culture," pointing out that niche publishers are succeeding where others have failed by closely targeting books to specific audiences. USE *illiterate.* • Not only is it managing to dent established titles but has also succeeded in converting a sector of the *alliterate* population to the reading habit. USE *illiterate.*

Alliterate, a verb, means to use or contain alliteration (the repetition of the same sounds at the beginning of words) in speech or writing. *Illiterate,* an adjective, means unable to read and write; violating established standards of speech or writing. SEE ALSO **literately**.

all the farther (further) Misused for *as far as.* • Oh, Kansas education; if you're not burning Harry Potter books or mishandling the material taught in science classes—that's *all the further* I'll go with that one—you're having your finances ravaged for no reason. USE *as far as.* • Sorry but this is *all the farther* I can help, as that solved my problem and so many things could be causing this new problem. USE *as far as.*

All the farther (further), dialectal for *as far as,* should not be found in anyone's writing.

allude Misused for *elude.* • Oak Ridge police are still searching for a man wanted on drug charges after he *alluded* capture last Monday. USE *eluded.* • I recognize him, but his name *alludes* me. USE *eludes.* • Detective Lincoln Rhymes, the foremost criminalist in the NYPD, is put on the trail of a cunning professional killer who has continually *alluded* the police. USE *eluded.*

Allude means to mention indirectly. *Elude* means to escape capture or detection; to dodge. SEE ALSO **refer**.

The sow, dubbed Babe by the Boston press, became famous as she alluded capture for two days by local police.

—Jeanne Miles, *The Caledonian-Record*

Herb Clay, 53, has been charged with alleged possession of a controlled substance, resisting a peace officer and fleeing or attempting to allude a peace officer, East St. Louis police have confirmed.

—Krista Wilkinson, *The Edwardsville Intelligencer*

This point obviously did not allude McDonald's officials when they presented the McCafé idea to Freeman in September.

—Julie O'Shea, *Mountain View Voice*

ally Misused for *allay.* • Only a comprehensive, independent and public inquiry will *ally* fears about their safety, and get to the root of this issue. USE *allay.* • Officials have further sought to *ally* concerns that the United States seeks to be a colonial power in Iraq, going so far as to dub General Jay Garner, who will be coordinating reconstruction and humanitarian efforts, as the "senior civilian administrator" rather than "military governor." USE *allay.*

The verb *ally* (ah-LIE) means to unite for a specific purpose; to relate. *Allay* (ah-LAY) means to quiet or calm; to lessen or alleviate.

(take) a look-see This phrase is one of the new illiteracies. Expressions like *a good read, a must-have,* and *a look-see* are favored today by the illiterati—smart, articulate people who find it fashionable to speak and write like an infant, like a "Dick and Jane" reader: • Folsom Lake College's new performing and visual arts center is giving the community an opportunity to *take a look-see.* • Apparently he's moving from one small first-division team to another, but has come to D.C. for *a look-see.* • We're just giving this streamlined homepage *a look-see* to determine if we like it or not. SEE ALSO **a (good) read**; **a must (miss)**.

alot Misspelling of *a lot.* • Programming is *alot* of fun and even more so if you can work on a program that is used by many people all over the world.

USE *a lot.* • I saw *alot* of him last season and know what he is capable of. USE *a lot.* • Technology has taken *alot* of the physical "labor" out of normal everyday activities. USE *a lot.*

Others misspell the word worse: • So in a sense *allot* of people are blind to tradition and think tradition in any form is evil. USE *a lot.* • I guess it's frustrating because boxing will lose *allot* of fans over this decision; even many of Oscar's critics had him winning the fight. USE *a lot.* • One thing *allot* of people don't realize is that Vince McMahon is right in your ear, he can talk to you at any given moment. USE *a lot.*

Some people, not a few college students among them, cannot even manage to spell two words, four letters correctly. SEE ALSO **alright**.

alot Misused for *allot.* • You still agreed to the Software License Agreement and like it or not must wait for Omega to *alot* resources to fix the Y2K problem, if and when they choose to do so. USE *allot.* • In addition, the queen had ordered the governor to *alot* land for Swiss settlers at these branches in Virginia. USE *allot.* • Since time is usually the reason given for not being able to do many things, you could *alot* time during the staff development for reflection, plans, and more. USE *allot.*

Allot means to assign, apportion, or distribute. *A lot* means many or a large number or amount of.

alphabeticalize Misused for *alphabetize.* • Find it quickly with our *alphabeticalized* list of all the Gateway sites. USE *alphabetized.* • There is an *alphabeticalized* directory of articles on the Parish Center main page available to guide viewers to any topic of interest. USE *alphabetized.* • How hard is it to *alphabeticalize* some files and put them in the right order on the shelf? USE *alphabetize.*

The verb meaning to arrange words or names in alphabetical (or alphabetic) order is *alphabetize,* not *alphabeticalize.*

> Selecting the data and sorting it by their last name and then re-selecting the data and sorting it by first name will give you a list alphabeticalized by first names.
>
> —University of California at Berkeley

Though the good people at the University of California may know how to arrange first and last names, they seem not to know that *alphabeticalize* is analphabetic.

alright Misspelling of *all right*. • It looks *alright* from this view, but Pooh's Bridge, near Hatfield, England, was recently condemned and rebuilt. USE *all right*. • With five games remaining, things are anything but *alright* along the banks of the Mississippi. USE *all right*. • "*Alright,* close No. 2 and 3," says the manager of the Mt. Hermon ski resort, Israel's only winter wonderland, as the sight of cable cars with legs and skis dangling from them disappears into sky soup. USE *All right*. • The next morning, I knew that everything would be *alright*. USE *all right*. • Would it be *alright* if I have it back to you with revisions sometime in the first week of July? USE *all right*.

The inclusion of *alright* in dictionaries is indefensible. If many more popular misspellings—of which there are scores—were also dictionary entries, these books would be censured by people more sensible than the makers of them.

Alright, choose your weapon.

—Ford "Built Tough" magazine ad

alter Misused for *altar*. • A religious *alter* was created, with candles representing God, the Spirit of Guidance, and each major religion. USE *altar*. • The main sacrificial *alter* is now closed due to vandals. USE *altar*.

And, of course, *altar* is sometimes misused for *alter*: • The popular TV teenager Lizzie McGuire hits the big screen with *The Lizzie McGuire Movie* complete with her animated *altar* ego. USE *alter*.

An *altar* is a platform where offerings or sacrifices to a god are made; a table or stand used in a religious service. To *alter* is to make different; to adjust or resew a garment for a better fit. An *alter ego* is a second side of oneself, a counterpart.

alterate Misused for *alter* (or similar words). • You must not *alterate* the button in any way; no changes to the graphics of the button or its size are allowed. USE *alter.* • Accidentals are added to the numbers if you *alterate* them by appending -, ! and +. USE *alter.* • In order to *alterate* this field, the user has to change a display setting for the composition window. USE *alter.*

Some people have a fondness for adding suffixes like *-ate* or *-ity* or *-ster* to words that they don't know the correct forms of, or that they hope to add some small significance to. *Alterate* is a barbarism. SEE ALSO **considerate**; **documentate**.

alterior Misused for *ulterior.* • A change of name upon marriage, dissolution, or divorce normally meets the court's requirements, provided no *alterior* motive is present. USE *ulterior.* • And yet it is this fact, this *alterior* position of the other, that draws the reader's care. USE *ulterior.*

Ulterior means beyond that which is evident or disclosed; lying beyond or outside; subsequent. *Alterior* means nothing at all; it is not a word that has a meaning.

alternate Misused for *alternative.* • Under the *alternate* bid submitted on Wednesday of last week, the fund's investors would have received just 5% of the roughly $4.6 billion their stakes were worth at the beginning of the year. USE *alternative.* • Perhaps the most common themes in *alternate* history are "What if the Nazis won World War II?" and "What if the Confederacy won the American Civil War?" USE *alternative.* • This *alternate* route adds 36 miles to your trip, so be prepared. USE *alternative.* • It is also acknowledged that the student attending an *alternate* school needs to be recognized, acknowledged, accepted, and understood. USE *alternative.* • The natural method involves abstaining from intercourse or using *alternate* methods of birth control during fertile periods. USE *alternative.*

Commentators on English usage have long complained about people confusing *alternate* with *alternative. Alternate* as a verb means to occur in succession or to move back and forth; as a noun, it means a person acting for another, a substitute; as an adjective, it means every other. The adjectival *alternate*—it ought to be clear by now—does not mean, as *alternative* does, providing a choice between two or more things; nor does it mean, as *alternative* does, relating to an undertaking or institution that appeals to nontraditional interests. As a noun, *alternative* is a choice between two or more than two possibilities.

If some people insist on maintaining the distinctions between *alternate* and *alternative,* it's because they prefer clarity to confusion, elegance to license.

altho Misused for *although.* • *Altho* it is covered with a water-tight roof and all doors and windows are closed, the Goodyear-Zeppelin dock at Akron, Ohio, is so large (43,000,000 cubic feet) that sudden changes of temperature cause clouds to form inside the hangar—and rain falls. USE *Although.* • Morse is my favorite mystery *altho* I like almost any of the UK mysteries and most of the regular dramas. USE *although.*

So, too, is *tho* misused for *though*: • Chrome's music score *tho* should really get some kind of an official award. USE *though.* • On the other hand *tho,* I've never actually seen one in that condition. USE *though.*

Spelling *although* or *though* with fewer letters ought to impress no one. It's not cute, it's not clever, it's not stylish, it's not smart. SEE ALSO **although**; **tho**.

although *Although* is a conjunction meaning even though or though or despite the fact that or regardless of the fact that (the last two are wordy phrases that ought never to be used). Many people use the word *while* where *although* (*even though* or *though*) is preferable; that is, *while* is best used, and least often misunderstood, in a temporal sense.

Others suggest that *although* should be reserved for the beginning of a sentence, and *though* for midsentence, but only the sound of the sentence should decide this; the grammar of either word in either position is irreproachable. SEE ALSO **altho**; **tho**; **while**.

altogether Misused for *all together.* • I keep seeing improvement from the girls and with districts next week, now is the time to put it *altogether.* USE *all together.* • I think the most powerful song that we sang *altogether* was "Turn, Turn, Turn." USE *all together.*

Unlike *alright* and *alot, altogether* is a perfectly good word, but it does not mean *all together. Altogether* means wholly or completely; in all; on the whole. *All together* means together; in a group; all at once.

alumnus Misused for *alumna.* • As an *alumnus,* she can attest to the educational and athletic experience a student-athlete can receive at Bellarmine. USE *alumna.* • My speech professor told me she was an *alumnus* of Moraine and many of the alumni return to teach at Moraine. USE *alumna.* • Margaret is a senior at West Virginia Wesleyan College and is an *alumnus* of Upward Bound. USE *alumna.*

Though many people today use *alumnus*: to mean males and females alike, *alumnus* is a male graduate of a school, college, or university; *alumna,* a female graduate. *Alumni* are the male or the male and female graduates of a school, college, or university; *alumnae,* the female graduates.

Alumni is also misused for *alumnus* (or *alumna*): • He is an *alumni* of Cal State LA where he studied biology and chemistry. USE *alumnus.* • The nominee must be an *alumni* of the college who has supported and/or been involved with the college since leaving Virginia Intermont. USE *alumnus* (or *alumna*). • As an *alumni* of the School you should already receive our bi-annual magazine, *Music @ Michigan.* USE *alumnus* (or *alumna*). • She is an *alumni* of Lincoln University, earning both her bachelor's and master's degrees in secondary education with a mathematics emphasis. USE *alumna.*

amature Misspelling of *amateur.* • I'm an *amature* chef and jack of many trades. USE *amateur.* • An *amature* mistake on Hershal's part can cause him to get an arm or leg broken or something worse. USE *amateur.* • But it has been proven he doesn't know squat and is a clueless *amature.* USE *amateur.*

Amateur, not *amature,* is the correct spelling.

ambivalate Misused for *be ambivalent.* • They *ambivalate* about making love, and planning to see each other again. USE *are ambivalent.* • Most of us vacillate and *ambivalate* about type on occasion. USE *are ambivalent.*

Ambivalate, another stillborn word from the social sciences, is meant to mean to vacillate between opposing interests, desires, or views, which, of course, is what the flourishing *be ambivalent* has long meant.

ambivalent Misused for *ambiguous.* • Although it clearly was not the intention of the administration to force the change for existing or already authorized projects, it is true that the language is *ambivalent.* USE *ambiguous.* • If we are of serious intent we should have watertight wording, not *ambivalent* wording. USE *ambiguous.*

And *ambiguous* is misused for *ambivalent*: • Even today when I look at photographs of the boat I have *ambiguous* feelings—a love-hate relationship! USE *ambivalent.* • And Allen's self-loathing, misanthropy, and *ambiguous* attitude toward women are hardly news. USE *ambivalent.* • *Ambiguous* feelings in Poland, for example, about military commitment in Iraq reflect the contradictory pulls of these impulses. USE *Ambivalent.*

Ambiguous means unclear; capable of being understood in more than one way. *Ambivalent* means having two different or contradictory feelings or views about someone or something. The meanings of these two words are decidedly different. Let us not waste the words we have under the false rubric, the artificial idealism, of liberalism or democracy, which as espoused by some, asserts one word may mean much the same as another. Neglecting or not knowing the distinctions between words can lead only to ambiguity and ambivalence at best, anarchy and turmoil at worst.

ameliorate Misused for *alleviate.* • The liberal Democratic model assumes that society can and should be adjusted to *ameliorate* suffering, especially of the underprivileged and the newcomers. USE *alleviate.* • One of the simplest and most efficient means to *ameliorate* pain and suffering is through the use of analgesics or pain medication. USE *alleviate.*

You do not *ameliorate* pain or suffering; you *alleviate* it. *Ameliorate* means to make better; to improve. *Alleviate* means to lessen; to make more bearable. SEE ALSO **amiliorate**.

amend Confused with *emend.* Both *amend* and *emend* derive from the Latin *emendare.* To *amend* is to make better or improve; to correct or revise ("Lubbock County Commissioners had to amend the county's sexually oriented business regulations based on a recent Supreme Court ruling"). To *emend,* more typically used in literary contexts, is to make improvements or corrections ("Calligraphers are free agents; they emend texts, and elongate graphs and employ variant or archaic forms for artistic ends"). The noun form of *amend* is *amendment*; the noun form of *emend* is *emendation.*

amendable Misused for *amenable.* • Defensor was *amendable* to Lacson's suggestion and added he was willing to shoulder the cost in the spirit of cooperation. USE *amenable.* • Change is never easy and the membership must be *amendable* to change. USE *amenable.* • Organizations that are more idea-driven than dollars-and-cents-driven can be more *amendable* to compromise. USE *amenable.*

Amendable has a meaning different from *amenable. Amendable* means able to be changed or improved for the better; correctable; alterable. *Amenable* means responsive to suggestion, advice, or authority; willing. Those unaware of the distinction deserve the *D.*

amiable Misused for *amicable.* • Following the public lecture, there will be *amiable* discussion over lunch with the speakers and registered faculty. USE *amicable.* • Following the divorce, he and the mother maintained an *amiable* relationship and were able to effectively manage his visitations with the children. USE *amicable.* • The couple agreed to seek an *amiable* divorce with neither party being at fault. USE *amicable.*

Amicable is also misused for *amiable*: • We seek an *amicable* person to assist our receptionist with general office duties. USE *amiable.*

Amiable means friendly; cordial; likeable. *Amicable* means showing goodwill or friendliness. *Amiable* is generally used to describe people; *amicable,* to describe occurrences, situations, or relationships between people.

amiable Misused for *amenable.* • Being *amiable* to this sort of thing, humans complied by kissing anytime two people happened to be under the mistletoe. USE *amenable.* • But new commissioner Mike Cox is *amiable* to some modification, though he didn't swallow all the industry suggestions. USE *amenable.* • Mr. Shier contacted the agents for the building, who said they were *amiable* to the idea. USE *amenable.*

Amiable (AY-mee-ah-ble) means friendly, good-natured, likeable. *Amenable* (ah-MEE-nah-ble) means responsive to advice, authority, or suggestion; willing. Though their pronunciations are similar, their meanings are not.

amiliorate Misspelling of *ameliorate.* • We're trying to figure out which ones can *amiliorate* the different sites in the brain, and then we can find which targets might not treat the disorder. USE *ameliorate.* • The Obama administration favors spending at this time to *amiliorate* the fiscal crisis and to do so in a manner that invests in long-term productivity that makes it easier to pay down the costs when the crisis abates. USE *ameliorate.* • Let us work to make changes for the *amilioration* of this beautiful continent. USE *amelioration.*

Ameliorate, amelioration, ameliorative are the only correct spellings. SEE ALSO **ameliorate.**

amongst Misused for *among. Amongst,* among the potentially bright, is preferable to *among,* but only because their potential has yet to be realized. • But we knew *amongst* ourselves that we could get the job done. USE *among.* • He ranked fourth on the team, and first *amongst* defensive linemen, with both his 81 tackles and 57 solos. USE *among.* • It does appear that awareness is up *amongst* consumers. USE *among.*

Amongst, like *amidst* and *whilst* and *unbeknownst,* is an archaic, pretentious term, at least in American English. Use *among* (*amid, while, unknown*): • But *unbeknownst* to them, the fire had already gone through the walls and into the attic space, where it was running rampant. USE *unknown.* • Players must penetrate Atombender's base, attempting to recover parts of the system password *whilst* avoiding deadly robots in a race against time. USE *while.* • Gallop on over to Marriott's Griffin Gate Resort, nestled *amidst* the lush, rolling green meadows of Kentucky's Bluegrass Country, for a romance, dining, or golf getaway and enjoy luxury accommodations and unbeatable rates. USE *amid.*

Although these words may seem more elegant than their more common counterparts, they are not. Using these archaic forms of *among, amid, unbeknown* (or *unknown*), and *while* is the mark of a sophomoric, not a sophisticated, writer or speaker. SEE ALSO **between**; **unbeknown**.

amoral Misused for *immoral.* • There's nothing inherently *amoral* or scandalous about manifesting your sexuality for a mass audience, especially when your job is to entertain. Use *immoral.* • AIDS is not a punishment or a retribution for *amoral* practices, but a problem which faces modern humankind: in 2002 in the world there were 3.2 million children infected with the virus. Use *immoral.*

Amoral means unconcerned with or incapable of distinguishing between right and wrong; beyond the scope of morality. *Immoral* means not conforming to the accepted standards of right and wrong; wicked; lewd.

amount Misused for *number.* • Prices are set at $10.00/month for a single board or $25/month for an unlimited *amount* of boards. Use *number.* • Buy a qualifying *amount* of books and save 10% on all your subsequent purchases of nondiscounted books. Use *number.* • All these methods will get you a minuscule *amount* of terrorists and a maximum *amount* of drug dealers instead. Use *number.* • The trends include aging of the population, a decrease in the *amount* of people who are available to work, an increase in the number of people who are willing to move to get a better-paying position, and a change in the way that work is being done. Use *number.* • In addition, actions taken to eliminate the *amount* of immigrants who are consuming U.S. jobs have created an underground economy and consequently lowered the wages for Americans as well as immigrants. Use *number.*

The word *number* is used with that which can be easily counted (or with count nouns); the word *amount* with that which cannot easily be counted (or with mass nouns). See also **less; much.**

> What was interesting to me, during the recall, was the amount of people that came out to hear Schwarzenegger.
>
> —U.S. Senator Dianne Feinstein
>
> If Senator Feinstein thinks of these people as a mass of people, "the masses," perhaps, and not as individuals, she might be able to convince us that *amount* is the correct word; if not, then not.

> I was moved by the amount of friends, enemies, and media who assumed they knew Rush, but later admitted to his two personas: one boisterous and confident while the other shy, and private.
>
> —Bob Parks, *American Daily*
>
> Friends, enemies, and media are all countable, but perhaps Parks does not count much; his writing certainly does not.

ampersand Use an ampersand (&) only in proper names—business names, book titles, and the like—that use it themselves; never use it in place of the word *and*. Aside from the hurried, the only people inclined to use & in place of *and* are those who have scant sense of self and scant sense of style, and believe using & somehow swells them both: • The complete first & second season is available now on a DVD four-volume set. USE *and*. • The Goldman Sachs Foundation announces $2.5 million in grants for international education projects in Europe, Africa, Asia & South America. USE *and*. • Read about our responsibilities and find passport information, visa regulations, travel tips, & voting procedures. USE *and*. • My idea is also to turn you on to writers' efforts, flaws & fortes, & my interviews reveal some of the passion, adventures & everyday labor that go into making a book happen. USE *and*.

a must (miss) Like all badly made terms, *a must (miss)* is no sooner said than it sounds stale, no sooner read, than it sours. In all its variations—*a must-have, a must-read, a must-see,* and so on—this phrase is altogether too *musty*. • A good soundtrack, but a dull story, bad acting and weak special effects make this *a must-miss*. • Phone interviewing skills are *a must-have* for most human resource professionals who spend a good portion of their day on the phone. • Is that business trip *a must*? • It is *a must-stop* location for portfolio-toting high school and college students from across the country. • Over 200 *must-do* summer events are listed. • Aux Delices is *a must-stop* for chowhounds. • If ever the Lightning faced *a must-win* game, this was it. SEE ALSO **a (good) read**; **(take) a look-see**.

an Misused for *a.* • After *an historic* day of grand jury testimony, Clinton called on the country—and independent counsel Kenneth W. Starr—to move on from the embarrassing episode. USE *a historic.* • *An hallucination* may be a sensory experience in which a person can see, hear, smell, taste, or feel something that is not there. USE *A hallucination.* • Search for *an hotel* in France. USE *a hotel.* • This is what I would call *an human* interest story. USE *a human.*

The correct form is *a historic,* not *an historic*. Similarly, *a hallucination* and *a hotel* and *a human* are correct; *an hallucination* and *an hotel* and *an human* are not. Conversely, *a heirloom* (like *a herb, a heir,* and *a heiress*) is incorrect. Since the *h* of *heirloom* is not pronounced, we say *an heirloom. A* is used before a consonant sound; *an* before a vowel sound. It's true that the correct wording was once *an historic,* but not since we have been pronouncing the *h* in this word and others. SEE ALSO **herb**; **historic**; **human**.

> At this point, the broken consensus represents, more than anything else, an historic opportunity.
>
> —Laura Carlsen, *CounterPunch*
>
> Gengaro's all-star pitching effort had an huge effect on the whole team.
>
> —Michael Cheung, *Yale Daily News*
>
> Potential banned activities include implanting human embryos in animal bodies, attempting to fertilize an human egg with animal sperm and conceiving children by harvesting eggs and sperm from fetuses.
>
> —Sheri Hall, *The Detroit News*
>
> There is no reason to—and every reason not to—use *an* before an aspirated *h*. Surely these writers do not say *an istoric, an uge, an uman,* but using *an* before these words suggests that they do and that we, their readers, should.

anaphalic Misused for *anaphylactic.* • Kid #2 is so allergic to wheat gluten she goes into *anaphalic* shock. USE *anaphylactic.* • He threw 500mg of Dextran in my IV and I had *anaphalic* shock. USE *anaphylactic.* • My daughter had an egg allergy, and my "brilliant" doctor insisted that she would be fine having the MMR: "We'll do it in the hospital and if she goes into *anaphalic* shock we can get Adrenalin straight into her system." USE *anaphylactic.*

The adjective of *anaphylaxis* is *anaphylactic* (*an*-ah-fah-LAK-tik), not, as some would have it, *anaphalic* (an-ah-FAL-ik).

and etc. (and et cetera) Misused for *etc.* • The money pays for trips to day camp, uniforms, training videos on topics such as drug awareness and youth protection, snorkeling gear, life jackets, fishing equipment, scholarships, *and etc.* DELETE *and.* • Many other advanced functions for mail service like antispam, auto-reply, mail block, forward, search, *and etc.,* are all in WMS-2208R's feature list. DELETE *and.*

The expression *and etc.* (or *and et cetera*) is redundant; use *etc.* or *et cetera* alone. *Et cetera* is Latin for and (*et*) the rest (*cetera*). SEE ALSO **ect.**; **et al.**; **etc., etc.**; **etcetera**.

anecdote Misused for *antidote.* • The best *anecdote* to a full day of shopping is sitting down to an unforgettable meal. USE *antidote.* • It had little bearing on the outcome but was a perfect *anecdote* to Friday's wildness. USE *antidote.* • The assassination attempt upset the late King Hussein, who threatened to sever diplomatic relations with Israel unless the Jewish state provided the *anecdote* countering the chemical agent. USE *antidote.* • The *anecdote* to violence is not turning our schools into prisons. USE *antidote.* • Nero tried to poison his mother three times, but she took an *anecdote* before eating. USE *antidote.* • Extracts of jewelweed have been shown in clinical studies to be an effective *anecdote* to poison ivy and oak rashes. USE *antidote.*

An *anecdote* is a short, interesting, or amusing story about a person or event. An *antidote* is a medicine that counteracts the effects of a poison; something that neutralizes an unpleasant situation or feeling.

angel Misspelling of *angle.* • The recommended numbers of lines and *angels* in the PIJ mesh are 100 and 11, respectively. USE *angles.* • The sum of two *angels* of a triangle is less than or equal to their remote exterior angle. USE *angles.*

And *angle* is a misspelling of *angel*: • Fully one third of the *angles* in heaven were deceived by Satan. USE *angels.* • The scene is a large village view with the *angles* on high and Scripture verses scattered in the sky. USE *angels.*

An *angel* is a celestial being; a seraph; a lovable, gentle person. An *angle,* a figure made by two lines diverging from a common point; a scheme.

anniversary *Anniversary* derives from the Latin *anniversarius,* returning yearly, and *annus* alone is Latin for year, so the word *year* in an expression such as *ten-year anniversary* is redundant: • Coming up on the *ten-year anniversary* of 9/11, the matters facing our nation's intelligence community and law enforcement agencies are significant. USE *tenth anniversary.* • Final rankings won't be available until the site's *second-year anniversary* on January 18, 2011. USE *second anniversary.*

annoyment Misused for *annoyance.* • If you hide this bauble on one of your pages, you do risk major *annoyment* to any of your visitors who lack a sense of humor. USE *annoyance.* • A minor crack in the finger can be a major source of *annoyment.* USE *annoyance.* • This portion of the site contains a few ramblings for your enjoyment/*annoyment.* USE *annoyance.* • The *annoyment* level goes up as the fun quotient drops during tourist season but on an average day you almost always see someone you know. USE *annoyance.* • What are these words that men mistakenly repeat over and over that are a source of *annoyment* and can actually make you appear to be stupid because you lack a vocabulary? USE *annoyance.*

Annoyment, an archaic variation of *annoyance,* has no place in today's English language, where words for being annoyed are already superabundant.

anonymous Misused for *unanimous.* • From what I can tell, it's all pretty *anonymous* among the teams. USE *unanimous.* • With *anonymous* agreement Bernie is officially in charge of the next lake party or social event. USE *unanimous.*

Though there is some similarity in sound between *anonymous* and *unanimous,* there is no similarity in meaning. *Anonymous* means unknown or unacknowledged, whereas *unanimous* means in complete agreement.

Antartica Misspelling of *Antarctica.* • Michael has run a marathon in every continent on the planet, including the icy tundra of *Antartica.* USE *Antarctica.* • It follows the emperor penguins of *Antartica* during their annual mating ritual season. USE *Antarctica.*

Two *c*'s are needed to correctly spell *Antarctica* (ant-ARK-ti-kah). SEE ALSO **artic**.

> A summer voyage to retrieve an aircraft abandoned in Antartica nearly 100 years ago has been put on hold.
>
> —ABC News, Australia

antithesis The pronunciation of *antithesis* is (an-TITH-i-sis), not (an-tee-THEE-sis).

anxious Misused for *eager.* • The Buffalo Sabres are *anxious* to get rookie Maxim Afinogenov back for the American Hockey League playoffs following Russia's elimination at the World Hockey Championships. USE *eager.* • The 50 people whose lives were changed when fire ravaged their homes at the Maryel Manor senior housing complex two months ago are *anxious* for things to return to the way they used to be. USE *eager.* • I'm not *anxious* to fly, but I have to be in California. USE *eager.*

Anxious is best reserved for feelings of dread, apprehension, or uneasiness; using it also as a synonym for *eager* can lead to confusion.

anymore *Anymore* (not *any more*) is used in the sense of today or nowadays when the sentence in which it appears is negative: "Gas isn't so expensive *anymore.*" *Anymore* in a nonnegative sentence like "Gas is so expensive *anymore*" is fairly common among speakers in the midwestern and western United States. People who care about how they speak, and about being understood, would do well to shun this dialectal usage.

anymoreso than Misused for *any more than.* • And let's not forget that being Jewish is no guarantor of appropriate behavior *anymoreso than* any other religious affiliation. USE *any more than.* • It is not beyond the limits of your intelligence to comprehend the differences between truth and deception, *anymoreso than* between right and wrong. USE *any more than.* • HumanKin do not want to destroy magical things *anymoreso than* OtherKin want to destroy human things. USE *any more than.* • Why should we be exposed to these egotistical and amateurish Karaoke singers *anymoreso than* all these poorly conditioned and ill-trained backyard wrestlers? USE *any more than.*

Any more than, not *anymoreso than,* is the correct wording.

anyways Misused for *anyway.* • What is a blog *anyways*? USE *anyway.* • What time is it, *anyways*? USE *anyway.* • *Anyways,* he was stealthy as a shadow, unlike some people. USE *Anyway.* • *Anyways,* I guess the best thing about birthdays is you get to hear from people you haven't heard from for a while. USE *Anyway.* • We are simply doing what we do *anyways*—securing software—and they have no say in the matter. USE *anyway.*

Labeling *anyways*—like *anywheres, somewheres,* and *nowheres*—dialectal, as many dictionaries do, is too kind; let them label it what it is: uneducated. SEE ALSO **in regards to**; **ways**; **with regards to**.

> He was executed somewheres around December 1974.
>
> —Howard Dean
>
> It was a night of peace and love and music (well that's what Ringo said anyways), and fans were taken on a mini tour of musical history spanning decades.
>
> —Kate Dingle, *The Palm Beach Post*

appraise Misused for *apprise.* • There is a thermocouple, which is a heat probe, connected to a digital controller, that keeps me *appraised* of the exact salt temps and can be used to control the temperature automatically, though I don't regularly use this feature. USE *apprised.* • Obviously, we cannot keep up with day-to-day changes, if any, in the methodology unless the vendor keeps us *appraised* of the changes and that is why we will cease showing numbers on his system. USE *apprised.*

The word *appraise* means to evaluate or estimate; *apprise,* to inform or notify. To use *appraise* when *apprise* is meant not only may confuse your audience but also may eventually eliminate from the language a unique word.

> And throughout it all Laing executives held meetings in residents' homes and City Councilman Alex Padilla's office to keep the neighborhood appraised of progress.
>
> —Gregory J. Wilcox, *Los Angeles Daily News*

appreciate Misused for *value* (or similar words). • I *appreciate* you, and what you do. USE *value.* • I know I've said it time and again, but I do *appreciate* you, my friend. USE *treasure.* • He's dedicating a lot of time to make sure our national finance effort is as strong as I know it's going to be. I *appreciate* you, Mercer. USE *thank.* • There are not enough words in the world to tell you how much I love you, how much I *appreciate* you, or how much I want to thank you. USE *admire.* • She keeps me straight on all my links and she doesn't miss a trick and I *appreciate* her very much. USE *respect.* • Tell your brothers that you *appreciate* them, but they need to back off. USE *love.*

You can *appreciate* an attribute or occurrence ("I appreciate her thoughtfulness"; "I appreciate your coming"), but not a person ("I appreciate you"; "I appreciate so many folks enduring the rain").

Using *appreciate* in the sense discouraged here is the mark of people who have no notion of eloquence and style, and scant appreciation of the limits of language.

> Thank you for your interest in Patrick Henry College. We appreciate you.
>
> —*The Trumpet of Liberty,* Patrick Henry College
>
> *The Trumpet* toots; it does not trumpet.

apropos Misused for *appropriate.* • They've had three years to get it right and the timing could not be more *apropos.* USE *appropriate.* • The setting will be *apropos,* since the museum currently has 48 paintings by 15 Highwaymen artists on exhibit in its art gallery. USE *appropriate.* • I think it was very *apropos* for the kind of person he is and the way he respects this organization, and the kind of respect the organization gives him. USE *appropriate.*

Apropos (*ap*-rah-POE) means in regard to; relevant. *Appropriate* means suitable or fitting.

architect Misused for *design* (or similar words). • Advanced modeling tools based on Visio enable developers to *architect* applications, design databases, and model business processes. USE *devise.* • You'd never ask an interior designer to *architect* a house, and you probably wouldn't go with an architect's opinion of a color scheme for the walls of your living space. USE *design.* • Howard Alan's vision is to *architect* buildings that are of the continuous present. USE *engineer.* • They were faced with the dilemma of how to *rearchitect* the existing site and deliver a high-quality application to their customers on a timely basis. USE *redesign.*

To *architect* is an absurdity. Not everyone can concoct an effervescent verb from some stolid noun. Though nouns do indeed occasionally become verbs, *architect* is hardly a good candidate, for many other verbs already provide more exacting definitions of what to *architect* seeks to define. A word not born of need begets only noise.

a (good) read *Read* as a noun is one of the shibboleths by which people who care about language identify people who do not. Today there are people who try to speak and write well, and there are people who have no such aspirations: • All the chapters are clearly structured, making them *an easy read for* both seasoned researchers and graduate students in second-language studies. USE *easily read by.* • Anyone who knows Massey knows what an interesting and thoughtful person he is, so it's stating the obvious to say every post is *a good read.* USE *stimulating read.* • Twists, turns and big suspense make this *a fantastic read* this summer, or anytime. USE *fantastic reading.*

artic Misspelling of *arctic.* • But by the afternoon, the wind rolled in like a blast straight from the *Artic.* USE *Arctic.* • However, to advocate the exploitation of the *Artic* National Wildlife Refuge and other protected spaces in the United States is irresponsible. USE *Arctic.* • In the film,

Adam plays Henry, an *artic* wildlife veterinarian who spends his spare time breaking the hearts of female tourists. USE *arctic.*

Arctic is spelled with two *c*'s: *arc, tic.* Only the hopelessly insular spell the word with one *c.* The pronunciation of *arctic* is (ARK-tik), not (AR-tik). SEE ALSO **Antartica**.

as Misused for *because* (or similar words). • Very little goes to waste, *as* almost the entire creature is edible. USE *since.* • That does not happen now, however, *as* there is just too much mail. USE *because.* • The situation may be worse, *as* 12 of the 43 schools surveyed did not respond. USE *for.* • They eat as much as they want, *as* restricting kids' calories can stunt growth and brain development. USE *since.* • *As* I haven't heard back from you, I am resending this email to you to ask for a couple minutes of your time. USE *Since.*

As instead of *because* or *since* or *for* is sometimes ambiguous for the word *while,* and therefore is best not used causally. What's more, *as* in this sense is colloquial; it is used by everyday, uninspired writers. Listen to TV commercials, especially those for pharmaceuticals, and many of them will declare: ". . . as this may cause an unsafe drop in blood pressure" (or some other malady, usually far worse than whatever the drug is purported to relieve). TV commercials, of course, are the utter antithesis of well-written, inspired English.

as Misused for *that.* • I don't know *as* I understand you. USE *that.* • Be sure and not speak of it at home, for I don't know *as* he knows it himself. USE *that.* • I don't know *as* I can tell you. USE *that.*

Neither in the sense of *because* nor in the sense of *that* should *as* be used. *As* instead of *that* is informal.

ascared Misused for *scared* (or similar words). Likely the result of people confusedly adding the initial *a* of *afraid* to the word *scared, ascared* is a disagreeable word.

ascetic Misused for *acetic.* • While the accident was contained to the southbound lanes, traffic was halted on all four lanes because of some spillage of *ascetic* acid solution, which was described to city-county Emergency Operations Center dispatchers as "paint thinner." USE *acetic.* • Citric acid seems to be the most dominant acid flavor, and I do not detect much in the way of *ascetic* acid. USE *acetic.*

Acetic means like, containing, or producing vinegar or acetic acid. *Ascetic* means self-denying or austere.

> The mummies in question are the remains of an obscure cult of mountain-dwelling Buddhist monks known as the Yamabashi—literally "he who lies in the mountain"—famous for their extremely acetic lifestyle.
>
> —Discovery Channel web page

ascetic Misused for *aesthetic.* • Installation of a new storm door takes about two hours and may greatly improve the *ascetic* beauty at the front entrance of your home. USE *aesthetic.* • The flowers are not just for *ascetic* pleasure, but have amazing flavoring qualities. USE *aesthetic.* • The use of such a team could give your products or services a leading edge in the marketplace by addressing safety, *ascetic,* and practical concerns all together. USE *aesthetic.*

Ascetic means pertaining to or characteristic of an ascetic; rigid in self-denial or devotions; austere; severe. *Aesthetic* relates to aesthetics or what is beautiful; artistic; pleasing in appearance. SEE ALSO **aesthetic.**

ascribe Misused for *subscribe.* • The Iraqi people did not *ascribe* to Saddam's thoughts, nor did the majority of them support his regime. USE *subscribe.* • Those in the center, on the other hand, believe the extremists are ideologically arrogant and are likely to *ascribe* to the philosophy espoused in the famous Indian legend The Blind Men and the Elephant. USE *subscribe.* • I know that some well-known popular bands *ascribe* to this theory, so I suspect that there is some truth to it. USE *subscribe.*

To *ascribe* is to attribute something to; to assign as a quality ("Most of the problems we ascribe to the 'drug problem' are really the problem of drug prohibition"; "Now is neither the time nor place to explore the complex relationship between belief and action, but suffice it to note that it is to our actions primarily that we ascribe the properties of 'moral' and 'immoral' "). To *subscribe* is to support or believe in; to pledge money; to sign one's name to a document; to sign up and pay for a regular publication or service. SEE ALSO **prescribe**.

> If legislators truly ascribe to the notion that "less government is preferable to more," a fresh look at the state and federal funding of unemployment compensation would seem an ideal fit.
>
> —Jon Zahm, *The Illinois Leader*
>
> Scribbler Zahm, a scribe indeed. Trust no one who does not know the meaning of his words.

as far as Misused for *as for* (or similar words). • *As far as* the "historical figure," Nathan Bedford Forrest has already been honored by the state, having Forrest County named in his honor. USE *As for*. • *As far as* looks, my taste is dark hair. USE *As for*. • The agency told legislative budget writers Tuesday the rebates will be a net neutral event, *as far as* impact on general fund revenues. USE *as for*. • But *as far as* the nastiness of the killings, I think we tried to steer toward creativity more than just being gratuitous. USE *as for*.

As for means concerning or with regard to. *As far as,* which means to the extent that, is an idiomatic phrase that, to make any sense at all, must conclude with the word *goes* (*go*) or *is* (*are*) *concerned*. To use *as far as* in the sense of *as for* exposes deplorable writing. But watch your dictionary, for before too terribly long, laxicographers will define *as far as* as *as for*.

assay Confused with *essay*. To *assay* is to determine the content or quality of; to analyze or evaluate ("To predict their deleterious effects, various in vivo or in vitro tests have been proposed to assay the xenoestrogenic activity"; "A lot of work was done in the past when they didn't even assay for gold because it wasn't what they were interested in"). To *essay* is to try out; attempt ("Such a ball can cramp a batsman, making it difficult for him to essay a positive stroke"). To *essay* seems an especially popular term among theater and movie critics, especially in India ("Mousumi, who is a model and started her acting career with KABK, is on cloud nine, as she is preparing herself to essay a new role in real life"; "I am proud to essay such a strong role and break the typecast that only a lady can be the main protagonist").

assent Misused for *ascent.* • The door had locked behind him and the small aircraft was beginning its *assent* into space. USE *ascent.* • Theme Park Inc. promises to include an ongoing narrative based around your projected *assent* up the corporate ladder. USE *ascent.* • Another steep *assent* puts you on top of the world among scenic high lakes, meadows, and snow-capped peaks. USE *ascent.*

Ascent means the act of rising or climbing; an upward slope; an advancement in status. *Assent* means agreement or consent.

assertation Misused for *assertion.* • I would dispute your *assertation.* USE *assertion.* • I can't say enough that this *assertation* is categorically, absolutely, and unconditionally wrong. USE *assertion.* • Given Miller's *assertation* that he knew of "at least three" teams willing to pay Boozer's $10.97 million salary, it appears that other teams have called to inquire about the forward. USE *assertion.*

Assertation, a thoroughly obsolete word used by fearfully modern people, is incorrect for *assertion. Assertation*—like the equally preposterous *documentate* (instead of *document*) and *opinionation* (instead of *opinion*)—is spoken or written by people who do not well know the words they use, by people who do not often read, by people who do not cavil over adding a syllable or two to a word: humanity lies elsewhere.

assiduous Misused for *acidulous.* • Duchamp himself developed a profound and *assiduous* wit throughout his artistic career, to the extent that his works have been described as forms of wit themselves. USE *acidulous.* • I enjoyed *Armageddon,* but it can't really be viewed as an *assiduous* commentary on the danger posed by asteroids and comets. USE *acidulous.* • From reading your many *assiduous* remarks, you are either a plant from Obama, a real left-wing nut, or just plain ignorant. USE *acidulous.*

Acidulous (ah-SIJ-ah-les) means caustic or sharp in speech or manner; sour or tart. *Assiduous* (ah-SIJ-oo-es) means diligent; persistent.

as such *As such* is an idiom that means in itself or in that capacity. The pronoun *such* in this expression must have a clear antecedent ("The *Times*' op-ed 'Trenton is in crisis' by Irwin S. Stoolmacher is a gross portrayal of the City of Trenton's administration. *As such,* it must be answered and corrected"—that is, as a gross portrayal of the City of Trenton's administration. "Written late in Janácek's life, this opera is a complex affair full of underlying tension and dramatic subtlety. *As such,* it proves a difficult piece for a company to master, requiring a balance of psychological strangeness and fairytale warmth"—that is, as a complex affair full of underlying tension and dramatic subtlety).

As such does not mean under these conditions, in these circumstances, however, therefore, for that reason, because of this, or any other transitional phrase. The following examples, all incorrect, show no identifiable antecedent: • Out of a possible 100, the oil giant earns an overall score of 96, compared to just 51 in January 2010. *As such,* we rate the stock a long-term buy. • This gap between dictionaries and the lexicon results from a balance that every dictionary must strike: It must be comprehensive enough to be a useful reference but concise enough to be printed, shipped, and used. *As such,* many infrequent words are omitted. • Mr. Kennedy has withdrawn his request for unemployment benefits. *As such,* the city has withdrawn its appeal.

assume Misused for *presume.* • I don't *assume* to know how my car works just because I drive one—I am not a mechanic. Use *presume.* • I believe (if I may *assume* to speak for anyone) they are annoyed, perturbed and generally disgusted with a particular kind of Christian. Use *presume.*

To *assume* is to suppose something to be so, and is based on possible evidence. To *presume* is to believe something to be so, and is based on probable evidence; to venture without authority or justification. See also **assumptious**.

assume Misused for *as soon.* • Last year was Lowe's worst in the majors, so it was somehow fitting that it was also a season Varitek would just *assume* forget. Use *as soon.* • Although it was fast becoming the entertainment and gambling Mecca of the world, the city was dogged by an image as a haven for crooks, thieves, and any other unsavory characteristic a city would just *assume* not be associated with. USE *as soon.* • However, I'd just *assume* not find out. USE *as soon.*

Assume, instead of *as soon,* is mind-numbingly inane. SEE ALSO **wearas.**

> The Red Sox want Rodriguez to re-structure his contract, and Scott Boras would just assume wash some of the slime off his skin before allowing that to happen.
>
> —Eric Wilbur, *The Boston Globe*
>
> I would just assume go out and deal with it right off the bat and try to cut down on what I'm going to have to do later on down the road.
>
> —Paul Merrill, Fox 23 News

assumptious It could be that those who use the rare *assumptious* (assuming or given to assumption) mean exactly that, but—given that some dictionaries offer presumption as one definition of *assumption,* and assumption as one definition of *presumption*—perhaps they mean the less restrained presumptuous (impertinently bold; forward): • Please do not allow any more judgmental, stereotypical, racist, or *assumptious* comments on these sites. • I hate when men assume that since I have a job I'd be "contributing cash to the relationship"; it's really quite *assumptious.* • I never said it was perfect but it is predictable though somewhat *assumptious,* but then isn't that what your entire belief in JC is?

There is a difference between *assume* and *presume,* between *assumption* and *presumption,* between *assumptious* and *presumptuous.* SEE ALSO **assume**; **presumptious**.

asterisk The pronunciation of *asterisk* is (AS-tah-*risk*), not (AS-tricks) or (AS-trick) or (AS-ter-iks).

as to Misused for *about* (or similar words). • One hint *as to* his possibly altered standing comes from the latest version of the *Encyclopaedia Britannica,* which, although Roget was an editor of the seventh edition and a contributor of more than 300,000 words to it, gives him somewhat short shrift today, with an entry of a mere twenty lines. Use *of.* • For example, testing of a graphics library will require a very different approach *as to* that of a calendar manager. Use *from.* • Depending on the night, the meal, and the energy of the evening, I also made distinctions *as to* the drink best suited to the occasion. Use *in.*

As to the phrase *as to whether,* delete *as to.* • If your browser is not secure, or there is any question *as to whether* or not it is, please download Netscape Navigator, Microsoft Internet Explorer, or an equivalent browser. Delete *as to.* • Yet there has been some question *as to whether* their hearts can take it. Delete *as to.*

Except when used to begin a sentence, *as to* is if not solecistic then certainly sloppy for a more precise *about* or *of, for* or *with, from* or *to, on* or *in.* This phrase, midsentence, identifies a person who, though he writes, doesn't much care to.

astronomy Misused for *astrology.* • We are raised in a highly Western civilized religion-based society where it is wrong and evil to believe in psychics and *astronomy* and horoscopes. Use *astrology.* • An official in the Presidential Security Service is paid to prepare *astronomical* horoscopes of the leaders of the nation. Use *astrological.*

Astrology is the study of the positions of the sun, moon, and stars to foretell the future or determine human affairs. *Astronomy* is the scientific study of the universe. See also **cosmology**.

as well (too) Do not use an ungainly *as well* or *too,* in the sense of *and* or *what's more,* to begin a sentence: • *As well,* Long Island is in a high-wind watch. Use *What's more.* • *As well,* if tonight is too short notice, I apologize. Delete *As well.* • *As well,* it's a coastal city with a major port, has farmland and agricultural land and is a powerhouse city of about seven million people. Use *Moreover.*

At other times, *as well* is even more awkwardly used: We don't negotiate with terrorists; *we don't advise others to do so as well.* Use *nor do we advise others to do so.*

as well or better than Misused for *as well as or better than.* • For many, it reduces seizure activity over time *as well, or better, than* it did initially. Use *as well as or better than.* • However, we believe that we are giving you an excellent product to work with as our reeds perform and last *as well or better than* any brand we know of. Use *as well as or better than.* • Studies have shown that students who work do just *as well or better than* non-working students and grades improve as students work more hours per week. Use *as well as or better than.*

So often, the word *as* either is used where it is not wanted or is not used where it is wanted. In comparative phrases like *as well as or better than,* the second *as* is quite as important as the first.

athlete The pronunciation of *athlete* is (ATH-leet), not (ATH-ah-leet).

augur Misused for *auger.* • For the past several weeks Goldstake field crews have been correlating mapped diamond and *augur* drill hole and surface trench data with the actual sites on the property. Use *auger.* • For the first three years that this operation was carried out, the City of Oconto used an off-the-shelf *augur* with a standard screw tip to drill the holes. Use *auger.* • Ten inches from the ground in each of the posts, make a hole 3 inches by 1 inch, by boring three holes with an inch *augur* and clearing them out. Use *auger.*

And *auger* is often used where *augur* should be: • Recent developments *auger* well for the public availability of a new class of drugs that appear to alleviate deficits in learning and memory and may also show promise in the treatment of schizophrenia. Use *augur.* • We do not *auger* future events, but rather focus upon present circumstances. Use *augur.*

An *auger* is a tool used to make holes; as a verb, it means to bore or drill. An *augur* is a soothsayer, prophet, or diviner; as a verb, it means to predict or presage. *Augury* is an omen or the interpretation of omens.

aural Misused for *oral.* • Feedback was in the form of weekly tutorials and *aural* remarks during reviews and written comment and marks for assessment of the students' work. Use *oral.* • The other class participants observe and offer both written and *aural* comments and suggestions. USE *oral.*

Aural means heard through the ears; relating to the ears or hearing. *Oral* means uttered by the mouth; relating to the mouth or speaking. Though the words are pronounced alike—they are homophones—their meanings differ. SEE ALSO **verbal**.

austentatious Misused for *ostentatious.* • Shanghai is an *austentatious* example of the incredible, burgeoning wealth of Asian markets. USE *ostentatious.* • I actually like this one better than the black, chromey one! It's more subtle, stylish IMHO. I think the chromey one is just a wee tad *austentatious.* USE *ostentatious.*

Although *austentatious* has been coined to mean marked by, or fond of, the conspicuous or vainglorious and sometimes pretentious display of all things related to Jane Austen, it also is the name of an off-Broadway musical, and is used, by some, to describe Australia. Still others use it to mean *ostentatious* (characterized by or given to ostentation; pretentious), which is its only disagreeable definition.

authentification Misused for *authentication.* • The Justice Ministry has been found to be testing a high-tech voice *authentification* system for surveillance of some violent and sexual offenders released on either bail or probation. USE *authentication.* • A certificate of *authentification* signed by the late Maris comes with the etching. USE *authentication.*

The verb is *authenticate,* and the noun is *authentication,* not *authentification.*

authuritis Misspelling of *arthritis.* • I have severe *authuritis* in both my knees, which limits me dramatically. USE *arthritis.* • She's real old now so it's not really surprising that she's having problems like that, not to mention *authuritis* and being completely stone deaf. USE *arthritis.*

Arthritis, not *authuritis,* is the correct word. The adjective is *arthritic,* not *authuritic*: • I use an Audio Tech 4033 condenser mic, which is so sensitive it can pick up an *authuritic* click from my elbow. USE *arthritic.*

avenge Confused with *revenge. Avenge* (a verb) implies getting even for a previous wrong or injustice, one often done to a third party ("Arshad believed he had to avenge a stain on his family's honor"; "Inmates had feared the guards would try to avenge the death of their colleague"). *Revenge* (a verb or a noun) implies a mean-spirited or malice-driven retaliation ("The *Independent* reported that Kulwant Singh did this in revenge after being spurned by Amex"; "A man was charged with shooting another man to death apparently out of revenge, just days after the victim had been acquitted of murdering the suspect's cousin").

averse Misused for *adverse.* • A good time for playing the good samaritan, contributing to a human cause and providing cheer to those facing *averse* circumstances. USE *adverse.* • In addition, dosage guidelines and *averse* effects of these therapies are presented. USE *adverse.* • Natural doesn't necessarily mean allergy-free, of course—fruits and plants can cause *averse* reactions on sensitive folk, just like the man-made stuff—but consider this: Everything your skin absorbs ends up in your bloodstream. USE *adverse.* • Despite the *averse* weather most caught well from the start with only four blanks recorded over the two days. USE *adverse.*

And *adverse* is sometimes used for *averse:* • Risk-*adverse* market participants need to know the most likely cost of environmental response and most likely value of the impaired property. USE *averse.*

The word *adverse* means antagonistic or adversarial; unfavorable or harmful. *Averse* means having a feeling of distaste, repugnance, or aversion; disinclined.

await for Misused for *await* or *wait for.* • He pauses, as if *awaiting for* a drummer to give him a rimshot. USE *waiting for.* • As he was leaving, the prince was cheered by a large crowd *awaiting for* his brief appearance. USE *awaiting.*

The verb *await* means to wait for, so to use *await for* is hardly necessary. SEE ALSO **for awhile**.

away Misspelling of *aweigh.* • As USS Cowpens arrives for the International Fleet Review, crew members man the rails while the 7th Fleet Band plays "Anchors *Away.*" USE *Aweigh.*

Aweigh (used of an anchor), not *away,* means hanging clear of the bottom of the sea. Similarly, you *weigh* (raise the anchor of the vessel from the sea floor), not *way,* anchor: • Ground tackle can become so firmly snagged on an underwater cable or pipe that attempting to *way* anchor can cause the boat to capsize. USE *weigh.*

awesome Misused for *excellent* (or similar words). • Our *awesome,* super child cross stitch will blow you away and help you to get more of what you deserve. USE *first-rate.* • These *awesome* calendars feature photos and illustrations and remind us of special occasions. USE *superlative.* • We went to Fire and Ice to eat which was *awesome* and then we drank and drank and drank. USE *excellent.*

Awesome ought to be used to mean inspiring awe, fear, or admiration; extremely impressive or intimidating. In the informal sense of excellent, it is a very poor, though very popular, choice of words. More than that, people who use *awesome* to mean excellent are, in fact, describing something that is, to keener minds, invariably mediocre or mindless, ridiculous or even repugnant. SEE ALSO **great**; **w00t**.

a whole nother Among educated speakers, *a whole nother* is sometimes used jocularly. Perhaps a clever person thought of this arrangement as an example of a tmesis, a rhetorical figure in which one word is made into two (*another* > *a nother*) or a word or phrase is added between parts of a compound word or between syllables of a word (*a whole nother*).

A delightful example of tmesis is found in the song "Wouldn't It Be Loverly" from *My Fair Lady*:

Oh so loverly sittin'
Abso-bloomin-lutely still.
I would never budge
Til Spring crept over the window sill.

Among less educated or slang-loving speakers, however, *a whole nother* is no longer clever; rather, it is just another example of ungrammatical English: • But we're talking about electric vehicles, and that's *a whole nother* ballgame because exactly two automakers sell mass-market EVs at the moment. • The program is designed to get kids interested in gardening—getting them to actually eat cabbage is *a whole nother* issue.

axed Misspelling of *asked.* • He *axed* me up a few days ago and I said that I'd be happy to be his stand-in. Use *asked.* • Once the gifts were exchanged, and we'd been introduced to all the cats, Art *axed* us about the "Mama Mia show." Use *asked.*

The misspelling probably stems from the mispronunciation. The pronunciation of *asked* is (ASKED), not (AKSD).

Bb

B

back slash Misused for *forward slash.* The *forward slash* (or *slash*) is the name of the / character on a computer keyboard. It leans forward. The *back slash* is the name of the \ character, which leans backward. SEE ALSO **slash**.

backwards Misused for *backward.* • Each state can be selected in order or random, so a *backwards* step or a jump of several steps is as simple to implement as a single step forward. USE *backward.* • It follows the lives of seven disparate people: a rock musician and his teenage groupie, two ruthless corporate sharks, an innocent *backwards* youth and his older brother, and a mysterious (and disarmingly droll) shaman. USE *backward.*

As an adverb, either *backwards* or *backward* is correct. As an adjective, only *backward* (in American English, if not in British English) is correct. SEE ALSO **afterwards**; **forwards**; **towards**.

bad Misused for *badly.* • In Britain you will never find a paper that speaks *bad* about that country. USE *badly.* • During pregnancy her calories will increase, but only if she eats *bad* will she get fat or crave even junkier foods. USE *badly.*

Bad is an adjective; *badly,* an adverb. Sensory verbs like *feel, taste,* and *smell* are followed by the adjective *bad,* not the adverb *badly*: • If the water is safe but smells *bad,* there are steps you can take to reduce or eliminate the problem. • Remember that lots of people say mean things because they feel *bad* about themselves. • Anytime potential government benefits flow to friends and relatives, it looks *bad.* SEE ALSO **feel badly**.

B

baneful Misused for *baleful.* • This historic practice has had a *baneful* effect on education and is not the fault of the coaches. Use *baleful.* • The *baneful* effects of total candidate immersion in vats of money at all levels is a truism, and it would strain readers' patience to labor it again. Use *baleful.*

Baleful means menacing or ominous, portending evil ("Europe's endless debt problems continue to have a baleful impact on stock-market sentiment across a nervously interconnected financial world"; "It is bad enough that some Pashtun areas may come under the Taliban's baleful influence"). *Baneful,* the stronger though less often used word, means harmful, destructive, or fatal ("From San Diego to Siesta Key, Florida, at least 37 people have died after mixing up baneful brews that in most of the cases cloaked them in invisible clouds of hydrogen sulfide so concentrated that one whiff can kill").

banister Misused for *baluster.* • His arms were wrapped around one of the vertical *banisters.* Use *balusters.*

And sometimes *baluster* is misused for *banister:* • If you actively ignore holding on to the *baluster* and you trip, then it is your fault. Use *banister.*

A *banister* is a handrail, especially on a staircase; a *baluster* is one of several posts that support the banister. A *balustrade* is both the banister and the balusters.

basicly Misspelling of *basically.* • *Basicly,* the philosophy is this: if you have a strong team then you should trade down some of your talent for youth during the off-season. Use *Basically.* • The IRW library allows reading *basicly* any type of color data (palette, images) in *basicly* any color space. Use *basically.*

The much written and much more spoken *basically* is used by people who do not think clearly; *basicly,* by people who do not think clearly or spell well.

bate Misused for *bait.* • A *bated* electric fence has a foodstuff attached to the wire fence strand that, when the deer sniffs or licks it, will shock them. Use *baited.* • Felipe Ortiz, 48, fishing in Colombia, cast a line into the teeth of a gale and suffocated when the *bated* hook blew back into his throat. USE *baited.*

And *bait* is misused for *bate*: • They produce an outstanding selection of finely crafted guards that can be combined with epee, generic schlager, and Del Tin practice rapier or *baited* rapier blades. USE *bated.*

To *bate* is to abate or lessen; to restrain; to flap the wings furiously; to blunt. To *bait* is to entice or lure; to torment; to tease; to feed an animal. As a noun, *bait* is food used to trap or lure an animal; an enticement. The idiom is *bated breath,* not *baited breath.*

bathos Confused with *pathos. Bathos* is a transition from dignified or grand to commonplace or laughable; an anticlimax ("Moving from lyric intensity—'My heart, my mind, my soul is yours'—to the bathos of the more mundane—'The order of the day is mud-mud-mud . . . '—it offers plenty of challenge even to Brewer's range and technique"; "At the end, the film flirts with bathos, but it's been absorbing enough along the way to maintain our good will"). *Pathos,* by contrast, is a quality in, for example, a work of art, that arouses feelings of pity or tenderness ("Although his major films were produced in the '50s and '60s, when the postwar landscape reflected a prosperous modernity, his virtually silent movies evoked the pathos of Buster Keaton and Charlie Chaplin"; "Comedy and pathos mingle brilliantly in Neil Simon's portrait of a widowed New York novelist who fears he may never love again").

bathotic Misspelling of *bathetic.* • Originally, I had planned some scathing comments on the death of the much-beloved-by-the-media John-John. But I've decided to leave the *bathotic* commemoration to just the title of this issue and be done with it. USE *bathetic.* • Here's my hypothesis: no one expected (certainly not the likes of a Galileo, or Marx, or Darwin, or Freud) that the Human Project would end, or end on such a *bathotic* note. USE *bathetic.* • From its hyperbolic style and *bathotic* self-importance many might conclude that the piece in question is a spoof of the kind familiar to readers of this paper. USE *bathetic.*

Bathotic is not the adjective of *bathos*; *bathetic* is.

B

beared Misused for *bore.* • Five stories about people living in the aftermath of the Twin Towers attack suggested the U.S. *beared* some responsibility for 9-11. Use *bore.* The past tense of the verb to *bear* is *bore,* not *beared.*

And the past participle is *borne,* not *beared.* • I have *beared* witness that Christ has died as payment for my sins and rose again. Use *borne.*

Present	Present Participle	Past	Past Participle
bear	bearing	bore	borne

beaurocrat Misspelling of *bureaucrat.* • The only difference is that the person who earned it will decide how it is spent instead of some *beaurocrat* in Washington. Use *bureaucrat.* • I am the expert when it comes to motorcycles, not some *beaurocrat* who's never even been near a bike. Use *bureaucrat.* • He was an academic *beaurocrat;* he taught at the academy three times a week. Use *bureaucrat.*

Bureaucrat (from French *bureau,* office, and Greek, *kratēs,* ruler), alone, is the spelling.

> We don't need beaurocrats to tell us what to teach!
>
> —Oxford University Press

beautify Misused for *beatify.* • Mr Lacy said it was remarkable that the letter, apparently foretelling her death, had emerged at the same time as the Pope had *beautified* Mother Teresa of Calcutta, who died in the same week as Diana. Use *beatified.* • The recently *beautified* and Polish-born pontiff had a long history of outreach to young people and the disaffected during his 26-year tenure as head of the Catholic Church. Use *beatified.*

And *beautification* is sometimes misused for *beatification*: • So what, it might be asked, are the political motivations for the *beautification* of John Paul II? Use *beatification.*

Beautify means to make beautiful. *Beatify* means to declare a deceased person to be in heaven and entitled to public veneration; to make blissfully happy.

> In order to encourage us in becoming holy, our Holy Father has canonized and beautified more persons during his pontificate than any of his predecessors on the Chair of Peter.
>
> —Bishop Paul S. Loverde, *Arlington Catholic Herald*
>
> It's true that beatification happens rarely, but not so rarely that Bishop Loverde and the *Catholic Herald,* for God's sake, shouldn't know the difference between *beatify* and *beautify*.

beckon call Misused for *beck and call.* • If your significant other has a load of homework or tests, don't expect that person to be at your *beckon call.* Use *beck and call.* • Many of Cox's customers have become unwilling and unknowing cyborgs at the *beckon call* of people all over the world. Use *beck and call.*

A *beck* is a gesture of beckoning; a wave or nod. To be at someone's *beck and call* is to be always ready to fulfill a wish. *Beckon call* is as incorrect, as ridiculous, as *for all intensive purposes* (instead of *for all intents and purposes*), *assume* (instead of *as soon*), *off the beat and path* (instead of *off the beaten path*), and *wearas* (instead of *whereas*).

beg the question Misused for *raise the question* (or similar words). Neither "to evade a question" nor "to raise a question" correctly defines this term. Derived from the Latin *petitio principii,* meaning "assuming, or laying claim to, a principle," *beg the question* is a form of logical fallacy in which an argument is based on a statement or claim that is itself unproved or questionable. That is, to *beg the question* is to take for granted, or assume, the truth of the point raised and yet to be proved.

But perhaps more important than what it does mean (since very few people use the term correctly thanks in large measure to the laxicographers who have entered the incorrect meanings into their dictionaries) is what it does not mean. It does not mean what these sentences suggest: • So the Packers' successful changeover *begs the question*: If they can do it, why can't other 4–3 teams (like the Eagles)? USE *raises the question.* • It also *begs the question* of what the six candidates running to replace Daley would have done differently. USE *makes us wonder.*

being that Misused for *since* (or similar words). • There is an especial irony in Bush criticizing Syria and Iran as illegitimate dictatorships, *seeing that* it was the United States which destroyed Syria's young parliamentary democracy in 1949. USE *since.* • This is a grand-scale project, *being that* it is a full curriculum covering math, science, social studies, language arts, physical education, art, and more! USE *in that.* • *Being that* the Stockton Record story never ever released the public information as to what revitalization idea did cause Stockton to win the State Enterprise Zone award, things have been changed. USE *Considering that.* • *Being as how* the year is 2003 and this is the "land of opportunity," I am both supportive of the ruling and shocked at how many people are against it. USE *Given that.*

Being that, like *seeing that, seeing as (how),* and *being as (how),* is uneducated English. Literate alternatives to these expressions include *because, considering that, given that, in that,* and *since.*

belie Misused for *betray* (or similar words). • Stress interviews can *belie* trouble within a company, such as a difficult boss, long hours, or impossible workload. USE *reveal.* • *The Return of the King*'s weaknesses do stem from exaggerations and intrusions that *belie* the screenwriters' misinterpretation of Tolkien's convictions. USE *betray.*

Belie means to give a false impression of; to contradict; to show to be false or wrong. *Betray* means to show unknowingly; to disclose; to reveal.

bellweather Misspelling of *bellwether.* • Barack Obama won Ohio in 2008, a *bellweather* state that helped propel him to victory. USE *bellwether.* • The commodity that is the *bellweather* for inflation has given a technical sell signal on the weekly chart. USE *bellwether.*

A *wether* is a castrated sheep or goat; a *bellwether* is a wether that leads the flock and has a bell hung round its neck; a leader; an indicator of future events or trends.

beloved The pronunciation of *beloved,* meaning dearly loved, is (bi-LUVD) or (bi-LUV-id). SEE ALSO **alleged**.

bemuse Misused for *amuse.* • This play will delight and *bemuse* you with its nimble humor. USE *amuse.* • Breakfast treats such as "Nuddy Nubble Abblestuffel," "Phantasmagoria," and a "Humpty Dumpty" house specialty continue to *bemuse* and entertain our guests. USE *amuse.*

Many clumsy writers will use *bemuse* and *amuse* together, perhaps to increase their chances of, with one word or the other, saying what they mean to say: • Back when he was living in Moe, Greg Domaszewicz used to *amuse and bemuse* friends with tales of flying saucers and alien abductions. • It will *bemuse, amuse,* and confuse—and, thanks to the Chapman brothers, this year's Turner Prize show might just turn a few stomachs too. • Enjoy this collection of poems, which will alternatively *amuse, bemuse,* and give you pause for thought.

Bemuse means to confuse or stupefy; to absorb in thought. *Amuse* is to entertain; to cause to laugh or smile. SEE ALSO **bemuse** in **appendix A**.

between Confused with *among. Between* is most often used with two objects or people ("Some of it is spewed by journalists who feign expertise in the Middle East, but couldn't tell you the difference between a Sunni or a Shiite"; "Some people might wonder about the connection between ethics and diversity"), *among* with three or more ("Terry was among 200 or so people who turned out for the TechExec"; "Rafe Esquith of Hobart Boulevard Elementary School was among 10 people honored by President Bush Wednesday"). *Between* is also the correct word to use if, no matter how many people or things are being discussed, one person or thing is being considered in relation to one other person or thing ("Even between provinces, there are differences in the way statistics are kept"—that is, between any one province and another; "The common link between the three destinations—and the perfume itself—is the watery floral accord"—that is, between any one destination and another). SEE ALSO **amongst**.

> Perhaps there's strife because there's some type of anger or disagreement among the boyfriend and girlfriend.
>
> —Dr. Alvin Poussaint, Harvard Medical School
>
> The redoubtable Dr. Poussaint misspoke; the strife, doubtless, is *between* the boyfriend and girlfriend.
>
> The team's offensive player of the year award for the second consecutive year was shared amongst two worthy recipients.
>
> —*The Willimantic Chronicle*
>
> However could this *Chronicle* writer use the affectation *amongst* with the word *two* alongside it—a high-flown word in a lowbrow sentence.

biannual Confused with *biennial. Biannual* means twice a year; semiannual ("You probably couldn't come up with a more rigorous test of a relationship than producing a biannual poetry journal"). *Biennial* means once in two years or lasting two years ("Crop producers in Manitoba are advised to be on the lookout next year for biennial wormwood, a native weed that appears to be making a comeback"). SEE ALSO **bimonthly**.

bicep Misused for *biceps*. • The victim suffered a deep stab wound on his *bicep*. USE *biceps*. • Were it not for a torn *bicep*, so much of Clark's life would have been different. USE *biceps*. • If you can lunge and bend your elbow at the same time, you can do a walking lunge with a *bicep* curl. USE *biceps*.

Biceps, a muscle with two heads, is the correct singular form. *Bicep,* which some people believe is the singular of *biceps,* is nonstandard. Linguists promote this error by calling it a back-formation, and lexicographers, by entering the word in their dictionaries. The plural of *biceps* is *biceps* or *bicepses*. SEE ALSO **quadricep**; **tricep**.

bidded Misused for *bid.* • The construction company WC&T Inc. recently *bidded* $854,000 to build the four multi-use fields. Use *bid.* • It is probably a fact that 9.999 out of 10 people have heard of, visited, or *bidded* on eBay. Use *bid.* • Please let us know in advance if you would like to be notified via sms/email if you have been *outbidded.* Use *outbid.*

If you are bidding someone good-bye, the correct past tense is *bade* (BAD or BADE), not *bid,* and certainly not *bidded*: • Before you left for Jakarta, you *bidded* me good-bye on MSN. Use *bade.* • The excellent crew on this flight then *bidded* us farewell. Use *bade.*

The past tense of *bid* is *bid* or *bade.* See also **forbid (forbidded)**.

Present	Present Participle	Past	Past Participle
bid (to offer)	bidding	bid	bid
bid (to utter, command)	bidding	bade	bidden

bimonthly Because *bimonthly* is commonly used to mean either twice a month or every other month, it may be better to use the phrase *twice a month* or *every other month. Semimonthly* also means twice a month, but some people may not know this word, for it is seldom used.

The same holds for *biweekly* and *biyearly*: *biweekly* may be used to mean either twice a week or every other week, and *biyearly* may be used to mean either twice a year or every other year. *Semiweekly* means twice a week, and *semiyearly* means twice a year. See also **biannual**.

bitter Misused for *embitter.* • The singer is a lover scorned and *bittered* by his emotional attachment to the woman. Use *embittered.* • Relations between the two countries had been strong for most of their 36-year relationship, though they have been *bittered* by a lengthy and ongoing landing rights dispute. Use *embittered.* • Despite all of my admiration for Gary, I think he is indeed *bittered* by the progress. Use *embittered.* • It highlights the humble beginnings of Facebook in a Harvard dorm room between a few buzzed friends *bittered* by the rejection of females. Use *embittered.*

To *embitter* is to stir bitter (angry or resentful) feelings in; to make bitter. To *bitter* is, also, to make bitter (acrid or pungent), but it is used to describe the taste of food or drink, not the feelings of a person.

bizarre Misused for *bazaar.* • For not only did they provide us with the use of their property for this charity *bizarre,* but they also are allowing us the use of their extensively stocked dungeon and their private clinic. USE *bazaar.* • It was like having a Middle Eastern *bizarre* right here in the middle of the Forest Mountains. USE *bazaar.*

Bizarre, an adjective, means weird or very odd; unexpected; fantastic or grotesque. *Bazaar,* a noun, is a market or street of shops, especially in Middle Eastern countries; a shop that sells a variety of goods; a sale of various items, often to raise money for a club or group.

blatant Misused for *flagrant.* • Moreover, to open it up to other Clinton scandals would put Lowell at the center of a *blatant* conflict of interest. USE *flagrant.* • Sometimes *blatant* injustice is committed in the name of security requirement or under the pretext of saving one's own country or even humanity. USE *flagrant.* • This *blatant* act of aggression against Syria, a fellow member of the OIC, must be condemned in the strongest terms as provocative, arrogant and dangerous. USE *flagrant.*

And *flagrant* is misused for *blatant:* • Straight-laced companies might have discouraged such *flagrant* displays of color, but not Yahoo! USE *blatant.* • Defensive end Greg Spires was flagged for a *flagrant* foul on Ramsey after Warren Sapp sacked the quarterback for a 2-yard loss near the end of the second quarter. USE *blatant.* • Having worked for them for the better part of a decade, I witnessed how managers told *flagrant* lies to get Apple's business. USE *blatant.*

Blatant means offensively loud or clamorous; conspicuous or obtrusive. *Flagrant* means glaringly offensive or deplorable; scandalous.

blessing in the sky Misused for *blessing in disguise.* • Triple H was a terrible champion in 2003, and it was a *blessing in the sky* when he finally lost to Bill Goldberg later in the year. USE *blessing in disguise.* • And like a *blessing in the sky,* I found out that Lennie, an ex-officemate, actually emcees professionally through her blog. USE *blessing in disguise.*

The correct expression is *blessing in disguise.*

blindsighted Misused for *blindsided.* • They say they're trying to improve our education, but they are being *blindsighted* by their own selfishness. USE *blindsided.* • Brokers, never knowing the current risk appetite of a given carrier, cannot afford to be *blindsighted* by a competitor. USE *blindsided.* • It's so easy to be *blindsighted* by romance, but the rose-colored glasses eventually have to come off. USE *blindsided.* • Innocent or dumb as I was, these issues *blindsighted* me. USE *blindsided.*

Blindsight, a noun, is the ability of blind people to respond to stimuli they are unable to see. *Blindside,* a verb, is to hit unexpectedly from a blind side; to attack, figuratively or literally, from an unseen or unexpected direction; to surprise unpleasantly. Why do you suppose some people say *blindsighted* when they mean *blindsided*? Is it not because they neither read nor listen well? Is it not because they feel one word is as good as another? Is it not because they are conned by lexlings who promote and applaud blind choice, blind chance?

blowed Misused for *blew.* • It *blowed* the roof off, top of porch and banisters, and picked up stuff from the back porch. USE *blew.* • The social networking giant *blowed* it off as nothing more than a scam to get money out of Zuckerberg. USE *blew.* The past tense of *blow* is *blew,* not *blowed.*

The past participle of *blow* is *blown,* not *blowed*: • He should have *blowed* it up. USE *blown.* • I was *blowed* away from the quality of sounds I was easily receiving by just applying the plugin on the track. USE *blown.*

Present	**Present Participle**	**Past**	**Past Participle**
blow	blowing	blew	blown

bought Misused for *brought.* • The lack of an appropriate memorial was *bought* to my attention by the Birmingham Air Raids Remembrance Association. USE *brought.* • They have been duping the people since the president was *bought* to power. USE *brought.* • These itinerant winemakers *bought* with them a wealth of viticulture and viniculture knowledge. USE *brought.*

Bought is the past tense of *buy*; *brought,* the past tense of *bring.* SEE ALSO **boughten**.

B

boughten Misused for *bought.* • If using store *boughten* veggies that are waxed, such as cucumbers and zucchini, it is best to peel them. USE *bought.* • Stocker cattle, either *boughten* or carried over from the previous year's calf crop, should also be culled. USE *bought.* • They can be *boughten* only by paying for both squares—you would have to pay for both squares #13 and #31 if you decided to buy one of them. USE *bought.*

The past participle, like the past tense, of *buy* is *bought,* not *boughten,* though the term is sometimes found in dialectal, that is, nonstandard, American English to mean store bought rather than homemade, altogether an unworthy distinction. SEE ALSO **bought**.

Present	Present Participle	Past	Past Participle
buy	buying	bought	bought

braggadocious Misused for *boastful* (or similar words). • We're full of it. We're vain. We're *braggadocious.* USE *conceited.* • As for that *braggadocious* young associate, his days at the firm were numbered. USE *bigheaded.* • He knew that being *braggadocious* would bring people to his fights and give black people pride. USE *arrogant.*

Though the noun *braggadocio* (a braggart) is a word, the adjective *braggadocious* is not. Let us admire those who use the word *braggadocio* and mock those who use *braggadocious.* SEE ALSO **trepidacious (trepidatious)**.

> I don't want to sound braggadocious, but I do have the biggest buildings in the city.
>
> —Donald Trump

breath Misused for *breathe.* • It sounds strange but we have to learn to *breath* properly. USE *breathe.* • The enriched oxygen seems to *breath* new life into tired aging skin, making it look more youthful and have a glow. USE *breathe.* • They possessed the equipment to *breath* in water and on land, and were one of the first amphibious animals. USE *breathe.*

The verb is *breathe* [BREETH]; the noun is *breath* [BRETH].

breech Misused for *breach.* • Although we will do our best to work with our customers in the event of a *breech* of policy, we will also take a firm line when necessary to protect our other customers and network. Use *breach.* • The vibrations created by the marching and the shouts of the people caused a *breech* in the wall large enough for Israel's army to march through. Use *breach.*

And *breach* is misused for *breech*: • Super-heated plasma from the reactor is injected into the *breach* of the rifle, where it is contained and focused by a magnetic field. Use *breech.* • If there is a *breach birth* the baby would take its first breath while its head was still in the birth canal. Use *breech birth.*

A *breach* is an act of breaking the law, terms of an agreement, or expected conduct; a break in relations; a gap in a wall or barrier. A *breech* is the part of a firearm at the back of the barrel; the buttocks; the lower part of a pulley block. A *breech birth* occurs when a baby's buttocks or feet are delivered first.

breech Misused for *broach.* • I really respect that kind of honesty, and have *breeched* the subject at times to encourage fellow pioneers to bring some integrity to the table in such matters. Use *broached.* • When discussing changes in the current severance package, *breech* the topic within the context of changes of other benefit plans. Use *broach.* • Since we've *breeched* the subject, I have to say the Associated Press poll shows John Kerry doing better with women by 1 percentage point than Al Gore did with women. Use *broached.*

Breech the noun has several meanings; as a verb, it has two meanings, both rarely used and little known: to put (a boy) in breeches; to provide a gun with a breech. *Broach* the verb has several definitions, but the one that's mistaken for *breech* means to raise for discussion.

bridal Misused for *bridle.* • Attached to the lead pole is a harness or *bridal,* which is used to attach the billboard to the pickup rope. Use *bridle.* • Featuring a horse with saddle and *bridal,* proud foal, posable rider, bucket, bag of oats, brush and trophy, this collection provides quality play for the imaginative young rider. Use *bridle.* • The existing trail was built as a *bridal* path in the 1930s along a traditional transportation corridor used by early settlers and Native Americans. Use *bridle.* • They take one incident at a time in isolation and not only don't they put them together, they *bridal* at the idea that they should be put together or dismiss the idea out of hand. Use *bridle.*

Bridal as a noun means a wedding or marriage ceremony; as an adjective, it means relating to a bride or wedding ceremony. *Bridle* as a noun means a horse's harness, and *bridle path* is a trail used for horseback riding; as a verb, it means to harness or restrain, or to show anger or resentment. See also **unbridaled.**

bring Misused for *take.* Few people bother to distinguish between *bring* and *take,* and fewer still, today, have any notion of their being, or of there ever having been, a distinction between these words' meanings. Still, the distinction should be observed, especially by those who value clarity, precision, and elegance in language.

Use *bring* to indicate movement toward the person who is speaking or being spoken to:

- But they have been forced to tell their guests to *bring* a gas bill with them if they want to get into Holyrood.

The action is toward the people doing the telling, so *bring* is correct.

- Picnicgoers are encouraged to *bring* their own instruments to the park.

The action is toward whoever is doing the encouraging, so *bring* is correct.

Use *take* to indicate movement away from the person who is speaking or being spoken to:

- The first-prize winner could *take* home more than $20,000.

The action is away from wherever the prize is awarded, so *take* is correct.

- Looking for an extra-special place to *take* the family this summer?

The action is away from one's home, so *take* is correct.

The same guidelines also apply to the verbs *come* and *go,* though they are less often confused than *bring* and *take.*

broach Misused for *brook.* • Believing themselves to be divinely inspired, they *broach* no dissent, and will argue with vehemence that they've been led by God. USE *brook.* • I will *broach* no arguments on the subject. USE *brook.* • They *broach* no nonsense from petty officialdom and would rather spend an hour by the roadside than pay a bribe to a policeman. USE *brook.*

Broach means to start a discussion about; to bring up; to announce. To *brook* is to put up with; to endure; to tolerate. *Brook* is usually used with the word *no*: "brook no dissent."

but what Misused for *that.* • There is no doubt *but what* this man had deep regrets. USE *that.* • There is no question *but what* his insightful comments will be missed. USE *that.*

Though seldom used today, *but what* means no more than *that.* The expression *but that* is common in negative expressions and wholly unobjectionable.

Cc

C

cachet Misused for *cache.* • U.S. authorities in California arrested him on December 12, 1995, when he was involved in preparations for an armed raid against Cuba and a *cachet* of weapons in his possession was seized. USE *cache.* • The brother of the political head of KLA was just arrested with a large *cachet* of arms and some $800,000 in cash, the first such arrest by NATO. USE *cache.* • With homebaked cake and a secret *cachet* of sweets, the bedrooms live up to the Latin name, meaning "everything is a dream." USE *cache.*

And *cache* is misused for *cachet*: • The Busch circuit, with costs of about half of Winston Cup's, lacks the so-called big names but has its own celebrity *cache.* USE *cachet.* • Slate talks about the brand name *cache* of Starbucks coffee, BMW cars, and Godiva chocolates for the middle class to outwardly demonstrate status. USE *cachet.*

Cachet (kah-SHAY) is a mark that indicates something is authentic, genuine, or superior; a distinction; a seal on a document; a commemorative design or motto stamped on an envelope; a medicinal wafer or capsule. *Cache* (KASH) is a hiding place for storing supplies, weapons, valuables, or other items; the items stored.

Because few people know the meanings of these two words, and fewer still the difference in their pronunciations, we can be sure that dictionaries will soon offer (KASH) as a variant pronunciation of *cachet,* and (kah-SHAY) as a variant of *cache.* Dictionaries: the new doomsday books.

> I think if Arnold had not been an action hero, and, say, he had been in 10 movies where he was the super villain, it may have hurt his celebrity cache a little bit.
>
> —John Orman, political science professor

> It has been described as the company's new bastard love child that is bound to give a brand cache—they just sound a bit naughty, perhaps explaining Cameron Diaz's current love affair with them.
>
> —Sarai Jacob, *The Oxford Student*
>
> We've been working very closely within Iraq to try to find cachets of cash, as we have found to date.
>
> —Juan Zarate, U.S. Department of Treasury
>
> Professors and students and government officials, equally untaught, do not know the difference between *cachet* and *cache*.

cacophony Misused for *mess* (or similar words). • Without a way to organize, house and label wires, the desk, baseboards and nooks behind the monitor or PC tower can become a *cacophony* of cluttered cables. USE *jumble.* • My kalua pork sandwich ($6.95) was a *cacophony* of flavors—tender pork chunks roasted in banana leaves accompanied by sweet mango pico and cilantro spread made interesting by the addition of musky rye seeds. USE *mix.* • Our city has become part of the *cacophony* of cities each with their own ordinances that conflict in substance with each other. USE *confusion.*

The word *cacophony* refers to noise—not to cables, not to flavors, not to cities—discordant, jarring noise. The meaning of *cacophony* is easily understood: the prefix *caco-* means bad, and the suffix *-phony* means sound. You might speak of "a cacophony of criticism" or "a cacophony of color," but in this sort of example, *cacophony* suggests a metaphorical dissonance.

> Legitimate business needs to have clear rules of the road. We really have a cacophony of laws.
>
> —Trevor Hughes, Network Advertising Initiative

cadillac Misused for *catalytic.* • We were a strong competitor throughout the competition, but then the *Cadillac* converter fell off, which hurt our emissions and place in the overall standings. USE *catalytic.* • 1997 Pontiac Trans Am WS6 (ram air) convertible, automatic black leather interior, red exterior with black top. A/C, ABS, cruise, cassette with 12 disk CD changer, keyless entry, always covered, second owner and 3" pipe from *cadillac* converter full-master exhaust. USE *catalytic.*

Cadillac (KAD-il-*ak*) is the name of a car. *Catalytic* (*kat*-ah-LI-tik), an adjective, means of or involving a catalyst. A *catalytic converter,* a device attached to automobile exhaust systems, converts harmful gases to harmless products.

caliper Misused for *caliber.* • A well-placed shot with a smaller *caliper* bullet is better than a badly placed shot with a big bore. USE *caliber.* • Chief Miller justified the purchase of the bullet-proof vests and gun stating that approximately an hour ago his officer took a .45-*caliper* gun from someone. USE *caliber.* • When and where am I going to meet anyone who shares my interests and is the *caliper* of person I'm looking for? USE *caliber.*

A *caliper* (KAL-i-per) is an instrument having two curved legs that is used to measure thickness or distance. A *caliber* (KAL-i-ber) is the diameter of a tube or gun barrel; a degree of worth or quality.

callus Misused for *callous.* • This might be a *callus* approach, but remember that one bad apple can spoil the basket. USE *callous.* • Otherwise, they are nothing but evil, pathetic, ignorant, mean-spirited, heartless, *callus,* cruel hypocrites with no compassion or empathy. USE *callous.* • It's scary that society has become so insensitive, so *callus* to violence. USE *callous.*

Callous is an adjective meaning hard-hearted, insensitive; *callus* is a noun meaning a thickening of the skin.

Calvary Misused for *cavalry.* • After months of anticipation, members of the 278th Armored *Calvary* Regiment said good-bye to loved ones. USE *Cavalry.* • The troops will be opposing the 1st *Calvary* Division, working as an enemy force during extremely lifelike fighting. USE *Cavalry.* • Beck said the charge, which wiped out the remaining Confederate troops at

Fort Collier and effectively ended the 1864 battle, was the largest *calvary* charge in American history. USE *cavalry*.

Calvary is the place where Jesus was crucified; *calvary*, with a lowercase *c*, is any representation of the crucifixion of Jesus; intense anguish or suffering. *Cavalry* is an army's combat troops, whether on horses or in armored vehicles. SEE ALSO **crucifiction**.

can Confused with *may*. *Can* expresses ability to do something ("The system incorporates a seven-inch camera shaped like a fish and connected to a cable that can be lowered up to 60 feet below the ice"; "In the classroom and out, male teachers are living proof that men can be just as smart—and nurturing—as women"). *May* expresses possibility or permission to do something ("Fencing along the Line of Control by India may hamper the peace process between two countries"; "You may attend only one grocery distribution site per seven days"). The words today are often used interchangeably, but the consequence of this is that the meaning of the sentences in which they are used is sometimes unclear and confusing. SEE ALSO **might**.

cannon Misused for *canon*. • Other fans of The Force have taken it upon themselves to distill it into a religious *cannon*, taking the film scripts as their scripture. USE *canon*. • The female writer's "battle for self-creation" and her struggle for a permanent spot in the literary *cannon*, involves her in a revisionary process. USE *canon*. • If jazz is to remain a living music any sort of inventive reinterpretation of its musical *cannon* is necessary and should be welcomed. USE *canon*.

A *cannon* is a piece of artillery; an automatic or laser gun; the loop on the top of a bell by which it is hung. *Canon* is a body of rules or principles; a decree issued by a church; a body of religious writings; the list of Roman Catholic saints; a Roman Catholic prayer; a complete set of artistic or literary works; a musical composition.

can't help but Misused for *can't help . . . -ing*. • We *can't help but go* back past the electric motor, past the telephone, all the way back to the first controlled fire, when our awed ancestors tried to figure out how to use a new tool. USE *can't help going*. • I *couldn't help but glance* into the room as Hartley worked her magic. USE *couldn't help glancing*. • With the stores chock-full of cupids, chocolates, and hearts of every size and description, I *can't help but smile and think* that all of those mushy poets, songwriters, and sentimentalists were on to something really good for us. USE *can't help smiling and thinking.* • As hopes of victory faded, Hyde *couldn't help but complain* bitterly about being sold out by Senate Republicans. USE *couldn't help complaining.* • Tymberly Wes Fields *can't help but laugh* when she thinks about her job. USE *can't help laughing.*

C

Popular though the expression is, *can't help but* is less defensible (since some critics maintain it is a double negative) than *can't help . . . -ing,* which also sounds better—and sound counts for something.

cantor Misused for *canter.* • The horses are well trained and responsive to all levels of riders, whether you want to walk, trot, *cantor,* or gallop. USE *canter.* • It was amazing how consistent the horse's *cantor* was. USE *canter.* • I know the tempos and rhythms that horses trot or *cantor* or gallop in, and I know the adagio nature of certain wire acts or trapeze acts. USE *canter.*

A *canter* is a slow, easy pace of a horse. A *cantor* is the singer of the liturgy in a synagogue.

can't seem to Misused for *seem unable to.* • Everyone at this photo shoot so obviously loves Melissa Etheridge that they *can't seem to* keep their hands off her. USE *seem unable to.* • Unlike Karen, who *can't seem to* get to Grace's office before 11 A.M. and complains at only having four hours for lunch, Megan is always striving to perfect her craft. USE *seems unable to.*

Though *can't seem to* is considered acceptable idiomatic English, it sounds awkward; *seem unable to* is more logical and more euphonious.

canvas Misused for *canvass.* • Extensive public workshops and meetings were held in 1998 to *canvas* the public's views about solid waste management. USE *canvass.* • In formulating Esap, Chidzero was determined to *canvas* opinion far and wide, drawing upon the expertise of as many as possible, and to be aware of the detailed circumstances impacting upon all facets of the economy. USE *canvass.* • The meeting was designed to *canvas* views of trends in the nuclear and regulatory fields against the background of changing economic and decision-making processes. USE *canvass.*

Canvas is a strong, heavy, unbleached cloth; *canvass* is a survey; as a verb, it means to survey or question.

capitol Misused for *capital.* • Additional words in the function name should begin with a single *capitol* letter. Use *capital.* • Newark is the *capitol* of stolen cars. Use *capital.* • The one city that didn't own a public utility was Kutztown, Pa., which is located between Philadelphia and Harrisburg, the *capitol* of the state and home of a full-time university. Use *capital.* • God has declared in his Word that whosoever wrongfully takes the life of an unborn child shall be guilty of a *capitol* crime. Use *capital.* • The whole point of capitalism is unabashed growth, the accumulation of *capitol,* wealth, and power. Use *capital.*

And *capital* is misused for *capitol*: • There were trees and limbs strewn all around the *capital* building, too. Use *capitol.*

The word *capital* has several meanings: a city, usually the seat of government of a country, state, or province; a crime punishable by death; principal or chief; a capital letter; a city or town associated with a particular activity or industry; wealth; a valuable resource. The word *capitol* has but one meaning: a building that houses a federal, state, or provincial legislature.

careen Misused for *career.* • Drivers cruise—or *careen*—down Woodland Hills as an alternative to Loop 323. Use *career.* • Is the band's decision to keep its follow-up down and dirty an effort to keep from *careening* too quickly toward pop stardom? Use *careering.*

Careen (kah-REEN) means to lean to one side; to lurch from side to side; to tilt a ship to clean or maintain the bottom of the hull ("A missile struck the Ch-47 Chinook and sent it careening into an Iraqi field"; "A pirate's least favorite part about coming to land was careening, or beaching the ship and cleaning the hull"). *Career* (kah-RIR) means to rush; to move at full speed ("While his friends fine-tune their parallel parking, 17-year-old James Sutton will be careering around racetracks at speeds in excess of 150 mph").

And *career* is sometimes misused for *careen*: • You can imagine it happening, the ship *careering* down the cliff in slow motion, sections of it peeling away, breaking off and showering the seabed. Use *careening.*

caret Misused for *carat.* • The gold detail is antiqued in 24 *caret* gold leaf. Use *carat.* • Until last summer, they had never sold a two-*caret* diamond and they had wondered why. Use *carat.*

And *carat* is misused for *caret*: • Leave the text *carat* in the field where you entered the ID. Use *caret.* • The *carat* (^) symbol acts as a dynamic left alignment position for all of the lines that contain it within a given text object. Use *caret.* • Use the *carat* symbol to indicate powers; for example, type as x^2 or as x^(1/3). Use *caret.*

A *caret* (^) is a symbol traditionally used to indicate where text is to be inserted in a document, but also is used in mathematical and computer-related notation. A *carat* is a unit of weight for precious stones and pearls; also spelled *karat,* it is a unit of measure of the purity of gold.

Carrot is also misused for *carat:* • The Gold Paralympic medals are made out of solid silver with a 24-*carrot* gold coating. Use *carat.*

A *carrot* is a plant or vegetable; an inducement.

catterwall Misspelling of *caterwaul.* • And the left won't respond as they only want issues to *catterwall* about, not solutions. Use *caterwaul.* • We are getting little to no sleep as she keeps us up all night with her moaning and *catterwalling.* Use *caterwauling.* • Since 1980, the life expectancy rate among men and women is ten years higher despite the *catterwalling* that we're all getting fatter. Use *caterwauling.* • If she left him out there, he'd raise the dead with his *catterwalling,* and if she let him in, well, God knew what would happen. Use *caterwauling.*

As a verb, *caterwaul* means to wail or moan like a cat in heat; to make a shrill, jarring sound. As a noun, it is a harsh, cacophonic noise. *Catterwall* is an unacceptable spelling.

celebrate Misused for *celibate.* • The idea of young girls forced into a state of chastity and working with so-called *celebrate* priests is also questioned in the film. Use *celibate.* • Some undertake strict vows to remain *celebrate* throughout life, never to accept service from others, and in this way lead a life of extreme hardship. Use *celibate.* • Many gay people never make it past acknowledging themselves as gay; they may remain *celebrate* throughout their lives or they may cave in to society and live a life that is not natural to them. Use *celibate.*

Celebrate, a verb, means to commemorate with festivity; to honor or mark with a celebration. *Celibate* is an unmarried person; one who vows to abstain from sexual intercourse.

cemetery Misused for *seminary.* • I once heard Dr. David A. Seamands from Asbury Theological *Cemetery* say that woman's ministry is fine and should not be discounted because of an obscure verse (1 Cor. 14:34–35) in the Bible. Use *Seminary.* • He was a graduate of Wheaton College and Westminster Theological *Cemetery,* Philadelphia. Use *Seminary.*

A *cemetery* is a graveyard. A *seminary* is a school that trains candidates to be priests, ministers, or rabbis.

centurion Misused for *centenarian.* • Aristophus was called Aris (pronounced Ayres) and lived to be a *centurion* in an age when this was rare. Use *centenarian.* • *Centurion* Lizzie Leonard of Tourlestrane died peacefully in Enniscrone last Thursday, January 10. Use *Centenarian.* • More than one million of these baby boomers are expected to live to be *centurions,* living to be 100 years old and older. Use *centenarians.*

Centurion is the commander of a century, a company of one hundred soldiers, in the Roman army; one who has scored or achieved 100 in any way. *Centenarian* is a person who is 100 years old or older.

chaff Misused for *chafe.* • Perhaps their new confidence in their ability to make decisions and tendency toward criticalness cause them to *chaff* at authority. Use *chafe.* • While you appreciate the vast history and resources of the Council, you also *chaff* at their sometimes stifling procedures, directives, and politics. Use *chafe.*

Chaff is the husks of grain separated in threshing; anything worthless; strips of metal used to confuse enemy radar; good-natured teasing. *Chafe* means to rub to make warm; to wear away or make sore by rubbing; to become annoyed or irritated because of some constraint.

chaise lounge Misused for *chaise longue.* • Just take a peek into any interior design magazine, and you will see touches such as Wenge dining tables, Italian marble floors, and microsuede *chaise lounges.* Use *chaise longues.* • Place upholstered chairs or a *chaise lounge* in the bedroom to provide a more inviting and personal feeling in the room. USE *chaise longue.* • Beautiful, sunny days were made for this elegant *chaise lounge.* USE *chaise longue.*

Chaise longue (shaz-LONG) is French for long chair. Lounging Americans, however, prefer *chaise lounge* (shaz-LOUNJ).

chalk full Misused for *chock-full.* • It's a great family film about Little League baseball that is *chalk full* of baseball action and delivers a powerful positive message. USE *chock-full.* • It is hard to tell the West Orange-Stark Lady Mustangs are not *chalk full* of seniors on their roster, especially on Monday against the Ozen Lady Panthers. USE *chock-full.*

Chock-full (or *chockfull*) means as full as possible. *Chalk* is a limestone composed of calcite from seashells and is used for drawing or writing on a chalkboard.

childish Misused for *childlike.* • To win his love you should assume a sweet and *childish* behavior. USE *childlike.* • The music and the choreography are a fine balance between *childish* awe and adult dreams, and never lapse into nauseous sentimentality. USE *childlike.*

Childish means immature; infantile. *Childlike* means naive; innocent; guileless.

choosed Misused for *chose.* • Thousands since the world begun never *choosed* to be but were lured and coerced into it. USE *chose.* • GENBAND's SAFARI C3 *choosed* by ImproWare AG for Advanced Multimedia. USE *chose.* • And out of all the forums available, you *choosed* punBB. USE *chose.*

The past tense of *choose* is *chose,* not *choosed.*

The past participle is *chosen,* not *choosed*: • I have *choosed* Dubai because I would like to explain how everything is going in the Middle East. USE *chosen.* • The teams were *choosed* randomly. USE *chosen.*

Use the past participle when an auxiliary verb like *have* or *were* precedes the verb.

Present	**Present Participle**	**Past**	**Past Participle**
choose	choosing	chose	chosen

chord Misused for *cord.* • Have your fireplace checked by a chimney sweep annually or after burning one *chord* of wood—whichever comes first. Use *cord.* • The central nervous system is made up of a brain, a spinal *chord,* and nerves. Use *cord.* • He discovered that this charge could be transferred to cork using an electrical *chord.* Use *cord.*

And *cord* is sometimes misused for *chord*: • It is simply a mathematical representation of a word that can also relate to a musical *cord.* Use *chord.*

A *chord* is usually three or more musical notes played or sung together in harmony. A *cord* is a thick string or thin rope; something that acts as a tie; a measure of wood cut for fuel; a ribbed fabric; an anatomical part resembling a cord; an insulated electrical cable.

C

circa Misused for *about* (or similar words). • *Avatar* might have a script worthy of Quentin Tarantino, *circa Pulp Fiction,* but based on the visuals in the trailer, we don't think that's going to make much of a difference. • Jack Black, *circa School of Rock,* would've appreciated this face-melter. • Perfect, CZJ can do the *National Velvet* part and AJ can give us her all *circa Who's Afraid of Virginia Woolf.*

What *circa* is meant to mean in these examples is not altogether clear. *Circa* ought only to be used before—never after—a date, and, occasionally, especially in Britain, a number, to indicate it is approximate ("The honey-colored Boston Chippendale mahogany chest, circa 1780, with a serpentine front and four graduated drawers went to the phone for $14,950"; "The Group says that it was anticipating a defence order of circa £1m in the current year but that this order is now expected to crystallise in the year").

clamor Misused for *clamber* • Joey is *clamoring* up the stairs in search of his family but returns, standing at the top of the stairs. Use *clambering.* • "Joe the Plumber" will likely *clamor* back into search engine trends and political water-cooler discussion this week after bashing his creator, Senator John McCain, for "trying to use" him. Use *clamber.* • After breakfast, we'd *clamor* into the boats—about 20 people per group, accompanied by local guides—and head off on our chosen tours. Use *clamber.*

Clamber (KLAM-ber) means to climb or move awkwardly or with difficulty, especially, using both hands and feet. *Clamor* (KLAM-er), as a verb, means to make a loud, sustained noise; to demand noisily or insistently.

C

class The antithesis of culture, *class* is a quality possessed by those who have neither elegance nor grace nor poise nor polish. • This always hurts me because I know who he is: a very intelligent, sensitive, *classy* human being. USE *admirable.*

Here's a description of a woman that no discerning man would ever wish to meet: • I am a shapely and petite, 31-year-old, exquisitely feminine, *classy* lady.

clean Misused for *cleanliness* (or similar words). • Add one cup to each gallon of warm water and sponge mop, then allow to dry for a fresh-smelling *clean* that kitchens and bathrooms deserve. USE *cleanliness.* • Just call or email us when you need a *clean.* USE *cleaning.*

Evidence that some people—marketers and advertisers more than most—have contempt for their audiences is their using the abomination *clean.* Some words are to be cherished, some to be questioned, and some, like the noun *clean,* to be disdained.

SuperMat clean is a clean you can see. . . . SuperMat clean is a clean you can feel. . . . SuperMat clean is a clean you can hear.

—Kleen-Tex Industries

Kleen-Tex is a company you can tease. . . . Kleen-Tex is a company you can mock. . . . Kleen-Tex is a company you can scorn.

Try Quilted Northern: 50 percent stronger for a confident clean.

—Quilted Northern toilet paper TV commercial

cliché The adjectival form of *cliché* is *cliché* or *clichéd*; either is correct. But despite the French origin of the word and the argument that *cliché* is a participle and no *-d* is needed to indicate past tense, *clichéd* does sound more like an English participle than *cliché* does: "clichéd writing" sounds more adjectival than "cliché writing"; "clichéd theme" sounds more adjectival than "cliché theme": • Despite the *cliché* theme of a shameless trip to Vegas, there are enough random elements thrown in to keep the film interesting. Use *clichéd.* • The obvious weakest link among the boys in Korn is lead singer Jonathan Davis, who not only cannot hold a note, sing a clear melody, or hit any decent range, but also writes some of the most *cliché* lyrics in modern rock. Use *clichéd.* • The book also suffers from patches of *cliché* writing (one character's "heart literally leaped into his throat," a rich neighborhood "smelled of old money," a person has vanished "like the wind," etc.), technical errors in the description of police procedure, and lapses of continuity. Use *clichéd.*

If we would rely less on speaking, writing, and even behaving in clichés, we might have less need to use the word, however it might be formed. See also **copyright**; **prejudice**.

> Most people in the U.S. picture the classic and cliché woman-flat-on-back kind of labor.
>
> —Susan Ashmore, *American Baby*
>
> From someone who uses *woman-flat-on-back* as a compound adjective—a sign of an unaccomplished, a clunky, writer—we cannot very well hope for *clichéd* instead of *cliché.*

click Misused for *clique.* • It is not uncommon to go places and see that certain social *clicks* exist; and most of the members of the *click* find it difficult to interact with members of other *clicks.* Use *cliques; clique.* • I have probably insulted or upset every little social *click* that exits in modern society today, but that was not my intention. Use *clique.*

A *clique* (KLEEK) is a small, exclusive group of people; a coterie. A *click* (KLICK) is a slight, sharp sound; the press of a computer mouse button; part of a mechanical locking device; a sound, such as *tsk,* made by the tongue against the soft palate.

climatic Misused for *climactic.* • The *climatic* battle to save the school is well done using appropriate weapons of choice: ketchup and mustard bottles and water balloons. Use *climactic.* • As Tarnas (1991) has suggested, humanity may be gathering for a *climatic* denouement, a unification of knowledge, of cultures, of faith and reason, of matter and spirituality, of art and science and religion, which have been increasingly fragmented and separated for almost 300 years. USE *climactic.* • From his first walk-on to his *climatic* battle scene, classical stage actor John Vickery plays the kind of villain that *Lion King* fans will happily boo. USE *climactic.* • By the time this becomes a plot point, Gibson has teamed up with his own clone and begun the *climatic* attack on Drucker's headquarters. USE *climactic.* • The final confrontation between Sabrina and Amanda may seem *anticlimatic* for some players. USE *anticlimactic.*

And *climactic* is misused for *climatic:* • The travel agent shall not be responsible for any injuries, damages, or losses caused to traveler in connection with terrorist activities, social or labor unrest, mechanical or construction difficulties, diseases, local laws, *climactic* conditions, abnormal conditions or developments, or any other actions, omissions, or conditions outside the travel agent's control. USE *climatic.*

Climatic means of or relating to climate. *Climactic* means relating to or constituting a climax.

> The climatic battle is indeed a big, clever pay-off.
>
> —Mike Ward, Richmond.com
>
> But until the climatic battle scenes and predictable reunion of mother and daughter, the missing in "The Missing" refers more to the absence of Maggie's father in her life.
>
> —Mike Ward, Richmond.com
>
> However many times *Ike* Ward uses it, *climatic battle* will never be correct.

cloths Misused for *clothes.* • All the doctor has to do is go over the area with a sort of brush, without the patient ever even taking his *cloths* off. USE *clothes.* • We got by with black-and-white TVs, hanging our wet *cloths* on a line to dry, washing dishes by hand, and throwing our potato peels in a pail instead of down the drain. USE *clothes.*

Cloth is a fabric such as cotton, silk, or wool. *Clothes* are wearing apparel and usually made of cloth.

> So maybe the quarterback of the football team is not hiding the Batmobile in the basement of his student-housing building. Maybe he doesn't wear the Flash's red spandex jumpsuit under his street cloths. But that doesn't mean he is not a superhero.
>
> —Heather Mathews, Portland State University *Vanguard*
>
> He may be a hero, but she, Ms. Mathews, does not seem to be. Heroes aren't simply noble warriors or sports figures, they are also common people who are uncommonly aware of how they use the language. They are people who, despite weak-willed lexicographers, descriptive linguists, peer-fearful adolescents, and others as pitiable, know the distinctions between words and observe them.

collaborate Misused for *corroborate*. • As our feedback reflects, we applaud some comments that *collaborate* our views on the proposals for further enhancement of relay services across the nation. USE *corroborate.* • At this point, we really only have Daniel's word and to back it up, it would be necessary to find Aerojet employees or White Sands people who could *collaborate* his statement. USE *corroborate.*

Whereas *collaborate* means to work together to accomplish something, *corroborate* means to confirm the truth of something. If people fail to enunciate their words, if they do not distinguish their liquid *l*'s from their liquid *r*'s, dictionary makers will one day dictate that these two words sound alike and mean the same.

collision Misused for *allision*. • The Canadian Navy said that the damage was likely from a *collision* with a dock, but had not happened while the *Victoria* was in Canadian possession. USE *allision.*

A *collision* (kah-LIZH-en) occurs when one object or person hits, and is hit by, another object or person. An *allision* (ah-LIZH-en) occurs when only one of the objects (usually a ship) is moving.

C

columnize Misused for *write.* • Anyway, let me know what your interests are, and if you want to *columnize* with us! Use *write.* • Whenever something frightening happens, columnists like me hasten to *columnize* about the anxieties of absentee parents; wire services follow the tragedy daily; and there is a hue and cry over the need for better regulation of the day-care profession. Use *write.*

Whatever is the point of *columnize*? Will we soon also have to endure *paragraphize* and *articleize*? Columnists write columns, articles; only the least able, or the most Corinthian, of them would say *columnize.*

comeupins Misspelling of *comeuppance.* • I'd like to see those responsible get their *comeupins.* Use *comeuppance.* • This is not funny, but know that everyone gets their *comeupins.* Use *comeuppance.* • You have to watch the video to see his excitement and giddiness that America got its *comeupins.* Use *comeuppance.*

Comeuppance (kum-UP-ence) is a punishment or result that is deserved; *comeupins* is the spelling that people, uncertain of, but also uninterested in, how the word is spelled, sometimes use.

comfrontable Misused for *comfortable.* • I don't feel *comfrontable* involving my friends because they are his friends. Use *comfortable.* • When does one become *comfrontable* in their own skin? Use *comfortable.* • At North Atlanta Scan Associates we are proud to offer comprehensive diagnostic imaging in a *comfrontable* environment. Use *comfortable.* • I enjoy good conversation and am *comfrontable* going out for drinks or relaxing at home watching movies. Use *comfortable.*

This spelling of *comfortable* is discomforting, for it suggests still further that in today's money-grubbing, entertainment-ridden, fear-induced society there is scant value in reading to oneself, scant value in thinking for oneself, scant value in being by oneself. See also **discomforture**.

commited Misspelling of *committed.* • Witnesses say the assault was *commited* in front of neighbors and a school bus full of children in a LaVerne neighborhood. Use *committed.* • Hastert says the United States must stay *commited* to Iraq and that it would be very irresponsible to pull coalition forces out prematurely. USE *committed.*

There are two *t*'s in *committed* and *committing,* but only one in *commit* and *commitment.*

commoditize Misused for *commodify* (or similar words). • I think this is where we start to find the sense of the deal as part of AOL's strategy to deploy and *commoditize* interactive services. USE *commodify.* • Thus IBM needs to *commoditize* enterprise software, and the best way to do this is by supporting open source. USE *commodify.* • Standardization tends to *commoditize* a product or technology. USE *commodify.* • Yeah, I have a fundamental belief that all technologies over time *commoditize.* USE *become commodities.*

Commodify means to turn into or treat as a commodity—which is also what *commoditize* is meant to mean. In other words, *commoditize* is likely a word born of error and ignorance, perhaps of people mispronouncing *commodify*. This is not, as descriptive linguists might maintain, an example of the evolution of English; it's an example of its devolution, its—when one word isn't distinguished from another (in this instance, a good word from a bad one)—commodification (*not* commoditization). And the commodification of the language can result only in the commodification of the people who use the language.

comparable The pronunciation of *comparable* is (KOM-per-ah-ble), not (kom-PAIR-ah-ble).

comparative Misused for *comparison* (or similar words). • How is this as a *comparative* to what has happened before? USE *comparison.* • Jimmy Carter has only one thing that will even cause his remembrance as a president—a *comparative* to measure the total incompetency of what we have today. USE *comparison.* • I read the story of the Lord Jesus in the boat on rough seas and I want to make a *comparative* to when we fall into sin and the water gets rough. USE *comparison.*

As a noun, *comparative* means a comparative adjective or adverb. You may speak of "a comparative review," "a comparative analysis," or "a comparative amount," but not "a comparative to what has happened" or "a comparative to measure" or "make a comparative to." *Comparative* is not a noun meaning comparison.

compassionated Misused for *compassionate* (or similar words). • We provide a 24-hour dignified, *compassionated* and dedicated funeral service. USE *compassionate.* • Dr. Hobson has a special interest in diseases of the breast and his sensitive and *compassionated* approach endears him to our breast patients who often face serious illnesses. USE *compassionate.* • Through house-to-house gatherings called Hope Parties, we are helping *compassionated* people like you learn more about this crisis, and providing opportunities to make a difference in the life of a hurting child. USE *compassionate.*

Though *compassionated,* in the sense of pitied or sympathized with, was used by Mary Wollstonecraft Shelley, Anne Brontë, Charles Dickens, Sinclair Lewis, Frederick Douglass, Herman Melville, Abraham Lincoln, and others in the past, it is not used today, in the sense of compassionate—except apparently by people who do not read Shelley, Brontë, Dickens, Lewis, Douglass, Melville, Lincoln.

> I've got a record, a record that is conservative and a record that is compassionated.
>
> —George W. Bush

compel Confused with *impel. Compel* means to force or constrain ("The groups that sued the EPA had sought to compel it to issue new standards for greenhouse gas emissions"). *Impel* means to urge or drive, through strong incentive or moral pressure, to do something ("May the care we give to making our streets and homes more resplendent impel us even more to predispose our soul to encounter him who will come to visit us"). We are typically *compelled* from without and *impelled* from within.

complaisant Misused for *complacent.* • Whether the positive changes as far as minorities are concerned will last is yet to be seen, but I think that we have to be careful that we don't get too *complaisant* about these things.

USE *complacent.* • It is vital for all of us to be most careful that we don't become *complaisant;* that we aren't willing to live with the good instead of striving for the best. USE *complacent.* • Have we become so smug, so *complaisant,* so sure that it can't happen here, that we can sit idly by and watch as it does, in fact, happen here? USE *complacent.*

Complacent means self-satisfied or contented; *complaisant,* eager to please.

complected Misused for *complexioned.* • The victim claims that two dark-*complected* males stole her tote bag from her. USE *complexioned.* • Hyperpigmentation and hyperpigmented lesions are more prominent components of photoaging in darker-*complected* individuals. USE *complexioned.* • The ancient Egyptians and Greeks had recognized that people from different places looked different, that the Egyptians were more darkly *complected* than the Greeks, and less darkly *complected* than the Nubians, and all of them were lighter than the Scythians. USE *complexioned.*

Complected is informal, substandard usage; *complexioned,* standard.

compliment Misused for *complement.* • Gamma Telecom has today announced the launch of Gamma Access, a new value-added service to *compliment* its expanding wholesale termination services. USE *complement.* • We *compliment* each other, so the cumulative result is greater than two individual funny performances. USE *complement.* • Orange is the *compliment* of blue, yellow is the *compliment* of purple, green is the *compliment* of red. USE *complement.* • The orange pure silk dress *compliments* her knitted orange mixed coat and matching hat. USE *complements.*

And *complement* is misused for *compliment:* • Watt was trying to be funny: Watt was *actually* paying them a *complement.* USE *compliment.* • So while we can't recommend *Our Lady of the Assassins,* we take some delight in the backhanded *complement* the film pays to Catholicism. USE *compliment.*

A *compliment* is a remark of praise or admiration; an act that shows respect or tribute. A *complement* is something that adds value or completes; one of two things that make a whole; a quantity of people who or things that completes a group or unit.

C

comprise Misused for *compose.* • Together, these four parts *comprise* the NGWS runtime architecture. USE *compose.* • Altogether 1,548 digitized segments *comprise* the shoreline system of the study area. USE *compose.* • The following states *comprise* the Eastern Region: Alabama, Georgia, Ohio, Maryland, Mississippi, Pennsylvania, Virginia, Tennessee, North Carolina, West Virginia, and eastern Kentucky. USE *compose.*

And *compose* is misused for *comprise*: • The album *composes* eleven songs, mostly mellow-sounding albeit sometimes romantic but never boring. USE *comprises.* • This page *composes* all the sentences with the polite forms. USE *comprises.* • The business immigrant category for Canada *composes* three components: self-employed immigrants, entrepreneurial immigrants, and investor immigrants. USE *comprises.*

The distinction, which is useful since observing it gives us a sense of the relationship of one thing to another, is thus: the whole *comprises* the parts ("The United States comprises fifty states"); the parts *compose* the whole ("Fifty states compose the United States").

Using *comprise* for *compose* or *compose* for *comprise* isn't likely to befuddle anyone for long, if at all, but knowing the distinction adds a refinement of meaning that is worth respecting.

Similarly, the whole correctly *consists* of its parts ("The Austin family consists of Jason, Renee, Camryn, and Gracyn"), and the parts correctly *constitute* the whole ("Take a moment to look around an office, or better said, the physical and virtual spaces that constitute an organization").

Comprises is also far better than the wordy *is comprised of* or *is composed of*: • The investment group *is comprised of* 9 members, each of which is responsible for a portion of the portfolio that parallels a sector of the Russell 3000 Index. USE *comprises.* • The list this year *is comprised of* 335 law firms. USE *comprises.* • The hydrogen atom *is composed of* a proton (which serves as the nucleus) and an electron. USE *comprises.* • Our Doctors Eye Center South *is composed of* board-certified optometric physicians and fellowship-trained and board-certified eye surgeons. USE *comprises.*

compulsory Misused for *compulsive.* • The Code also sets out what are not disabilities, such as substance abuse, *compulsory* gambling, self-imposed body adornments, or normal deviations in height, weight, and strength.

Use *compulsive.* • Sven Hassel must be characterized as a *compulsory* liar, with a habit to dress up in uniforms, with lots of medals. Use *compulsive.* • But while Mr. Theberge puts up warning signs with this perspective I disagree with him in the sense that it is not just the artists who are becoming *compulsory* consumers of technology. Use *compulsive.*

Compulsory means obligatory; mandatory. *Compulsive* means something that is compelling; obsessive.

concave Confused with *convex. Concave* means curved inward, like the inside of a ball ("Mike Russell said his daughter, delivered by caesarean section, didn't turn pink and her stomach was concave, so sunken it appeared to touch her backbone"). *Convex* means curved outward, like the surface of a ball ("Unlike traditional toothbrushes that have a concave or flat bristle surface, the new Curvex toothbrush has a patented convex head and tapered bristle array that is designed to better contact the surfaces of teeth, front and back"). A cave is *concave*; a mound, *convex.*

concensus Misspelling of *consensus.* • The *concensus* in Ottawa is the banks have not made that case, despite extensive public relations campaigns and behind-the-scenes lobbying. Use *consensus.* • *Concensus* is a sportsmanlike approach to group decision-making, which avoids the win/lose situation sometimes caused by voting. Use *Consensus.* • V2#11 includes a look by Carrie Menkel-Meadow at the evaluation process and the need for development of a *concensus* on how to evaluate ADR programs and how to understand the evaluations. Use *consensus.*

Though a common misspelling, people would do well to remember that the only *c* in *consensus* is the one that begins the word.

confident Misused for *confidant.* • He was a *confident* to his sister, three years his junior. Use *confidant.* • A *confident* to the queen in the early years of her reign, he had been suffering from liver cancer. Use *confidant.*

Confident means assured; full of confidence. A *confidant* is a trusted friend with whom one shares intimacies.

conflicted Misused for *torn* (or similar words). • Many such parents *feel conflicted* about segregating their children in special classes but think they have no alternative. USE *have conflicting feelings.* • The single most important element to a successful production of *Julius Caesar* is to see Brutus as a truly honorable, yet *conflicted* soul whose actions belie his intentions. USE *torn.* • My guess is that you have underlying and perhaps *conflicted* feelings about the way this change occurred. USE *conflicting.* • A *conflicted* relationship with a partner often means there is a nonexistent sex life. USE *uneasy.* • Our Western science and religion are *conflicted,* reflecting our Judaic and Christian mix of philosophy, theory, and practice. USE *in conflict.*

And some people apparently use *conflicted* to mean war-torn or embattled. • RONCO involvement in humanitarian demining in *conflicted* countries evolves from 20 years' experience with worldwide development and humanitarian assistance contracts. USE *war-torn.* • The war on drugs cannot alone explain why the U.S. is sending 60 Black Hawk and Huey helicopters to this *conflicted* nation. USE *embattled.*

If the people who use *conflicted* instead of conflicting, torn, or uneasy, mean to suggest they also are *afflicted*—with what horror one can only wonder—there may be reason to forgive this usage. If not, there is none.

confused The pronunciation of *confused* is (kon-FYOOZD), not (kon-FYOOZ-ed). The pronunciation of *confusedly,* however, is (kon-FYOO-zed-lee), not (kon-FYOOZD-lee).

congenial Misused for *congenital.* • DiGeorge's syndrome is a *congenial* defect resulting in absence of a thymus. USE *congenital.* • These chronic defects include *congenial* heart disease, anomalies of the urinary tract and genitals, and spina bifida. USE *congenital.* • Should this examination disclose any genetic or *congenial* defect, the seller must be contacted within 48 hours and the problem must be verified by seller's veterinarian. USE *congenital.* • It may not be easy, given that once a *congenial* liar, always a *congenial* liar. USE *congenital.*

Congenial means compatible; having the same qualities or interests; agreeable. *Congenital* means existing from birth; inherent or well established.

> Jake and Alyssa (Arp) Laughlin shared the story of their baby son, Cole, and his struggle with a congenial heart defect.
>
> —*North Scott Press*

congenial Misused for *genial.* • My *congenial* taxi driver, Mohsen, insisted that we approach the Old City from a little-used side road that provided the most dramatic vista. Use *genial.* • He is pleasant, *congenial,* and engaging, making him very easy to work with. Use *genial.* • It requires a *congenial* climate and suitable soil for the seed to grow into a tree. Use *genial.*

Congenial means compatible; having similar tastes or temperament; well suited to one's needs. *Genial* means affable or friendly; mild and favorable to growth.

congradulate Misspelling of *congratulate.* • Over 3000 wrestlers signed already; *congradulation* to all of you. Use *congratulation.* • Pro K-9 would like to *congradulate* Officer McClure and Officer Nelson and their K-9 partners Oky and Nash. Use *congratulate.* • U.S. Secretary of Defense William Cohen . . . and Russian Minister of Defense Igor Sergeyev *congradulate* each other on the recently signed agreement. Use *congratulate.*

Despite how it is often pronounced, *congratulate* is spelled with a *t,* not a *d.* The proper pronunciation is (kon-GRACH-ah-late) or (kon-GRAJ-ah-late).

connect Misused for *connection* (or similar words). • We also knew there was no *connect* that had been perceived with anything that was going on in the homeland. Use *connection.* • Here's a *connect* to their list, and we may just weigh in with a few recommendations to ease your tired reading eyes. Use *link.*

Connect as a noun is an atrocity. When one more syllable gives us *connection,* or one fewer, *link,* there can be no need to turn the verb *connect* into a noun. This miscreation very likely stems from the noun *disconnect,* itself an abomination. See also **disconnect**; **disconnected (from)**.

connotate Misused for *connote.* • I think the difference between the words denotate and *connotate* is one of those important distinctions people need to know about words. Use *connote.* • The reference to "God's eyes" is an Old Testament term used to *connotate* divine oversight of God in the life of an individual or group of people. Use *connote.* • Obviously, therefore, a white elephant in India's cultural context can never *connotate* redundancy, as it would in the West. Use *connote.* • In common usage in the Usui Shiki Ryoho and Usui/Tibetan systems in the West, Reiki "Mastery" does not *connotate* advanced spiritual development, enlightenment, superior moral character, or virtue. Use *connote.*

Connotate is, or ought to be, obsolete. *Connote,* to suggest or imply meaning in addition to the explicit meaning, is the word to use. See also **denotate**.

connote Confused with *denote. Connote* means to refer to implicitly; to suggest ("I had grown up in a culture where academic titles are at a premium and connote awe and respect"). *Denote* means to refer to explicitly; to mean ("The showy red flowers will denote the school building as a drug-free building").

conscience Misused for *conscious.* • Jobs are primarily given to people out of happenstance rather than *conscience* efforts if there is no mandate to do otherwise. Use *conscious.* • Throughout our difficult and trying lives, we are faced with a number of situations whose full understanding goes beyond our *conscience* thoughts. Use *conscious.* • Your spirit makes you *God-conscience,* your soul makes you *self-conscience,* and your body makes you *physical-conscience* of the world around you. Use *God-conscious; self-conscious; physical-conscious* • First, an eating disorder is an illness that affects several million of the U.S. population because society has driven many people to be *self-conscience* about their appearance. Use *self-conscious.* • Truly artistic paintings are deep *subconscience* attempts to explain your thoughts. Use *subconscious.*

And *conscious* is sometimes misused for *conscience:* • It is based on the honor system, so let your *conscious* be your guide. Use *conscience.*

Conscience, in brief, is the inner sense of right or wrong that influences one's actions and behavior; equally briefly, *conscious* (an adjective) means having an awareness of oneself and one's environment.

consequence Misused for *discipline* (or similar words) • Be willing to *consequence* defiant or resistant individuals. Use *punish.* • With these ideas in mind, Fay concludes that the most effective way to *consequence* is to lock in the empathy and then lower the boom. Use *discipline.* • My probation officer/case worker may choose to *consequence* me for not showing up. Use *discipline.* • This dilemma contributed significantly to the fit of Ivan's ongoing substance use since the parents were reluctant to *consequence* Ivan's behavior. Use *punish.*

Not yet in many dictionaries, the politically correct, though completely inane and pathetic, to *consequence* is increasingly used by psychologists and human resource personnel, themselves perhaps often inane and pathetic.

considerate Misused for *consider.* • I have been trying to convince teamers to *considerate* that proposal. Use *consider.* • The only black law school that's worth *considerating* is probably Howard. Use *considering.* • Which is the safest way to go, especially when *considerating* future updates? Use *considering.*

Considerate (kon-SID-er-it) is an adjective, and *consider* is a verb. Were *considerate* a verb, it would be pronounced (kon-SID-er-*ate*), which should be enough to dissuade anyone from using this horrid, unspeakable word. See also **alterate**; **documentate**.

consul Confused with *council. Consul* is a government official who represents his country's business interests in a foreign country ("French Vice Consul Olivier Arribe is in this city on a goodwill visit with Utah's political, religious, business, and education leaders"). *Council* is a legislative body or group of delegates who administer, discuss, consult, or advise ("Harpersville Town Council members will ask Mayor Gloria Tate to resign Monday following her arrest last week"). See also **council**.

contemn Misused for *condemn.* • The Armenian president thanked the House of Representatives for its preceding decision to *contemn* the Armenian genocide by the Turks. Use *condemn.* • When the French captured the Castle of St. Andrews, Knox as a prisoner was *contemned* to row in the French galleys for nineteen months. USE *condemned.*

To *condemn* (kon-DEM) is to censure or express disapproval of; to convict or sentence; to doom; to declare unsuitable for public use ("I condemn this vicious attack and extend my sympathies to the families"; "The district has not yet filed to condemn the property through eminent domain, but has notified Vavrina it intends to do so"; "Eddie Crawford, 56, was condemned to die in 1983 for the death of his two-year-old niece"). To *contemn* (kon-TEM) is to treat with scorn or contempt; to despise ("Such forms do not teach students to write well; they teach students to contemn all writing"; "He must have learned to contemn euphony and symmetry, with its benison of restfulness, and to delight in monotony of orchestral color and monotony of dynamics and monotony of harmonic device").

contemptible Misused for *contemptuous.* • Flaubert had a pessimistic view of life, and he was *contemptible* of middle-class society. USE *contemptuous.* • This word was mostly used by "in" crowds, i.e., popular groups to distinguish themselves from others who are *contemptible* of being "popular" and show this by deliberately seeming as though they have "lost it." USE *contemptuous.* • He socked me hard in the stomach. I doubled over, but that *contemptible* smile never left my face. USE *contemptuous.*

And *contemptuous* is misused for *contemptible*: • Manzotti's interpretation does expose the novel's *contemptuous* intentions with regard to the genealogy of the Pirobutirro family, but an additional layer of interpretation is also possible. USE *contemptible.*

Contemptible means deserving contempt; disgraceful. *Contemptuous* means showing contempt; disdainful. The indignation or contempt that people who use these words feel is wholly lost when the words are confused—a very good reason not to confuse them.

continuous Misused for *continual.* • He also criticizes the *continuous* equipment failures and the poor design of the delivery elevators, which sometimes leave crushed books. USE *continual.* • But after *continuous* self-reflection and adjustments, we now stand firmly on the road of reform. USE *continual.* • The ongoing concern over crippling attacks necessitates the *continuous* upgrade of antivirus software to ensure maximum protection in the enterprise. USE *continual.*

Continuous means without interruption, whereas *continual* means recurring at intervals. Though a distinction that is perhaps seldom observed, such subtlety can only enrich our writing and refine our thinking.

contretemps The pronunciation of *contretemps* is (KON-trah-*tan*), not (KON-trah-*temps*).

conversate Misused for *converse* (or similar words). • Receive bulletins about news articles and *conversate* with our readers. USE *converse.* • Despite this busy workload, he still manages to make time to *conversate* with others. USE *talk.* • San Diego Mommies is a place for local mommies and mommies-to-be to congregate and *conversate* about anything and everything under the sun. USE *chat.* • I am looking for an intelligent young man who loves to cook and *conversate.* USE *communicate.*

Over the past few years, this ridiculous word has cleaved to young adults, sports figures, and, now, others ill advised. Any dictionary that eventually adds this word born of imbecility to its pages is a dictionary to be disdained. As it is, we ought to consider whether we can gainfully consult a dictionary that includes the comical, the infantile *humongous* or *ginormous.* SEE ALSO **humongous**; and **ginormous** in **appendix A**.

convey back Misused for *convey.* • If you are not convinced the deaf person has understood the content of the conversation or question, ask the person to *convey back* to you a condensed version. DELETE *back.* • They typically *convey back* to the property owner the results of those meetings. DELETE *back.* • I want to *convey back* to the author or web designer my appreciation of what they have given me. DELETE *back.*

You *convey to*; you do not *convey back to*. The word *back* is superfluous. SEE ALSO **re- back**.

convince Misused for *persuade.* • In order to *convince* them, Jobs will need to talk about all the device's specs. USE *persuade.* • Daly went to Gless's house with champagne and balloons to *convince* her to take the role of Christine Cagney. USE *persuade.* • Now, we have Michael Pollan, a journalist I greatly admire, giving us new rules to follow when we eat and Jonathan Safran Foer sneaking onto butchering facilities to *convince* us all to be vegetarians. USE *persuade*.

And *persuade* is occasionally misused for *convince*: • Nobody is ever *persuaded* of anything. USE *convinced*. • Religion by its nature requires that people be *persuaded* of its truth. USE *convinced*.

There is a difference between *convince*—which is being used where *persuade* is better suited—and *persuade*. *Convince* means create belief in; *persuade*, induce or talk into. We are *convinced of* and *persuaded to*. Many people do not observe the distinction between *persuade* and *convince*, and that in part is due to dictionaries that use one word to define the other. Buy your dictionary deliberately.

cooperate Misused for *corporate*. • Churches, whether any of us want to admit it or not, are *cooperate*, even down to the suits and ties. USE *corporate*. • Do you guys disbelieve that big *cooperate* companies have control over the government? USE *corporate*. • A blog is a personal website maintained by individuals or *cooperate* organizations. USE *corporate*.

Cooperate (koh-OP-ah-*rate*) means to work together for a common purpose, whereas *corporate* (KOR-per-it) means incorporated or relating to a corporation.

copulation Misused for *cooperation*. Though not a common error—what unspeakable progeny would we know if it were?—misusing *copulation* (the act of sexual intercourse) for *cooperation* (a joint effort) does happen: "Losing its candor, valor, and taste in schools and the spirit of academic copulation is fastly evading . . . ."

copyright Misused for *copyrighted*. • Baker and others said they sympathized with efforts by the recording and motion picture industries to protect *copyright* material, but insisted on their own rights to protect the privacy of subscribers. USE *copyrighted*. • The country's copyright agency has given its blessing to all downloading of *copyright* music, no matter the source. USE *copyrighted*.

The adjectival form is *copyrighted*, not *copyright*. SEE ALSO **cliché**; **copywrite**.

copywrite Misspelling of *copyright.* • For books that are out of *copywrite* in many cases the entire book is available to download and read for free. USE *copyright.* • Authorities have been unable to shut Pirate Bay down, despite the fact that the men have been charged with *copywrite* infringement. USE *copyright.*

Copyright is the only permissible spelling of the legal right given to publish or perform literary, artistic, or musical works. *Copywrite* means to write advertising or promotional copy. SEE ALSO **copyright**.

core Misused for *corps.* • The Marine *Core* is only for the real men of the United States of America. USE *Corps.* • Within the ROTC *core* of cadets, experienced cadets take on leadership responsibilities and roles inside the detachment. USE *corps.*

Core (KOR), as a noun, is the central or innermost part of something; the most important part; the central part of an apple or other fruit; a section of the earth's strata; the main memory of a computer; the central part of a nuclear reactor. As an adjective, *core* means principal or central. *Corps* (KOR), not (KORPZ), is a group of people involved in some organization; a military force or branch of the armed forces.

corporal Misused for *corporeal.* • The beauty of the political order, however, is that it revolves around *corporal* not spiritual qualities. USE *corporeal.* • We allow for the evolution of man's body, of that part which is *corporal* and tangible, under the guidance of God, but we affirm that man's soul was created specially. USE *corporeal.*

And sometimes *corporeal* is misused for *corporal*: • Parties can also be held criminally liable for their actions, in which case they may be subjected to a number of criminal sanctions including fines, imprisonment, or *corporeal* punishment. USE *corporal.* • Two patients with minimal *corporeal* injury who did not undergo exploration did well. USE *corporal.*

Corporal (KOR-por-el) means relating to the body. *Corporeal* (kor-POR-ee-el) means relating to the physical world; tangible. The words are not interchangeable.

correctify Misused for *correct.* • Please let me know what else I need to do to help *correctify* this situation. USE *correct.* • Your attempt to politically *correctify* my language to your standards is absurd and if "geek" or "enthusiast" or "tekkie" bothers you so much perhaps you are in the wrong forum, because this is after all a geek forum. USE *correct.* • *Correctify* me if I'm wrong, but I don't see a driveshaft either. USE *Correct.* • Well, most of us can't and we all hope that it is *correctified* quickly. USE *corrected.*

Correctify, instead of *correct* or, possibly, *rectify,* is nonstandard and unnecessary.

cosmology Misused for *cosmetology.* • You'll enjoy the best food, finest fashions, all the attentions of an esthetician, *cosmologist,* hairdresser, and personal trainer. USE *cosmetologist.* • Late in the afternoon of November 17, 1993, Hales drove to Sylvina's Hair Emporium in Laurel, where his wife of twenty-five years, Donna Elaine Hales, worked as a *cosmologist,* to drive her home after work. USE *cosmetologist.*

And *cosmetology* is misused for *cosmology:* • I recently read an article—I think it was in the *Journal of Astrology and Cosmetology*—that a new asteroid had been discovered and was being named Xantiusia. USE *Cosmology.*

Cosmetology is the study of cosmetics and the application of them. *Cosmology* is the scientific study of the universe. SEE ALSO **astronomy**.

could care less Misused for *couldn't care less.* • However, if your clients are like most small business owners, they *could care less* about the technical details on blocking well-known ports, SMTP support, and dynamic HTML. USE *couldn't care less.* • Okay, okay, we know—you *could care less* about our formative years, when Tommy took apart and rebuilt our dad's heap over and over again—each time having a few extra parts, until eventually there was nothing left to disassemble. USE *couldn't care less.* • Then you end up with a site that makes you happy but that everyone else on the planet *could care less* about. USE *could not care less.* • What could be more fascinating than knowing what really matters to American women—what they adore, detest, and *could care less* about? USE *couldn't care less.*

However it is meant, whatever the speaker's intention and inflection, the phrase *could care less* means just the opposite of the one it is so often misused for. Though hardly elegant English, *couldn't care less* means that

C

apathy reigns in regard to whatever is being discussed; *could care less* clearly means that there is still interest.

could of Misused for *could have.* • Defensively, I thought we played as well as we *could of* at this stage. USE *could have.* • Cottrell believes that if Acclamation had had a clear run in the King's Stand at Ascot, he *could of* won instead of slitting Australian speedster Choiser and Air Wave. USE *could have.* • If she did not have a gun, she *could of* got hurt. USE *could have.* • He *could of* told us what went on with that woman. USE *could have.*

Because *could've* (like *should've* and *would've*) is the term many people say, *could of* (*should of, would of*) is the term many people write: • The football season is over. *Could of, should of, would of,* are all irrelevant points right now. USE *Could've, should've, would've.* Similarly, *may of, might of,* and *must of* are incorrect. SEE ALSO **would have**.

council Misused for *counsel.* • Addario is legal *council* for the Canadian Conference of the Arts, the country's largest arts lobby group. USE *counsel.* • The adviser shall give *council* to the president and *council* on matters concerning PHC. USE *counsel.* • Lawyers for Oba Chandler argued before the Supreme Court this morning that their client had ineffective *council* in his murder trial. USE *counsel.*

And *counsel* is misused for *council*: • Syria asked the UN Security *Counsel* to condemn the act of aggression, which, they say, has no justification at all. USE *Council.*

A *council* is a group of people, legislative body, or body of delegates that deliberates over matters. *Counsel* is advice or a person who gives advice, such as a lawyer. SEE ALSO **consul**.

coupon The pronunciation of *coupon* is (KOO-pon), not (KYOO-pon).

course Misused for *coarse.* • Later, Stalin, in his rude and *course* manner, would develop that which Lenin began, as shown in dealings with Roosevelt and with Hitler. USE *coarse.* • The foundation may consist of rock, *course*-grained material (sand and gravel), fine-grained material (silt and clay), or a combination of all three. USE *coarse.* • Light gray hair tumbled over her *course* face and it was obvious she was never a beauty. USE *coarse.*

And *coarse* is misused for *course*: • September 11 dramatically altered the *coarse* of events. USE *course.* • If you are one of those who wants to know more about golf *coarse* equipment this is the place to look. USE *course.* • An hors d'oeuvre hour will start the event off, followed by a five-*coarse* meal, complete with wine service. USE *course.* • The successful completion of the prescribed CAT-I *coarse* is a prerequisite for graduation in the academic *coarse.* USE *course.* • Such variations reflect the many changes in the dialects of the region over the *coarse* of time. USE *course.* • The tip of Mud Island and its shrimp boat wreck soon passed by and we were free to leave the channel and set a more direct *coarse* to Rockport. USE *course.*

Course means a route or direction; a duration of time; a mode of action or behavior; the manner in which something develops; a mealtime dish or set of dishes; an area of land where a game or sport is played; a series of lectures or medical treatments. *Coarse* means rough in texture; consisting of large particles; not fine or elegant in structure; of inferior quality; rude or vulgar.

cowtow Misspelling of *kowtow* (*kow-tow*). • The officials clearly *cowtow* to superstars and favor the home team ridiculously. USE *kowtow.* • While some will use this investment as an argument that the Gates Foundation will *cow-tow* to Monsanto's interests, there is another aspect to stock ownership that is worth bringing up. USE *kow-tow.* • It's the biggest public service scam in town, and the officials who *cow-tow* to this situation know it, protect it, and expand it. USE *kow-tow.* • Should we *cowtow* to the Deep South, if it's to our own detriment? USE *kow-tow.*

Kow-tow (or *kowtow*) is the correct spelling. *Cow-tow* (or *cowtow*) is a spelling that only bovine linguists would be "mooved" by. SEE ALSO **kowtow**; **kowtowed**.

credible Misused for *credulous.* • Teach us not to be gullible and *credible,* swallowing every line that comes along. USE *credulous.* • I have asked Dr. Wilkinson more than once to name an ancient writer who was not, on occasion, *credible,* gullible, and superstitious. USE *credulous.* • This is the paperback of the movie by Sun Classic Pictures, a company notorious for semislick movies aimed at *credible* and gullible audiences. Use *credulous.*

Credible means believable, plausible. *Credulous* means believing too readily, gullible.

creditable Misused for *credible.* • It's reporting that is really not based on information that came from a *creditable* source. Use *credible.* • Even with this highly *creditable* threat that could result in a terrorist attack anywhere in Israel, including the area in which the homosexual parade will take place, Israeli authorities will still bring in around 10,000 police to guard the homosexual parade. Use *credible.* • He takes a lesson from E. L. Doctorow and fashions a *creditable* story around a detective hired to find out what really happened to George Reeves (Ben Affleck). Use *credible.*

The two words have two meanings. *Credible* means believable; plausible. *Creditable* means worthy of credit; deserving of modest praise or commendation. Years ago *creditable* meant bringing honor or esteem (that is, the praise was unreserved).

Dictionaries, today, do not necessarily tell us the correct meaning of words; they simply tell us how people use words—hardly a good measure of meaning.

criterion Misused for *criteria.* • Product designers have to consider a number of *criterion* to determine the best shielding solution for their product. Use *criteria.* • If we classify "the election defaults" as "not a candidate," quorum would satisfy these *criterion.* Use *criteria.*

And even more common, *criteria* is misused for *criterion*: • The following formulas return an average from a range of cells based on a single *criteria.* Use *criterion.* • One *criteria* was based on how many research articles were published in highly regarded international journals. Use *criterion.*

Criterion is singular; *criteria,* or *criterions,* is plural. See also **phenomenon**.

cronically Misspelling of *chronically.* • I am *cronically* upbeat, environmentally aware, and enjoy group activities. Use *chronically.* • The kids are underprivileged, many are living in homeless shelters like the Road Home, and Palmer Court (housing for *cronically* homeless families). Use *chronically.*

Chronically, with an *h,* is the correct spelling.

crucifiction Misspelling of *crucifixion.* • This is the account of the *crucifiction* of Jesus as written by John. Use *crucifixion.* • After the *crucifiction,* the Apostles begin spreading the teachings of Jesus, first in Judea and Galilee, then to the gentiles in Greece, Rome, and elsewhere. Use *crucifixion.*

Crucifixion refers to the execution of Jesus on a cross at Calvary; execution on a cross; extremely painful suffering. If you believe Jesus did not die on the cross, that he simply lost consciousness there, you might make a case for spelling the word *crucifiction;* otherwise, *crucifixion* is correct. See also **Calvary**.

crumble Confused with *crumple.* To *crumble* is to break apart or disintegrate ("That day, terrorists foolishly thought that they could cause America to crumble by destroying the financial towers and the innocent people within them"). To *crumple* is to crinkle; to collapse; to be upset ("If you made a typo and had to crumple up a piece of paper and rewrite a memo, you would not be expected to pay for that sheet of paper out of your own pocket"; "Mr. Bush's face crumpled, and he stuttered the reply 'Oh, I'm so sorry'"). As the examples illustrate, *crumble* suggests severe or widespread damage, whereas *crumple* suggests slight or insignificant damage.

cue Misused for *queue.* • Can you put my project back in the *cue* once you receive my documents and check? Use *queue.* • After about five minutes we reached the front of the *cue.* Use *queue.*

And *queue* is sometimes misused for *cue*: • This was a great idea on his part and I wish more people would take his *queue* and offer to do some documentation. Use *cue.*

A *cue* (KYOO) is a long stick used in the game of billiards or pool; a signal or hint to do or say something; a gesture. A *queue* (KYOO) is a line of waiting people or vehicles; a braid of hair.

currant Misspelling of *current.* • It is appropriate for young and fit individuals and is adapted to the athlete's *currant* needs. USE *current.* • This internal command is used to display and change the *currant* time. USE *current.* • Electrical *currant* is equal to the flow of water, and voltage is equal to the pressure. USE *current.*

Current, as an adjective, means at the present time; contemporary; circulating; prevalent. As a noun, it means the flow of air or water; the flow or amount of electricity; a general tendency or course. *Currant* is a small, seedless raisin; a shrub.

Dd

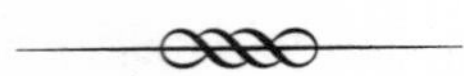

D

dairy Misspelling of *diary.* • "It's a wonder I haven't abandoned all my ideas," Anne wrote in her *dairy,* "they seem so absurd and impractical." Use *diary.*

And *diary* is misused for *dairy*: • Under the compact, a commission of *diary* farmers and bureaucrats sets the minimum farm price that processors must pay for milk. Use *dairy.*

The adjective *dairy* means of or relating to milk and milk products. The noun *diary* is a journal of one's own thoughts, feelings, and experiences; a book of such writing.

dalmation Misspelling of *dalmatian.* • This page is dedicated to all *dalmations.* I love all *dalmations* and hope you will too. Use *dalmatians.* • One of the newest additions to the Disney Series is this adorable set of salt and pepper shakers from the recent Disney movie *102 Dalmations.* Use *Dalmatians.* • Boone, a *Dalmation* belonging to Jeanette Weaver Hutchinson, receives some attention Friday at the Wheatland Cluster Dog Show at the Bicentennial Center. Use *Dalmatian.*

Dalmation persists as a common misspelling of *dalmatian.*

deabilitate Misused for *debilitate.* • I woke up with a nice *deabilitating* headache this morning. Use *debilitating.* • Osteoporosis is a huge problem that will *deabilitate* a large baby boomer population of women. Use *debilitate.* • Heroin is just one of those drugs that doesn't totally *deabilitate* you like alcohol. Use *debilitate.*

Debilitate (di-BIL-i-*tate*), not *deabilitate* (*dee*-ah-BIL-i-tate), means to make weak; enfeeble. See also **disabilitate**.

debacle The pronunciation of *debacle* is (di-BAHK-el), not (DEB-i-kel).

debark (disbark) Misused for *disembark.* • In this painting by Samuel B. Waugh, Irish immigrants *debark* at New York in 1847. Use *disembark.* • Taiwan travelers from Jinmen Island wearing masks *debark* at a ferry dock Wednesday in Xiamen, a coastal city in southeastern China's Fujian Province. Use *disembark.* • It was the kind of airport typical of many European cities: the passengers *debark* from the plane at some distance from the terminal and are brought in by buses. Use *disembark.* • A Muslim woman feeds her children as they wait to *disbark* from the Philippine Navy ship BRP *Dagupan City.* Use *disembark.*

You might *debark* logs or trees, or, others, despicably, dogs, but you never *debark* or *disbark* a plane, train, or boat. Clearly some people cannot be bothered to pronounce polysyllabic words.

debone Misused for *bone.* As *shell* means to remove the shell from, so *bone* means to remove the bones from. Because people, for decades, have mistakenly used *debone* to mean to remove the bones from, most dictionaries now include this definition with no qualifying remarks—further evidence that the word *dictionary* may, before long, mean rubbish; rot; claptrap; tripe.

decant Misused for *descant.* • It has an optional brass quintet, percussion, organ fanfare at the beginning, then 5 stanzas (1 in 4 parts for choir), soprano *decant* on the last stanza. Use *descant.* • Kurt can also *decant* on early modern and modern Europe, the early-modern Atlantic world, comparative European imperialism, and modern South Asia. Use *descant.*

To *decant* (di-KANT) is to pour liquid from one container to another, usually so as not to disturb the sediment ("Conventional wisdom has it that fine wines should be decanted before serving in order to let the wine breathe"). To *descant* (DES-kant) is to discourse on a subject; to sing or play melodiously. As a noun, a *descant* is a comment or criticism; a melody or counterpoint sung or played above the basic melody ("She descants on, among other things, her own upbringing as a mass-media consumer, her relationship with Steyer, and the fact that she misses her parents"; "The word descant is also used to indicate the high range, as in descant recorder").

decimate Misused for *destroy* (or similar words). • A trial enabled the company to *decimate* the workforce at its Taupo mill this year—100 more jobs are at risk next year. USE *reduce.* • Bulldogs *decimate* cougars. USE *thrash.* • Inexperience and injury may *decimate* some wrestling teams, but the Bears have held their ground through a difficult start to the season despite some new faces. USE *weaken.* • If he doesn't go for the deal, we'll just *decimate* him. Flat out just *decimate* him. USE *crush.*

Originally, *decimate* meant to kill one person in ten. Today, the word has come to mean to kill or destroy a large part of. You cannot correctly, as in these illustrations, use *decimate* to mean, simply, damage or defeat. And you do not *decimate* a single person, home, or idea.

> Sugar and citrus producers say eliminating tariffs could decimate farmers in the Sunshine State.
>
> —Tamara Lush, *St. Petersburg Times*
>
> Why do students decimate their bodies with alcohol one night a year?
>
> —Adam Pulver, *The Tufts Daily*
>
> But now many of the homes are decimated.
>
> —Gary Tuckman, CNN reporter
>
> Examples of the absurd use of *decimate* are abundant. People who do not distinguish *decimate* from *destroy* or *damage* or other words also do not distinguish their writing.

declaim Misused for *disclaim.* • His friends and neighbors vehemently *declaimed* the idea as absurd. USE *disclaimed.* • They're folks who hide behind pseudonyms to defame, *declaim,* and disdain. USE *disclaim.* • It was genuine pleasure, even validation, to have my father *declaim* my music sensibilities, my mother dismiss my gravity-defying afro as barbarian, and my grandparents denounce my politics as either utopian or communist. USE *disclaim.*

Declaim means to speak formally in public; *disclaim* means to deny or renounce. SEE ALSO **elocute**.

> It's no surprise that the mayor who required fast-food restaurants to display caloric content of every menu item would declaim food trucks.
>
> —Michael C. Moynihan, *The Wall Street Journal*

de facto Confused with *de jure. De facto* (di-FAK-toe) means existing in fact though not in law ("Hill is even serving as de facto mayor of the district where his battalion is stationed"). *De jure* (dee-JOOR-ee) means by right or law ("He was also incensed that Sharansky had voted for a new law that would give Orthodox rabbis de jure control over religious conversions inside Israel").

definate Misspelling of *definite.* • We have written to the Department (of the Environment) to look for funding and we have had no *definate* indication. USE *definite.* • Their entry-level, $8 Merlot is fine, but its Winemaker's Select line is a *definate* step up. USE *definite.* • I *definately* would like a serious relationship when the time is right. USE *definitely.* • If Larry Summers is for it then I am *definately* not! USE *definitely.*

Definate is a common misspelling—made by common people, that is, people who pay scant attention to the words they use—of *definite.* Being able to pronounce a word is half what it takes to express yourself; being able to spell it, the other. SEE ALSO **definite**; **indefinate**.

definite Misused for *definitive.* • The medical examiner concluded there was *definite* evidence of sexual abuse. USE *definitive.* • And since there is no *definite* authority on English language, you can use the word, of course as long as you know and acknowledge it is "grittier" than "ground." USE *definitive.* • Download *Lennon: The Definite Biography,* Revised and Updated, from Usenet. USE *Definitive.*

Although the meanings of these two words overlap—both mean precisely defined or explicit—*definitive* means authoritative or conclusive, whereas *definite* does not. SEE ALSO **definate**.

degradate Misused for *degrade.* • Materials used in cars, airplanes, tools, constructions, electronic equipment can *degradate* gradually or fail suddenly.

USE *degrade.* • Its electric generating capacity may *degradate* gradually between 0 and 20 percent over its useful life. USE *degrade.* • We seem to *degradate* psychiatry and psychiatric patients no less than we denounce the legislation of mind-expanding drugs. USE *degrade.*

Occasionally, *degradate* is meant to mean something other than *degrade*: • Are we to *degradate* to the Stone Age to adopt a code of religiousness that many of us do not want? USE *revert.* • This is a read for men and women; it's tough, but tough is what it takes to get people to communicate, instead of *degradate.* USE *separate.*

To *degrade* is to treat with contempt or disrespect; to lessen in rank or in value; to wear down, decompose, or deteriorate. *Degradate* is nonsense.

delegate Misused for *relegate.* • We can read this verse in a couple of seconds, and it's a summation that the beast was speaking, it was eventually slain, and finally, it was *delegated* to hell. USE *relegated.* • The problem here is the public's access to and their channel time allotments on Channel 12 have been *delegated* to third place within the PEG equation. USE *relegated.*

To *delegate* is to authorize another person to act as one's representative; to entrust a task or responsibility to another. To *relegate* is to assign to a particular place or position, class or category; to assign to an inferior position; to banish. Watch this word. One day soon, our worst dictionaries will tell us that *delegate* does mean *relegate.*

deliberative Misused for *deliberate.* • But the status quo is unacceptable to me and to the governor, so we are going to make thoughtful, *deliberative* changes in personnel, practices, and programs. USE *deliberate.* • He doesn't usually react or respond in a visceral way, he's very *deliberative.* USE *deliberate.* • I think he's going to go about this in a very *deliberative* fashion. USE *deliberate.*

Deliberate—which means thoughtful, premeditated, considered, not impulsive—does not mean *deliberative*—which means relating to discussion or consideration. There are *deliberate* people, *deliberate* lies, *deliberate* attempts, but *deliberative* bodies, *deliberative* sessions, *deliberative* processes. *Deliberate* typically applies to one or two people; *deliberative* typically applies to a group of people.

delusion Confused with *illusion.* An *illusion* is a false perception of reality; something that tricks the mind ("Beware of the illusion of perfection"; "Are we interested in security or just the illusion of it?"). A *delusion* is a false belief held despite strong evidence that indicates its falsity ("The delusion of grandeur was reinforced by his nickname, King James"; "It can cause hallucination, delusion, and disorganized speech patterns, otherwise known as thought disorders"). SEE ALSO **illusion.**

D

demur Misused for *demure.* • The always delicate and *demur* Helen Hunt graced the stage to hand out the Best Actor award and I was happy to see Roberto Benigni win for the second time in the evening. USE *demure.* • During athletic competitions, Armour, a Memphis, Tennessee, native, is anything but *demur.* USE *demure.* • With her flaming red hair this model could be a *demur* woman or a cabaret dancer complete with black stockings and garter. USE *demure.*

Demur (di-MUR) means to object; to have scruples; to hesitate. *Demure* (di-MYOOR) means modest, reserved, decorous; affectedly shy or modest.

denotate Misused for *denote.* • Synths also *denotate* the nightmarish moment of the action. USE *denote.* • In real situations labels can be names for the objects or may *denotate* specific features or functions of them. USE *denote.* • Letters *i, j, k, l, m, n* often *denotate* subscripts of arrays. USE *denote.*

Denotate is also sometimes used for *detonate*: • The alleged al-Qaeda plot to build and *denotate* a "dirty" bomb is a grim reminder of the widespread proliferation of nuclear materials. USE *detonate.* • TNT is less powerful, harder to *denotate,* more difficult to make, but cheaper, less poisonous, unaffected by dampness, and less dense. USE *detonate.*

As *connote* is preferable to *connotate,* so *denote* is to *denotate. Denote* means to signify or refer to explicitly; to be a sign of; indicate. It does not mean, as *detonate* does, to explode or cause to explode. SEE ALSO **connotate**.

denounce Misused for *renounce.* • The idea was if you can have a Klan member *denounce* his membership because he is in love, then love can conquer all. USE *renounce.* • The Iowa constituent opens his letter by announcing his desire to *denounce* his citizenship in favor of becoming an illegal alien. USE *renounce.*

To *denounce* is to publicly condemn or criticize. To *renounce* is to reject or give up.

depravation Misused for *deprivation.* • At times, members of 1st Battalion, 7th Marines battled Hussein's Republican Guard troops, sandstorms, the searing Iraqi sun, slow mail, sleep *depravation,* and no days off. USE *deprivation.* • John Sayles has something to say in *Casa de los Babys* about the relentless poverty afflicting Mexico, about the tragedy of children growing up among such *depravation,* about Americans and their condescending attitudes, about the plight of mothers forced to give up their babies and the emotional trauma suffered by women who desperately want children but can't have them. USE *deprivation.* • India has gone through decades of want and *depravation.* USE *deprivation.* • He is also a graduate of Ranger School, a rigorous school that includes sleep and food *depravation.* USE *deprivation.*

Depravation means moral corruption; a depraved or corrupt act. *Deprivation* means loss; the state of being deprived; privation.

> Annie Dillard says in her *The Writing Life,* "The writing life is colorless to the point of sensory depravation."
>
> —Philip Yancy, as quoted in ChristianityToday.com
>
> If we believe Dillard wrote *deprivation* and Yancy said *deprivation,* we must wonder at how deprived of depravity, or old-fashioned fun, perhaps, the good people at *Christianity Today* are.

deprive Misused for *deprave.* • It is said that they are the most evil race in the Warhammer World because they derive pleasure in performing the most *deprived* acts just because it causes suffering to others. USE *depraved.* • Fifteen years after thousands were killed in a poison gas leak at a Union Carbide Corp.'s pesticide plant in Bhopal, survivors and relatives of victims sued the company on Monday for "*deprived* indifference to human life." USE *depraved.*

To *deprive* is to take something away from; to deny. To *deprave* is to make immoral or corrupt.

descry Misused for *decry*. • Other Oates critics *descry* a closed world of fatal impossibility. Use *decry.* • Certain poets are badly represented, and many critics will want to *descry* the travesty done their favorite. Use *decry.* • Metropolitan critics, however, continued to *descry* the "obsession with landscape." Use *decry.*

Decry (di-KRI) means to ridicule or condemn; *descry* (di-SKRI) means to catch sight of; to detect or discover. *Descry* is a so-called literary word, and it is so-called literary people who typically misuse it.

desirous Misused for *desirable.* • The woman was beautiful, sexy, and *desirous,* but she wasn't what he needed. Use *desirable.* • We have to silence our bodies when we negotiate wanting to be *desirous* and sexual and having to play the role of a good girl. Use *desirable.*

Desirable means arousing desire; worth doing, having, or seeking. *Desirous* means having desire or longing for, and it is often used in the phrase *is desirous of* ("It means we are not apathetic enough to let things be and are desirous of a better high school"). *Is desirous of,* however, is wordy for *desire* alone.

despaired Misused for *discouraged* (or similar words). • The overall social scenario *despaired* him and he decided to retire in seclusion on a bhitt (dune). Use *discouraged.* • It *despaired* him to see her struggle with the words. Use *disheartened.* • The thought of another hour of walking *despaired* her, as she was still carrying her guitar, but she tried not to show it. Use *discouraged.* • This *despaired* us, for there were reports of Mobius's war efforts turning toward us. Use *discouraged.* • In a group I ran the game for, the characters creation *despaired* me a bit. Use *disheartened.*

To *despair* means to lose all hope; to lose heart or be overcome by a sense of futility or defeat. You may use a personal pronoun (*me, him, her, them,* or *us*) after *discourage* or *dishearten,* but not after *despair.*

As the meaning of one word distinguishes it from the meaning of another, so the words we use distinguish each of us from others. Language, how we express ourselves as much as what we express, is designed to discriminate; it distinguishes, it defines, it identifies. We choose our friends, we choose our work, and we choose our words.

dessert Misused for *desert.* • At points we hit totally barren *dessert,* no vegetation to be seen whatsoever. USE *desert.* • So why do we lock them up for 30 years?—probably not to protect us from them, but for retribution or just *desserts.* USE *deserts.* • Who knew being stranded on a *desserted* island could be so humorous? USE *deserted.* • Taliban military forces *desserted* the capital of Kabul today, after a series of stunning military victories by opposition forces. USE *deserted.*

Dessert has one meaning: a usually sweet dish that is served at the end of a meal. The noun *desert* means barren or arid land with sparse vegetation; desolate; deserved reward or punishment. The verb means to abandon or withdraw from.

destruct Misused for *destroy* (or similar words). • A port was *destructed.* USE *obliterated.* • Aboriginal communities were *destructed* and displaced, which has had an indelible effect on their cultural practices and existence. USE *destroyed.* • If quarantined disease organisms are detected, the cut flower must be reconditioned, *destructed,* or returned to the shipper. USE *destroyed.* • National programs should be established to identify and/or label, collect, dispose, and *destruct* PCB-containing articles. USE *destroy.*

Though obsolete, the verb *destruct* is in use today by people insufficiently familiar with the English language. Of course, *autodestruct* and *self-destruct* are popularly and correctly used, as is, in computer terminology, the *destruct* class object.

dethaw (unthaw) Misused for *thaw.* • Allow cuts of venison to *unthaw* in the refrigerator in heavily salted water after removing the meat from the freezer for 24–48 hours. USE *thaw.* • Some stores opened at midnight, others at 3, 4, 5, and 6 A.M., but at every store thousands of shoppers were happy to *unthaw* once doors opened. USE *thaw.* • Will she be able to *unthaw* his heart? USE *thaw.* • Flaherty urges homeowners to call a plumber rather than trying to *dethaw* frozen pipes with a blow dryer or lighter. USE *thaw.* • How long would it take for frozen beefsteak to *dethaw* in the fridge? USE *thaw.*

To *thaw* is to change a solid to a liquid by warming; to lose stiffness or numbness or frozenness by being warmed; to abandon a cold or reserved manner. To *dethaw* and to *unthaw* are solecisms.

device Misused for *devise.* • He *deviced* a new plan based on the contemporary Gothic pointed arch, and "ribs" that would support the ceiling. USE *devised.* • They have to *device* a strategy so that the visitor comes again and again. USE *devise.*

Device (di-VIS)—a contrivance; plan; scheme; technique; trick—is a noun; *devise* (di-VIZ)—to contrive; plan; invent—a verb. SEE ALSO **advice**.

dialate Misspelling of *dilate.* • Can a boy's pupils *dialate* when he is talking to you and likes you? USE *dilate.* • My baby was supposed to be born on January 1 of 2006 and I still havent started to *dialate* or anything. USE *dilate.*

The pronunciation of *dilate* is (di-LATE or DI-late), not (di-ah-LATE or DI-ah-late). The word has two syllables, not three.

dialectical Confused with *dialectal. Dialectical,* the adjectival form of *dialectic,* means relating to dialectics, a method of argument ("In his book *At The Origins of Modern Atheism,* Michael J. Buckley argues that modern atheism and modern theism are two poles in the same dialectical movement of Western thought"). *Dialectal,* the adjectival form of *dialect,* means relating to dialect, a regional variety of a language ("Mr. Mubarak avoided Zine el-Abidine ben Ali of Tunisia's gambit of giving his speech in dialectal Arabic"). That is, *dialectical* deals with logic, and *dialectal* with language. It may be that *dialectics* (or *dialectic*) is also occasionally confused with *dialect.*

dialog The spelling *dialogue* is preferable to *dialog,* a variant spelling that people who have a distaste for the English language—people, that is, who truncate the spelling of words; use clichés, idioms, or slang bottomlessly; speak in monosyllables whenever possible; and, if they read, read simply to be entertained—are wont to use. SEE ALSO **monolog**.

didn't (hadn't; shouldn't) ought to Misused for *ought not to.* • You *didn't ought to* make me do something like that. USE *ought not to.* • Now, maybe all this *shouldn't ought to* be true. USE *ought not to.* • He was searched, and though nothing was found, it was decided that he *shouldn't ought to* return to the store. USE *ought not to.* • We *hadn't ought to* fool ourselves or fool the public in the sense that if we charge ourselves for the demolition debris for the high school we will be adding about $1,250,000 to the high school project. USE *ought not to.*

These expressions are illiteracies. Use *ought not to*. SEE ALSO **ought not**.

differential Misused for *difference.* • The answer is not to arm the police: it is surely to learn the obvious lesson from Sir Robert and restore a *differential* between robbery and murder. USE *difference.* • The consensual relationships that are of concern are those romantic and/or sexual relationships in which both parties appear to have consented, but where there is a definite power *differential* between the two parties. USE *difference.* • With 35 seconds left, FBCA turned the ball over, but with a 5 second *differential* between the shot clock and game clock they elected to play tough defense. USE *difference.*

Differential is not simply a synonym for *difference,* as many dictionaries maintain, and in the examples shown here, *difference* is the word wanted. *Differential* is often used in regard to differences in price and, more correct and specialized still, mathematical increments.

> There's a minor advantage when you look at polls toward one or the other, depending on which issue, but apart from Iraq, which has fallen on the list of concerns, there really isn't a big differential between the candidates.
>
> —Ron Brownstein
>
> Political analyst Brownstein evidently believes that *differential,* instead of *difference,* makes his vapid thought a more inviting sentence.

different from (different than; different to) *Different than* is peculiarly an American expression and the least supportable of the three; *different to* is widely used in Britain though not in the United States; and *different from* is popular in both British and American English. The OED records examples of *different to* from 1526, *different from* from 1590, and *different than* from 1644.

diffuse Misused for *defuse.* • After confirming a bomb report, DeBenedet scans the possible explosive, secures the area, and decides whether to detonate or *diffuse* the bomb. Use *defuse.* • *Diffuse* your conversation about this difficult topic with a little humor—it will put you both at ease. Use *Defuse.* • Taiwan's newly elected president is steering a moderate political course to *diffuse* tension between his nation and mainland China. Use *defuse.* • If you encounter a bear, do not run! Slowly back away to try to put distance between you and the bear to *diffuse* the situation. Use *defuse.*

Diffuse means to spread over a wide area, disseminate; to make less brilliant, soften. As an adjective, it means widely spread or scattered; verbose or unclear. *Defuse* means to remove the fuse from (a bomb); reduce the danger or tension in.

dilemma Confused with *predicament* (or similar words). A *dilemma* offers a choice between two equally unappealing outcomes ("So the dilemma is having to back a dictator like Mubarak, or open the door to something worse"). A *predicament* does not suggest a choice of any kind, simply a bothersome or vexing problem ("It's hard to know which is the better analogy for our predicament in Iraq: Vietnam or Israel").

dilemna Misspelling of *dilemma.* • Adding Choo to the lineup will bring about an interesting *dilemna* for Manny Acta. Use *dilemma.* • This may be the epitome of the value investor's *dilemna.* Use *dilemma.* • Orestes was handed an impossible moral *dilemna*—avenge his father only by the blood crime of killing his mum. Use *dilemma.*

Although some people were apparently taught that the spelling of *dilemma* is *dilemna, dilemma* (there's an Emma in every *dilemma*) alone is the correct spelling.

D

dis (diss) Misused for *disrespect* (or similar words). • This issue addresses five other means of *dissing* employees: buck passing, procrastination, inattentiveness, impatience, and public reprimands. USE *disrespecting.* • More bad news for Leonardo DiCaprio: ABC News is *dissing* him big-time. USE *dismissing.* • Governor Bill Owens made a media splash Monday, playing TV critic and *dissing* first lady of TV news Barbara Walters on national television. USE *disparaging.* • Watch Letterman stir up trouble with a Top 10 list or by *dissing* the soft drink Dr Pepper as "liquid manure." USE *denigrating.* • Franzen, despised and envied by all writers for his talent, his luck, his good looks, and his marketing acumen, essentially *dissed* the Oprah award for being lowbrow. USE *dismissed.*

Haven't we all had quite enough of this prefix aspiring to be a word? Are we to allow *un* and *anti, non* and *pre* to follow? People are increasingly mono- and disyllabic as it is; let's rail against this foolishness, this affront, this *dis.*

If you speak in monosyllables, you likely think in monosyllables. Complex thoughts, well-reasoned arguments, a keen understanding of self and society—each and all of them lost, squandered, forfeited. SEE ALSO **def** in **appendix A**.

disabilitate Misused for *debilitate.* • Sleep disorders like apnea, narcolepsy, and insomnia can be dangerous and *disabilitating.* USE *debilitating.* • Many who suffer from a *disabilitating* illness swear that this wonderful machine has changed their life. USE *debilitating.* • Also, note that microwave and lower-frequency EMF weapons are in wide use today as so-called nonlethal weapons to disorient and *disabilitate* people. USE *debilitate.* • Back pain can cause severe suffering and *disabilitate* anybody. USE *debilitate.*

Disabilitate, an apparent muddle (or "blend," as a linguist might say) of *disability* and *debilitate,* is incorrect for *debilitate,* which means to enfeeble or enervate. SEE ALSO **deabilitate**.

disburse Misused for *disperse.* • Arrested and charged with failure to *disburse,* unlawful assembly, and failure to give their names (some had given their names, however), bail was set at $2,000 for most rescuers.

USE *disperse.* • An explosion at 10:12 P.M. Tucson time outside the Hut, 305 North Herbert Avenue, sent spectators running and activated nearly 500 extra police officers in full riot gear to *disburse* the crowd. USE *disperse.* • While all these were taking place, the RDO was continuing to request people to *disburse.* USE *disperse.*

And *disperse* is misused for *disburse*: • The National Heritage Foundation is the entity that will hold and *disperse* funds, and the Child Adoption Funds Organization is the facilitator of the process. USE *disburse.*

Disburse means to pay out; expend. *Disperse* means to spread or distribute over a wide area; to scatter in different directions; to cause to vanish or disappear.

The nouns are *disbursement* and *dispersion*: • Tuesday and Wednesday are less desirable because deliveries conflict with activities surrounding the packaging and *disbursement* of the bags. USE *dispersion.*

D

discomforture Misused for *discomfiture.* • However, the reason for your obvious *discomforture* is unclear to even someone as smart and learned as I am. USE *discomfiture.* • The women just now are discussing the relative merits of men and women much to the *discomforture* of the men. USE *discomfiture.*

Discomforture has no known meaning. The actual word, *discomfiture,* means frustration or embarrassment. SEE ALSO **comfrontable.**

disconnect Misused for *gap* (or similar words). • In other words, there's a *disconnect* between Dubya's policies and his governance. USE *disparity.* • We identified a $1.1B projected shortfall and continued to track the *disconnect* between projected and actual sales for subsequent months. USE *variance.* • Throughout this decade there has developed a widening *disconnect* between what we expect our national defense forces to do, and the resources supplied to accomplish those missions. USE *gap.* • A communications *disconnect* or gap exists between our operations commanders and our logisticians. DELETE *disconnect or.*

In this brash but silly sense of a gap, misunderstanding, miscommunication, or disparity, *disconnect* is to be reviled. Even if we must concede to its usage as a noun in the sense of a computer modem or electrical line disconnection, let that be the end of it. All further development of this word produces only grotesqueries. SEE ALSO **connect**; **disconnected (from)**.

disconnected (from) Misused for *unconnected (to)*. • I believe they are *disconnected* events. USE *unconnected.* • Many with movement disorders experience seemingly *disconnected* symptoms such as depression, lack of concentration, poor memory function, incontinence. USE *unconnected.* • Distance runner Corey De Leon was born with his esophagus *disconnected from* his stomach. USE *unconnected to.*

You can be *disconnected* from a phone call, from the Internet, from gas or power, but events and symptoms, for example, are *unconnected.* The term *disconnected* is most often used to describe something deliberately separated or disengaged. SEE ALSO **connect**; **disconnect**.

discrete Misused for *discreet.* • Our goal is to provide you with a simple, secure, and *discrete* method of obtaining Viagra from the privacy of your own home. USE *discreet.* • Condom King has twelve different name brands in an assortment of styles; you pick the desired quantity, pay once, and have them mailed to your home *discretely* on a monthly basis. USE *discreetly.* • The individual briefing must be provided as inconspicuously and *discretely* as possible. USE *discreetly.*

The homonyms *discrete* and *discreet* are often confused. Whereas *discrete* means distinct or separate, *discreet* means circumspect or prudent.

discrimitory Misused for *discriminatory.* • It is illegal in the United States to make any *discrimitory* remarks, and post pictures of people without written and direct permission. USE *discriminatory.* • No hate-related, pornographic or *discrimitory* sites will be allowed. USE *discriminatory.* • He grew up in a tough neighborhood, and succeeded in becoming a doctor despite *discrimitory* circumstances. USE *discriminatory.*

The fast-paced occasionally mispronounce *discriminatory,* and the slow-minded often misspell it.

> Non-discrimitory policy: St. Marys School recruits and admits students of any race, color, or ethnic origin to all the rights, privliges, programs, and activities.
>
> —Clyde St. Mary's Catholic School
>
> Since it—in large, bold type—proclaims its *Non-discrimitory* policy, St. Mary's must attract people who neither understand nor care the word is *discriminatory*; who neither understand nor care the word is *privilege;* who neither understand nor care the word is *St. Mary's*—nondiscriminating people all.

discuss (explain) about Misused for *discuss (explain).* • Captain Erickson introduced himself and *explained about* what it means to become a commissioned officer in the air force. DELETE *about.* • Our guide *discussed about* the types of methods that are used in the factory. DELETE *about.* • One speaker also *mentioned about* marketing. DELETE *about.* • The two men *discussed about* Greek–Turkish relations, the Cyprus issue, developments in the Middle East, and the crisis in southern Serbia. DELETE *about.* • Here is where you can *discuss about* the polls and see their results. DELETE *about.* • As HIV/AIDS is still considered a social taboo, no one is willing to *discuss about* it openly. DELETE *about.*

You may *talk about,* but you may not *discuss about,* and you may not *explain about* (of course a sentence like this is perfectly acceptable: "Keller Fay finds that people discuss about a dozen brands each day"). This misusage is fairly common among people still learning the English language, but people who have spoken the language all of their lives also use this disturbing solecism. SEE ALSO **discussed**.

discussed Misused for *disgust.* • She didn't feel pity for him, she felt *discussed.* USE *disgust.* • She figured that she better try and please him even though she felt *discussed* for him. USE *disgust.*

How, we must wonder, do the people who spell *disgust discussed* spell the past tense—*discusseded*? Yes, it appears so: • I was *discusseded* not just by some of that woman's policies, but also by the fact that people are using the thing to spam. USE *disgusted.* SEE ALSO **discuss (explain) about**.

D

disguard Misused for *discard.* • As the new energies approach, many people feel a need to *disguard* the old and get themselves together. USE *discard.* • This was the first book I read after I became a Christian—a true story that I will never forget, and a book that I will never *disguard.* USE *discard.* • Clean and *disguard* stems of mushrooms and put in a ziplock bag. USE *discard.*

Discard means to get rid of, throw away, or reject; *disguard* is useless idiocy.

disingenuine Misused for *disingenuous.* • CEOs can and should use notes, teleprompters, or any other aids they may need to effectively convey their message, but never to a point where their messages may appear *disingenuine.* USE *disingenuous.* • I find particularly declarative Christians tiresome, as it seems to smack of being *disingenuine.* USE *disingenuous.* • This effectively renders them powerless to expose *disingenuine* comments or outright falsehoods expressed by candidates during the election campaign. USE *disingenuous.*

Disingenuous (*dis*-in-JEN-yoo-es) means insincere or calculating. *Disingenuine* means nothing; it is a confused mix of *disingenuous* and *genuine*. SEE ALSO **disingenuous**.

disingenuous Misused for *naive* (or similar words). • This is a *disingenuous* comparison, because Governor Wallace was trying to deny constitutional rights, while Governor James is defending local judge Roy Moore's constitutional right to the free exercise of his religion. USE *naive.* • It's unfortunate because the study was *disingenuous*; it didn't account for the fact that we have other divisions that pay salaries and benefits. USE *uninformed.*

Disingenuous means lacking in frankness or candor; insincere or calculating. It does not mean naive or uninformed. SEE ALSO **disingenuine**.

disinterest Misused for *indifference* (or similar words). • We would have named it Apathy.com, but we like the concept: take the typical American voter's *disinterest in* politics, and make more money on it. USE *indifference to.* • For Washingtonians, pop culture is a threat, a Pied Piper leading Americans down the road to *disinterest.* USE *apathy.* • The lack of fights is not a result of *disinterest* from nationally based promoters, according to Don Hazelton, executive director of the Miccosukee Boxing Commission. USE *uninterest.* • Finally, there was lots of talk at Cannes this year about the lack of a Hollywood presence, whether due to the festival's inattention or industry *disinterest.* USE *indifference.*

Disinterest means without bias or impartial; it does not now mean uninterest or indifference. To use *disinterest* in the sense of uninterest is to forsake the word itself and, in effect, is a diminution of the foremost way in which we maintain our humanity: using language effectively.

> We have let the liberal paradigm define the debate, and the result is the false stereotyping of Conservatives as disinterested in the suffering of this nation's at-risk kids.
>
> —Former U.S. Representative Tom DeLay
>
> As middle school and high school children are tested before they are allowed to graduate, so elected officials ought to be tested before they are allowed to serve.

disparate Misused for *desperate.* • In retaliation to its military and political losses in different corners of the country, the TPLF regime is taking *disparate* measures such as killing and imprisoning of civilians in the country. USE *desperate.* • It is a known fact that *disparate* people do *disparate* things and our government has played a major role in our lives being in a *disparate* state. USE *desperate.*

Disparate (DIS-per-it), not (dis-PAR-it), means distinct or different. *Desperate* (DES-per-it) means so overwhelmed by hopelessness or anxiety as to behave rashly or violently; frantic; having a great need; extremely difficult, dangerous, or serious.

D

displace Misused for *misplace.* • A weak attack or defense will only serve to create an air of *displaced* confidence on the part of your partner. USE *misplaced.*

To *misplace* is to mislay; to bestow confidence or some other quality on a person or idea undeserving of it. To *displace* is to move from a usual place; to force to leave a country; to supplant; to discharge from a position.

disprefer Misused for *dislike* (or similar words). • It's interesting as a spelling pronunciation, preferred by some speakers, *dispreferred* by others. USE *not.* • They never spontaneously produce them; in fact, they strongly *disprefer* them. USE *object to.* • In a pinch, you can fax it to me, but I *disprefer* faxes because of deficient legibility. USE *dislike.* • Other things being equal, we should *disprefer blogs to journalism.* USE *prefer journalism to blogs.*

Among linguists and their lackeys, disaffected as they often are from sense and thoughtfulness, *disprefer* actually does exist. No sentence is improved, none made true or clear, by using *disprefer* instead of some other wording.

The findings demonstrate that children disprefer learning a different, unrelated meaning for a known word when that word is used in a linguistic context that fails to bias strongly for a new meaning.

—Devin Casenhiser, graduate student in linguistics

Regarding "well-motivated," I have a distinct dispreference for "well motivated" in this situation.

—Gabe Doyle, graduate student in linguistics

These sentences, scarcely intelligible as they are, should dissuade all of us from having much faith in linguists and their pronouncements. If linguists want to use a word like *disprefer* or *dispreference,* let them first learn how to write a readable sentence.

dissemble Misused for *disassemble.* • When asked about the U.S. decision to *dissemble* the American plane in China and fly it out on a Russian cargo plane, Powell said that was the preference because the Russian cargo plane is readily available and it is the plane that is best able to handle this kind of mission. Use *disassemble.* • If the engine happens to be going through a rebuild, it would be best to have this done before all components are installed even though you can install this kit without having to *dissemble* the entire engine. Use *disassemble.* • They code-named Weems the Modular Man due to the ability to *dissemble* and reassemble his body, and due to the number of detachable components of his body. Use *disassemble.*

Dissemble means to disguise or hide behind a false appearance; to feign. *Disassemble* means to take apart; to break up randomly.

> People that had been trained in some instances to disassemble—that means not tell the truth.
>
> —U.S. President George W. Bush
>
> Like others who speak before sizeable audiences, Bush has a responsibility to speak well. The worse a person speaks, the smaller his audience deserves to be.

dissent Misused for *descent.* • Her *dissent* into madness is hastened by his cruelty. Use *descent.* • It occurs when one's best friend moves out of state and you are left behind, when a person is left in the wake of unrequited love, or when a seemingly healthy marriage finds itself in a steep *dissent* toward divorce. Use *descent.* • Through it all Jay maintains his Darwinian place, planning in his mind how he'll trample and smash the slow-moving secretarial pool if they impede his *dissent* down the stairwell. Use *descent.*

And occasionally *descent* is misused for *dissent*: • Duke's political *descent* and felony plea have alienated even longtime supporters in America, including those who once saw him as the ticket to the mainstream. Use *dissent.* • When is political *descent* unpatriotic? Use *dissent.*

Dissent is a difference of opinion or belief from that commonly held; nonconformity. *Descent* means a descending; a downward slope; a way down; a decline into an undesirable state; ancestry or lineage.

divert Misused for *avert.* • If ever there was a time for peaceful demonstrations to *divert* war, now is that time. USE *avert.* • Negotiators from both sides said Monday that a last-minute deal could *divert* a strike. USE *avert.* • Her small breasts peeked through the foaming ocean, and Helen had to *divert* her eyes. USE *avert.*

And *avert* is confused for *divert*: • Rosario said the need for the parapet is to *avert* the river waters from overflowing into the Pantal area community, especially during high tide and typhoons. USE *divert.*

Avert means to turn away; to ward off or prevent. *Divert* means to turn aside; to distract the attention of; to entertain or amuse.

divorcé Misused for *divorcée.* • It is not accidental that she is a *divorcé* and takes care of her two kids alone. USE *divorcée.*

And *divorcée* is sometimes misused for *divorcé:* • A has-been *divorcée* gets a chance at redemption when he is asked to coach the local high school girls basketball team. USE *divorcé.*

A divorced man is a *divorcé*. A divorced woman is a *divorcée*. SEE ALSO **fiancé**.

documentate Misused for *document.* • These data are *documentated* by three machine-readable portable document files. USE *documented.* • We provide fully *documentated* results with a publication-quality print and stained gel (wet or dry). USE *documented.* • It is the aim to experience and *documentate* the impact on rural areas, urban development, and social organizational structures. USE *document.* • During this expedition we were able to closely *documentate* the breeding and the birth of these frogs. USE *document.*

Not only a noun, *document* is also a verb. Aside from *document,* the English language admits the words *documentary, documentation, documental, documentable, documenter, documentalist, documentarian,* and even *documentarist.* Barred is *documentate.* SEE ALSO **alterate**; **considerate**.

domesticated Misused for *domestic.* • I have selected three rituals that are clear examples of *domesticated* violence. Use *domestic.* • Supernaturalists have generally displayed a willingness, if not an eagerness, to suffer and die, and to cause others to suffer and die, to defend, maintain, and extend their doctrinal dominions against all enemies, foreign or *domesticated,* actual or hallucinated. Use *domestic.*

Both *domestic* and *domesticated* refer to tame animals. *Domestic* also means relating to family or home life; relating to a country's internal affairs; native to or made in a particular country. *Domesticated* also means adapted to domestic or home life; naturalized.

dominate Misused for *dominant.* • Certain actions are recognized as *dominate* behavior; deep growling tones are aggressive while high-pitched whining tones are submissive. Use *dominant.* • Behavior data suggested that the experimental treatment caused *dominate* monkeys to exhibit increases in *dominate* behavior and subordinate monkeys manifested increased submission. Use *dominant.*

Dominate, to rule or control through superior power or authority, is a verb; *dominant,* exercising authority or control, an adjective. See also **predominate**.

done (finished; completed) All three words are interchangeable. Some years ago, officiators of language usage decried the use of *done* to mean either *finished* or *completed,* but few people today are undone by *done.*

When speaking of a thoroughly cooked meal, *done* may be the best word to use. If you want your writing to have a more elegant tone, *finished* or *completed* is the better word. See also **out loud**.

donut Misused for *doughnut.* • If they handed out delicious *donuts* with each search, I'd leave Google in a New York minute. Use *doughnut.*

Doughnut is the correct word, and *donut,* a variant spelling—a perverted spelling. The people who spell *doughnuts donuts* are the people who eat them.

doormat Misused for *dormant.* • It lies *doormat* for 14 days and then kills your hard drive. Use *dormant.* • The part of the brain, normally activated when people look at other faces, remains *doormat* in those with autism. Use *dormant.* • My husband has this disease and he had to take meds for 9 months so the TB would stay *doormat.* Use *dormant.* • We may continue to read God's word yet somehow the words remain *doormat* and half dead in our souls. Use *dormant.*

Yes, some people do write *doormat* (a mat placed before or inside a door for wiping dirt from the shoes) when they mean *dormant* (marked by a suspension of activity).

dose Misused for *douse.* • He was *dosed* with water, chased by dogs, and threatened to be shot. Use *doused.* • It's basically fried white rice, onions, red pepper, and black beans, liberally *dosed* with hot sauce. Use *doused.* • He said the family at first attempted to *dose* the fire with water, but once a bedroom door was opened, the flames "took off." Use *douse.*

To *douse* (DOUS) is to immerse, to plunge into liquid; to wet thoroughly; to extinguish (a fire). To *dose* (DOS) is to give someone a specified quantity of medicine; to prescribe (medicine) in certain amounts.

do to (do to the fact) Misused for *due to* (or similar words) • *Do to* a current departure from Los Angeles for a weekend press event, she will not be available today for the interview. Use *Owing to.* • Amare, as you all know, ended up being the ninth overall pick in the 2002 NBA draft, the only high schooler chosen in the first round, largely *do to the fact that* both Anthony and Bosh decided to give college a year. Use *because.* • *Do to the fact* some individuals desire to spam others, all email features were eliminated. Use *Since.* • Peterson also argued *do to* the publicity surrounding the case, his client cannot get a fair trial in Ada County. Use *owing to.*

Although *due to* is the expression meant in these examples, it is ungrammatical. *Do to* is astonishingly incorrect; *due to,* more commonly incorrect. Instead of *do to,* use *due to;* instead of *due to,* use, at least in these examples, *owing to, because,* or *since.* See also **due to**.

doubtlessly Misused for *doubtless.* • HTC will *doubtlessly* be as promiscuous about their Windows Phone 7 smartphones as they have with their Android ones. Use *doubtless.* • Rose is *doubtlessly* motivated by last weekend's experience at the Travelers Championship. Use *doubtless.* • *Dinner for Schmucks* will *doubtlessly* be the weirdest comedy of the summer. Use *doubtless.*

All six collegiate dictionaries in the Fiske Ranking of College Dictionaries (see appendix B) record *doubtlessly* as an adverb, as they do *doubtless.* None of them maintains that *doubtlessly* is awkward or unnecessary and that *doubtless* is the better adverb to use. Other adverbs also do not use an *-ly* ending: *seldomly, thusly,* and *muchly,* for example. See also **-ly**.

D

doubt that Misused for *doubt whether.* • We *doubt that* anything on this year's MTV Video Music Awards will top that special moment in 1999 when Diana Ross copped a feel from Lil' Kim, but we'll be watching just in case. Use *doubt whether.* • Naturally they *doubt that* this can be pulled off. Use *doubt whether.* • And given the thoroughness of our inventory work, we *doubt that* any such evidence will be forthcoming. Use *doubt whether.* • In fact, we *doubt that* Iraq will take the sensible steps necessary to obtain the lifting, or the suspension, of sanctions as long as Saddam Hussein remains in power. Use *doubt whether.*

Arcanum though it may be, the idiom is *doubt whether* unless the sentence is a negative one, whereupon *doubt that* is correct.

The conjunction following *doubt* or *doubtful* is *that* in negative or interrogative statements, and *whether* or *if* in positive statements.

douse Misused for *dowse.* • This phenomenon, often hinted at, but rarely spoken of openly in the trade, is something akin to an ability to *douse* for water. Use *dowse.* • According to records, he could *douse* for gold and silver, cure sick horses, and speak with animals. Use *dowse.*

Douse (DOUS) means to drench; to immerse or plunge into liquid. *Dowse* (DOUZ) means to search for water or minerals with a divining, or dowsing, rod.

downtalk (down talk) Misused for *disparage* (or similar words). • A lot of people *down talk* our military; they don't realize that if we don't have this, they can't talk at all. Use *vilify*. • Why *down talk* religion? Religion is a faith, a belief. Use *denigrate*. • So many uninformed people *down talk* the tapes and equipment, and others call themselves "Eight Track Nuts" to describe their interest in the format. USE *sneer at.* • Also, I've seen other car forums where people *downtalk* Japanese cars yet praise the Elise, and it just makes me wonder, since the B18C and 2ZZ are both Japanese engines. USE *ridicule.* • The Fed as a whole does not like to *downtalk* the economy, but the data is not matching what their yak has been saying. USE *criticize.*

And sometimes *downtalk* is used instead of *talk down to*: • Anderson himself doesn't exactly *downtalk* his class of women, but he does try to explain things in housewife terms. USE *talk down to.*

One word or two, *downtalk* is as much as some people can manage. Words such as *vilify* and *denigrate, malign* and *defame* may be unknown or misused by people who know and use *baby talk.*

doyen Misused for *doyenne.* • In my estimation, she is a *doyen* of physical fitness. USE *doyenne.* • In an era with few opportunities for women in cricket (and many deep-seated prejudices) she became a *doyen* of the sport. USE *doyenne.*

And *doyenne* is sometimes used for *doyen*: • He is a *doyenne* of the panel show circuit, appearing on *Have I Got News for You, Mock the Week, Armando Iannucci's Charm Offensive, 8 Out of 10 Cats, QI,* and (gulp) *FAQ U.* USE *doyen.*

A *doyen* (doi-EN) is a man who is the senior member of a group, whereas a *doyenne* (doi-EN) is a woman who is the senior member of a group.

dribble Misused for *drivel.* • The diatribe given by that pro-union guy at the Twilight Zone was nothing short of intellectual *dribble.* USE *drivel.* • Salepeople talk *dribble.* USE *drivel.*

Dribble is drool; the bouncing of a basketball. *Drivel,* which also means drool, is more often used to mean silly talk, nonsense.

drug Misused for *dragged.* • Who *drug* up the past? I would personally like to thank this person. USE *dragged.* • I've been kicked, beat, and *drug* through the dirt by many a man and want someone who knows how to treat a woman. USE *dragged.* • Our girls are not part of this presidential process, and I'm not going to let them get *drug* in. USE *dragged.*

Dragged, not *drug,* is the past tense of *drag.*

> I think if you felt that your name was going to be drug through the mud and it would do great damage to your career, it would last a long period of time, one might make that decision.
>
> —Johnnie Cochran, attorney
>
> I mean, that seems to be a category all in itself to me, that, yes, your name is going to be drug through the mud, but you've got an accusation that's so severe that most of us consider one of the worst crimes.
>
> —Jann Carl, correspondent with *Entertainment Tonight*
>
> Two minutes after Cochran used the word *drug,* an illiteracy in the sense used here, Ms. Carl, being interviewed on the same program, did as well. The only impression Cochran and Carl were likely to have made is how hopelessly inarticulate, how easily influenced, how quickly confused they are.

due Misused for *do.* • If you also reduce the core voltage of the CPU, you could probably get away with just one large heat sink and *due* away with the fan altogether. USE *do.* • As it stands now, the university will have to make *due* with half that amount. USE *do.* • Since boats are a luxury item (not a necessity), consumers can *due* without them. USE *do.* • It's always good to see people *due* something for America, and ask for nothing in return. USE *do.*

Though pronounced the same, these two words differ in meaning, spelling, and part of speech. As an adjective, *due* has several meanings: payable immediately; owed; appropriate; expected at a certain time; adequate; and so on. As a verb, *do* has many meanings: to perform; to work on; to fulfill; to carry out; to solve; to produce; to exert; and so on. SEE ALSO **do to**.

With Floyd batting .391, the Mets have been able to make due with Mike Piazza batting .198.

—Lee Jenkins, *The New York Times*

When he mistakes one word, one meaning, for another, Jenkins himself does not make do. He makes doo-doo.

duel Misused for *dual.* • Each team is allowed three foreign players, but Skinnon, an Italian-American who has *duel* citizenship, counts as an Italian. USE *dual.* • Unlike Final Fantasy 7, you can use a *duel* shock controller and you will feel every bit of vibration. USE *dual.* • For *duel*-use facilities, high collateral damage refers to significant effects on the environment, facilities, and infrastructure that are not related to war-making ability. USE *dual.* • A *duel*-diagnosis patient is someone who has both a drug problem as well as some sort of mental issue along with it. USE *dual.*

And *dual* for *duel*: • U.S. President George Bush, who was once challenged to a *dual* by Ramadan, has welcomed the Iraqi's capture. USE *duel.*

A *duel* is a combat with deadly weapons, usually to settle a point of honor; a contest between two persons or groups. *Dual* means consisting of two parts; having two purposes.

The affair caused rifts within families. People fought duals over it. There was talk of civil war.

—NPR's *Writer's Almanac*

A compelling account of the Dreyfus affair, a story of courageous behavior by some and despicable behavior by others, has as its denouement a mistake that unsettles every reader more attentive than the writer.

due to Misused for *owing to* (or similar words). • *Due to* the transformer fire at our 31st Street and 23rd Avenue location, we have to merge our offices. USE *Owing to.* • The Crusaders' game against Bulloch Academy on Friday night was postponed at half *due to* a lightning storm. Use *because of.* • Pakistan had to cancel the South Asian Federation Games *due to* India's refusal to participate. Use *because of.* • Business suffers and commuters work longer *due to* poor rail services. Use *owing to.* • The plan was intended to be used through 2010, but *due to* rapid growth, it became outdated. Use *because of.*

D

Traditionalists and stylists have long railed against using *due to* as a preposition. If *due to* can be replaced by *attributable to,* the phrase is perfectly good; if not, use *because of* or *owing to.* You could not say "*Attributable to* the transformer fire . . ."; *owing to* or *because of* is the correct phrase. You could, however, use *attributable to* in this sentence: "She said her success was entirely *due to* the devotion of her fans."

The correct use of *due to* is normally found after some form of the verb *to be,* whether stated, as in "The only changes *were due to* injuries after Greg Williams beat out Jomo Legins for one starting safety spot after two games," or elliptic, "Despite a month-long delay [*that was*] *due to* equipment and software installation glitches, 258 testing sites around the stations had no visible problems with the testing procedure."

Due to also, of course, means scheduled to ("It is due to dock with the 16-nation orbital platform early on Monday") or expected ("He is due to arrive October 19"). See also **do to (do to the fact)**.

duplicitous Misused for *duplicate* (or similar words). • Some of you will receive *duplicitous* copies of this issue as you've already signed up to receive this electronically. Use *duplicate.*

Duplicate, duplicative, duplicatory, or *duplicatable,* not *duplicitous,* is the adjectival form of the noun *duplicate* or *duplication,* which means a replica or copy of. *Duplicitous* means deceptive or misleading.

Ee

E

each other Misused for *one another.* • Testimony from a former Los Angeles police officer to investigators looking into police corruption has opened a window into an ominous world where allegedly corrupt cops brazenly rewarded *each other* for their actions. USE *one another.*

And *one another* is often misused for *each other:* • Both sides of the brain depend on *one another*. USE *each other.*

And in this next example, the writer doesn't quite know what to do: • After their long distraction, the two presumptive nominees finally get to concentrate on *one another,* and they are losing no time trying to define each other. USE *each other.*

Each other is properly used when only two people, groups, or things are being referred to ("It took both parties some time to get used to each other"); *one another,* when three or more are ("This is because languages reinforce one another and provide tools to strengthen skills").

This is a distinction worth observing. Although some texts and commentators suggest the distinction between *each other* and *one another* is artificial, more important than a phrase's historical, or even present-day, usage is maintaining clarity. Along with observing and maintaining, let us strive for better comprehension and clarity by, if need be, devising distinctions between words.

ebullient The pronunciation of *ebullient* is (i-BOOL-yent), not (EB-yah-lent).

economical Misused for *economic.* • The European Information Technology Observatory analyzes the current European ICT Market and contains a statistical and *economical* forecast for the next years. Use *economic.* • Tax, Policy, and Research is responsible for the statewide revenue estimation process, all state revenue legislation and legislative proposals affecting the department, and department *economical* data analysis. Use *economic.* • The site provides information on monetary policies, *economical* indicators, and currency rates. Use *economic.* • This resulted in a gradual decline and 400 years of *economical* downfall. Use *economic.* • It is strange that the industrialized and developed countries in Europe and the United States have been recording unprecedented *economical* growth while the rest of the world is undergoing destabilizing *economical* turmoil. Use *economic.*

Even though *geographic* and *geographical, pharmacologic* and *pharmacological, theoretic* and *theoretical,* and other such pairs are synonymous, *economic* does not necessarily mean *economical. Economic* means pertaining to an economy or the science of economics; thrifty, inexpensive, cost-effective. *Economical* has only the latter definition.

ecscape (excape) Misspelling of *escape.* • He should just sit in jail to *ecscape* again and kill once more? Use *escape.* • He may be able to *ecscape* me, but he won't be able to *ecscape* everyone else. Use *escape.* • Also, she is an *ecscape* artist and I don't think pins would be a good idea with her. Use *escape.* • Another point to add is suicide is used as a way to *excape* a problem or fear or just *excape* from life itself. Use *escape.* • Many people come to our chat rooms because the need to *excape* from the everyday life and have some fun. Use *escape.* • The reset button on this page or the Esc (*Excape*) key on the keyboard will clear all entries. Use *Escape.*

Escape is the correct spelling, and (i-SKAPE), not (ek-SKAPE) or (eks-SKAPE), the correct pronunciation.

ecstacy Misspelling of *ecstasy.* • Gospel trio the Emotions are filmed in rapturous *ecstacy* in a decrepit storefront church. Use *ecstasy.* • Human life must know *ecstacy*. Use *ecstasy.*

Ecstacy is not a variant spelling of *ecstasy;* it is a misspelling. So-called variant spellings are nothing other than misspellings.

ect. Misspelling of *etc.* • The skeletons look like skeletons, angels like angels, *ect.* USE *etc.* • Special Olympics event includes downhill skiing, cross country, *ect.,* for over 650 athlete volunteers. USE *etc.*

Of course, *ect., ect.* is doubly wrong: • We are extremely busy, and I really like the fact that our division encompasses work from a wide range of areas, like civil litigation, claims, sanity (mental illness) cases, public administrator cases, contracts, zoning issues, bankruptcy cases, guardianship cases, *ect., ect.* USE *etc.* SEE ALSO **and etc.**; **et al.**; **etc., etc.**; **etcetera**.

edify Confused with *enlighten.* To *edify* is to instruct or improve, especially morally or spiritually ("It could mean a thing like bad language, dirty stories, unkind remarks, and gossip, anything that does not edify or build someone up"). *Enlighten* means to furnish knowledge or insight to; to make clear; to inform ("The media's role is to enlighten the public").

effort Misused for *try* (or similar words). • Can we *effort* to spread democracy in the Middle East? USE *attempt.* • Now, the Texas Department of Public Safety is *efforting* an even tougher cell law. USE *trying.* • Butler also said he'll continue to *effort* what current sheriff Tom Burgoyne has done, detaining illegal aliens, and getting drugs off the streets. USE *attempt.*

Though the noun *effort* means energy, whether physical or mental, exerted to do something, the online and "open" Wiktionary recognizes *effort* as a rare verb meaning to make an effort; the *Oxford English Dictionary* offers *effort* as an obsolete verb meaning to strengthen, fortify; and the 1913 *Webster's Dictionary* records *effort* as an obsolete verb meaning to stimulate. Not one of the dictionaries in the Fiske Ranking of College Dictionaries (see appendix B) includes the verb to *effort.*

> So we are efforting to ask some of those people to talk with us.
>
> —Brook Baldwin, CNN anchor

eke out Today the phrasal verb *eke out* has two meanings: its original meaning to make something last by being economical ("We watched our mothers eke out rations and improvise"); and its more recent meaning to supplement with effort ("Most of the land lies fallow and many families eke out income by cutting down what's left of indigenous trees to sell as charcoal").

A third meaning, its worst, is taking hold among sportscasters and those who imitate their cant: • Akron hit four foul shots in the final seven seconds to *eke out* a 71–67 Mid-American Conference triumph before 281 at Alumni Arena. • Prairie used a 63–39 rebounding advantage to help it *eke out* the close victory.

Eke out in these examples is meant to mean to scrape; squeak (the most likely derivation of this sense of *eke,* since the words rhyme); squeeze; or sneak by, in, or out.

elder (eldest) Misused for *older (oldest).* • This building has the distinction of being not only the *eldest* building in the city but also in southern Illinois. USE *oldest.* • And if the younger ox wanted to "slack off," the *elder* animal would keep him going so the job would be completed. USE *older.*

Elder is properly used when referring to two people; *eldest* when referring to three or more people. *Older* is used when referring to two people, animals, or objects; *oldest* when referring to three or more people, animals, or objects.

When speaking of an individual, *elder* signifies relatively advanced age as well as accomplishment ("As an elder statesman among rodeo athletes, Woolman also would like the top competitors to be able to focus more on major rodeos so they can travel less and win more"). Advanced age alone is better expressed with *older* or *elderly* ("That would leave more shots for people in high-risk groups like the elderly and children").

electronical Misused for *electronic.* • The deceased, according to the obit, had done his own automobile repairs until cars "became so *electronical.*" USE *electronic.* • *Electronical* technicians realized that changing the environment's temperature to a colder climate could increase effective and efficient work output. USE *Electronic.* • KEMA Quality tests and certifies low-voltage equipment and electrical components, *electronical* and medical products as well as management systems. USE *electronic.*

Electronical is an adjective that people unfamiliar with the English language might use. *Electronic* is the adjective that refers to electrons or relates to anything produced by means of electronics.

elegy Confused with *eulogy.* An *elegy* is a mournful poem or song, especially one written as a lament for a dead person ("The decadence conveyed in Eliot's *Waste Land* is like an elegy of our modern civilization"). A *eulogy* is a speech written in praise of a dead person; a funeral oration ("Steve Milley Sr. turns to the casket as he gives the eulogy at the funeral of his son, army lieutenant Scott Milley").

elicit Misused for *illicit.* • Lovemaking for pleasure exists only in a fantasy world—either with porno flicks, an *elicit* affair between a teacher and student, or a fling between two emotional desperadoes. USE *illicit.* • Anyway, it appears that the label is really nothing but a pathetic front for untold *elicit* and illegal operations. USE *illicit.* • And the entertainment industry said, let's make television shows and movies that promote profanity, violence, and *elicit* sex. USE *illicit.*

Elicit is a verb meaning to draw out or evoke; *illicit* is an adjective meaning unlawful or improper.

elocute Misused for *declaim* (or similar words). • Speakers *elocute* from dispatch boxes once used in Britain's House of Commons. USE *declaim.* • Even in casual conversation, if you could call it that, he doesn't so much chat as *elocute.* USE *declaim.*

To be able to *declaim* is a valuable and rare skill, unlike being able to *elocute,* which every babbler is perfectly capable of. Lopped from the noun *elocution, elocute* is severed from its force and effectiveness; it neither describes nor inspires elocution. SEE ALSO **agress**; **declaim**; **enthuse**; **precip**.

email (e-mail) This is largely a matter of house style or personal preference. *Email,* however, is preferable for at least two reasons:

(1) *Email* is as understandable as *e-mail*; that is, very few people misunderstand what the nonhyphenated word means or would pronounce it (EM-ail); (2) many compound words evolve from two words to a

hyphenated word to a single word: *electronic mail, e-mail, email.* By god, the language does evolve.

Some dictionaries list the word as **e-mail (email)**—that is, they prefer the hyphenated spelling but allow the nonhyphenated. Other dictionaries allow *e-mail* only and do not bother to mention the spelling *email,* which further illustrates how dictionaries are a hotchpotch of inconsistencies and absurdities.

Electronic mail, of course, is not alone in its evolution to becoming one word. Many words have changed similarly. For instance, *lowercase* was initially two words (the bottom or lower drawer in a cabinet that housed the small letters of metal type in a compositor's shop). *Lower case* became *lower-case,* became *lowercase.*

In the computer field, where a wholly unknown term may be widely known within months, we have *data base, data-base, database,* and *on line, on-line, online,* to name but two terms that have evolved speedily.

embarass Misspelling of *embarrass.* • They're not going to come up with anything that's going to *embarass* DHHR, because that's who they work for. USE *embarrass.* • If I am wrong about this, I would totally *embarass* the both of us and possibly ruin our friendship. USE *embarrass.* • Do we have two councilmen here trying to *embarass* me tonight? USE *embarrass.* • Now that that little *embarassment* is out of the way, I can smoothly segue into another *embarrasment*—last night's Bennett Hockey Team's loss to the Discovery Channel, a townie team. USE *embarrassment.*

Embarrass has two *r*'s and two *s*'s, which is likely the easiest way to remember how the word is spelled for those who seem unable to.

embetterment Misused for *betterment* (or similar words). • You are struggling sometimes to see some sign of *embetterment,* but know that the improvements are not too far behind the resolution you have made. USE *betterment.* • The primary objective of the foundation, then, is the introduction and cultivation of universal ethical and spiritual principles through a natural, holistic, and multidisciplinary approach centered on individual *embetterment.* USE *improvement.* • These two actions, taken together on the same day, made a powerful statement: the *embetterment* of persons with disability was now a global priority. USE *betterment.*

• Firstly, CSI, in my view, is what the business embodiment has been doing, and continues to do, outside of its main commercial functions for the *embetterment* of the society. USE *advancement.*

Embetterment is the product of careless people confusing *embitterment* with *betterment,* the word they surely mean to use.

emigrate Misused for *immigrate.* • Bush announced Friday that his government would tighten a ban on American tourism and other restrictions against the island, and would allow more Cubans to *emigrate* to the United States. USE *immigrate.* • Subsequently, these peoples are drawn to urban centers, even being compelled to *emigrate* to them, suffering readily observable consequences for their quality of life and for their ability to preserve their specific identity. USE *immigrate.*

Some people, perhaps not clever enough to distinguish between *emigrate* and *immigrate,* prefer using *out-migrate* and *in-migrate*: • Given the level of attractiveness, as long as a region's relative wage is below its long-run level, native and foreign workers are assumed to *out-migrate.* USE *emigrate.* • Of all the individuals who *out-migrate,* at most 25 percent return to their communities ten years later. USE *emigrate.* • Honolulu ranks 43rd among 152 U.S. cities for the number of people who *in-migrate* from other cities and countries to become new residents. USE *immigrate.* • That shortage encouraged African Americans to *in-migrate* from southern cities into the larger industrialized cities of the North in search of that elusive "better life." USE *immigrate.*

People who *emigrate* leave one place or country for another; those who *immigrate* arrive at one place or country from another. You *emigrate from* and *immigrate to.*

eminent Misused for *imminent.* • Anyone reading one of her romances is in *eminent* danger of addiction. USE *imminent.* • Lester Brown, president of the Worldwatch Institute based in Washington, D.C., said the solution to *eminent* water shortages can be found in a water-pricing policy that reflects the real value of water and in research into energy-efficient irrigation technologies. USE *imminent.*

And *imminent* is misused for *eminent.* • One *imminent* scholar of its recent history, Charles Cruickshank (1979), says that deception is the art of misleading an enemy into doing something or not doing something so that his strategic or tactical position will be weakened. Use *eminent.* • City Manager Ted Staton said the city is trying to find a solution to appease fraternity members but it ultimately could use its power of *imminent* domain to obtain the house. Use *eminent.*

Eminent means lofty; renowned or distinguished. *Eminent domain* is the right of a government to take private property. *Imminent* means impending or about to occur. See also **immanent**.

emphasize Misspelling of *empathize.* • *Emphasize* with his feelings, then lead by example: you feel like yelling and stamping your feet, but that wouldn't be fair to everyone else nearby. Use *empathize.* • Residents of the island say they understand the danger associated with where they live and can *emphasize* with others. Use *empathize.* • Being an avid golfer, and clearly out of my element on the course, I can *emphasize* with this uncomfortable feeling. Use *empathize.*

To *emphasize* is to stress or express forcefully. To *empathize* is to be able to appreciate what another is feeling or experiencing.

enarmored Misspelling of *enamored.* • When he becomes *enarmored* of a young bride-to-be (Madge Bellamy) who is visiting a neighboring estate, Legendre resorts to black magic to make her his own. Use *enamored.* • For those, like myself, who are *enarmored* by the Tucson poet, it is a refreshing visit to an old friend who also has strong connections to Mexico. Use *enamored.*

Enamored (i-NAM-erd), not *enarmored* (i-NAR-merd), means to be captivated or charmed by; to be in love with.

encourageable (incourageable) Misspelling of *incorrigible.* • You drove in silence to my condo in Gold Coast, where you would prove to be the most *incourageable* and thankless of all my progeny. Use *incorrigible.* • The five words that describe me best are: feisty, stubborn, strong, *incourageable,* independent. Use *incorrigible.* • You're *encourageable.* How could you have spent so much of your time chasing skirts with all that other stuff happening around you? Use *incorrigible.*

Incorrigible refers to someone who's not improvable or manageable. *Encourageable* (or *incourageable*), a word only to the witless, refers to someone who's simply not able.

endue Misused for *endure* (or similar words). • This leads to the self-certain, self-sustained hero who can *endue* hardship in the name of a chosen principle. USE *endure.* • Pasteuria spores can *endue* long periods of drought. USE *endure.* • Riders begin the ride in snow, *endue* 110 degree heat in the canyons, and traverse the American river. USE *endure.*

Endue, not a common word, means to endow with a quality or faculty; to put on or assume; to clothe. *Endure* means to undergo; to carry on despite suffering or hardship.

enervate Misused for *energize* (or similar words). • Even the hurricanes, the torrential downpours, skies solid black with furious clouds, could do nothing but *enervate* and invigorate me. USE *energize.* • Fashion is photography's Frankenstein monster; a hideous parody of the photographic art rudely constructed with bits and pieces discarded from other art forms, which seeks not to elevate, illuminate, invigorate, *enervate,* or inspire but exists only to serve its own purpose: to sell a rather ordinary garment at a grossly inflated price. USE *energize.* • Mitchell plays his curmudgeonly role with a vitality and energy that seem to *enervate* the rest of the cast. USE *invigorate.* • Any disease process anywhere in the body is affected, at least in part, by the ability of the nervous system to *enervate* and enliven that area. USE *invigorate.*

Enervate—never *innervate,* which means to supply a body part with nerves—is an antonym, not a synonym, for *invigorate* or *energize. Enervate* means to weaken or enfeeble, to debilitate or deplete the energy of.

> That aspect of it in particular is not to my taste, although on the whole, I believe it's been a very successful and enervating and exciting convention.
>
> —Ben Affleck, actor

Not only did Affleck embarrass himself by saying *enervating* when he meant *invigorating,* or perhaps, *energizing,* he, embarrassing himself further, chided one or two people who questioned his use of the word.

enjoin Misused for *join.* • Welcome, I hope you *enjoin* our group. Use *join.* • And please *enjoin* us on our special wedding day this December 20 and 28. Use *join.* • Everyone is welcome on this page! It's not important that you're a fan, if you like the music, please *enjoin* us! Use *join.*

Enjoin, hardly a synonym for *join,* means to prohibit or forbid; to order.

en masse The pronunciation of *en masse* is (on MAS), not (en MAS). See also **en route**.

enormacy Misused for *enormity* (or *enormousness*). • I can almost come to grips with and accept the *enormacy* of the universe. Use *enormousness.* • The sheer *enormacy* of the event still makes me feel it never happened. Use *enormousness.* • The *enormacy* of the city then really took its form and without a car Mexico City is one hell of a walk. Use *enormousness.* • However, through the *enormacy* of the sin, they may have to wait their time in purgatory until they have made up for the sin. Use *enormity.*

There are two words: *enormousness,* which means hugeness, immensity; and *enormity,* which means great wickedness, a monstrous offense. *Enormacy,* an arrangement of letters that some people may think encompasses both hugeness and great wickedness, is meaningless, not a word at all. See also **enormity**.

enormity Misused for *enormousness* (or similar words). • Ms. Hall believes that God's *enormity* and universality are best communicated through science, which the characters in *Joan of Arcadia* will discuss at least as often as they talk about religion. Use *enormousness.* • The idea of testing athletes was dropped because of cost and the *enormity* of the task of administering tests in a truly random manner. USE *enormousness.* • Many regional projects, breathtaking in their *enormity* and vision, are acting as magnets to the international real estate industry. USE *enormousness.*

Enormity means monstrous wickedness. *Enormousness* means immensity. Though these two words were once synonyms, *enormity* in the sense of *enormousness* has been archaic for some centuries.

> And the enormity of the honor that you have bestowed upon him is still sinking in.
>
> —Lynne Cheney, wife of former U.S. Vice President Dick Cheney
>
> Enough of this misusage. *Enormity* is a word like no other; let us not disembowel it by using it as a synonym for *enormousness,* which of course, is sated with synonyms. More than most, politicians—and their wives—ought to know the correct meaning of *enormity*.

en route The pronunciation of *en route* is (on ROOT), not (en ROUT) though *route* alone, as in Route I-95, is pronounced (ROOT) or (ROUT). SEE ALSO **en masse**; **on route**.

ensure Misused for *assure.* • They have the best track record and they *ensured* us of the broadest distribution of television viewers. USE *assured.* • How can you *ensure* us that the Beijing declaration on commitments for children will be realized and implemented? USE *assure.* • Biology teacher Jon Pettingill said teachers and staff were advised to tell students the facts and *ensure* them the school was safe. USE *assure.* • I want to *ensure* you that I will get a satisfactory answer and bring it to the House. USE *assure.*

As there is a distinction between the words *insure* and *ensure,* so there is between *assure* and *ensure.* To *assure* is to declare confidently; to give confidence to; to promise or guarantee. To *ensure,* to make certain. In British English, *assure* means to insure, to cover by insurance. SEE ALSO **insure**.

enthuse Misused for *excite* (or similar words). • Ed Spangler, a partner with the retail-consulting unit of Arthur Andersen, adds that retailers who lead in customer service, whether large or small, often give employees the chance to have a stake in the company, and always *enthuse* them about its culture of service. USE *excite.* • A renewed doctrinal, theological, and spiritual proclamation of the Christian message, aimed primarily to *enthuse* and purify the conscience of the baptized, cannot be achieved through irresponsible or indolent improvisation. USE *galvanize.* • Book Fairs provide a wide selection of books that *enthuse* children, parents, and teachers alike. USE *animate.* • Good interpersonal and time management skills are essential, as is the capacity to *enthuse* others and to work successfully in a variety of teams. USE *motivate.* • It can be a way in for some boys, and whatever we can we use as a hook to *enthuse* boys and girls. USE *stimulate.*

What's worse, *enthuse* is sometimes used to mean talk excitedly or be excited: • Scientists can stand up and *enthuse* about their work but it's really important that they question it, too. USE *talk excitedly.* • Angel's free-kick apart, there was precious little else to *enthuse* about in the opening 45 minutes, with the halftime whistle being greeted by boos from sections of the Holte End. USE *be excited.*

Enthuse, a malformation capable only of misshaping whatever sentence it appears in, is one of those words that reveal more than their users may suppose. Aside from expressing its irregular meaning, *enthuse* exposes its users as slapdash speakers and indifferent writers. SEE ALSO **aggress**; **elocute**.

enthused Misused for *infused.* • Go through the quotes and feel yourself *enthused* with the spirit of patriotism. USE *infused.* • Shrouded by these fantastic memories, his heart was *enthused* with joy. USE *infused.* • The French "citizens" became *enthused* with nationalism when defending their motherland against armed forces of other monarchal states. USE *infused.* • Darkest of all "indie" records, with lyrical themes that cover serial killers, self-mutilation, loss, and longing, even the production is *enthused* with misery. USE *infused.*

Infuse means to fill or permeate; to imbue or steep. The disagreeable *enthuse* means, among those who use the term, to feel or show enthusiasm. In these examples, *infuse* is the correct word, the proper meaning. SEE ALSO **enthuse**; **infusement**.

entomology Misused for *etymology.* • A Gemini Mercury and an Aquarian Mercury will talk for hours sharing perspectives on world peace, the digital divide or the *entomology* of words, while a Virgo Mercury and a Capricorn Mercury may go over details of the work to be accomplished in the next week. USE *etymology.* • By systematically teaching students stems of words, their meanings, and their uses, students are able to internalize the *entomology* of words, often revealing hidden meanings and stimulating thought and discussions about words. USE *etymology.*

What's worse, some people misspell *entomology entymology* and misuse it for *etymology*: • Upon successful completion of this unit, the learner will be able to trace the *entymology* of words. USE *etymology.* • If Yiddish dies, Yinglish dies with it, and where would we be without an *entymology* of words like schlemiel, schmuck, putz, yold, bullvan, yenta, shmooze, schlep, schpiel, yentz, chutzpah, meshuga, schlemazel, mazel tov, and if you can think of others, add them to the list. USE *etymology.* • Trent. Uncertain *entymology.* May have been given to those known for traveling, one who lived near one of various rivers named Trent in England or from a town named Trent near Dorset. USE *etymology.*

Entomology is the study of insects; *etymology* is the study of the origins of words.

envious Misused for *enviable.* • The tax law change raises the amount farmers can deduct for certain farm-related purchases, while placing some producers in the *envious* position of deciding whether they want to pay income tax at all—at least for now. USE *enviable.* • Either way, we need not peer too closely into the world of George Lucas to see he leads a normal life with a normal family but with a particularly unique and *envious* job. USE *enviable.*

Enviable means evoking feelings of envy. *Envious* means feeling, showing, or characterized by envy. Most often, it is people who are *envious,* things that are *enviable.*

envisualize Misused for *visualize.* • You really have to *envisualize* these results carefully. Use *visualize.* • Alternately, you can look at a map of the United States, point to Illinois, and *envisualize* it as a cornflake. Use *visualize.* • I *envisualize* love and the joy of it, and it is there. Use *visualize.* • I like to *envisualize* perfume as a piece of precious jewelry, created through an artisan process. Use *visualize.*

We have *visualize* and *envision,* but not *envisualize.* Linguists call this a "lexical blend"; the rest of us call it ignorance.

epicenter Misused for *center.* • Pocatello is a secret arts *epicenter* with a long, and colorful, literary tradition. Use *center.* • The club—which began operations on the East Side, near where Lapeer and Third Street stand today—served as the *epicenter* of the community's German population. Use *center.*

The *epicenter* is the point on the Earth's surface directly above the origin of an earthquake. It does not mean the center or most central point.

epigraph Misused for *epitaph.* • The *epigraph* etched on Moses Carver's headstone might not be comforting to visitors when they enter the Carver Cemetery at the George Washington Carver National Monument, but it certainly reminds them of where they are. Use *epitaph.* • In the southeastern side the cemetery hosts, among others, the tomb of Andrea Costa, with an *epigraph* written by poet Giovanni Pascoli. Use *epitaph.*

An *epigraph* is an inscription on a statue or building; a motto or quotation at the beginning of a literary work. An *epitaph* is an inscription on a tomb or gravestone and in memory of the person buried there; a literary piece commemorating a deceased person.

epithet Confused with *insult* (or similar words). An *epithet* need not be a disparaging or abusive term though, because many people think it must be, it often is ("If you wonder where this came from, consider their epithet 'sand nigger'"; "In Washington, D.C., a government official used the word 'niggardly,' which is not a racial epithet but happens to sound like one, and was forced to resign"). An *epithet* can also be an innocuous term or name used to describe a person or thing; a descriptive title ("The 'iron' in the epithet 'Iron Chancellor' given to Germany's Otto von Bismarck is a way of describing absolute military power"; "Oddest of the bacterial bunch was the West Nile Isle virus—a deceptively exotic epithet that concealed a legacy of astonishing doom").

epitome The pronunciation of *epitome* is (i-PIT-ah-mee), not (EP-i-tome).

equally as Misused for *equally* or *as.* • Newer categories of antidepressant drugs are *equally as* effective as older-generation antidepressants. USE *as.* • If Windows applications, which include macro programming languages, are run on an OS/2 machine, then the OS/2 machine is *equally as* susceptible to macro viruses as a Windows machine. USE *as.* • A banana and whole-wheat bagel would be cheaper and *equally as* nutritious. USE *equally* or *as.* • I think you'll find the Democrats *equally as* aggressive. USE *equally* or *as.*

Since the word *as* means equally, *equally as* is redundant. Use either *equally* or *as* but not both words.

> I can't make a distinction because they're both equally as bad, and equally as evil, and equally as destructive.
>
> —U.S. President George W. Bush
>
> Both *both* and *as* (and perhaps the *and*s) turn Bush's otherwise capably spoken sentence into near blather.

equanimous The pronunciation of *equanimous* is (ee-KWAN-i-mes), not (*ek*-whah-NIM-es).

equivocable Misused for *equivocal.* • At this time it is *equivocable* whether or not the presumptive myoblast and the satellite cell are functionally identical and at the same stage of myogenic differentiation. USE *equivocal.* • Emotions and dispositions are in no way *equivocable.* USE *equivocal.* • As an aside, Joan Rivers, on *Johnny Carson,* said she was always *equivocable* about the women's movement. USE *equivocal.*

Equivocable is in no lexicon. Equally idiotic is *equivocably* for *unequivocally.* Many people, as the next few examples make clear, think *equivocably* means *unequivocally*—allowing no doubt; unambiguously.

• I can state most *equivocably* that we are committed to our membership and zoos in general by way of publications. USE *unequivocally.* • However, what I can *equivocably* state is many thousands of hours of solo are required. USE *unequivocally.* • Regarding a flat Earth, the Bible doesn't *equivocably* state that it is flat. USE *unequivocally.*

Others think *equivocable* means *equivalent*: • Jim was also awarded the lot at a value of $25,000 and Sue was awarded an *equivocable* amount of cash of $25,000 from the parties' savings. USE *equivalent.*

eruption Misused for *irruption.* • This study establishes that the *eruption* of crows and ravens in the last decade or so is very large. USE *irruption.* • This is the second front of the Revolution: an *eruption* of meaningful content and innovative design that puts the means of production to use for something other than a fast buck. USE *irruption.* • There has been an *eruption* of silent film on video and cable, including a six-cassette series entitled *The Origins of American Film,* jointly produced by the Smithsonian Institution and the Library of Congress. USE *irruption.*

And *irruption* is sometimes misused for *eruption*: • Located at the base of the 11,000 foot-high Irazu Volcano, the area has been nearly destroyed by *irruptions* and earthquakes three separate times. USE *eruptions.*

An *eruption* is a sudden, violent outburst; an explosion; a rash or blemish on the skin; the emergence of a tooth through the gums. An *irruption* is a sudden, violent entrance; a bursting in; a rapid and irregular increase in number.

The verb forms *erupt* and *irrupt* are also sometimes misused, though we can hardly be surprised by this when dictionaries offer, as some do, erupt as one of the meanings of *irrupt.*

escape goat Misused for *scapegoat.* • But the reality is that the only real *escape goat* is staring at us when we look in the mirror; it's simply ourselves. USE *scapegoat.* • Jennifer was John's *escape goat* when he couldn't bring himself to leave Caroline. USE *scapegoat.*

The correct word for a person who is blamed for the actions of others is *scapegoat,* not *escape goat,* though the word does derive from the Hebrew term for "goat that escapes."

escortment Misused for *escort* (or similar words). • Police officers should have not only been there for *escortment,* but actually for the forensic interviewing of the child. USE *escorting.* • An *escortment* of ten guards circled around them in an intricate pattern. USE *escort.* • Examples are the deployment of troops for protection from attacks or military *escortment* of food and medicine transports. USE *escorts.* • They can also probably argue it was safer for him to be stuck in the port-a-potty until the workers had halted what work they needed to to ensure his proper *escortment* from the premises. USE *escort.*

Though the OED gives a 1775 example of *escortment* ("One of the warriors was sent to accompany me, by way of escortment"), the word has fallen into desuetude. *Escort* or *escorting* effectively says what the less pronounceable, the more alveolar *escortment* only used to.

esoteric Confused with *exoteric. Esoteric* means understood only by a chosen few or the initiated; recondite; private ("The Constitution of the United States is not some esoteric document, written to be understood only by people with high IQs and postgraduate education"). *Exoteric* means understood by the public or uninitiated; external; popular ("It is an exoteric music; that is, it's meant to be easily comprehended and performed by anyone with little musical training").

especial Confused with *special. Special* means distinctive; peculiar; particular or specific to someone or something ("I have a special interest in blue eye fluorescence"). *Especial* means preeminent, exceptional, or outstanding ("Such issues have posed especial difficulties in Africa, the region with the highest incidence of poverty, as well as in Latin America"). Journalists and other writers have forsaken the word *especial,* using *special* almost exclusively. What's more, to be *special* is hardly a compliment. Are we not, today, all drearily *special*?

especially The pronunciation of *especially* is (i-SPESH-ah-lee), not (ek-SPESH-ah-lee).

et al. Misused for *etc.* • Instead, Mpath *et al.* are shifting away from a subscription model to an advertising strategy, still offering premium pay-to-play services but relying more on free game and chat areas to attract hordes. USE *etc.* • It also reminded the UN that there are a ton of issues on which the UN wants the U.S.'s help: AIDS, the sex trade, *et al.* USE *etc.* • Allegations are that he was told to go on leave due to a host of issues, such as the issue of temple demolition, row over the issue of headship in the department of general surgery, *et al.* USE *etc.*

Et al., from the Latin *et alii,* means and others; *etc.,* from the Latin *et cetera,* means and the rest—that is, and other things. SEE ALSO **and etc.**

etc., etc. Misused for *etc.* • There was news about Iraq, about Afghanistan's leader visiting the States, *etc., etc.* USE *etc.* • They made all the usual boasts: Vibram soles, nubuk upper leather, Gore-Tex for waterproofing, antimicrobial lining, *etc., etc.* USE *etc.* • Now I'm a good liberal, too, and I believe that helping people, respecting diversity, saving the environment, *etc., etc.,* are good things. USE *etc.*

The expression *etc., etc.* is always unnecessary—two (or more) *etc.* do not suggest anything more than one does—always a mark of callow writers and inept editors. SEE ALSO **and etc.**; **ect.**; **et al.**; **etcetera**.

etcetera The correct spelling, *et cetera,* not *etcetera,* is Latin for and the rest, or and others. The pronunciation of *etcetera* is (et SET-er-*ah*), not (ek SET-rah). As a convenient end-of-sentence device to use instead of well-considered remarks, *etcetera* (or *etcetera, etcetera*) should be shunned: • We've yet to determine how that fire has occurred, whether it's spontaneous combustion, *etcetera.* • So how do you feel this study will impact how you deal with your son's autism, *etcetera*? • I felt nearly naked on the blocks and the whole sensation of water rushing over body, *etcetera,* was a weird feeling. • The list will most certainly include the ever-popular vow to lose weight, exercise more, quit smoking, save money, *etcetera, etcetera, etcetera.* SEE ALSO **and etc.**; **ect.**; **et al.**; **etc., etc.**

every day Misused for *everyday.* • Hieroglyphics were not for *every day* writing. USE *everyday.* • Do you find yourself overwhelmed with the *every day* tasks of running your business? USE *everyday.*

And *everyday* is misused for *every day*: • The odd thing is that though I see her *everyday,* I doubt I'd recognize her if I ran into her at the mall. Use *every day*.

Everyday, as an adjective, means common or ordinary. *Every day,* as an adverbial phrase, means each day. Almost all language, whether written or spoken, is today everyday; the misuse of these two terms, a fair example of that.

evidences Only as a verb (to attest or prove; to indicate clearly) acting on a singular noun can *evidences* be considered correct ("We at Carroll celebrate the award, recognizing the energy, dedication, and achievement on the part of Bruce, which this award evidences"; "This tournament evidences the positive impact that the new West Boulevard YMCA will have in this Y community"). But *evidences* as a noun (a thing or things that help form a conclusion; an indication or sign) is insupportable: • Sometimes, when the water recedes, so do the *evidences* of all but the trashiest of the trash—but that doesn't mean it isn't there. • By now, the defense is leading and the prosecutors are seeking for more *evidences* to support the charges against him. • In my own life, I've seen too many *evidences* of healing through prayer to doubt Owens' claim. • Guns, illegal drugs and other *evidences* that have been kept at the evidence custodian of the prosecutors' offices are already blighted or decaying.

Indeed, *evidences* is used by people—whether from Pakistan or Virginia—insufficiently familiar with the English language.

evoke Misused for *invoke*. • This is a country of profound religiosity and personal piety—a place where small, charismatic, and Pentecostal places of worship with names like the "Temple of Fire End Time Church" seem to inhabit every corner and where someone like Taylor, a Baptist, could *evoke* God's name at every turn with a straight face—and, for a time, get away with it. Use *invoke*. • One must even stir the porridge in the proper direction, so as not to *evoke* evil spirits. Use *invoke*. • Coordination is never easy, but it tends to work better when the leader is perceived as an honest broker and can *evoke* the authority of the White House. Use *invoke*.

And *invoke* is misused for *evoke*: • As the dollar slides, dire prognostications of an investors' strike *invoke* comparisons between the U.S. economy and Enron. Use *evoke.* • The first winter storm of the year might *invoke* memories of last year's treacherous winter. Use *evoke.*

To *invoke* means to call on God or another for help or support; to cite as pertinent or as an authority; to summon an evil spirit; to ask for solemnly. To *evoke* means to elicit or call to mind; to provoke a feeling; to re-create with the imagination.

Evoke does not mean *invoke* though some dictionaries, mimicking the public misusage of this word, insist it does.

evolute Misused for *evolve.* • A language *evolutes* toward precision or at least it used to do. Use *evolves.* • If man *evolutes* from the animals, man would certainly be like the animals in everything. Use *evolves.*

Those who applaud that the language *evolves* might soon applaud that the language *evolutes.* But some already do: • As I have said before, "Language *evolutes* and names evolve," and this applies to spellings, too. • All this goes to prove that the language *evolutes* and cannot be taken literally, not even the spelling of it.

Evolve, not *evolute,* is the correct verb.

exacting Misused for *exact.* • This T is an *exacting* replica of the car that finished first in the 1909 New-Seattle race. Use *exact.* • Iraq's a loser because it has no end game; Afghanistan's tolerable to the American public because there's an *exacting* target. Use *exact.* • Such nations as France, England, Germany, the Soviet Union, America knew to an *exacting* number, the manpower, armor, artillery, aircraft of each Arab/Muslim nation. Use *exact.*

Exacting means making rigorous demands; requiring great care or attention. *Exact* means accurate or correct; precise.

exalt Misused for *exult.* • Those that finish the journey will *exalt* in their triumph, and rightly so. Use *exult.* • As parents we are delegated to the sidelines, to watch as our children *exalt* in tackling new sports and activities. Use *exult.* • As we share stories, we *exalt* in the joy of completed journeys, solved problems, and happy endings. Use *exult.*

And *exult* is misused for *exalt*: • Because of his obedience, Jesus was *exulted* to a position of fame second only to Jehovah himself. USE *exalted.*

To *exalt* is to hold someone in high regard; to raise someone to a high standard; to make noble or glorify. To *exult* is to celebrate; to show jubilation.

exasperate Misused for *exacerbate.* • Poor illustrations of the white shark also abounded, *exasperating* the problem. USE *exacerbating.* • Generally the kinds of things people need to be aware of are possibilities of skin irritation, sensitization, stimulating effects that could *exasperate* a high blood pressure condition, hormonal effects that are unwanted during pregnancy, photosensitization and using an herb that speeds up the action of an organ when that organ's function is already severely damaged. USE *exacerbate.* • During the flight you should drink plenty of nonalcoholic beverages (alcohol at any time can cause dehydration and swelling of sinus membranes, and when flying it will just *exasperate* the effects of dry cabin air). USE *exacerbate.* • The only two alternatives in this case are to raise taxes or cut spending—both of which serve to *exasperate* rather than temper recessions. USE *exacerbate.*

Exasperate (ig-ZAS-pah-*rate*) means to annoy greatly or make angry; *exacerbate* (ig-ZAS-er-*bate*), to aggravate or make worse. A dictionary that records that both words mean to aggravate or increase the severity of is a dictionary to shun—or shed. SEE ALSO **aggravate**.

> A mother of five, Christine continued to gain weight with each pregnancy, exasperating a weight problem she says she had her whole life.
>
> —Caritas St. Elizabeth's Medical Center

exceed Misused for *accede.* • If for any reason I were to *exceed* to requests that are being made by the unions, then no doubt that material can also then be provided to the appropriate authority. USE *accede.* • And given that His Honor was not going to *exceed* to the wishes the child had expressed, he took the view that it was an appropriate case given the age and maturity of the child to speak to the child. USE *accede.* • Henry did have a third child, a son, named Edward VI, who *exceeded* to the throne after his father's death, but he died at the age of 15. Use *acceded.*

Exceed means to surpass; to go beyond what is required or expected. *Accede* means give one's consent to; to concede or agree to a request, demand, or treaty; to come into an office or position of authority. See also **supersede**.

excell Misspelling of *excel.* • They've come a long way since taking the court together in the third grade, but they're still going strong, mesh beautifully, and *excell* in a sport they both love. Use *excel.* • According to police, the daughter of the businessman, who did not *excell* in her studies, was denied a prefectship. Use *excel.* • However, Brian is committed to *excell* against South Africa, and I am confident that he will perform at the Cricket World Cup tournament. Use *excel.* See also **accel (accell)**.

Though the noun *excellence* is spelled with two *l*'s, the verb *excel* has but one *l.*

except Misused for *accept.* • You never know, so please *except* my apologies. Use *accept.* • But I'll *except* your eternal gratitude, friendship, and patronage in return. Use *accept.* • All major credit cards are *excepted.* Use *accepted.* • We *except* all ad offers. Use *accept.*

The confusion between *except*—which means excluding or otherwise than—and *accept*—which means to receive something offered or to agree to something—is most often, though not always, due to a lapse of carefulness rather than a lack of cognition. Carelessness, however, is easily just as irresponsible as misunderstanding.

exceptionable Misused for *exceptional.* • Other musicians participating in the concert included venerable musicians from the Moscow conservatory, performers on the Dombra (the national instrument of Kazakhstan), and Aiman Musahodzhaeva, an *exceptionable* lady and the foremost violinist in Kazakhstan. Use *exceptional.* • The tomb is in *exceptionable* condition and really worth the cost. Use *exceptional.* • In addition to *exceptionable* quality food and service, the caterers provide uniformed waiters/waitresses, cooking facilities, trestles, tablecloths, crockery, cutlery, serviettes, condiments, and bread sticks and rolls. Use *exceptional.* • Transicoil LVDT pressure transducers provide high accuracy and *exceptionable* reliability at moderate prices. USE *exceptional.* • You will treasure this print, not only for its *exceptionable* beauty but also for the memory of Nelson, Sarazen, and Snead. USE *exceptional.* • Our highly educated and experienced staff in education and computer science takes pride in providing schools/colleges, government agencies, and private businesses with *exceptionable* quality service and support that everyone wants and can expect from us. USE *exceptional.*

Exceptionable means objectionable; *exceptional* means something quite different: uncommon or extraordinary.

excite Misused for *incite.* • Then Jack and several of his like-minded persons *excite* a riot and Jack gets to the guardhouse. USE *incite.* • The function of government is to calm, rather than to *excite* agitation. USE *incite.*

To *excite* is to arouse strong feelings in; to stir or stimulate; to elicit. To *incite* is to provoke; to urge or encourage to take (often violent) action.

Some emotions and states can be either *excited* or *incited,* depending on whether they are welcomed or unwelcomed: • The bill, currently in draft form at the House of Representatives, defines pornography as acts that *incite* sexual desire. • An aphrodisiac is a substance thought to *excite* sexual desire.

exercise Misused for *exorcise.* • So when Sinkhorn's squad takes the field as the No. 2 seed against the seventh-seeded Flashes in the first home playoff game in program history, it will have an opportunity to *exercise* the demons of nearly a decade in the making. USE *exorcise.* • When a witch doctor dances, it is to *exercise* evil spirits from the sick person. USE *exorcise.*

And *exorcise* is occasionally used for *exercise*: • It's also odd that a group would be telling us we shouldn't *exorcise* our right to free speech and assembly. USE *exercise.*

To *exorcise* (EK-sor-*siz*) is to rid, through prayer, ceremony, or incantation, a person or place of an evil spirit. To *exercise* (EK-ser-*siz*) is to engage in a program of physical activity; to employ; to exert; to carry out; to upset or vex.

exhileration Misspelling of *exhilaration.* • Or if the child who for the first time bravely put his whole head under the rolling wave before it crashed, would in later years remember the *exhileration* he felt. USE *exhilaration.* • This was a more exciting journey where the atma (soul) soared to new heights and there was a sense of *exhileration* instead of the peace and calm and contentedness of Muar! USE *exhilaration.*

Exhilaration, not *exhileration* (and certainly not *acceleration*) is the correct spelling. SEE ALSO **accelerate**.

E

existance Misspelling of *existence.* • Altogether, thirty-eight students are enrolled in four horticulture program classes during its first term of *existance.* USE *existence.* • The same reports were seized on by environmentalists as evidence that *co-existance* was impossible and growing crops such as GM rape would cause contamination. USE *co-existence.* • The alleged *existance* of biological, chemical, and nuclear weapons that posed an imminent danger to the Western world was one of the main reasons for the U.S.-led war that toppled the Iraqi leader. USE *existence.*

Existence (three *e*'s: beginning, middle, and end), not *existance,* is the correct spelling.

exotic Confused with *erotic. Erotic* means of or relating to sexual desire; amatory ("But those images of the city may soon have to make way for a new project called Erotichesky Peterburg, or Erotic Petersburg, that aims to highlight the city's sensual pleasures"). *Exotic* means foreign; strikingly strange or fascinating ("However, selling and keeping the more exotic creatures such as Burmese pythons and Gila monsters could become illegal under a proposed Lake County Health Department ordinance").

expatriot Misused for *expatriate.* • Integration of political refugees is an important issue in Switzerland, a small country with a large number of *expatriot* residents. USE *expatriate.* • We open with Adolfo Olaechea, a 52-year-old Peruvian *expatriot* living in London, England. USE *expatriate.* • "April is the cruelest month," begins T. S. Eliot's most famous poem, and it is ironic that, as an *expatriot,* he never had to suffer the agony of the Internal Revenue Service and April 15 in America. USE *expatriate.*

Expatriots (people who no longer love or support their country) are likely few, but the number of *expatriates* (people who—though they may love their country—live in another one) ever increases.

expiate Misused for *expatiate.* • The wise man from America *expiated* at length on two issues: first, that everyone should live according to their means and second, that there should be an international division of labor. USE *expatiated.* • At great length Dedwood *expiated* on the glories of the city, on the magnificent work that was being accomplished there, on the grandeur of the buildings. USE *expatiated.* • It would be a mistake, we think, to *expiate* on what may be the merit of these paintings, or to do more than point out that many of them are very summary in their impressionistic statement of the pictorial facts. USE *expatiate.* • There was still a growing, if grudging, respect for his uncanny ability to *expiate* on exciting new issues in the philosophy and praxis of dialectical materialism. USE *expatiate.*

To *expiate* (EK-spee-*ate*) is to atone for sins; to make amends. To *expatiate* (ik-SPAY-shee-*ate*) is to speak or write at length.

> Assorted obscure Southern musicians—a guy named "16 Horsepower" was a favorite—and not-so-obscure writers (Harry Crews) pontificate, ruminate, meditate, and expiate on their rural home country from the farms, honky-tonks, churches, jails, and junkyards of the Southland.
>
> —Roger Moore, *Orlando Sentinel*

expire Misused for *retire* (or similar words). • CNN.com will *expire* this article on 06/12/2003. USE *remove.* • He thought that T13 should probably vote to *expire* the document if there were no issues with this action. USE *retire.* • Authors wouldn't be able to *expire* documents, only to request that the documents be *expired.* USE *delete; deleted.*

Expire means to end or terminate; to cease to be valid; to die; to exhale. Let us disabuse information technology professionals and their peers of the belief that it should also mean to retire, remove, or delete.

explicit Confused with *implicit. Explicit* means distinctly stated; definite ("A row erupted today over an explicit new booklet on puberty aimed at nine-year-old schoolchildren"). *Implicit* means implied; suggested or understood; without question ("The letter contained an implicit threat that Democrats had sufficient strength to block the bill under Senate rules").

expose Misused for *exposé.* • A movie about the dawn of Facebook sounds as thrilling as an *expose* into the minds behind Super Mario Bros. USE *exposé.* • The subject is an *expose* on the alarming rate of sex trafficking within American borders. USE *exposé.*

When the acute accent spells the difference between two words, their meanings and pronunciations, it is indispensable. Other words, traditionally spelled with the acute accent, can sometimes be spelled without it. *Cliché,* for example, though preferable with the accent, can be spelled *cliche* without many people confusing it for another word. SEE ALSO **cliché.**

expresso Misspelling of *espresso.* • While 90 percent of the coffee sold in cafés was *expresso,* it represented only 5 percent for Starbucks. USE *espresso.* • Since then, the Wykoop House has been purchased by Saugerties couple Wendy Ricks and Mark Colligan, who plan to turn it into an *expresso* bar, Internet café, and gourmet ice cream shop. USE *espresso.*

The word is spelled *espresso* (i-SPRES-oh), not *expresso* (ex-PRES-oh).

extant Misused for *extent.* • These efforts demonstrate the *extant* to which Kao-tsung cherished certain types of jade, and, by implication, the impact that his personal taste had on the content of the palace collection. USE *extent.* • Another indication of the *extant* of the problem is the support market for sprays, dips, etc., to rid your pet of unwanted parasites. USE *extent.* • We will prosecute any and all violators to the full *extant* of the law. USE *extent.*

And *extent* is sometimes misused for *extant:* • From this perspective, one could say that, of the currently *extent* species, man must be one of the oldest, having had the time to adapt to most environments. USE *extant.* • This tune is a simplified phrase from one of the *extent* fragments of ancient Greek music. USE *extant.* • Ginkgo biloba is the only *extent* species of ginkgos today, but many ginkgo relatives have been found in fossil records, dating back over 300 million years. USE *extant.* • Sulphur is widespread around the southern and southwestern sides of an *extent* volcano, Koh-e-Sultan. USE *extant.*

Extant means still in existence; not extinct. *Extent* means range, size, breadth, or scope of something.

extract Misused for *exact.* • However, uncertainty certainly is not *extracting* a toll from the American housing market. USE *exacting.* • We have taken it upon ourselves to promise to *extract* vengeance for them. USE *exact.* • It is not a time for demonstrating the coalition's power or *extracting* revenge from a beaten despot. USE *exacting.*

To *exact* is to demand (a payment); to inflict. To *extract* is to remove or draw out; to obtain by force; to obtain by mechanical or chemical action; to derive information from a source; to deduce.

extraordinary The pronunciation of *extraordinary* is (ek-STROR-din-*air*-ee), not (*ek*-strah-OR-din-air-ee).

extremify Misused for *hyperbolize* (or similar words). • Indeed, a relatively small portion of senators *extremify* their public ideology during this decade. USE *exaggerate.* • To *extremify the* example: if I'm having a debate with someone who is speaking in Latin, what would it profit me to attempt to answer them in English? USE *give an extreme.*

In using *extremify,* people acknowledge their inability to think well. We use incorrect words, counterfeit words, simple assemblages when we cannot think of the better built words available to us.

extrenuating Misused for *extenuating.* • Some *extrenuating* circumstances are present to help make it a little tougher. USE *extenuating.* • A bid is a binding contract that is not negotiable outside of *extrenuating* circumstances. USE *extenuating.* • Due to *extrenuating* circumstances, Epsilon's website will no longer be available at this address. USE *extenuating.*

• Killing should be considered murder by default, unless it can be shown that it was justified due to circumstances, an accident, or some other *extrenuating* reason. Use *extenuating*.

No one who reads, or who reads carefully, could possibly say or write *extrenuating*. Instead of judging one another by how much money we earn or by how big our house is, let us judge one another by more telling talents, such as by whether and how well we read.

Ff

F

fair Confused with *fare.* A *fare* is a charge for transportation or a passenger transported for a fee; food and drink; goods or services offered to the public ("Staff asked them to pay the fare but they refused, before the man threatened to come back and stab them"; "Lester's offers a variety of beer and wine in the afternoons and evenings as well as coffee and light edible fare in the morning and throughout the day"). A *fair* is a gathering for the exchange of goods; an exhibition or event ("Will County Healthy Families Illinois will be sponsoring a free community resource fair Monday"; "Finger Lakes Community College is seeking employers to set up booths free of charge at a summer job fair at the school").

famest Misused for *most famous.* • I'm the *famest,* but I'm also the poorest. USE *most famous.* • What are some of the *famest* dance choreographers in the world. USE *most famous.*

Nor is *most famest* correct: • Who is Connecticut's *most famest* person? USE *most famous.*

The only acceptable superlative of *famous* is *most famous.*

farther Misused for *further.* • If you want just one reason, look no *farther* than free throws. USE *further.* • Earlier this week, he stunned the court by musing about the possibility of breaking the company into three parts, going even *farther* than the government had proposed. USE *further.*

Further is also misused for *farther*: • While meteors typically streak through our atmosphere in a second or two and are sometimes much brighter than even a bright comet (when they are called fireballs), comets are much *further* away than the moon and move slowly with respect to the background stars from night to night, rising and setting each day just as do the sun, the moon, the planets, and the stars. USE *farther.* • The field in this type of magnet is zero at dead center, but grows linearly as you move *further* away from the center. USE *farther.*

Although many people use the words interchangeably, *farther* is best used to refer to physical distance, and *further,* figuratively, to refer to extent or degree.

fateful Misused for *fatal.* • The representative of Fiji added that most deaths and *fateful* injuries would have been preventable if suitable intervention had been developed. USE *fatal.* • For those of us who knew him more personally, we have all lost a dear and genuine friend, with whom one could talk about the most abstract philosophical issues and with the same ease move to more mundane problems in life—which usually paled in comparison with his endless and brave struggle against his *fateful* illness. USE *fatal.*

Fatal means resulting in death; disastrous. *Fateful* means determined by fate; prophetic; significant. Several dictionaries maintain that *fatal* also means *fateful,* but the true meaning of this is that dictionaries are unreliable.

far gone conclusion Misused for *foregone conclusion.* • As we got older, the concept of "happily ever after" became a *far gone conclusion* eclipsed by reality. USE *foregone conclusion.* • It is a *far gone conclusion* that there is no biblical or scientific reason to accept evolution. USE *foregone conclusion.*

A *foregone conclusion* is a result considered inevitable or certain. A *far gone conclusion* is nonsense, the sort of monstrosity that people who neither read nor think tend to use.

favorite Misused for *favor.* • In other words, I'll *favorite* your blog if you *favorite* mine. USE *favor.* • On my wall, Facebook claims I *favorited* about 30 YouTube videos—many of which I never *favorited.* USE *favored.* • I have been a Twitter user for over a year now and I have never *favorited* a single update. USE *favored.* • I came here from Graywolf's blog, so I've *favorited* him, you and Oilman. USE *favored.*

Social networking and dating sites have adopted the verb to *favorite* as a way for its clients to show preference for people, events, blogs, products, services, and more. Other than being an Internet-inspired word, to *favorite* means nothing that to *favor* does not mean, and has not meant for many hundreds of years: to regard or treat with favor, friendship, or approval.

And now it is clear that *favorite* is being used in other, nonnetworking and nondating, contexts: • Plus it was overwhelmingly obvious that my mom *favorited* her over me. USE *favored.* • Kristin Davis went wide-eyed at the sheer volume of clothes to choose a favorite from, but ultimately *favorited* her big, frou-frou Vera Wang dress from Charlotte's wedding to the WASPy and highly unsuitable Trey. USE *favored.*

F

This is nothing to celebrate, as lexicographers and other imposters no doubt do; this is another example of the lessening of our language. Newly coined words are only as valuable as they are useful. To *favorite* is not useful. Very likely to *favorite* was thought of by someone unfamiliar with to *favor.*

fawn Misused for *faun.* • Claude Débussy (1862–1918), whose style is called Impressionist, used tone color and nontraditional scales in his *Prelude to the Afternoon of a Fawn* (1894). USE *Faun.* • I like to characterize the period following 9/11 as a "Pan Period" because silhouettes during the past four seasons since the fall of '01 have been dominated by a juxtaposition that rivals the body of the mythic *fawn.* USE *faun.*

And *faun* is misused for *fawn*: • Fans of classic rock will *faun* over this album while guitar enthusiasts will perhaps adore it. USE *fawn.*

A *fawn* is a young deer; to *fawn* is to act servilely or obsequiously; to attempt to please. A *faun* is a god in Roman mythology, half man and half goat.

fearful Misused for *fearsome.* • We were either viewed as the pitiful refugees or we were looked at as the horrible and *fearful* terrorists. USE *fearsome.* • Nigerian gangs in South Africa have now become the most *fearful* immigrants in South Africa. USE *fearsome.* • Their bond was so strong that when they crossed over, it made them the most powerful and *fearful* vampires known to man or vampire. USE *fearsome.*

Though many dictionaries declare that *fearful* and *fearsome* are synonyms, dictionaries—it must be remembered—merely record how people use the language. And the public is a fool.

It is far better to use *fearful* to mean afraid or frightened, and *fearsome* to mean causing fear. If we allow one word to mean much the same as another, we have fewer words that matter. If we have fewer words, nuance and knowledge are lost.

February The pronunciation of *February* is (FEB-roo-*er*-ee), not (FEB-yoo-*er*-ee).

feel badly Misused for *feel bad.* • And when she loses, I think she'll *feel very badly.* USE *feel very bad.* • I *feel badly* because I understand Connie is upset with me because I think we joked about her departure from CBS. USE *feel bad.* • Our resident Sexdoc Dr. William Fitzgerald has advice for a woman whose husband is constantly making her *feel badly* about her body—in and out of bed. USE *feel bad.*

The distinction should be maintained between *feel bad* and *feel badly.* The former is meant to describe an emotional or a physical condition; the latter, touch. However, like so many other expressions, the distinction between these two is not always, and may even be seldom, observed. SEE ALSO **bad**.

> While any customer mistake is regrettable, we feel particularly badly about the mistakes we made here.
>
> —Kristin Lemkau, J. P. Morgan Chase chief communications officer

felicitate Misused for *facilitate.* • CEPA will *felicitate* trade and ensure removal of nontariff barriers. USE *facilitate.* • Lord Shiva created Lord Brahma to *felicitate* the process of creation and bestowed him with all these eighteen learnings. USE *facilitate.* • The newly launched offerings are designed to provide an effective solution to the increasing challenges of risk measurement and management faced by banks the world over and to *felicitate* the adoption of quantitative techniques and international best practices in risk management. USE *facilitate.*

Facilitate (fah-SIL-i-*tate*) means to make easier; *felicitate* (fi-LIS-i-*tate*), a less common word, means to congratulate.

fiancé Misused for *fiancée.* • Mel Gibson refuses to marry his *fiancé* Maria Ortiz after Maria secretly recorded his conversations to humiliate Gibson and destroy his career. USE *fiancée.* • The woman identified on Facebook as his *fiancé,* Jodi Newcity, also referenced his long shifts. USE *fiancée.*

And *fiancée* is misused for *fiancé:* • Her *fiancée* is an investment banker. USE *fiancé.* • The *Real Housewives of Atlanta* actress and a well-known model married her *fiancée* in a private wedding ceremony last weekend. USE *fiancé.*

A man engaged to be married is a *fiancé.* A woman engaged to be married is a *fiancée.* The pronunciation of *fiancé,* like *fiancée,* is (*fee*-an-SAY). The pronunciation (FEE-ahns) is ridiculous and wrong. SEE ALSO **divorcé**.

finely Misused for *finally.* • Ronald Reagan was quoted as saying, "Those that have known freedom and lost it, have never regained it," and we are seeing the loss of our freedoms *finely* come to fruition. USE *finally.* • It looks like I can *finely* stop complaining about the cold and start complaining about the heat. USE *finally.* • When war *finely* began, the Republicans, under the name of "unconditional Union men," took complete control of the new state. USE *finally.*

Both adverbs, *finely* means in a fine manner, discriminatingly, or in small parts, and *finally* means in conclusion or conclusively.

first off Misused for *first.* • *First off,* design a simple letterhead that you'll use throughout your packet pages. USE *First.* • *First off,* I want to thank everyone for being here this morning. USE *First.* • Jerry, *first off,* this is a great forum, and thanks for providing us all with such great info. USE *first.*

First off—like *first of all* and *in the first place* and *first and foremost* and *firstly*—is a thoughtless expression that people use only because they hear others using it. The *off* is meaningless. At least most people seem to have the great good sense not to say *second off.* SEE ALSO **start off (out)**.

fiscal Misused for *physical. Fiscal* (FIS-kel), of or relating to finances or revenue, and *physical* (FIZ-i-kel), of or relating to the body or material world, are as different in meaning as they are in spelling.

fixing to The expression *fixing to* means planning to (do something) or on the verge of (doing something). Though it may sound improper, it is not; *fixing to* is southern ("Now, she's nine months pregnant and fixing to have the baby, so we're fixing to rush her to the hospital"; "As you read this, the cold air from Canada is fixing to crash into the wet storm system coming up the Atlantic coast"; "If you're fixing to lie, if you're fixing to conceal, if it's not your intent to impede an investigation, why do you invite the agents in?").

Much regional English sounds incorrect to people from other areas, and indeed much of it can be called incorrect. Some of these expressions, however, like *fixing to,* though they sound incorrect are, instead, merely informal or casual. Still, anyone who wishes to make a favorable impression on others would be well advised to shun the regionalism *fixing to.*

flaccid The pronunciation of *flaccid* is (FLAK-sid), not (FLA-sid).

flare Misused for *flair.* • Wahlberg shows plenty of *flare* in the sensational exposé *Boogie Nights.* USE *flair.* • Jane is an accomplished actress who has a natural talent and *flare* for performing. USE *flair.* • Glasgow's music seems to be a mixture of the best parts of everywhere else. Dirt from Detroit, cheekiness from Chicago, style from Paris, and *flare* from New York. USE *flair.* • With precision, *flare,* and panache she has demonstrated before hundreds of thousands of spectators across the globe. USE *flair.*

Flair means natural ability or aptitude; style; flamboyance. *Flare,* as a verb, means to blaze brightly; to burst out in anger. As a noun, it means a flame.

flaunt Misused for *flout.* • Companies regularly *flaunt* the laws, collecting and disseminating personal information. USE *flout.* • North Korea continues to *flaunt* international law by speeding ahead with their nuclear program with no consequences whatsoever. USE *flout.* • The regime has shown little political will to stop the narcotics exports from Burma and prevent illicit drug money from enriching those who would *flaunt* international rules and profit by destroying the lives of millions. USE *flout.* • Leave it up to the Rocky Mountain volleyball team to *flaunt* convention. USE *flout.*

To *flaunt* is to show off or exhibit ostentatiously; to *flout* is to disobey or show contempt for.

> That flaunts industry convention, in which agents provide a package of services for a commission. It also flaunts the law, at least in a technical sense.
>
> —Loren Steffy, *Houston Chronicle*
>
> The problem, however, is that older adults appear to flaunt safe sex practices. For instance, the researchers note, 50-year-olds are six times less likely to use a condom than men in their 20s.
>
> —Frederik Joelving, Reuters
>
> Steffy and Joelving *flaunt* their unfamiliarity with the difference in meaning between *flaunt* and *flout*.

flotsam Confused with *jetsam. Flotsam* is the wreckage from a ship or its cargo found at sea; odds and ends; people who live on the fringes of society ("The federal government is considering several measures to reduce the flotilla of flotsam that's clogging seas around northern Australia, the vast bulk of it coming from countries to our north"; "Police never enter the Zone, an urban wasteland peopled by society's flotsam"). *Jetsam* is cargo thrown overboard to lighten a ship in distress; such material washed ashore; discarded items ("Jetsam was the luggage, furniture and fittings thrown overboard to lighten the ship when it was being shipwrecked").

flounder Misused for *founder.* • Staff writer P. J. Connolly muses over Apple's ill-fated OpenDoc and wonders why a *floundering* ship would toss women and children overboard to stay above water. Use *foundering.* • Sparks fly when Dawson manages to talk Rose out of jumping overboard, but tragedy awaits as the unsinkable ship hits an iceberg and begins to *flounder.* Use *founder.* • After starring roles in *The Krays* (with brother Martin), *The Bodyguard* (with Kevin Costner), and heist caper *Killing Zoe,* his acting career *floundered.* Use *foundered.* • Unfortunately, while the business thrived, the marriage *floundered;* in late 1997, Pete and Linda divorced after 33 years together. Use *foundered.*

To *flounder* is to move clumsily or thrash about; to struggle confusedly. To *founder* is to fill with water and sink; to cave in; to fail or collapse.

flush Misused for *flesh.* • We also appreciate the need for business executives to *flush out* an idea before proceeding into anything too robustly and quickly. Use *flesh out.* • I take these masks, using them for comic effect or using them to *flush out* story or create atmosphere. Use *flesh out.* • Frequent brainstorming sessions between the contractor and customer can *flush out* details, and new ideas can be implemented immediately. Use *flesh out.*

To *flesh out* is to realize; to fill out or give substance to. To *flush out* is to force an animal or person into the open.

font Misused for *fount.* • He was a *font* of stories about ancient feuds, ward fights, canny pols, and the funny and desperate moments the political life dishes out. Use *fount.* • So it's no wonder that the Democrats seek one of their own, a *font* of wisdom who can divine what is wrong and point the way forward. Use *fount.*

And *fount* is sometimes misused for *font*: • It was agreed that responses to each question would not exceed 10 pages in length using a 12-point Times Roman *fount* with one-and-one-half spacing and one-inch margins. Use *font.*

In the United States, a *font* (FONT) is a set of type of one face and size, and a *fount* (FOUNT) is a fountain, or a source of something—knowledge, for example. These are two different words, with two different pronunciations and two different meanings. Let the laxicographers mix them up if they must; let the rest of us understand that it is language, and our ability to use it, that best identify us as human. The less well we use the language, the less thoughtful, cogent, and communicative we likely are—indeed, the less humanity we likely have.

for all intense (intensive) (of) purposes Misused for *for all intents and purposes.* • *For all intense purposes* asthma is behind me unless I come upon a stressful situation or dust. Use *For all intents and purposes.* • While many may shun from any comparison to the men, the fact is that the WUSA, *for all intensive purposes,* will be imitating the structure of MLS. USE *for all intents and purposes.* • Only in this play a cookie is a biscuit because *for all intense purposes* the play is delivered in a foreign language. USE *for all intents and purposes.* • We have been waiting since March 6, 2004, and we have not seen it, so may we presume that *for all intense of purposes* we are never going to see it? USE *for all intents and purposes.*

For all intents and purposes means in effect or virtually, either of which is a better phrase to use. *For all intense (intensive) (of) purposes* is a meaningless mash.

for awhile Misused for *awhile* (*for a while*). • They've been around *for awhile,* they happen with some frequency in these parts, and as long as you're willing to crouch idiotically beneath a friendly desk, you're as prepared as humanly possible. USE *for a while* or *awhile.* • Just need to get away from it all and take it easy *for awhile*? USE *for a while* or *awhile.* • Considered to be the logo for the Louisiana Tech Drumline, the name was dropped *for awhile.* USE *for a while* or *awhile.*

Awhile, an adverb, means for a short time or for a while and hence does not need the *for* preceding it. Using one phrase for the other is, or ought to be, frowned upon. SEE ALSO **await for**.

foray The pronunciation of *foray* is (FOR-ay), not (for-AY).

forbid (forbidded) Misused for *forbade.* • Their parents *forbidded* them to be together. USE *forbade.* • My ex-husband stopped visiting our kids, because his wife *forbidded* him to see them. USE *forbade.*

Nor is *forbid* the past participle: • She was *forbid* from helping him get back onto his feet. USE *forbidden.*

The past tense of *forbid* is *forbade* (for-BAD), not *forbid* and not *forbidded.* The past participle is *forbidden.* SEE ALSO **bidded**.

Present	Present Participle	Past	Past Participle
forbid	forbidding	forbade	forbidden

forcefully Misused for *forcibly* • LAPD *forcefully* breaks up melee after concert. Use *forcibly.* • Hong Kong is a colony that Great Britain *forcefully* took from China about 150 years ago when China was weak and intimidated by the strengths of the Western world. Use *forcibly.* • On Monday, Thai police arrested more than 200 Pak villagers who had *forcefully* broken into the Government House compound on Sunday. Use *forcibly.* • In all territories, members of minority groups have been *forcefully* evicted from their homes, violently attacked, robbed, threatened, dismissed from their jobs, and, in some cases, killed. Use *forcibly.* • This morning at 10 A.M., the Serbian police *forcefully* evicted Xhavit Goraj and his family from their apartment at the Bregu i Djelli quarter of Prishtina. Use *forcibly.*

To the diminution of us all, the meanings of these two words often trespass on each other: *forcefully* means persuasively or vigorously or effectively; *forcibly* most often describes actions involving physical force. Both *forceful* and *forcible* mean having or using force or strength, but the former is reserved for metaphorical or abstract force (such as a *forceful* speaker), whereas the latter is reserved for physical or exceptional force (such as a *forcible* eviction).

forebear Misused for *forbear.* • Equity, however, enters injunctions or decrees directing someone either to act or to *forebear* from acting. Use *forbear.* • I'm going to *forebear* from writing a long, goofy column today and instead will just extend my thanks to Mark for his dedication. Use *forbear.* • Due to the weakness of their faith and their utter lack of wisdom, they were not able to *forebear.* Use *forbear.*

Forbear, a verb, means to refrain from or resist; to control oneself under provocation. *Forebear,* a noun, is an ancestor. Ignore all dictionaries that would have you believe *forbear* is also a noun having the same meaning as *forebear.*

forego Misused for *forgo.* • NASA officials decided Friday to *forego* any extra inspections on shuttle *Endeavor*'s twin orbital maneuvering engine pods, avoiding a potential delay in its planned late November launch on a space station crew rotation mission. Use *forgo.* • The researchers looked at the proportion of young people who reported *foregoing* medical care, their reasons for doing so, and their risk for health problems. USE *forgoing.* • What better way to fund the government than to *forego* all those deductions and all that loophole lawyering? USE *forgo.* • Lacking digital IDs, we *forego* the convenience of single sign-on—swiping your card rather than trying to remember names and passwords. And we *forego* the security of knowing, with some degree of assurance, who sent a message. USE *forgo.*

Forego means to precede; to go before. *Forgo* means to do without; abstain from; renounce. Some dictionaries offer the spelling *forego* as a variant of *forgo,* but this is only because so many people have confused the words for so long—and dictionaries are merely a compilation of people's language usage, however incorrect or cretinous.

forewarn Misused for *warn.* • I will *forewarn* readers that the following is a discussion of feminists and liberals, some of whom are adolescents attending public high schools. USE *warn.* • We're trying to be proactive and *forewarn* students that if they plan to drink they need to go somewhere else. USE *warn.* • I want to *forewarn* potential ticket buyers: I'm not going to be playing an acoustic version of "Thunder Road." USE *warn.*

To *warn*—to notify or make aware of in advance—renders the word *forewarn* unnecessary, useless. People often use the phrase *warn in advance,* which many know is a silly redundancy, but to *forewarn,* which means to warn in advance, is equally silly, equally redundant. *Forewarn in advance,* were someone to use it, would be irrefutably foolish.

forgot Misused for *forgotten.* • I think he has *forgot* about me. USE *forgotten.* • We haven't *forgot* about you but unfortunately the resolution is taking more time than we had hoped. USE *forgotten.* • As his eyes rolled toward the object of his affection, the garden, he saw the lone standing figure that he had *forgot* about earlier. USE *forgotten.* • I often do that since by morning I will have *forgot* the details of the dream. USE *forgotten.*

The past tense of *forget,* an irregular verb, is *forgot,* and the past participle of *forget* is *forgotten*. That is, after auxiliary verbs like *has* or *have* or *had* (as in the examples shown), *forgotten,* not *forgot,* is required.

Present	**Present Participle**	**Past**	**Past Participle**
forget	forgetting	forgot	forgotten

formerly Misused for *formally.* • Many companies embark on a strategic planning process, either *formerly* or informally. USE *formally.* • Customer Solutions *formerly* announces the release of a new and innovative approach to bag tags and label product design, development and distribution. USE *formally.* • Hospital and/or rehabilitation professionals need to immediately inform the school that they are presently caring for one of their students and to have the family and/or attending physician *formerly* request that the school come in and evaluate the child. USE *formally.* • This is the album that *formerly* introduces the ethnic experimentation that will be part of Gabriel's work since then, combined with atmospheric melodies. USE *formally.*

Formerly means at an earlier time, erstwhile, once; *formally,* officially, properly, or ceremoniously.

forsaked Misused for *forsook.* • For the project Sheen *forsaked* his Los Angeles base—home to his daughter Lily, 12, with the actress Kate Beckinsale—to revisit his roots. USE *forsook.* • A society where women *forsaked* makeup and clothing (creams, high heels, nylons, etc.) would indeed be an interesting one. USE *forsook.* The past tense of *forsake* is *forsook,* not *forsaked.*

And the past participle is *forsaken,* not *forsaked*: • All my friends have *forsaked* me. USE *forsaken.* • If he had *forsaked* us, and waited for us to believe in Him and worship Him then that would be unfair. USE *forsaken.*

Present	**Present Participle**	**Past**	**Past Participle**
forsake	forsaking	forsook	forsaken

forte Misused for *forte. Forte* (FORT) means one's strong point; the strongest part of the blade of a sword. *Forte* (FOR-tay) is a musical notation meaning loud or forceful.

F

Misguided, impressionable people think the words, though spelled the same, are pronounced the same. They are two different words (one of French derivation, one of Italian), and they have two different pronunciations.

fortuitous Misused for *fortunate* (or similar words). • Some of these days, now that we are a dominant, if not *the* dominant power in the world, we may have to make good without allies or time or *fortuitous* circumstances to assist us. USE *fortunate.* • Apparently the first precondition has been achieved, as evidenced in the Palestinian participation in the Madrid Conference as part of the Jordanian delegation, and by their acceptance of the Oslo Agreement, in the hope that more *fortuitous* circumstances would develop in the future. USE *fortunate.* • State employees looked on today's results not only as *fortuitous* for themselves, but the services they provide as well. USE *fortunate.* • Payne's timing in volunteering for Saudi Arabia was simultaneously awful and *fortuitous:* His departure was right before the Christmas rush. USE *lucky.*

Fortuitous means happening by chance, accidental or unplanned. It does not mean—despite the efforts of a good many bothersome people—fortunate or lucky.

forward Misused for *foreword.* • Cynthia teams up with Roopster Roux to write the *forward* for *Roopster Roux presents . . . Modern Day Fairy Tales.* USE *foreword.* • The *forward* consists of three sections. USE *foreword.* • As he points out in the *forward* of the book, you will find the inches and centimeters approach to measurements used in his illustrations. USE *foreword.* • Exclusive *forward* for Mario Puzo's *The Godfather* by bestselling crime novelist Stuart Woods. USE *foreword.*

Authors often confuse *forward* with *foreword. Forward* has a number of meanings, most of which people are familiar with. Among its meanings, however, is not introductory remarks in, say, a book; this meaning belongs to *foreword.*

forwards Misused for *forward.* • The paddle tip describes a figure-eight pattern and each stage of the cycle produces *forwards* movement. USE *forward.* • Each click will accelerate the clock in a *forwards* direction. USE *forward.*

As an adverb, either *forwards* or *forward* is correct. As an adjective, only *forward* (in American English, if not in British English) is correct. SEE ALSO **afterwards**; **backwards**; **towards**.

fourty Misspelling of *forty.* • The Pats enter the holiday break in second place in the East Division with a 20-13-0-1 record and *fourty*-one points. USE *forty.* • *Fourty*-two-year-old Rick Armbruster was last seen in a bar in Indian River on October 11. USE *Forty.*

Forty, not *fourty,* is the correct spelling.

fowl Misused for *foul.* • If it has a *fowl* smell, you should reject that wine. USE *foul.* • I believe that while even Potter's author shows murder as a *fowl* act, young people just don't need to read about any more violence. USE *foul.*

And *foul* is misused for *fowl*: • They used these assays in seven TMJ patients who had described recent contact with domestic *foul* (chickens, pigeons, etc.) or pet birds (canaries, etc.), plus ten other TMJ patients who had no close contact with birds (controls). USE *fowl.*

Fowl is any of several large, domestic birds used for food; the flesh of these birds. *Foul* means offensive to the senses; stinking; filthy; putrid; obscene; abominable; inclement; not according to the rules of a game; dishonest.

fraud Misused for *defraud.* • He *frauded* the city. USE *defrauded.* • If you were *frauded* by GrandTechDigital with false capacity we need you to send messages to other eBay members to warn them to test! USE *defrauded.* • I have been *frauded* by companies who were trying to represent these companies. USE *defrauded.* • I still want to hear more stories from some buyers who have been *frauded.* USE *defrauded.*

The verb is *defraud;* the noun is *fraud.* Some people are wont to disregard prefixes and suffixes, thinking, perhaps, the root of a word is or should be quite enough to convey a word's correct meaning; others cannot be bothered to pronounce any word that is disyllabic.

fraudulate Misused for *fraudulent.* • The banking industry right now is hurting pretty bad from *fraudulate* loans booked, high LTV loans booked, and the increase in adjustable-rate mortgages that don't meet the banks' debt-to-income ratio anymore. USE *fraudulent.* • What is more unfortunate is that these people are learning such weak and *fraudulate* techniques, masquerading as authentic Aikijutsu. USE *fraudulent.* • I have confidence in the card company but this *fraudulate* hoodia deal has got to be stopped. USE *fraudulent.* • All I have received from them are lies, threats, blackmail, and *fraudulate* activity. USE *fraudulent.*

Fraudulate is also used by some people as a verb: • They can only *fraudulate* so many votes before they just can't keep up with the turnout! • In other words, those who *fraudulate* their research have no high regard for those from whom they wish recognition. • It is illegal to steal, illegal to murder, illegal to *fraudulate* on your taxes.

Whether adjective or verb, *fraudulate* is utter nonsense, and those who use this word are utterly nonsensical.

friend Misused for *befriend.* • That said, if you've read this and agree, do *friend* me. USE *befriend.* • Did they *friend* you or did you *friend* them? USE *befriend.* • I *friend* people for a variety of reasons; some *friend* me back, some don't. USE *befriend.*

To *friend* is being used instead of *befriend* or, perhaps, *ask to be my friend.*

In some ways, the verb *friend* corresponds to the verb *fuck*: "do fuck me . . . ," "did they fuck you . . . did you fuck them?" "I fuck people . . . some fuck me back." Monosyllabic labiodentals both, *fuck* and *friend* are different only in that *fuck,* in the sense of to make love, is a powerful, meaningful word, whereas *friend,* in the sense of to befriend, has no more power or meaning than every other sense of *fuck.* SEE ALSO **fuck**.

friendly Misused for *friendily.* • We saw him twice, and he smiled brightly and genuinely both times and spoke *friendly* to us. USE *friendily.* • The man gestured *friendly,* but the young woman just frowned in suspicion. USE *friendily.*

Others misuse *friendily* for *friendly*: • The staff was very *friendily* and helpful. USE *friendly*. • Using the n900, I forgot how much more user-*friendily* Android was. USE *friendly*.

Friendly is the adjective; *friendily*, awkward to pronounce though it may be, the adverb.

from whence Misused for *whence*. • If the children represent where society is going, then the elderly represent *from whence* we came. USE *whence*. • But I kept thinking about what I'd seen on the sunporch that morning when I wandered in to look out over Lake Margrethe, *from whence* our weather usually comes. USE *whence*. • It's as much for what the industry has grown into as for *from whence* it came that the mechanical engineering society is honoring the Blue Box. USE *whence*. • But *from whence* came this utter restfulness and nobility? USE *whence*.

From whence is redundant for *whence*, which means from what place, from where.

fuck Avoid scatological phrases and swear words: • *Shit*, we wouldn't even see the damn thing from here, where people in the culturally diverse school I work at barely scrape by well beneath the poverty level. • It occurred to me today that I was a little harsh on myself yesterday, talking of my young creative writing graduate school self as an arrogant snot-nosed little *shit*. • *Fuck*. If you're an anchor in Philadelphia and you hate Barbaro, can you please email me? • Of course, leave it to Boston's own Ron Borges to *piss* all over everything. • And to be real, this endless string of *bullshit* is starting to cast a pretty dark cloud over the hip-hop world. • Neighbors who usually trail their hounds with sandwich bags keep hands in pockets; the canine *turdsicles* skitter over frozen earth.

Swear words are among the least expressive words available to us. They are boring and boorish at once. Using scatological phrases and swear words no longer shocks anyone and suggests only that you are not clever enough to think of better, more meaningful words. Very likely, your writing is no more readable than you yourself are companionable. SEE ALSO **friend**.

F

fulsome Misused for *abundant* (or similar words). • As White House aides expressed their glee when independent counsel Kenneth Starr resigned last month, one top official broke ranks, offering Starr *fulsome* praise. Use *gushing*. • In remarks to Fox Business network, Palin didn't exactly offer *fulsome* praise to Bachmann. Use *abundant.* • At no point in his broadcasts did Jones disclose that there was a financial consideration underpinning his *fulsome* editorial support. Use *enthusiastic*. • European leaders marked Reagan's death with unusually *fulsome* praise. Use *effusive*. • The newspaper that published his columns checked his entire oeuvre, and it turns out that Goeglein's thefts were frequent and *fulsome*. Use *numerous.*

Fulsome means insincere, offensively flattering, not, as is meant in these examples, abundant, effusive, or enthusiastic.

> Under certain circumstances, after the sampling part of that process is taken . . . it's supposed to go forward with a more fulsome process.
>
> —Theodore Olson, attorney for George W. Bush
>
> Full or complete is what Olson meant, not *fulsome,* which means insincere or offensive. If someone is to make such an error, it's best not to do so, as Olson did, before the U.S. Supreme Court.

fundage Misused for *funds* (or similar words). • That left me with very little access to emergency *fundage* if needed. Use *funds*. • From its NYC HQ, the fund will offer between $5,000 and $500,000 to start-ups getting into developing for the Apple product, with *fundage* granted dependent on just how complex the mooted App may be. Use *funding*. • If so, it's tax time and I have a small amount of *fundage* to expend. Use *money*.

Though slang to some, *fundage* is thought by others, the acutely impoverished, to be an acceptable synonym for funds or money.

Gg

gaff Misused for *gaffe.* • Ironically, that refusal to disclose his background leads to his professional demise, when an innocent verbal *gaff* in a classroom is instead viewed as a deliberate racist comment. USE *gaffe.* • Gifford chatted about some of the politically incorrect remarks he had heard on TV over the years, seemingly inspired by Russ Limbaugh's recent *gaff* on TV. USE *gaffe.*

A *gaffe* is a social blunder; an embarrassing mistake. A *gaff* is a large hook on a pole used to land large fish; a pole attached to a ship's mast used to extend a sail; a metal spur attached to the leg of a fighting cock; a climbing hook used by workers.

gail Misused for *gale.* • It's been a long week and I'm not feeling like driving to Cape Ann in a *gail.* USE *gale.* • Despite heavy downpours, dropping temps, and *gail* winds, we managed to get a few hours in today and the bite was on! USE *gale.* • The only weather concern over here, short of a hurricane, is very strong *gail*-force tradewinds. USE *gale.* • Before she understood the words, Laura would go into *gails* of laughter over her dad's silly chatter. USE *gales.*

Gale is a strong wind; a forceful outburst. *Gail,* when capitalized, is a name.

gambit Misused for *gamut.* • This video runs the *gambit* of instructional techniques used against various weapons and in real situations. USE *gamut.* • We've tested water all around the world and found that it runs the *gambit* from rock hard to baby bottom soft. USE *gamut.*

Gambit is an opening move in the game of chess in which a piece is sacrificed to get an advantage; an opening maneuver or remark intended to gain an advantage. *Gamut* is a full range of something; all recognized musical notes. To *run the gamut* is to go through the complete range of something.

gambol Misused for *gamble.* • But wealthy men were *gamboling* away their homes and livestock against futures in the tulip-growing industry! Use *gambling.* • Initial intentions are to offer the developed product to major gaming sites for a portion of the advertising revenues as well as develop interest in the *gamboling* industry. Use *gambling.*

To *gambol* is to skip or leap about playfully; to frolic. To *gamble* is to play games of chance; to bet; to take a risk or put at risk.

gauntlet Misused for *gantlet.* • If the odds are against her, they're against him as well and the *gauntlet* of bullets they run on the way to Phoenix is spectacular. Use *gantlet.* • Prince, who is told by Eastwood that he is coming, sets up an incredible police *gauntlet,* hundreds of cops who riddle the bus as it roars into the city. Use *gantlet.* • The new year is just around the corner, but first you have to get through the *gauntlet* of activities. Use *gantlet.*

And *gantlet* is misused for *gauntlet*: • A loss next week will provide the opportunity for him to throw down the *gantlet* publicly. Use *gauntlet.* • For heavy degreasing or cleaning jobs, where your hands are likely to be submerged in solvent, use thicker, over 10 mil, gloves with a *gantlet.* Use *gauntlet.*

A *gantlet* (GANT-lit) is a form of punishment in which a person had to run between two rows of men who struck him with clubs or sticks; a severe trial or ordeal; two railroad tracks that converge into one so that one rail of each track is within the rails of the other. A *gauntlet* (GONT-lit) is a medieval glove covered with metal plates; a fortified glove with a flared cuff; a challenge. *Take up the gauntlet* and *throw down the gauntlet* mean, respectively, to accept a challenge and to issue a challenge.

Many dictionaries today, however, use the spelling *gauntlet* for the word *gantlet.* Some dictionaries maintain that either word may be spelled either or both ways, but what sense can there be to this? Let us promote clarity, a notion lost on lexicographers, by spelling the glove *gauntlet* and the punishment *gantlet.*

gentile Misused for *genteel.* • When men open the doors for ladies and girls, they exhibit a respect for women and encourage their daughters to behave in a feminine and *gentile* fashion. Use *genteel.* • Compared to the strongly etched drama of Shakespeare, Jane Austen's books were more refined, *gentile,* and civilized, and as such Patrick Doyle's score is more elegant and restrained than the tempestuous moods he created for *Henry V* or the exuberant sunniness of *Much Ado About Nothing.* Use *genteel.*

And *gentile* is also misused for *gentle*: • He one of the nicest guys on our team; he's polite, articulate, *gentile.* Use *gentle.* • After the history our people have had, leave it to the Japanese to be forever kind and *gentile.* Use *gentle.*

Gentile (JEN-tile) means any person not a Jew; a Christian; somebody who is not Mormon; someone who does not believe in God. *Genteel* (jen-TEEL) means well-mannered and refined; excessively or pretentiously refined. *Gentle* (JEN-til) means kind; considerate; tender.

gibe Misused for *jibe.* • The Federalist Society would have no reason to do this because the technical, expensive accrediting process does not *gibe* with its mission. Use *jibe.* • While it may be pleasant to think so, it doesn't really *gibe* with reality. Use *jibe.*

And *jibe* is misused for *gibe*: • He jovially *jibed* at his Indian publishers for having made so many mistakes. Use *gibed.* • Chugging up the river side by side, the passengers cheered and *jibed* at one another. Use *gibed.*

To *jibe* is slang for agree. To *gibe* is to scoff or jeer at. As a noun, a *gibe* is an insulting remark. See also **jive.**

gift . . . (with) Misused for *give* (or similar words). • *Gift* her a soft Pashmina wrap to keep her cozy and she will know that you really care. Use *Give.* • *Gift* them with something that will last a lifetime! *Gift* them with a winning résumé from us. Use *Give.* • Keep them all for yourself or *gift* them for the holidays. Use *give.* • Keeping alive this charming tradition not only gives family and friends an opportunity to *gift* the bride but also to share some personal, intimate moments while the bride ends her single life and begins on her road to marriage. Use *buy a gift for.* • If you have one specific cause in mind you can *gift* stocks and shares to CAF, naming the charity you wish to benefit from the proceeds. Use *donate.*

Though *gift* as a verb is an antiquated form, the use of it today is nonsense, even offensive. When we have words such as *give* and *donate* or *make a gift of, gift* the verb is patent commercialese for *buy* or *purchase.* SEE ALSO **shop (it) against**.

(he) goes Only the adolescent or the addle-brained prefer this gruesome *goes* to acknowledge; admit; announce; assert; asseverate; aver; avow; comment; confess; cry; declare; disclose; divulge; exclaim; mention; note; observe; proclaim; pronounce; remark; reveal; say; state; utter. • They say they don't know anything, and then they *go,* "If we hear anything, we'll call you." USE *say*. • He walked into the room, and she *goes,* "Guess what?" USE *exclaims*. • I asked what do you like about her, and he *went,* "I don't know." USE *confessed*. • And then he *goes,* "I don't want to see you anymore." USE *announces*. SEE ALSO **like**.

G

go (move; proceed) forward These useless expressions are spoken and written by people who seem unable to remember that the English language has both a present and a future tense. *Going forward, moving forward,* and the like are used instead of, or along with, present- or future-tense expressions. This may mean that, before long, people will not easily be able to distinguish between the present and the future, or that they may not be able to think in terms of the future. Already, there is evidence of this, for many of us are without imagination and foresight: • *Going forward,* the companies will conduct business under the name TechTeam. DELETE *Going forward*. • We have a lot of small players *going forward* and they're getting bullied out of games and we're not playing to their strengths. DELETE *going forward*.

> What else are you working on, musicwise, going forward?
>
> —Brooke Anderson, CNN reporter
>
> We are looking for moderate growth in the U.S. economy going forward.
>
> —Ben Bernanke, Federal Reserve Board chairman

> This experience will change me forever going forward.
>
> —Sheldon Yellen, Belfor CEO
>
> And going forward we will continue to keep the U.S. public fully updated.
>
> —President Barack Obama
>
> We're looking forward to moving forward positively.
>
> —U.S. Senator Tom Price
>
> Each individual woman is welcome to proceed forward if she can afford to do that.
>
> —Suzette Malveaux, lawyer

gone (went) missing Misused for *disappeared* (or similar words). • The boy *went missing* Monday, the day after his birthday. Use *disappeared.* • The estranged husband of a woman who *went missing* five years ago has been charged with her murder. Use *vanished.* • In heavily Democratic Fulton County, in downtown Atlanta, 67 memory cards from the voting machines *went missing,* delaying certification of the results there. Use *were misplaced.* • When a $250,000 boat *went missing* while docked at the foot of Grand Street in Alameda, police seemed lost at sea. Use *was stolen.* • A large and potentially hazardous asteroid that *went missing* almost 66 years ago was rediscovered by astronomers on Wednesday morning. Use *was lost.* • Fifteen people aboard the ship reportedly *went missing.* Use *were missing.* • Many *went missing* after joining the militant groups, while others disappeared after being picked up by security forces for questioning. Use *deserted.* • The prisoner *went missing* around lunchtime, but prison staff did not notice his absence until early evening. Use *absconded.* • She's a grown woman, and reasonable people can and should understand that if they are going to *go missing,* they are going to cause public outcry. Use *disappear.*

Gone (went) missing is the phrase to use if you dislike subtlety and exactitude, honesty and insight. Use it also if you're easily influenced, disposed to speak as others speak and think as others think, and receptive to every malodorous term that wafts your way.

People are so dull-witted and impressionable that today, in this country, the popularity of *gone* or *went missing* has soared. Words such as *disappeared, vanished, misplaced, stolen, lost, deserted,* and *absconded* are less often heard today because *went missing* has less meaning, or less exact meaning, than any of them, and people, especially the media, politicians, and businesspeople, are loath to express themselves clearly. What's more, *went missing* sounds willful or deliberate, and sometimes that connotation is accurate, but the child who has been kidnapped is hardly agreeable to having been so.

Gone (went) missing appeals to people because it's largely meaningless and because it's a fad term. Few people who are conscious of how they speak, of the words they use, say *gone* or *went missing.*

good Misused for *well.* • I tried to play my heart out and did the best I could; we really all did *good.* Use *well.* • He is funny and sings *good* enough to give us a pleasant performance. Use *well.* • What programs run *good* with other programs? Use *well.* • Currently the 2-in-1 Comfort Shorty is my favorite pen/stylus combo: It looks good, it writes *good,* and it has a nice price. Use *well.* • Here in the mountains, the radar doesn't work too *good.* Use *well.*

Well, not *good,* is the word that accompanies the verbs shown in the examples. *Well* may be used as an adjective or an adverb. *Good* is always an adjective and should never modify a verb.

With sensory verbs like *feel, taste, smell,* and linking verbs like *be, appear,* and *seem, good* is the word to use ("At the starting line, you could tell she wasn't feeling too good"; "We felt good about ourselves last year when we beat them twice"; "Corn yields appear good, but harvesting is still behind its average pace"; "Our first obligation is to ensure that the water tastes good"; "So far everything seems good").

People who use *good* where *well* should be are soulless speakers, hopeless writers.

gorilla Misused for *guerrilla.* • Kelly ran his pizza operation in a very competitive arena where *gorilla* marketing played a major role in controlling his market share. Use *guerrilla.* • There is no way for a country to defend itself against the U.S. other than to fight using *gorilla* warfare. Use *guerrilla.*

A *gorilla* is a large and powerful ape; a person who is regarded as, or who looks like, a gorilla; a thug. A *guerrilla* (or *guerilla*) is a member of a band of volunteer soldiers bent on defeating a more established enemy; a terrorist. As an adjective, *guerrilla* relates to unconventional marketing practices (*guerrilla marketing*), or drama about political or social issues that is usually performed outside (*guerrilla theater*).

gourmand Confused with *gourmet.* A *gourmand* (goor-MOND) is a lover of food who likely eats to excess ("They savored French words with all the gusto of a Parisian gourmand"). A *gourmet* (goor-MAY) is a connoisseur of foods and drinks; an epicure ("Thailand is a gourmet's paradise"). As an adjective, *gourmet* means of or relating to fine foods ("Add gourmet food to the point-and-click world of Amazon.com").

graduated Misused for *graduated from.* • The study showed 83 percent of Latinos and 80 percent of blacks failed the 10th-grade math exam, which will be a requirement to *graduate* high school in 2003. Use *graduate from.* • I *graduated* high school by taking the GED exam. Use *graduated from.* • Older cohorts of the population were much less likely to have *graduated* high school than younger cohorts. Of those born in the years 1938 to 1943, only about 76 percent *graduated* high school; of those born between 1973 and 1978, 88 percent had *graduated* high school. Use *graduated from.*

The use of *graduated,* instead of *graduated from* (or, perhaps, *was graduated from*), displays a remarkable lack of learning. More than many solecisms, *graduated* taints the talker and, with each new reader, ridicules the writer.

After graduating high school in 1985, Kravits received an acting scholarship to the University of Maryland and spent the next six years doing theater in Washington, D.C., before moving to New York City, where he acted in commercials and small theater productions.

—Jason Lynch and Allison Singh Gee, *People*

Two people are apparently not enough to write a grammatically correct sentence at *People* magazine, where the writing is so often reminiscent of someone who never did graduate *from* high school.

grammer Misspelling of *grammar.* • I've found a few things to teach *grammer,* parts of speech, and that sort of thing for her grade level. USE *grammar.* • One's abilities with basic *grammer* and usage are every bit as important as one's abilities with grooming and cleanliness. USE *grammar.*

Grammar is the correct spelling.

This site has a great deal of information about the basics of English grammer.

—Mid-Continent Public Library

The basics of English *grammar* surely include knowing how to spell the word.

granite Misused for *granted.* • Prior to this experience of observation and teaching, I took for *granite* lessons, never once stopping and questioning where they came from. USE *granted.* • Literacy is clearly very valuable as it helps us complete many activities we take for *granite,* such as using the Internet, filling out applications, earning our driver's license, looking up phone numbers, and voting. USE *granted.*

Granite is a very hard igneous rock often used in buildings. To *take for granted* is to assume something is true without question, or to fail to appreciate the worth of someone or something.

> Despite their easy Primary race, Smith and Caiola said they aren't taking anything for granite.
>
> —Jeff Werner, *Yardley News*

great That which is called *great* is seldom more than *good,* and that which is *good* is scarcely mentionable. *Great* (as well as more contemporary, if less sensible, words like *phat* and *bad* and *w00t*) is one of several words that people rely on to express favorable emotions. Among these English-language prattlers, however, there is scant subtlety of emotion and little distinction in thought. SEE ALSO **awesome**; **w00t**.

greatful Misused for *grateful.* • All of the men are in good condition, and we're really *greatful* for that. USE *grateful.* • While they are *greatful* for all the outpouring of support, they do not wish that another home be built on that site. USE *grateful.* • And he seemed *greatful* for the praise. USE *grateful.* • We really get to do a lot of hands-on things, to talk to people, and it's exciting too, because they're so *greatful* for it. USE *grateful.*

Grateful means thankful or expressing gratitude. Though *great* is a word, an adjective, *greatful* is not.

gregorious Misused for *gregarious.* • My father, a man of discipline, is *gregorious* and helpful. USE *gregarious.* • In the story he talks about how Walt was *gregorious* and athletic, and so were the other guys. USE *gregarious.* • Moore has a rather *gregorious* personality, and as a result, he counts many Greene Countians, including other politicians, as his friends. USE *gregarious.*

Gregarious (gri-GAIR-ee-es) means sociable; fond of the company of others. *Gregorious,* in the sense of *gregarious,* is wholly incorrect.

grief Misused for *grieve.* • It is a pity and I *grief* over this every once in a while. USE *grieve.* • Do they not use sounds to annoy someone when they *grief*? USE *grieve.* • *Griefers* don't have fun unless they *grief.* USE *Grievers; grieve.*

Grief is the noun; *grieve,* the verb. A person who grieves is a griever, not a griefer. Good grieve!

grizzly Misused for *grisly* • When a popular youth pastor is accused of a *grizzly* crime, MacLaren won't rest until she finds the truth. USE *grisly.* • The American recalls every *grizzly* detail and so does Monty, who also hasn't forgotten what playing for your country can do to an individual. USE *grisly.* • Although a bit *grizzly* in light of recent events, it presents a fascinating case study to pose to high school and university students. USE *grisly.* • There hasn't been a national tragedy in my memory that wasn't coupled with *grizzly,* awful humor, told at the expense of the most injured, often within hours of the injury itself. USE *grisly.*

And *grisly* is sometimes misused for *grizzly*: • Managing to glance back you see it is in fact a giant *grisly* bear snarling ferociously and wanting to destroy you. USE *grizzly.* • If Joe liked a person, they would often be treated to a joke and a complimenting slap on the back by one of Joe's greasy, *grisly*-bear-sized paws. USE *grizzly.*

Grizzly means grayish; a North American brown bear. *Grisly,* causing horror or disgust.

grocery The pronunciation of *grocery* is (GRO-sah-ree), not (GRO-shree).

grow As business jargon, *grow* has hypertrophied into something ugly and ungainly: • We merged Navision Software and Damgaard to *grow* the business, to take us closer to our goal. USE *expand.* • The coupons and strategies on this page are just a fraction of the useful strategies that may be used to *grow* profits. USE *increase.* • These are just two examples of our plans to diversify and *grow* income from our existing and new customer base. USE *earn.*

guesstimate Misused for *guess* (or similar words). • If you would like a *guesstimate* of time required for your site, we would be happy to give you one. USE *estimate.* • Yet with just a few moments of thought you can make a surprisingly good *guesstimate.* USE *guess.* • They were asked to guess what the contents were and *guesstimate* how many objects were in the envelope. USE *guess.* • We know that at this time you may not know the exact style or quantities, but a *guesstimate* of the extent of your participation will help us in the planning. Use *estimate.*

Guesstimate is a perfectly ridiculous merger that people who are uncomfortable with using *guess* will turn to. Most of us prefer knowing to not knowing, or at least we prefer letting others believe we are knowledgeable. *Guesstimate* adds authority to a *guess,* leeway to an *estimate.*

guild Misused for *gild.* • I need to mend some damage and clean then *guild* the frame. Use *gild.* • While many can appreciate the effort to *reguild* the walls of Adams dining hall, we'd rather be able to sit down to a hot breakfast. Use *regild.*

Gild, a verb, means to cover with a thin sheet of gold. *Guild,* a noun, is an association of people who have much the same job or interests. According to some dictionaries, *gild* is a variant spelling of *guild,* but it is far better to spell the two words in two ways.

Hh

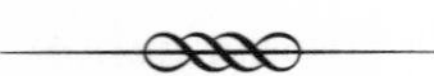

hail and hardy Misused for *hale and hearty.* • We are *hail and hardy* and wise enough not to ride. Use *hale and hearty.* • She is *hail and hardy,* exercises every day, and is very active. Use *hale and hearty.*

Others manage to use one of the two correct words: • Jacob Schirf, of Nicktown, is *hale and hardy* at age 75. Use *hale and hearty.* • Many people visualize a successful salesperson as a *hail and hearty* person with an outgoing personality. Use *hale and hearty.*

Hale and hearty is an idiom meaning strong and healthy; fit and robust. See also **hale**; **hardy**.

hairbrained Misused for *harebrained.* • Hitler can be seen as coming up with all sorts of *hairbrained* schemes, but they all had the virtue that they conceivably could have affected the eventual outcome of the war, and only *hairbrained* schemes had that promise. Use *harebrained.* • The small voices of *hairbrained* ideas are very easy to hear. Use *harebrained.* • Grove, Barrett, Gelsinger, and Co. still know how to design and build great semiconductors, so how come none of them is saying "no" to the marketing department when they come up with their latest *hairbrained* scheme to launch a crappy chipset that doesn't work, or a processor that can't be delivered? Use *harebrained.*

Harebrained means foolish; flighty; having or showing no more sense than a hare. People who use *hairbrained* have less sense still. See also **harrass**.

hale Misused for *hail.* The Indians have a superstitious fear of northern rain because they thought that snow and *hale* are pieces of the bones of people who died a long time ago. Use *hail.* • But then I found that the easiest way to do these missions is to *hale* a cab. Use *hail.*

And *hail* is sometimes misused for *hale*: • I look fit, healthy, and *hail,* although my generous curves remain the same. USE *hale.*

Hail is a form of frozen rain; as a noun, it also is a greeting or shout to someone; as a verb, to *hail* means to greet or call out to get someone's attention. *Hale* means sound, healthy. SEE ALSO **hail and hardy**; **hardy**.

hangar Misused for *hanger.* • An over-the-door clothes *hangar* will expand your hanging capabilities. USE *hanger.* • Another challenge, more recently, was who invented the clothes *hangar*? USE *hanger.* • You hang your clothes on the *hangar* and put your shoes in the bag. USE *hanger.*

A *hangar* is a building that houses airplanes and the like. A *hanger* is a device used for hanging clothes or other items.

H

harbringer Misspelling of *harbinger.* • Cirrus clouds are almost always a *harbringer* of bad weather. USE *harbinger.* • I hate to be a *harbringer* of more bad news, but get ready and start saving. USE *harbinger.* • No caution-minded bride thinks of carrying a bouquet made up solely of red and white flowers—that floral combination is a *harbringer* of death. USE *harbinger.* • These struggles in the "developing" world could possibly serve as a *harbringer* of the future in the West. USE *harbinger.*

A *harbinger* is a herald; someone who or something that foretells the future. The barbarous *harbringer* is a slayer of sense, a taker of souls.

hardly . . . than Misused for *hardly . . . when.* • At Rome he had learned Latin and Greek, and *hardly* had he left the school of rhetoric *than* he ventured on a commentary on Abdias the Prophet. USE *hardly . . . when.* • *Hardly* had the surgeons opened me up *than* my aorta, an artery that runs from heart to head, ruptured. USE *Hardly . . . when.*

The expression *no sooner . . . than* is correct, but *hardly . . . than,* despite its currency, is incorrect. This error is also found in the phrases *scarcely . . . than* and *barely . . . than,* both of which require *when,* not *than.* SEE ALSO **no sooner . . . then (when)**; **not hardly (barely**; **scarcely)**.

hardy Misused for *hearty.* • Menu items include favorite Mexican entrées that will appease any *hardy* appetite. USE *hearty.* • Located in the Blue

Ridge Mountains of Virginia, our beautiful stone lodge offers a warm and *hardy* welcome to park visitors. USE *hearty.* • If you are hungry for a *hardy* meal, chances are your labor is still in the early phase and you will be able to digest this meal without difficulty. USE *hearty.* • He smiled *hardily* at her. USE *heartily.*

And *hearty* is sometimes misused for *hardy*: • All three are excellent beginner herbs and they are *hearty* perennials that do well in the Chicagoland area. USE *hardy.*

Hardy means robust, vigorous; daring, courageous; able to survive difficult or winter conditions. *Hearty* means warm, friendly; enthusiastic; unrestrained; strong, healthy; nourishing, satisfying; needing or enjoying a good deal of food. SEE ALSO **hail and hardy**; **hale**.

> It's a task hardily joined by heavyweights Microsoft and Yahoo, along with an ever-expanding list of smaller players.
>
> —Steven Levy, *Newsweek*

harrass Misspelling of *harass.* • I'm a teacher and we have noticed the increased incidence of children, especially girls, using the text buttons of cellphones to bully and *harrass.* USE *harass.* • And they don't *harrass* me nearly as often; I can live with that. USE *harass.* • As with most abusers he feels he's done nothing wrong and to this day he continues to *harrass* me. USE *harass.*

Harass has but one *r.* Clever people—those who spell the word correctly, perhaps—pronounce it (hah-RASS); others pronounce it (HAIR-es). SEE ALSO **hairbrained**.

hawk Misused for *hock.* • Despite the finance minister's declaration that we are in *hawk* up to our eyeballs, the government continues to ignore the perilous fiscal situation we have created and continues to sustain in land claim settlements. USE *hock.* • Often a new contract, written in a foreign language, is forced on the employee once she's in *hawk* for her fees and far away from home. USE *hock.* • If Susan dies, *hawk* her things. USE *hock.*

Slang though it may be, *hock* means to pawn; *in hock* means in debt.

Hawk, of course, is a bird of prey; a person who preys on others; a person who favors military action.

heal Misused for *heel.* • Thomas, who has been bothered by a slight tear in his Achilles *heal,* said he plans to practice Friday. USE *heel.* • Fragments of a child's shoe *heal* attached with wooden pegs were also recovered. USE *heel.* It often occurs in women who wear thin-soled, tight, narrow high-*healed* shoes. • USE *heeled.*

To *heal* is to make well or restore health; to cause a wound to be repaired; to recover or reconcile. A *heel* is the back part of a foot; the part of a stocking or shoe that covers the heel; something that resembles a heel; a cad.

H

healthy Misused for *healthful.* • Thus, when New England travels to Denver to open its season next Monday night, Drew Bledsoe will be healthy and Terry Glenn will be healthy and Bruce Armstrong will be as healthy as a guy can be after he's played pro football for nearly a dozen years and Ben Coates will be healthy and everyone else on offense who matters will be healthy, and that is a *healthy* situation. USE *healthful.* • What's more, Mrs. deBarra always thought that granola bars and popcorn were *healthy* snacks. USE *healthful.*

The distinction between these two words is becoming increasingly rarefied. Still, the difference in their meanings is worth observing. Let us use *healthy* to mean enjoying good health, and *healthful* to mean contributing to or promoting good health.

heart-rendering Misused for *heartrending.* • These *heart-rendering* statistics might lead you or a friend to adopt some simple preventive measures that could save your lives. USE *heartrending.* • This is one of the most *heart-rendering* books I've read. USE *heartrending.* • The loss of life is described with *heart-rendering* details of loss and mourning. USE *heartrending.*

To *rend* means to tear something apart; to cause emotional pain or distress to. To *render,* quite a different word, means to provide or give; to make; to depict; to translate; to perform; to melt down fat; to process an animal carcass.

Whether it is a singles or seniors meeting, a women's or men's conference, or a family church event, Venna keeps the excitement of accomplishment alive with entertaining stories and heart-rendering messages that touch the soul.

—Venna Bishop

Speaker Venna Bishop "delivers dynamic programs that improve attitudes, strengthen character, create vivid visual images, instill patriotism, address overcoming fears, cultivate teamwork," and promote the maltreatment of the English language.

heartship Misused for *hardship.* • Your financial *heartship* may be their crucible to true adulthood. USE *hardship.* • We each have to write a letter telling what *heartship* there would be to us if he doesn't get the visa. USE *hardship.* • In spite of *heartship,* she was a happy woman, content and thankful for all she had. USE *hardship.*

This misusage further signals the future of the English language. If people continue to heed laxicographers and descriptive linguists (fascinated as they are by this kind of "new usage"), the words will not matter. "Any spelling, any usage, any meaning"—the motto of all ding-a-linguists.

hecticity Misused for *frenzy* (or similar words). • By now I am accustomed to all the *hecticity* of these events. USE *stir.* • Since the concept of alienation is too wide and varied, I refined my goal by concentrating on the *hecticity* of contemporary urban life, and the artist's role in creating cultural change in the form of public works that can find a larger audience. USE *franticness.* • But even if I was miserable and discouraged—in the *hecticity* of departure I'd left my warm jacket at home, so I had to bundle up as best I could with every shirt I'd brought and a paper-thin rain shell—many others weren't. USE *disorder.* • Amid the *hecticity* of existence, we perceive the celestial bodies as phenomena that calm and reassure. USE *chaos.* • With people around the globe suffering from what we here call *hecticity,* a pace and schedule so hectic it hurts, here is a book that considers the "disease" to be one that organizational leaders must recognize as serious—yet addressable. Use *tumult.*

This is an abominable word—one that a silly celebrity or a descriptive linguist might love. As you see, many words readily mean what *hecticity* struggles to. That this word is used by a few impressionable people is hardly reason for more discriminating ones to embrace it. Not all words are worthy.

heighth Misused for *height* • Martinville girls have *heighth,* talent. Use *height.* • In the high jump, senior Matt Kenny of Red Cloud placed sixth with a *heighth* of 6-2. Use *height.* • This perspective from the center of the Lorenz barn gives an idea of the *heighth* and breadth Dan Otto and Bruce Conley talk about when envisioning a country cathedral. Use *height.* • In the case of dollhouse furniture, your main concern will be the size of the tabletop and the *heighth* of the legs. Use *height.* • Also check the *heighth* of their fifth-wheel hitches (ask about minimum *heighth*); most new trucks have increased their ride *heighth* up to 4 inches over the past three years. Use *height.* • Students will learn how to estimate the *heighth* of a tree. Use *height.*

Though *heighth* has a history, today the standard spelling is *height,* and the correct pronunciation is (HIGHT), not (HIGHTH).

heinous The pronunciation of *heinous* is (HAY-nes), not (HEE-nes).

herb The pronunciation of *herb* is (ERB), not (HURB). See also **an.**

hereinafter Misused for *hereafter.* • Consciousness is the key assuredly; who made it, to what end is of less importance in our present tense as we'll have plenty of time to debate it in the *hereinafter* however we choose to define it. Use *hereafter.* • Briefly, I believe that more stringent requirements should not be placed on digital broadcasters as opposed to regular broadcasters, but the digital broadcasters should have to comply with all present and *hereinafter* adopted regulations on each of their broadcast streams. Use *hereafter.*

Hereinafter means in the following part of a document or speech. *Hereafter* means the state after death; after or following this; in the future.

heroine Misused for *heroin* • All *heroine* that is available in Europe is of Afghan origin. USE *heroin*. • It's easy to overdose on *heroine*, which can cause a coma and/or death. USE *heroin*.

A *heroine* is the principal female character in a novel or story; a woman of outstanding courage and strength of character. *Heroin* is a highly addictive drug derived from morphine.

> My distracting point with drugs was during my second year in the faculty of commerce and by the second term I was constantly injecting myself with cocaine and occasionally sniffing heroine.
>
> —Reham Wafy, Teen Stuff Online
>
> That ending *e* makes quite a difference. All who believe that meaning matters little, that spelling matters less, that usage matters least, consider our fair *heroin*.

hey Certain words do not belong to the realm of writing, or at least nonfiction writing: the juvenile *hey* is clearly one of them. • They talk about what a steal that was, but—*hey!*—that was almost 40 years ago. DELETE *hey*. • *Hey*, I'm not saying Zambrano and Clement are bad. DELETE *Hey*. • Converse is drawing heat from antigun folks for its new sneaker called Loaded Weapon. *Hey*, it could be worse; could be the name of a new diaper. DELETE *Hey*. • *Hey*, why abandon a game plan that appeals so beautifully to the baser instincts of fellow Americans? DELETE *Hey*. • Please accept my apology for sounding so painfully like an agent, but *hey*, these are the business facts of the situation. DELETE *hey*. SEE ALSO **I'll tell you**; **like**; **OK (okay)**; **so**; **well**.

> Hey, I'm hardly against men pitching in around the house and helping with kids, or listening to their wives concerns (in fact as a mother of three with another little one on the way, I'm all for it).
>
> —Betsy Hart, *Jewish World Review*

> Hey, in a country where not actually winning the popular vote can lead to the Oval Office, it pays to aim low.
>
> —Kimberly Reyes, *Entertainment*
>
> *Hey* is exclamatory, but only less than able writers—however friendly they wish to appear—would use it, in effect, as an inverted exclamation mark with which to capture our flagging attention.

Perhaps the best way to discourage people from using *hey* is to respond with a hearty, lubricious *diddle, diddle*?

hiatus The pronunciation of *hiatus* is (hi-AY-tes), not (hee-AY-tes).

him (me) . . . -ing Misused for *his (my) . . . -ing.* • Aside from *him* being an athlete and *me* being an athlete, he's my husband and I'm here to show support for him. USE *his; my.* • Senator Lugar, I very much appreciate *you for* joining us. USE *your.* • So what name do you belong to, if you don't mind *me* asking? USE *my.* • I do vaguely remember *him* being badly spoken. USE *his.* • Any chance of *me* being sent that $1,400 before the end of the month? USE *my.* • Do you mind *us* going? USE *our.* • There is no prohibition against *them* making this information available either to the FDA or to their customers. USE *their.*

Use the possessive pronoun, not the personal pronoun, before verbal nouns ending in *-ing.*

historic Misused for *historical.* • Imperiled by habitat loss, invading species, and other known and unknown dangers, up to a third of U.S. amphibians have disappeared in part of their *historic* ranges. USE *historical.* • Miller Dunwiddie Architects earned AIA Minnesota's 2001 Firm Award by providing clients with technical expertise, design savvy, and *historic* authenticity. USE *historical.* • Mexico's peso currency fell to a new *historic* closing low on Wednesday, weakened by fears of a jump in inflation. USE *historical.* • Partisan differences over both national security and domestic issues are at a *historic* high a year before election day, according to an in-depth voter poll by the Pew Research Center for the People and the Press. Use *historical.*

And *historical* is sometimes misused for *historic:* • The highly publicized murder was a *historical* turning point in New York's fight against lawlessness, prompting police programs that led to dramatic crime reductions. Use *historic.* • This was a *historical* day for Antrim midfielder Edel Mason, as she became the first player to have won an intermediate medal with two counties, namely Down and Antrim. Use *historic.*

Historical means relating to history, whereas *historic* means having importance in history. It's especially unsettling when the word *historic* is used to describe events that are nothing of the sort—indeed, wholly unimportant or forgettable: • It is a *historic* piece of mail; it's the most ambitious single piece of political mail ever undertaken. Delete *historic.* • Sampson wouldn't reveal proposals, but says the meeting will *be historic and* address recent scandals in college basketball. Delete *be historic and.* • All the scoring chances didn't mean much, though, even if it was a *historic* night with some of Hollywood's pretty people. Delete *historic.* See also **an**.

H

hoi polloi Misused for *hoity-toity* (or similar words). • And can the Knights exact a whangy-twangy revenge on the snobby *hoi-polloi* society group that caused Tubby's to be closed down in the first place, while eluding the doofus cops who are hot on their trail at every turn? Use *hoity-toity.* • Soon nurses, handing out programs—when you get a bit this good, you just have to run with it—are seating tuxedoed and fur-draped members of the *hoi polloi.* Use *elite.*

Greek for the many, *hoi polloi,* which has come to mean the common people or the masses, is sometimes confused with *hoity-toity,* dialectal for snobbish, pompous, or pretentiously self-important. That is, some people use *hoi polloi* thinking it means the opposite of what it actually does mean.

hold up Misused for *holed up.* • Plans take a turn for the worst when everyone is forced to spend the night *hold up* inside the diner at the hands of a ruthless prison escapee. Use *holed up.* • Russian forces bombarded the tiny town from the ground and the air Monday to dislodge dozens of Chechen fighters *hold up* inside the local police station. Use *holed up.*

• Barajas appeared unaffected by the first stun gun shot, used his machete to cut the wires of the second shot, and charged police on the third shot, jumping through the window of a house where he had been *hold up* for about seven hours. USE *holed up*.

To *hold up* is to rob, often at gunpoint; to prevent from falling; to halt or delay; to remain vital or strong or lasting. To *hole up* is to hide oneself.

homage *Homage* is better pronounced (OM-ij), as *heir* is better pronounced (AIR) and *herb* (ERB). Most dictionaries today show (HOM-ij) as the first listed pronunciation, but this may mean only that it's how the word is most often pronounced, not that it's preferable to (OM-ij). Or it may mean nothing much at all:

- *Merriam-Webster's Collegiate Dictionary* shows 'ä-mij first and 'hä-mij second but in their Explanatory Notes write "A second-place variant is not to be regarded as less acceptable than the pronunciation that is given first."

- The *Oxford American Dictionary,* which shows '(h)ämij, writes "The more common pronunciation is listed first, if this can be determined, but many variants are so common and widespread as to be of equal status."

hone Misused for *home.* • Several companies *hone* in on web performance. USE *home.* • UCSF researchers develop a faster way to *hone* in on cancer genes. USE *home.* • Sun.net will enable resellers to *hone* in on searches. USE *home.*

To *hone* is to sharpen or perfect, whereas to *home in* is to move or be guided toward a goal or destination. No dictionary that maintains that *home in* is synonymous with *hone in* ought to be consulted further.

> It was a simpler recommendation to simply say everyone over age fifty get vaccinated than to try to hone in on the specific chronic illnesses that would be in that group.
>
> —Dr. Julie Gerberding, director, CDC

Home in, not *hone in,* is what Dr. Gerberding means to say. One must wonder what other words, what other data, she and the CDC have spoken or written that are not quite correct, not quite accurate, not quite meant.

They're not just looking for personality; they hone in on those key personality traits.

—Client in an eHarmony.com TV commercial

Having well-spoken clients is not among eHarmony's key concerns.

H

hopefully Misused for *I hope* (or similar phrases). • I'm really enjoying it at the moment and *hopefully* that will carry on. Use *I hope.* • Unfortunately, it happened; *hopefully,* he won't have to regret it for the rest of his life. Use *we hope.* • But a few are like me—*hopefully* a future professor who will go on into grad school. Use *I hope.* • This time, *hopefully,* people realize we have more time and resources and money. Use *let's hope.* • *Hopefully* this helps people see what Susquehannock soccer is all about. Use *We hope.*

Hopefully means in a hopeful manner; it does not mean I hope or let's hope or it is to be hoped. Incorrectly using *hopefully*—all most people have any knowledge of—tells a good deal about a person's relationship with the English language. A person who uses *hopefully* correctly—as in: • So much of nature speaks *hopefully* to me, from the singing of the birds, the laughter of children, to the occasional straight drive on the golf course. • United substitute Diego Forlan ran *hopefully* toward it but collapsed under Martin Keown's challenge. • More often the white-crowned sparrow sang *hopefully* in the night.—is clearly conscious of how he speaks and writes; he who uses it as in the earlier examples is likely unconscious of a good deal more than this one misusage. See also **thankfully**.

horde Misused for *hoard.* • A gang of Wakamba tribesmen raided one of the Yaaku villages, killing many and stealing their *horde* of ivory. Use *hoard.* • But we also understand that most companies will *horde* their knowledge and refuse to share it for fear of losing some of that control.

Use *hoard.* • The idea behind it was to create discussion on why people *horde* possessions and the meanings attached to the objects. Use *hoard.* • They *horde* hockey cards and pore over their favorite players' stats. Use *hoard.*

A *hoard* is a hidden stock of something; a cache. As a verb, *hoard* means to accumulate a hoard; to keep hidden or private. A *horde* is a large group of people; a crowd; a nomadic tribe.

how's about Misused for *how about.* • *How's about* rattling off our top five Expos of all-time? Use *How about.* • *How's about* a monthly column in the food section devoted to just local and regional wines? Use *How about.*

How about is an idiom for what do you think about or how do you feel about. *How's about* is sloppy speech, dreadful writing that makes no sense whatever ("how is about"; "how has about").

human The pronunciation of *human* is (HYOO-men), not (YOO-men). See also **an**.

humongous Misused for *huge* (or similar words). • There are lengths of natural cherry and red and white cedar, and three pine tie beams 23 feet long, the center one *humongous* at 13 by 15 inches, with two sets of step dovetail pockets cut into it. Use *huge.* • Surfing the online GTS scene you'll find giantesses galore—in reality, photos of normal-size women manipulated to appear *humongous.* Use *gigantic.* • Somehow the Prides found time (and a vacant computer) in this madhouse to compile their evaluations in a *humongous* and amazingly complete atlas to all educational software available for personal computers and CD-ROM platforms. Use *mammoth.*

Not quite a misusage, *humongous* is altogether a monstrosity. It is a hideous, ugly word. And though it's not fair to say that people who use the word are hideous and ugly as well, at some point we come to be—or at the least are known by—what we say, what we write. See also **conversate**.

hung Misused for *hanged.* • Engram, a repeat felon, attacked Laurie, raped her, and *hung* her by an electrical extension cord until she was dead. Use *hanged.* • Both were pregnant, and by the law of those times they could not be *hung* until they had their babies. Use *hanged.* • Those who continue to protest will have their businesses confiscated and will be brought to justice and could be *hung* by their necks until they are dead. Use *hanged.*

Today, the word *hanged* is used only in the sense of to execute by suspending from the neck. In our slipshod society, however, *hung* is used just as often to mean this; our only solace can be that fewer hangings occur today.

> He went upstairs and, using belts to fashion a noose, hung himself from the door in his bedroom, Don Hooton said. . . . In August 1989, Eric Elofson of Bakersfield, Calif., hung himself from a tree in his front yard.
>
> —Jere Longman, *The New York Times*
>
> Even the sad horror of someone's having hanged himself is made bathetic when we are told he *hung* himself.

hurdle Misused for *hurl.* • Ward inadvertently deflected the ball into the path of Abbey, who had no problem *hurdling* the ball past Warner from close range, for his fourth goal of the season. Use *hurling.* • A blazing fireball came *hurdling* toward him. Use *hurling.* • Without these, it would be difficult, if not impossible, to detect a round object, like a baseball, *hurdling* toward you at 90 miles per hour. Use *hurling.*

To *hurdle* is to run in a race while jumping over hurdles; to clear a barrier; to overcome a difficulty. To *hurl* is to throw something, such as a ball, with great force; to push or shove violently; to yell; to vomit. See also **hurtle**.

hurtle Misused for *hurdle.* • It's the last *hurtle* between me and 100 percent linux on the desktop at work. Use *hurdle.* • One major *hurtle* Lipinski has been working on is making the building's computerized utility system more efficient. Use *hurdle.* • Federal legislation that would curb preexisting condition exclusions in health care policies cleared a huge *hurtle* in the U.S. Senate and is confronting a new and ominous obstacle in an expanded health care bill, HR 995. Use *hurdle.*

And *hurdle* is misused for *hurtle*: • They also project the path of the clouds of particles and magnetic fields *hurdling* through space at a million miles or more an hour. USE *hurtling*.

To *hurtle* is to move swiftly; to collide. To *hurdle* is to jump over hurdles, or barriers, while running; to overcome an obstacle or difficulty. SEE ALSO **hurdle**.

> In the world of Hollywood action movies, hoist ropes are never far from snapping in two, sending the car and its passengers hurdling down the shaft.
>
> —Tom Harris, Howstuffworks.com
>
> The basic idea of a seatbelt is very simple: It keeps you from flying through the windshield or hurdling toward the dashboard when your car comes to an abrupt stop.
>
> —Tom Harris, Howstuffworks.com
>
> For all Mr. Harris does know, he seems not to know that *hurdle* means something quite different from *hurtle*. Would he similarly confuse a hoist rope with a drawstring, a seat belt with a sanding belt?

hypothecate Misused for *hypothesize*. • Now is no time to speculate or *hypothecate*, but rather a time for action. USE *hypothesize*. • You can *hypothecate* that no one would have protested if there was no draft, but that is a meaningless hypothetical since the war could not be fought without the draft. USE *hypothesize*. • I *hypothecate* that the law of these United States of America as written before the American Civil War was mostly constitutionally sound, but that much which purports to be "statutory" or "code law" and Acts of Congress is highly suspect. USE *hypothesize*.

To *hypothesize* is to make a hypothesis, a tentative or uncertain explanation; to assume or suppose. To *hypothecate*, a legal term, means to pledge (property) as collateral without transferring possession or title.

H

Ii

I (he) Misused for *me (him)*. • If you have a problem, please see *Dana or I*. Use *Dana or me*. • He does not jump but can, at times, challenge *her or I*. Use *her or me*. • You can use the CWA Constitution and file charges against *he, she, or them*. Use *him, her, or them*.

Some people, people who think rather highly of themselves, perhaps, tend to use a nominative pronoun (such as *I*) when an objective pronoun (such as *me*) is required. • Last December, *him and President Clinton* came up with another solution. Use *President Clinton and he*. • He even spends the night every day but I don't mind because *she and him* always go somewhere for a few hours every day so I get time to myself. Use *she and he*. • Let's see who is more ready to die, *they or us*. Use *they or we*. • A railway carriage charm is the name for speed pills that *he and them* used to take. Use *he and they*. • My thought on this one is that *they, or him or her or whoever*, is a religious fanatic. Use *they, or he or she or whoever*.

Whereas others, people who do not think much at all, we might easily imagine, use an objective pronoun instead of a nominative. See also **it's me**.

In the meantime, me and my friends and my conservative colleagues will continue to use legal organizations to advocate that point of view.

—Former U.S. representative Tom DeLay

Without a prepared speech to read from, Congressman DeLay speaks like any other ignoramus.

You teach a child to read, and he or her will be able to pass a literacy test.

—U.S. President George W. Bush

It takes an extraordinary mind to mix nominative with objective personal pronouns. President Bush, it is clear, may not be able to pass a literacy test.

idle Misused for *idol.* • I've done tons of research about Billy the Kid; I guess you could say he's my *idle.* USE *idol.* • Inundated as we are by rival pop *idle* shows, it ought to be self-evident to the record-buying public that the whole purpose of manufactured pop bands is simply to separate fools from their money. USE *idol.*

Idle, as an adjective, means having no value or significance; unfounded; unemployed or unoccupied; lazy; not in use. *Idol,* a noun, means an image of a god; a heathen deity; someone who is very highly admired; something without substance.

i.e. Misused for *e.g.* • He has at least one physical feature with inherent comic value, *i.e.,* Jim Carrey's grin, John Cusack's pout, and Ben Stiller's slouch. USE *e.g.* • Also, unlike other popular diet books, *Metabolize* does not focus on one dietary component to the exclusion of others (*i.e.,* all protein, no carbohydrates). USE *e.g.* • Do you find that you use sex as a way of dealing with feelings (*i.e.,* stress, loneliness, sadness, fear, anger)? USE *e.g.* • Up until two decades ago, "awesome" was reserved for the sublime: *i.e.,* an F5 tornado or God. USE *e.g.*

The difference between *i.e.* and *e.g.* is the difference between the phrases *that is* and *for example*; the first is for stating an equivalence, the second for stating an illustration. Only scientists and academicians (who have their own perverse rules of style and composition and seldom seem able to write a readable sentence) have any reason to use *i.e.* (or *e.g.*); the rest of us should use *that is* (or *for example*).

Still another admonition is never use *i.e.* (or *e.g.* or *for example* or *for instance* or *such as* or *like*) along with *etc.* or *et cetera* (much less *etc., etc.* or *etcetera, etcetera*). Only one of these forms is ever required: • Why is every other Greek noun used as a term in rhetoric in a nominative form: *i.e.,* tmesis, syncope, litotes, *etc., etc.,* but this one exception is in the accusative case? DELETE *etc., etc.* • There is an entrepreneur in Texas that has some land upon which he has placed various "wild" animals *such as* sheep, deer, wild pigs, *etc.* DELETE *etc.* SEE ALSO **a.k.a.**

if Misused for *whether.* • People will have sex *if* it's legal or not. USE *whether.* • It almost seems silly to ask *if* Valdosta can win the state championship. USE *whether.* • By monitoring how hard the heart is beating, the device can figure out *if* the patient is resting or climbing stairs and adjust the flow of blood accordingly. USE *whether.*

Traditionally, *if* introduces a single condition, whereas *whether* (or *whether or not*) introduces two or more possibilities. Today, *if* or *whether* is permissible, though *whether* is the better choice when describing two or more alternatives. Just remember that *if* should not be used when doing so may cause misunderstanding.

if . . . then Misused for *if.* • *If* the nation's indicators of economic progress are obsolete, *then* they consign us to continually resorting to policies that cannot succeed because they aren't addressing the right problems. DELETE *then.* • If you believe the rumors, *then* Charlie Sheen is dead to *Two and a Half Men.* DELETE *then.* • If you haven't heard the truth, *then* it doesn't matter if you lose the data. DELETE *then.*

In certain mathematical or computer expressions, *if . . . then* is the necessary expression; in prose, the understood *then,* when explicitly stated, is often an encumbrance to grace and elegance.

I'll tell you; let me tell you; I've got to tell you (something) It may be that few people use these dull-witted expressions in their writing, but a great many people use them in their speaking. Few expressions define a person as quickly as these: • *I gotta tell you,* anyone can put up a shingle and call themselves a tax preparer. DELETE *I gotta tell you.* • *I'll tell you something,* when you get your sense of humor back, you know you are really getting better. DELETE *I'll tell you something.* • *I'm telling you,* the disparities aren't nearly so many that gay folks and straight folks can't still come together and make music. DELETE *I'm telling you.* • *Lemme tell you,* if Fred Thompson is running for president, he is going about it quite deftly. DELETE *Lemme tell you.*

Of course, these phrases are usually spoken "I'll tell ya," "lemme tell ya," and "I've gotta tell ya," which only strengthens the impression that the people who use them pay scant attention to what they say and still less to how they say it. SEE ALSO **hey; OK (okay)**.

illicit Misused for *elicit.* • It is interesting to note that sugar placed directly over the diaphragm or on the Crown Chakra will not *illicit* a reaction of any kind in a balanced body. USE *elicit.* • It can *illicit* a response from a child who is ill or a person who has been in a coma. USE *elicit.* • I love any film that can *illicit* debate, and *Session 9* is one film that will have anyone who has seen it talking for some time. USE *elicit.* • Several vaccine strategies have been designed in order to *illicit* a heightened immune response. USE *elicit.*

Illicit means forbidden by law or custom; unlawful. *Elicit* means to call forth, draw out, or provoke; to arrive at by logic.

illiterate Misused for *iterate.* • I could *illiterate* them here but I think you and most other thinking people know exactly what those crimes might be. USE *iterate.* • This is a good example of how I try to take things and *illiterate* them so that they can stick in your mind. USE *iterate.*

Iterate (IT-ah-*rate*), a verb, means to repeat. *Illiterate* (i-LIT-er-it), an adjective, means uneducated, ignorant.

Occasionally, *illiterate* is erroneously used to mean illustrate or mention: • As I *illiterated* in my earlier post, North Korea is probably close to economic collapse. USE *illustrated.*

Illiterated, by the bye, is an obsolete (a senseless) formation: • From comments from other computer-*illiterated* people, blogging is easier than any computer application—even easier than email. • Never has man listened to the simple, the children, the righteous, the *illiterated,* and the powerless. • You're obsessed with your hatred of Bush, and anyone who disagrees with you is labeled *illiterated,* stupid, ignorant.

illusion Misused for *allusion.* • It is Latin for "touch me not," and is an *illusion* to the Gospel of St. John where Jesus says to Mary Magdelene, "Touch me not, for I am not yet ascended to my Father." USE *allusion.*

• There are several ways to begin your paper. You may begin with: 1. A paradoxical or intriguing statement. 2. An arresting statistic or shocking statement. 3. A question. 4. A quotation or literary *illusion.* USE *allusion.* • Even in the description of the drawbridge and passing barges it makes a literary *illusion* to the mythological River Styx. USE *allusion.*

And *allusion* is misused for *illusion*: • This house is run by a command central computer system that vacuums, cooks, cleans, creates optical *allusion* vacation scenes on your family room wall. USE *illusion.* • This is what intrigues me about photography: the compelling *allusion* of reality. USE *illusion.* • Holograms are a great way to trick people. They look so real, but in reality there is nothing there. Parabolas play a big part in creating this magical *allusion.* USE *illusion.*

I

Allusion is an indirect or passing reference; a hint. *Illusion* is an incorrect perception of reality; a false belief or idea; a mirage, hallucination, or trick. SEE ALSO **delusion**.

illustrative The preferred pronunciation of *illustrative* is (i-LUS-trah-tiv), not (IL-ah-*stray*-tiv). As there are variant spellings—that is to say, misspellings—so there are variant pronunciations.

imaginate Misused for *imagine* (or *imaginative*). • It is the place where you want to be, place that you *imaginate,* place you are in when you dream. USE *imagine.* • I *imaginate* many people took the Friday off as well. USE *imagine.* • *Down to Earth,* by Gavin Chafin and Steve Wood: an extremely funny and *imaginate* strip that takes place, at various times, in Heaven, Hell, and a small diner out in the middle of nowhere. USE *imaginative.*

The obsolete *imaginate* is an adjective meaning imaginative or a verb meaning to imagine. If some people use the word today it's not because they are familiar with the sixteenth-century use of this word. It's because they are unfamiliar with the word and believe adding a suffix to *imagine* somehow increases the word's value as it does their own.

imbibe Misused for *eat* (or similar words). • Generally, you should be living a clean life, and only *imbibing* food substances that are fresh, light, and pure. USE *eating.* • Because of the scarcity of staff and the lack of time to properly *imbibe* food, I resorted then to giving myself an IV shot of vitamin C with calcium. USE *ingest.* • If we *imbibe* these "substantial," higher-calorie meals on a regular basis, we'll pack on the pounds in stored body fat. USE *consume.*

To *imbibe* is to drink; to take in as if by drinking; to absorb or assimilate. It does not mean to eat or consume.

imbibe Misused for *imbue.* • And all of a sudden they've been *imbibed* with these amazing powers. USE *imbued.* • Speeches ensued in which the palindrome was explained to those not *imbibed* with the spirit of Python Monty. USE *imbued.* • If you're Louisiana-born, Alabama-based Billy Reid, you go back to doing what you do best: making all-American clothes *imbibed* with southern luxury, down home charm, and downtown hipness. USE *imbued.*

Imbue means to inspire or influence thoroughly; to pervade or permeate or saturate; to stain or dye deeply. *Imbibe* means to drink, especially alcohol; to absorb liquid or moisture; to take in or assimilate ideas or facts. *Imbibe* did once mean to saturate or imbue, but it is today an archaic usage, and no one now, we can be confident, who uses *imbibe* for *imbue* is cognizant of this much earlier meaning.

immanent Misused for *imminent.* • The truth is Iraq did not have weapons that represented an *immanent* threat. USE *imminent.* • Here the yips of a few autograph-seekers and the flashes of a few bulbs might be enough to convince viewers of Alex's *immanent* celebrity. USE *imminent.* • The threat is real. It's not *immanent,* but there are still terrorists out there who would like to repeat what happened on September 11. USE *imminent.*

Immanent means inherent or existing within. *Imminent* means about to occur; impending; threatening. SEE ALSO **eminent**.

> Again, in U.S. Senate and House Committee hearings, the FDA conceded that the packaging and recalled drug violations were minor and posed no immanent health hazard to the public.
>
> —W. Lloyd Eldridge, *The Tullahoma News*
>
> The *imminent* hazard, if not to our health, is to our humanity. Using the English language badly is hazardous to our humanity.

immerge Misused for *emerge.* • But fear not, the hangover monster will soon go back to its cave, but threatens to *re-immerge* next weekend. USE *re-emerge.* • As far as personality disorders there are theories that there are some personality traits that we can either exhibit automatically or will *immerge* under some stimulus. USE *emerge.* • We are those stubborn little caterpillars that given the grace of God, we may *immerge* beautiful butterflies. USE *emerge.* • As the seeds start to develop in this unisexual plant, bear in mind that they have an 18-month germination factor and the embryo starts to *immerge* in the fall. USE *emerge.*

Immerge means to submerge or immerse in or as if in a liquid; *emerge,* much the opposite of *immerge,* means to rise from or as if from immersion; to come forth or become evident.

immunity Confused with *impunity. Immunity* means exemption from legal prosecution; freedom from something unpleasant or burdensome; resistance to or protection against a disease ("A Northampton County judge has granted immunity from prosecution for a reluctant witness in the John Hirko Jr. trial, making it more likely he will testify"; "He cited a study conducted several years ago in which 85 percent of children who had one shot without the booster developed protective immunity against the flu"). *Impunity* means exemption from punishment or harm ("At times he has operated with the impunity of a man who has nothing to lose"; "In too many cases, these crimes have been committed with impunity, which has only encouraged others to flout the laws of humanity").

immure Misused for *inure.* • So *immured* to pain and scarred from years of squig hunting is the madcap that he is hard to wound and much more formidable than the average redeye. USE *inured.* • Violence today seems to have become a hallmark of modern society; it is so pervasive that many children are becoming *immured* to it. USE *inured.* • We can even get *immured* to low-level constant pain because our brain starts to presume it is a constant that it need not process. USE *inured.*

Immure is to enclose within or as if within walls; to imprison or confine. *Inure* is to make used to something difficult, painful, or unpleasant; to habituate.

impactful Misused for *influential* (or similar words). • Positive and *impactful* progress requires confidence, strategic vision, and the energetic change agents who will lead the way to new paths of success. USE *effective.* • Let Exclusive show you how our motivational, *impactful,* focused campaigns can translate into revenue growth and expanded opportunities. USE *powerful.* • He said his job is to attract audiences with quality content; it's the advertisers' job to make their marketing messages *impactful.* USE *memorable.* • This could be the most *impactful* Congress in thirty years. USE *influential.*

The verb *impact* is criticized, and rightly so, but the adjective *impactful,* often used by businesspeople and marketers, is condemnable.

impassible Misused for *impassable.* • Some beach segments of the route can be *impassible* at high tide. USE *impassable.* • There are hundreds of yards of trails that are *impassible.* USE *impassable.* • Roads weren't *impassible,* but many motorists weren't slowing down enough. USE *impassable.*

Impassible means unable to feel pain or suffering; impassive. *Impassable* means impossible to pass or travel over. SEE ALSO **passible**.

impatient Misused for *inpatient.* • A study of two programs in Washington State found that for every $1.00 the state spent, $9.70 was returned through *impatient* treatment while $23.33 was garnered through outpatient programs. USE *inpatient.* • When home is not enough, hospice *impatient* care is available for short-term symptom management and respite care. USE *inpatient.*

An *impatient* person is irritable; edgy; intolerant. An *inpatient* is a person hospitalized for treatment.

impermeable Misused for *impervious.* • We are the best of the best, *impermeable* to disease and age. USE *impervious.* • It does not matter how much he hurt me because I love him; he is strong, powerful, *impermeable* to pain and to love. USE *impervious.*

Both *impermeable* and *impervious* mean impenetrable, but *impermeable* also means not allowing fluids to pass through, and *impervious* also means not affected by.

impetuous Misused for *impetus.* • This gave the market a bid into the close Friday, and provided the *impetuous* for the positive numbers seen in the market this week. Use *impetus.* • The main *impetuous* of the contract was to prepare and then implement a move of over 300 computers from a San Francisco office to a Concord office. Use *impetus.* • So, there is an *impetuous* to move forward according to schedule. Use *impetus.* • What was the *impetuous* behind lifting the tariffs? Use *impetus.*

Impetuous, an adjective, means acting impulsively or rashly; moving with force and energy. *Impetus,* a noun, means the force or momentum to accomplish something; a stimulus.

imply Misused for *infer.* • What does it mean that Zaccheus was a chief tax-collector? What can we *imply* about him for that? Use *infer.* • What can we *imply* from Rav Sheishes' initial statement that bar Pivli fulfilled Rebbi Yehudah's Torah obligation? Use *infer.* • You cannot *imply* from this that I reject all forms of control on liberty. Use *infer.*

To *imply* is to suggest; to *infer* is to conclude. Speakers *imply*; hearers *infer.* Some dictionaries, continuing their disservice to us all, consider these two words synonymic, defining one with the other. *The first thing we do, let's kick all the laxicographers.*

imput Misspelling of *input.* • We learned it is too late to have much *imput* once the plan has been set and the funding is in place. Use *input.* • Members of the board want the Vero Beach City Council to have their *imput* before the plan is implemented. Use *input.* • The league also received *imput* from WCHA observer Denny Davis of Duluth. Use *input.*

Imput is a misspelling of *input.*

incalcitrant Misused for *recalcitrant.* • He must balance the demands of his government, which is reluctant to amend its *incalcitrant* position in the climate negotiations. Use *recalcitrant.* • He remains as arrogant and *incalcitrant* as ever, hiding it behind the veil of confession. Use *recalcitrant.* • On the other hand, fierce, *incalcitrant* voices, while having no potency for the pious, may be quite influential for young, unsure intellectuals. Use *recalcitrant.*

Recalcitrant means resistant to authority; difficult to manage. *Incalcitrant* is meaningless.

incent Misused for *encourage* (or similar words). • How do you *incent* a CEO to innovate? USE *encourage.* • Reduce prices by 20 percent for standard configurations and 10 percent for nonstandard configurations to drive more volume and to *incent* customers to buy standard configurations. USE *motivate.* • A compensation program needs to be developed to *incent* employees to retire at an older age. USE *persuade.* • The VSI bonus program is designed to *incent* a person to join, to stay with VSI over a long period of time, and to tell friends about all the benefits a VSI membership provides! USE *inspire.*

Incentivize instead of *motivate* or *encourage* is quite bad enough, but *incent* is execrable. SEE ALSO **incentivize**; **precip**.

incentivize Misused for *motivate* (or similar words). • Just as public shareholders seek to align their interests with management, private owners can also use options to *incentivize* management. USE *motivate.* • Understand that you're going to have to *incentivize* private businesses to get them back there, otherwise they will not go. USE *goad.* • In the face of diminished competitive barriers and an economy where profitability depends on a broad customer base, companies of necessity will offer frequent customer awards to *incentivize* repeat business. USE *stimulate.*

The English language often welcomes nouns and adjectives being made into verbs—for instance, *computerize, jeopardize, criticize.* However, other *-ize* formations are less welcome—*finalize, prioritize,* and *incentivize*—especially if words already exist that have much the same meaning. Moreover, the polysyllabic *incentivize* sounds idiotic; *motivate, incite, inspire, stir* are more euphonious, more sound.

Worse still, by a syllable, is the frightful *disincentivize,* instead of, say, *discourage* or *deter.* SEE ALSO **incent**.

incidary Misused for *incendiary.* • These balloons were launched from the home islands of Japan, allowed to ascend into the prevailing worldwide winds and be carried all the way to the West Coast region of the United

States of America, where some of these *incidary* devices landed and caused fires. Use *incendiary.* • I remember having to look through stock in work for any packages or *incidary* devices. Use *incendiary.* • The Germans never firebombed, they used *incidary* bombs, but never on the scale that the Allies employed them. Use *incendiary.* • Your statement is weak and *incidary* rhetoric. Use *incendiary.*

This sort of mistake, failing to pronounce or to write one or two syllables in a word—desyllabification—occurs often among people who rarely read and scarcely write, among the hurried and the harebrained. See also **incindiary**.

incidently Misused for *incidentally.* • *Incidently,* most people seem to think that the simple edition is just as good as the more expensive travelers' edition, which doesn't really contain anything more that is useful than the basic edition does. Use *Incidentally.* • *Incidently,* research supports this position. Use *Incidentally.* • *Incidently,* many women consider affection and conversation are preconditions for sexual fulfillment. Use *Incidentally.*

Incidentally means as a minor or less important matter; parenthetically, by the way. *Incidently* means so as to depend on something else; concomitantly.

incidents Misused for *incidence.* • It is in the interest of everyone in the county that the *incidents* of disease and unwanted pregnancy be minimized or eliminated. Use *incidence.* • A recent study by the Minnesota Department of Health reveals higher *incidents* of cancer and cancer-related death in the state's minority population. Use *incidence.* • Problems associated with large student populations include increased *incidents* of crime or violence, increased student absences, high academic failure rates, and low graduation rates. Use *incidence.*

Incidents is the plural of *incident,* which is an occurrence; a minor disturbance. *Incidence* is the frequency or rate of an often undesirable occurrence.

incindiary Misspelling of *incendiary.* • The St. John's County Sheriff's Office bomb squad was called in to investigate and disarm the suspected *incindiary* device as city police secured the area. Use *incendiary.* • Sadly, the ad was deemed too *incindiary* by Allen and he refused to run it, evidence that Allen has far better taste than we do. Use *incendiary.* See also **incidary**.

The correct spelling is *incendiary,* not *incindiary.*

inclimate Misused for *inclement.* • O'Dell pointed out that the large room can also be used as a gym for PE classes forced inside by *inclimate* weather. Use *inclement.* • The 2003-04 Missouri Volleyball Season Celebration has been postponed due to Sunday's *inclimate* weather conditions. Use *inclement.* • Indeed, the facility bustles, especially during the winter months, when *inclimate* weather forces many climbers and athletes away from outdoor sports. Use *inclement.* • I will have an *inclimate* weather message on the voice mail letting you know if the dojo will be closed. Use *inclement.*

If laxicographers continue to compile dictionaries, *inclimate* will soon be listed as a variant spelling of *inclement.*

> The ceremony was rescheduled for the following Sunday, but had to be cancelled again due to inclimate weather.
>
> —Luke O'Neill, *The Hyde Park Townsman*
>
> Rebuke Luke, the *Townsman*'s editors should, for in one short sentence he manages to make four grammatical errors.

inclination Misused for *inkling.* • I had a bit of an *inclination* of what was coming along. Use *inkling.* • Obviously they had no *inclination* of how to run a successful business. Use *inkling.* • Has he no *inclination* of why normally law-abiding citizens are forced into a course of civil disobedience? Use *inkling.* • We hear, unsurprisingly, given his results, that he works very hard but likes to devote his weekends to his family but we get no *inclination* of why he is so brilliant and how we lesser mortals can learn from his successes and his failures, assuming, if we dare, that he has ever failed at anything. Use *inkling.*

An *inclination* is a tendency to behave or feel in a certain way; an interest in, or propensity toward, something; a slope or slant; an angle at which a straight line deviates from a horizontal or vertical plane. An *inkling* is a hint or suspicion; a vague idea or understanding of something.

incomparable The pronunciation of *incomparable* is (in-KOM-par-ah-ble), not (in-kom-PAIR-ah-ble).

incompatible Misused for *incomparable.* • I have never seen anything like it, so the view was *incompatible* to me. USE *incomparable.* • She wonderfully combined *incompatible* beauty with cleverness and common sense and was always very kind toward her close friends. USE *incomparable.*

Incompatible means unable to get along or live together; unable to coexist. *Incomparable* means without equal; unable to be compared.

> Still, a science fiction novel by the incompatible Ms. McCaffrey is always a winning treat and readers will relish and crave the next book.
>
> —Harriet Klausner
>
> As bad as the novel is this review of it by the incomparable Ms. Klausner.

incredulous Misused for *incredible.* • It is *incredulous* that we learned about the third American Media employee from a televised news conference rather than from appropriate governmental agencies. USE *incredible.* • The class is designed to introduce the *incredulous* ways acrylics can be used! USE *incredible.* • Really, how do action-thrillers get away with the most *incredulous* and unbelievable scenes pitting humans against a gazillion bullets, C4 mushroom-shape explosions, super-durable sports cars, and deranged killer robots? USE *incredible.*

Incredulous means unwilling to admit or accept what is offered as true; not credulous; skeptical. *Incredible* means hard to believe.

indefatigable The pronunciation of *indefatigable* is (*in*-di-FAT-i-gah-ble), not (*in*-dee-fah-TEE-gah-ble).

indefinate Misspelling of *indefinite.* • The controversial singer/actress has been put on an *indefinate* hiatus on *Gossip Girl* beginning with the midseason finale. USE *indefinite.* • The Vancouver Canucks announced today that they have granted Rick Rypien an *indefinate* leave of absence for personal matters. USE *indefinite.*

The correct spelling is *indefinite.* SEE ALSO **definate**.

indignity Misused for *indignation.* • If he felt *indignity* over one man's 40-year-old statue then how would the Kurds feel over the loss of one of their 10,000 year old cities? USE *indignation.* • "A Dwarf has no business acting as nurse-maid to an Elf!" he stated firmly, beard bristling with *indignity* at the suggestion. USE *indignation.* • What they have done has aroused the *indignity* and strong dissatisfaction of the Chinese people. USE *indignation.* • The story's strengths are its elaborate paintings of righteous *indignity,* pompous historical pride, professional jealousy, and nonstop conflict. USE *indignation.*

Indignity is something that wounds one's self-respect or dignity ("After the indignity of seeing its economy overtaken by China's earlier this year, Japan has clawed back a little pride, beating its east Asian rival to produce the world's most powerful computer for the first time in seven years"; "The poor guy had already suffered the indignity of being literally the last player anyone wanted for their team"). *Indignation* is anger or contempt for a perceived injustice or unfairness.

indispensible Misspelling of *indispensable.* • Holmes said the Yoders, beyond their natural athletic talent, played an *indispensible* role for this year's team. USE *indispensable.* • A water chart is *indispensible,* and a bird chart helpful. USE *indispensable.* • This is an *indispensible* fact of a functional economy, and the free market does not account for it at all. USE *indispensable.*

Only able spellers know that *indispensable* ends in *-able,* not *-ible.*

> The problem is that Arafat was and is the indispensible Palestinian political figure; recent polls show that his popularity remains undimmed.
>
> —Cameron W. Barr, *The Christian Science Monitor*
>
> In his indispensible history, *In Nevada: The Land, the People, God, and Chance,* David Thomson describes the burgeoning of Las Vegas to big-city status.
>
> —Richard Corliss, *Time*
>
> Even the mighty *Monitor* and the unshakable *Time* do not know their *i*'s from their *a*'s, one vowel from another.

indite Misused for *indict.* • Three Mountain State University student athletes are out on bail after being *indited* on federal drug charges. USE *indicted.* • Unfortunately, he lacks the power to *indite* her and put her behind bars. USE *indict.* • The police arrested the performers of the play, *inditing* them under Article 159 of the Turkish penal code, under the grounds that the play was an insult to the Turkish armed forces. USE *indicting.* • They want to *indite* Cheney for war crimes. USE *indict.*

Though both *indite* and *indict* are pronounced (in-DITE), their definitions differ. *Indite* means to write or compose, whereas *indict* means to charge with an offense or crime.

Similarly, *inditement* is often misused for *indictment*: • Based on all the information that has come to light regarding Mayor Kilpatrick's misdeeds and now criminal *inditement,* do you feel he should resign as mayor? USE *indictment.*

inducive Misused for *conducive.* • This fear running through the system is not *inducive* to happiness at a most fundamental level. USE *conducive.* • Practicing meditation and yoga is similar to reading a book, because they are all *inducive* to mind and body relaxation. USE *conducive.* • So many hats must indeed be difficult to wear and cannot be *inducive* to efficiency or job satisfaction. USE *conducive.* • Our open spaces, sunshine, clean environment have been *inducive* to sport, in which we have also excelled. USE *conducive.* • Some of the instruments that are *inducive* to meditation are the tamboura, Tibetan singing bowl, the flute, and the sitar. USE *conducive.*

Induce is a word, as is *inducible,* but *inducive* is not, nor should it be. *Conducive* (or *conduce*) is the word to use when you mean contributes or tends to something.

inexplained Misused for *unexplained.* • There was an *inexplained* plane crash in Poland. USE *unexplained.* • Unfortunately, Multimania-Lycos' free site was removed by Lycos on October 15, 2006, for some *inexplained* reason. USE *unexplained.*

Perhaps a confusion between *unexplained* and *inexplicable, inexplained* is inadmissible as an alternative to either word.

infantalize Misspelling of *infantilize.* • To argue that the "very occasional inconvenience" that contemporary racism represents for many blacks is enough to deter black students from pursuing their educational goals is, according to McWhorter, to *infantalize* an entire race. USE *infantilize.* • "Compliant" isn't much better—it still puts the patient in a one-down, *infantalized* position. USE *infantilized.*

To treat someone as, or reduce someone to, an infant is to *infantilize* him. A person may be *infantile,* not *infantale.*

infect Misused for *infest.* • Crabs, or pubic lice, are insects that *infect* pubic hair, hairy parts of the chest, armpits, upper eyelashes, and the head. USE *infest.* • Fungi (wood rot) and subterranean termites *infecting* wood are retarded in their growth when the moisture content of the wood is lower than 20 percent. USE *infesting.*

And *infest* is misused for *infect:* • She urged the participants to be polite in delivering the message to the people and advised female students to be content with what their parents provide for them and desist from soliciting help from men who could take advantage of them and *infest* them with the HIV virus. USE *infect.*

Infect means to contaminate with a disease-producing organism; to affect or instill with one's feelings or beliefs. *Infest* means to overrun or be present in large numbers.

infestate Misused for *infest.* • First, he tried leaving out food for them to enjoy and *infestate,* sort of sharing the wealth. USE *infest.* • Droppers *infestate* computers with viruses, exploits, and data miners. USE *infest.* • They migrate up from below ground over foundations, support members, conduits, etc., in contact with the ground, in search of moist wooden structural members, which they *infestate* and digest causing eventual disintegration and collapse. USE *infest.*

Infestation is the noun, and *infest,* not *infestate,* is the verb.

infinitesimal Misused for *infinite* (or similar words). • We are also part of a macrocosmic world of planets and stars and *infinitesimally* huge distances of space and time to which we are connected in vitally important ways. USE *infinitely.* • Everything we see within the universe is made up of an *infinitesimally* large number of combinations of the 100 different kinds of atoms. USE *infinitely.* • Having that passion, having that religion, having the maxims to live and love by, is the key to embracing life's *infinitesimal* beauty. USE *infinite.* • Then she starts in on undergrads in general: how they have no clue and are *infinitesimally* stupid. USE *infinitely.*

Infinitesimal means extremely small, not, like *infinite,* extremely large or limitless.

> Each play produces a small loss, but in an extraordinarily rare event, the payoff is infinitesimally large.
>
> —Dr. Bill Brody, president, Johns Hopkins University

inflammable Misused for *nonflammable. Inflammable,* like *flammable,* means easily set on fire. *Nonflammable* means not easily set on fire. Since the consequences of not knowing the definition of *inflammable* are potentially severe, most people quickly learn the meaning of this word.

influence The pronunciation of *influence* is (IN-floo-ence), not (in-FLOO-ence).

infusement Misused for *infusion.* • Unfortunately, selling a sister station is a one-time *infusement* of capital. USE *infusion.* • He's generally not a fan of federal involvement, but he hopes that the Byrd grant will provide an *infusement* of energy. USE *infusion.*

And there are examples in which the intended meaning of *infusement* is a little less clear: • The goals of the GeroRich Program include: to provide faculty with educational resources in gerontology to promote ease of *infusement* within existing curricula. • There are (at least) three types of rituals: those with spiritual *infusement,* those that act as a rite of passage, and those that are merely repetitious.

The word is *infusion,* the introduction of a new element or quality into something. *Infusement* means nothing at all—though, to those who say nothing at all, it might indeed mean something. SEE ALSO **enthused**.

> Theoretically, this four-year infusement of money would be enough to get the new system up and running with state-of-the-art equipment.
>
> —John Fox, *Cincinnati CityBeat*
>
> Mr. Fox might improve his credibility as a writer were he, on occasion, to look up the meaning of words he is shamelessly sure of. He would not have found *infusement* in his dictionary, though if he—along with others as careless—continues to use the "word," we shamefully one day will.

ingenious Misused for *ingenuous.* • One day she is childlike, naive, *ingenious,* a girl of ten. USE *ingenuous.* • When his work succeeds, it appears artless and *ingenious,* and intimate rather than regional. USE *ingenuous.* • Is this intended as an *ingenious* but misguided fantasy for midaged women who want to believe someone like Jack Nicholson could fall for an experienced woman like Diane Keaton and never look back at the twiggy twentysomethings who came before? USE *ingenuous.*

Ingenious means brilliant or clever; *ingenuous,* naive or artless.

ingenuitive Misused for *ingenious* (or similar words). • I contest that atonal jazz is neither *ingenuitive* nor daring. USE *ingenious.* • I love the outdoors, gardening and baking, sewing, being *ingenuitive,* but not for survival purposes. USE *clever.* • What is the most *ingenuitive* use you have found for a 12v relay? USE *inventive.* • I enjoyed watching the movie, it was entertaining, but far from *ingenuitive.* USE *imaginative.*

There is no adjectival form of *ingenuity,* which, we might gather, is what *ingenuitive* strives to be. Perhaps some misbegotten amalgamation of *ingenious* and *intuitive, ingenuitive* is nonstandard, that is, it is incorrect, for words like *ingenious, inventive,* and *clever.*

ingenuity The pronunciation of *ingenuity* is (*in*-jah-NOO-i-tee), not (*an*-jah-NOO-i-tee). An ingenue (AN-jah-noo) is a naive, artless girl or an actress playing one.

inimical Misused for *inimitable.* • John also had a one-year run as the host of a daily three-minute syndicated radio rant called *Rotten Day,* commenting on rock history in his unique and *inimical* style. USE *inimitable.* • But before that, the well-known TV gardener Jeff Turner will keep the audience entertained in his own *inimical* way. USE *inimitable.*

Inimical (i-NIM-i-kel) means tending to harm or injure; unfriendly; hostile. *Inimitable* (i-NIM-i-tah-ble) means defying imitation; matchless.

And *inimicable,* a nonword, not a nonce word, is mistaken for *inimical* by some and for *inimitable* by others: • In general, however, anti-Semitism refers to the denouncement in speech or writing of Jewish culture, traditions, and attitudes as being *inimicable* to a nation's welfare. USE *inimical.* • Firstly, he was born with an *inimicable* name, one of a kind. USE *inimitable.*

in memoriam Misused for *immemorial.* • No other part of Europe can match either the "new" or the "old" Ireland, an island that's been here since time *in memoriam.* USE *immemorial.* • From time *in memoriam,* we have been dysfunctional peoples within the family of countries that make up our world. USE *immemorial.* • Since time *in memoriam,* desperate patients have tried one or another magic potion that promises to actually "grow hair." USE *immemorial.*

Immemorial means extending beyond the limits of memory or recorded history. *In memoriam* means in memory of; an obituary.

innoculate Misspelling of *inoculate.* • You may wish to experiment with Sulphur Shelf on Cherry Logs and *innoculate* pine tree seedlings with Chanterelle spawn. USE *inoculate.* • We are faced with the real possibility of attack with biological weapons, and have drawn up plans to *innoculate* the entire unvaccinated segment of this country. USE *inoculate.*

Inoculate has one *n,* not two.

in regards to Misused for *in regard to.* • PalmGear.com will assume no responsibility for software submitted by any developer *in regards to* usability and/or damage that it may cause. USE *in regard to.* • I also encourage you to contact any of my clients for a recommendation *in regards to* my performance, competency, support, and service levels. USE *in regard to.* • *In regards to* the development or recovery of binocular vision, vision therapy is much more successful than surgery or glasses alone. USE *In regard to.* • Modern research tends to show that more universal educational attainment has not led to a more equal society *in regards to* equity in the distribution of high social class. USE *in regard to.* • Please exercise good judgment *in regards to* what information you wish to transmit to Hyatt via this medium. USE *in regard to.*

In regards to, like *with regards to,* is an example of egregious English. That these forms of *in regard to* and *with regard to* can be found in the writing and speech of some otherwise articulate people is ever startling.

The word *regards* is correct only in the expressions *(give her my) regards,* meaning greetings or affection, and *as regards,* meaning regarding or concerning ("As regards atheism, one mistake often made, even by many experts, is a failure to differentiate atheism from disbelief and indifference to religion"). SEE ALSO **anyways**; **with regards to**.

insidious Misused for *invidious.* • Space is sold to the advertisers for the purpose of making announcements concerning their own business and may not be used for attacking or making *insidious* comparisons with other advertisers, firms, institutions, or persons. USE *invidious.* • The important (and *insidious*) distinction is that in this case Lucasfilm, which has a stake in the specific ways in which their properties are used, also shares that right to users' intellectual property. USE *invidious.* • Genetic information can be used as the basis for *insidious* discrimination. USE *invidious.*

Insidious—which means treacherous; harmful but enticing; spreading slowly and in a subtle manner—is not infrequently confused for the less often used *invidious*—which means provoking ill will or animosity, giving offense; discriminatory.

insight Misused for *incite.* • This book will rock the comfortable mainliner, anger the traditional independent, *insight* to riot the hard-core bureaucrat, and motivate to action those who hunger to see what God is about in this world. USE *incite.* • Amazon spokesperson Dale Cheeseman stated that the company did not want to be linked to any publications that might *insight* terrorism, or those who harbor terrorists. USE *incite.* • This is not sloppy journalism but a targeted, calculated scheme to *insight* anger and create a sense of resentment among Muslim citizens against the government. USE *incite.*

Insight (IN-*site*), a noun, is an intuitive understanding of a person or situation; a deep perception of something. *Incite* (in-SITE), a verb, is to stir or rouse; to urge on.

> Isn't Moore concerned about insighting the same fear in people that he criticizes the media for creating?
>
> —Anna Kaufman, *The Daily Californian*
>
> The *Daily Californian* "is run entirely by current or recently-graduated UC Berkeley students," but perhaps Kaufman should return to grammar school.

insure Misused for *ensure.* • What we must do is *insure* that Mr. Taylor is the last president of Liberia to enjoy unlimited authority. USE *ensure.* • The time off will likely *insure* that the injured throwing shoulder will make a 100 percent recovery while Plummer is out with the foot injury. USE *ensure.* • In just such ways did Ted Hughes *insure* that his persona as a poet would survive him and would slowly work its way into the consciousness of posterity. USE *ensure.*

Ensure means to make certain. *Insure* is best reserved for matters of insurance: to issue or acquire insurance for. SEE ALSO **ensure.**

intense Confused with *intensive. Intense* means in a high degree; zealous; showing strong emotion ("Capturing fabulous moments and behind-the-scenes dramas, these pictures reflect the filmmaker's intense personality"; "Gamers applaud the Midway Sports trademark arcade-style gameplay and intense action but also want to experience their favorite teams, players, and stadiums in an authentic professional sports context"). *Intensive* means increasing in degree or amount; concentrated or thorough; especially attentive care ("The Duchess of York's former aide Jane Andrews is in intensive care after being rushed to hospital in a critical condition"; "And foreign students enrolled in Lewis & Clark College's intensive English-language program dropped 30 percent since last fall").

interesting The pronunciation of *interesting* is (IN-tri-sting), not (IN-ter-es-ting).

interpretate Misused for *interpret.* • Doesn't it take legal debate in court between two opposing sides to *interpretate* that law, when it comes under question? USE *interpret.* • If the server sends an answer of at least 262 bytes, the client will badly *interpretate* the input and the execution flow will continue from the address pointed by the 4 bytes at the offset 204 of the answer. USE *interpret.* • In conclusion, data on ketamine were inconsistent and difficult to *interpretate* with only one of four trials showing improved analgesia with preemptive treatment. USE *interpret.* • Chameleon Design prides itself on being able to *interpretate* the client's brief and offer a quality service at a reasonable price. USE *interpret.*

Though *interpretation* is the noun form, the correct verb form is *interpret,* not *interpretate.*

intrepity Misused for *intrepidity.* • To receive the medal, one must demonstrate distinguished gallantry or *intrepity,* at the risk of life, above and beyond the call of duty. Use *intrepidity.* • He had prided himself on his audacious *intrepity,* his macho veneer, his sneering in the face of anything this world had to throw at him . . . even he could leer at the mouth of death, with no worry in his head of the blackness beyond. Use *intrepidity.* • As in the past, the performance of Mansfield and its crack crew was marked by the *intrepity* and aggressive application of naval power which can be executed only be truly knowledgeable professionals. Use *intrepidity.*

To misspell or mispronounce *intrepidity* as *intrepity* may diminish the courage and mock the fearlessness of whomever the word is used to describe; it certainly diminishes and mocks the person misusing the word.

intrest Misspelling of *interest.* • We also feature adjustable *intrest* rates. Use *interest.* • And judging by the current lack of *intrest* in FoxPro, the company could very well be down to two before the year's end. Use *interest.* • Carbosoft also does custom programming; if you are *intrested* please send what you need done, how fast you need it programmed, and the operating system it is for and we will respond within 48 hours with a price quote. Use *interested.*

That some people spell the word *intrest* is as remarkable as it is wrong. Words are not always spelled as they are sometimes pronounced.

inuendo Misspelling of *innuendo.* • From *Desperate Housewives* to *Real Housewives of Atlanta,* humor mills, gossip benches, and *inuendo*-ville seem to thrive on that little word that Tammy Wynette made so famous "d-i-v-o-r-c-e." Use *innuendo.* • There's a danger of sounding terribly pious, but the Left don't deal in smear, gossip, and *inuendo.* Use *innuendo.*

Innuendo has two *n*'s, at the start of the word, not one.

investigatable Misused for *investigable.* • I wished them to explore, then define *investigatable* questions, conduct experiments, and write a conclusion reporting what they had learned. Use *investigable.* • Ask questions, both *investigatable* and *noninvestigatable,* about objects and events observed. Use *investigable*; *noninvestigable.* • Statistics are not easy to find in the book but it appears that the PCC rejects far more complaints as "outside its remit" than does the Australian Press Council (in 1995, for example, only 476 of 2,508 complaints were deemed *investigatable*). Use *investigable.* • The cruelty case must fit certain criteria before it is deemed *investigatable.* Use *investigable.* • The sphere of modern science is the systematizable, the organizable, and the empirically *investigatable.*

Investigable is correct, as is *investigative.* Incorrect is *investigatable.*

invigorment Misused for *invigoration.* • Some people inhale the mist of H_2O_2 for lung problems or squirt their bodies down after showers for *invigorment.* Use *invigoration.* • If the principles and ethics are enunciated clearly, a separation and distinction made from the lapses of the past, then we can set the conditions for a *re-invigorment* of the party. Use *re-invigoration.*

Invigoration is the quality of being active or vigorous. *Invigorment* is an unendurable locution.

invisible Misused for *indivisible.* • I pledge allegiance to the flag and to the republic for which it stands, one nation, *invisible,* with liberty and justice for all. Use *indivisible.*

Invisible means unable to be seen. *Indivisible* means unable to be divided.

invite Misused for *invitation.* • In order to use boxee, you need an *invite.* Use *invitation.* • It just strikes me as naive to expect blokes to take feminist issues like maternity leave and universal day care seriously when the majority of young women do not consider themselves feminists—they run from the term like they're Bill Henson getting an *invite* to Miranda Devine's Christmas drinks. Use *invitation.* • That incredible four-day run is a big reason the Bulldogs scored an *invite* into this year's preseason NIT. Use *invitation.*

Invite is a verb; it is not a noun—except among the foolish who eagerly abbreviate or shorten any polysyllabic word they are impatient to pronounce or unable to remember. See also **enthuse**; **precip**.

irradiate Misused for *eradicate.* • In 1980, the World Health Organization declared that smallpox had been completely *irradiated* and, since then, there has not been a single natural case of the disease anywhere in the world. USE *eradicated.* • Rotary has been one of the primary contributors to a worldwide and highly successful campaign to *irradiate* polio from the world. USE *eradicate.* • Efforts continue to virtually *irradiate* polio and measles, and Qatar was one of the first countries to have added anti-influenza vaccine B to their newborns' comprehensive immunization programs. USE *eradicate.* • "AIDS: Search for the Cure" WCN will chronicle the quest of Bill Gates to *irradiate* Aids in Africa, reporting on the progress of his parents who have done more than tackle this problem with mere money. USE *eradicate.*

To *irradiate* (i-RAY-dee-*ate*) means to expose to or treat with radiation; to illuminate or shed light on. To *eradicate* (i-RAD-i-*kate*) means to destroy or put an end to; to tear up by the roots.

irregardless Misused for *regardless* (or similar words). • *Irregardless* of trees, they should be cleared a minimum of once a year because of birds and animals depositing debris in your gutters. USE *Regardless.* • Would you like to have one e-mail address *irregardless* of how many times you switch jobs or Internet providers? USE *regardless.* • All children can learn. All children—*irregardless* of their ethnicity, *irregardless* of their socioeconomic status, all children can achieve academic success once you teach them how to learn and how to use a standard set of tools. USE *regardless.*

Using *irregardless* is a sign of a shoddy speaker, a third-rate writer, a thoughtless thinker.

> Every single moment of your life you are faced with a choice irregardless of your station in life, irregardless of your status, irregardless of your circumstances or your limitations.
>
> —Diana Rogers, Crystal Clear Reflections
>
> *Irregardless* is nonstandard used once, illiterate used twice, barbarous three times.

irrelevant Misused for *irreverent.* • It was full of *irrelevant* fun almost to the point of Marx Brothers-style of antics, with a small dose of the horrors of war thrown in. Use *irreverent.* • *Vancouver: Secrets of the City*: an *irrelevant* look at the lesser-known side of British Columbia's largest city. Use *irreverent.* • Andy Armstrong takes an *irrelevant* look at motoring and motorsport. Use *irreverent.* • His *irrelevant* style of humor is both witty and makes us think of how we see ourselves. Use *irreverent.*

Irrelevant means not relating to the subject; not pertinent. *Irreverent* means lacking reverence, disrespectful; critical of what is generally accepted; satirical.

irrevocable The pronunciation of *irrevocable* is (i-REV-ah-kah-ble), not (ir-ah-VOH-kah-ble).

isle Misused for *aisle.* • He led the men gently down the *isle* and showed them where they would be seated. Use *aisle.* • Every little girl dreams about walking down the *isle.* Use *aisle.* • In this manner the user can turn on the light and view any documents or light their way in a dark area, such as a theater *isle.* Use *aisle.*

An *aisle* is a passageway usually between rows of seats; an *isle,* an island.

issueize (issueization) Misused for *become a concern* (or similar words). • The overuse of antibiotics, though a problem for many years, has only become *issueized* in the past ten years. Use *a problem.* • Whether we like it or not, whether it makes prudent development sense or not, in the donor countries increasingly we see *an issuization of funding strategies.* Use *funding strategies becoming a worry.* • That's how citizens make change; they take something they're upset about and they *issueize* it. Use *make it a concern.*

Many people object to the frequent use of *issue* and *has issues with* instead of, for example, *problem* or *difficulty* or *dislike.* Consider then how disagreeable a word like *issueization* is to sensible people. *Issueization* (or *issuization*), like *issueize* (or *issuize*), is apparently meant to mean turning (something) into an issue, a problem, concern, or worry. Occasionally it may also mean issuance or issuing, though in other instances, it's not altogether clear what the word is meant to mean—a very good reason not to use it.

is when (is where) *Is when* (like *is where*), when introducing a definition or explanation, is a device that only the least able of writers use: • *Parent Week is when* parents come to the school and get a taste of what their children are doing. USE *During Parent Week.* • *A bribe is when* I offer to give you something and in return you give me something. USE *In a bribe.* • *Spring is when* the pond begins to awaken from its long winter dormancy as signs of life reappear with longer days. USE *With spring.* • *The Tufts Career Network is where alumni* serve as mentors for students looking for their first jobs. USE *Alumni at the Tufts Career Network.* • A case in point *is where the Talmud says* that Jesus of Nazareth was a student of Yehoshua ben Perahia, a sage who died at least 100 years before. USE *is the Talmud's saying.*

it's Misused for *its.* • By now, even the most out of touch among you must realize that the government of the United States is at war against *it's* own people. USE *its.* • You'll get a chance to read my world-famous Speed Seduction Newsletters, hear Real Audio Clips from seminars and products, hear testimonials in their own voices from satisfied customers just like you, join the Speed Seduction private email discussion group, sign up for the Seduction tip of the week, learn all about the Speed Seduction Home Study Course that is turning the world of dating and seduction on *it's* ear, and much, much more. USE *its.* • Freemasonry requires that *it's* members confess a belief in a supreme being. USE *its.* • Our customers have been absolutely spellbound by *it's* results. USE *its.*

Most often, this confusion is simply a matter of carelessness, but in the end, all good writing is careful writing. *It's* is a contraction for *it is* or *it has; its,* the possessive of *it,* indicates belonging or relating to.

it's me Misused for *It's I.* • It's *him*! How can it be *him*? USE *he; he.* • If circumstances had been different, it might have been *them* here today—not *us*. USE *they; we.* • We logged on using a different name, so Blue Nile wouldn't know it was *us*. USE *we.* • It was *us* looking at them looking at us. USE *we.* • How do you know it is *her*? USE *she.*

A pronoun that refers to the subject of a sentence or phrase and that follows a form of the verb *to be* is correctly nominative—though we might excuse *it's me*. People do argue for both expressions. If you prefer *It's I* or *This is I,* you might also consider using the startlingly correct *I am he*. SEE ALSO **I (he)**.

ivy tower Misused for *ivory tower*. • Pope Benedict often reminds me of someone who basically lives in an *Ivy Tower* world. USE *Ivory Tower.* • If some scholar in an *ivy tower* is out there somewhere making this comparison, I don't want to know about it. USE *ivory tower.*

The correct expression for a place of refuge or study is *ivory,* not *ivy, tower*.

Jj

jaundra Misspelling of *genre.* • All ephemera is inspected by three experts in the appropriate *jaundra.* Use *genre.* • That's why I can't wait to have it playing 24/7 so I can really experience yet another *jaundra* of thought and music. Use *genre.* • He goes on to detail the characters in the movie and why he chose to make a film in this *jaundra.* Use *genre.*

Genre, not *jaundra,* is the correct spelling of the word that means a type or class, a style of artistic composition.

J

jewelery Misspelling of *jewelry.* • No matter which team wins the 2003 World Series, a former Tulsa Drillers player will be wearing new *jewelery* next year. Use *jewelry.* • This site includes beaded *jewelery* and hemp *jewelery.* Use *jewelry.* • The line will include jeans, T-shirts, *jewelery,* lingerie, and a fragrance. Use *jewelry.*

Jewelry is the American spelling, not *jewelery* or *jewellery,* which is the only correct spelling in British English.

jibberish Misspelling of *gibberish.* • I wouldn't want to be anywhere near you when a Kentucky fan who knows you and your *jibberish* crosses your path. Use *gibberish.* • That is because nothing in trustworthy historical documentation supports such *jibberish.* Use *gibberish.* • So much arrogant and ignorant *jibberish* from the far right spewing out lies and deceptions created in their dark and twisted lizard brains. Use *gibberish.*

The spelling *jibberish* is *gibberish. Gibber* (JIB-er), not *jibber,* means to talk foolishly or unintelligibly.

jive Misused for *jibe.* • It may also be that your circadian rhythm doesn't *jive* with your lifestyle. Use *jibe.* • So this does not *jive* with your remarks so give us some facts or you need to be careful with your statements. Use *jibe.*

To *jive* is to dance to or play jazz or swing. To *jibe* is to agree or be in harmony. SEE ALSO **gibe**.

judicial Confused with *judicious. Judicial* means relating to judges and courts of law; befitting a judge; fair and unbiased ("The judicial branch hears cases that challenge or require interpretation of the legislation passed by Congress and signed by the president"). *Judicious* means showing good judgment or wisdom; careful ("Judicious use of insecticides is essential for natural enemy conservation and for the enhancement of natural biological control").

Kk

kindergarden Misspelling of *kindergarten.* • I blame my *kindergarden* teacher forcing me to sit in the back of the class. USE *kindergarten.* • Summer Daze here at the Y is a supervised and activity-planned summer child care for kids going into *kindergarden* through seventh grade. USE *kindergarten.*

Kindergarten, from the German for "children's garden," not *kindergarden,* is the correct spelling.

K

knelt (kneeled) Either *knelt* or *kneeled, leapt* or *leaped, gelt* or *gelded,* or as a further illustration, *blest* or *blessed* is correct, though using *-t* instead of *-ed* to form the past tense or past participle of these verbs may sound quaint, if not incorrect, to modern ears. Other verbs insist on the *-t* ending. We say, or should say, *swept,* never *sweeped,* and *kept,* never *keeped.*

knotical Misused for *nautical.* • This third S/V Olapa Survey spent five weeks looking for NF at sites every six *knotical* miles along the Atlantic reef crest. USE *nautical.* • As a tropical disturbance strengthens, pressure drops, and winds increase to 20 *knotical* miles per hour, it becomes known as a tropical depression. USE *nautical.*

Though the speed of a ship is measured in *knots,* the distance traveled is specified by the word *nautical* (relating to ships, sailors, or the sea), not *knotical.*

kowtow The pronunciation of *kowtow* is (kou-TOU), not (kou-TOH). SEE ALSO **cowtow**; **kowtowed**.

kowtowed Misused for *cowed.* • Scott Morgan smacks the *LA Times* for being *kowtowed* by Holder's threat. USE *cowed.* • Are they so *kowtowed* by "doctors" that they vacate their own authority? Use *cowed.* • Lee Myung-bak and the U.S. president, Barack Obama, spoke in Washington of how they will not be *kowtowed* by North Korea's nuclear threats. Use *cowed.*

To *cow* is to intimidate or frighten. To *kowtow* is to kneel and touch the ground with the forehead to show respect or submission; to act in a servile manner.

This is further evidence that much language change is due simply to people not knowing, and apparently not caring to know, what the words they use mean. Not for one instant is this an evolution of language; it is the crumbling of language, the ruin of meaning, the slaying of sense. See also **cowtow**; **kowtow**.

kudo Misused for *kudos* (or similar words). • It is obviously Formula One influenced—he deserves *a great kudo.* Use *kudos.* • Or will banks have to spin off new operations that will be allowed to form without using the Big Brother AML systems? *Another kudo* for Congress, I guess. Use *More kudos.* • Incidentally, Art's award was presented to the best journalist of any size paper competing, quite *a kudo*. Use *an honor.*

Kudos is praise or acclaim for an achievement; the word is singular. The spelling *kudo* exists only in some descriptive dictionaries, the nether regions of English usage, which certainly does *not* legitimize its use.

> Despite rain, cold, lack of outhouses, and "three large vultures circling" the camp, he receives the ultimate kudo: "You made my life larger."
>
> —Galye Keck, *The Washington Post*
>
> The "ultimate kudo" belongs to cuckoo Keck, who makes our lives smaller with her sloppy writing. Bad usage atrophies our thoughts and feelings; it shrinks our ability to speak clearly and withers our ability to write well.

Ll

L

laconic Misused for *emotionless* (or similar words). • His tone of speech is *laconic* and pithy. Use *dispassionate.* • "Death Watch," a *laconic* litany of medical patients who were given faulty terminal diagnoses, delivers a shorthand version of hope and fatalism run awry because of human error. Use *unemotional.* • Glenn behaved in the familiar way of the sexist Australian pig and the fact he was a bushie (speaking with a dinky-di *laconic* Aussie voice, vowels as wide as the brown plains are endless) made it worse. Use *emotionless.* • She may not be pushing comedic boundaries, but her irreverence and *laconic* delivery make you feel you are in the company of the best kind of pub raconteur. Use *deadpan.*

When a word takes on a new meaning—often a wholly incorrect and inappropriate meaning—laxicographers and ding-a-linguists, bungling, clumsy arbiters of the language, call it a "semantic shift" or "semantic drift."

The meaning of the word *laconic* is terse, concise; using few words. It does not mean unemotional, affectless, or dispassionate.

lamblaste Misspelling of *lambaste.* • In just the past decade, America was *lamblasted* for not doing more to prevent atrocities in Somalia, the Balkans, Zaire, etc. Use *lambasted.* • Not only was he being *lamblasted* by the press, there were people at NBC who were questioning his ability to portray Charles Ingalls, happily married frontiersman and devoted father. Use *lambasted.* • Do I not *lamblaste* Brahmins for having become a degenerated class? Use *lambaste.*

To *lambaste* (lam-BASTE) is to criticize someone severely, to scold or berate. *Lamblaste* means nothing other than that its user is an inattentive listener, an infrequent reader.

> Bush lamblasted "activist judges"—presumably those justices from Vermont, Massachusetts and New Jersey—for "redefining marriage by court order, without regard for the will of the people."
>
> —*The Cornell Daily Sun*

landlover Misused for *landlubber.* • As one in our party is allergic to seafood, we asked if there was any *landlover* items on the menu. USE *landlubber.* • Any seaman or *landlover* will enjoy using this seaworthy tamper! USE *landlubber.*

A person unfamiliar with the sea or sailing is called a *landlubber.*

languaging Some people, linguists and therapists especially it may be, use *language* as a verb meaning to communicate by language; to express in language: • *Languaging* is obviously not just verbal—but tacit as well. • The delight of defamiliarization is one of the genuine pleasures of *languaging.* • Julie discusses the embedded negativity and racial inconsistencies that exist in *languaging.* • Powerful, progressive *languaging* dramatically alters the speaker's life.

How *languaging* differs from language or using (or the use of) language few can communicate. SEE ALSO **relanguage**.

later Misused for *latter.* • The real confrontation came in the *later* sixteenth century, as the church faced the radical challenge of Protestantism. USE *latter.* • But Bloomberg reported that investors sold the shares and bought those of archrival Foundry Networks, Inc., as the former's sales growth slowed to the *later's* level. USE *latter's.*

Later means at a later time; subsequently. *Latter* means near the end; the second of two people or things mentioned. *Latter,* however, ought not to be used to mean the last of three or more people or things mentioned.

laudatory Misused for *laudable.* • Kansas earned a *laudatory* No. 15 ranking, while Missouri came in blah and blaher at 28. USE *laudable.* • While maintaining "family values" is a *laudatory,* if ambiguous, goal, we have to wonder if it is worth rewriting the Constitution for. Use *laudable.*

Laudable means worthy of being lauded; praiseworthy. *Laudatory* means expressing praise; eulogistic ("The event was filled with laudatory speeches and kernels of advice that were particularly poignant for 2011's graduates"; "Plenty of laudatory remarks were made and memories shared at the services").

laxadaisical Misused for *lackadaisical.* • Winstone is a good actor but here he seems *laxadaisical,* as if he isn't much interested in what's going on. Use *lackadaisical.* • The Kapha-type person is slow, methodical, and thorough; if imbalanced, they can become *laxadaisical* and inert. Use *lackadaisical.* • No longer does that *laxadaisical* attitude that once filled the men's basketball locker room exist. Use *lackadaisical.*

Though some people might, on occasion, allow, even applaud, the spelling *laxicographer* (a hopelessly descriptive dictionary maker), no one should allow the misspelling *laxadaisical.*

lead Misused for *led.* • Not only did she have a successful career on stage, screen, radio, and television, she *lead* the way for many women to become leaders in their fields of endeavor. Use *led.* • The Pirates *lead* 6 to 2 going into the top of the 4th before the Astros' bats came alive with 9 runs in that inning and 6 more in the top of the 5th. Use *led.*

Led (LED) is the past tense of *lead* (LEED): to direct the course of; to guide; to be in charge; to be at the forefront of. *Lead* (LED) is a heavy, soft, bluish-gray metal.

learnings Misused for *lesson* (or similar words). • And the *learnings* we get from our employee telework program are embedded in the networking services we sell to customers. Use *knowledge.* • The early days are certainly handing us some painful *learnings,* but then sport is not about instant gratification. Use *lessons.* • Many of these "skills" fit in with the "essential *learnings*" the district wants the kids to take with them when they graduate from high school. Use *aptitudes.* • For journalists, change brings new challenges and new *learnings.* Use *insight.*

Learning no one can find fault with, but *learnings* is a different word, and a ridiculous one. *Learning* has been made plural so as to include the meanings of a dozen other words, more precise words. People are impatient with, even intolerant of, exactitude and nicety. We are no more careful of our words than we are caring for one another. The less exact our words, the less clear our thoughts, the less sincere our sentences, the less honest our behavior.

leave Misused for *let.* • I'm *leaving* this go for another time. USE *letting.* • So please can you show some respect and *leave* us go about our day-to-day while we try to deal with the situation as best we can. USE *let.* • Until we hear some more facts, I'd be inclined to *leave* it lie, rather than assume it's operational and begin discussion on just where it is best employed. USE *let.*

Leave means to go away from, whereas *let* means to permit or allow. *Leave* to mean *let* is incorrect (except in the phrase *leave me alone*). SEE ALSO **leave alone**.

leave alone Misused for *let alone* (or similar words). • How can people like you and me ever hope to come to any sort of grips with social theory, *leave alone* Social Theory? USE *let alone.* • I recall while in grade 10, the teacher blushed so much while teaching us about the male and female reproductive organs that she did not even go through the chapter, *leave alone* the sex part. USE *let alone.*

"Leave us alone" is perfectly good English, but "leave alone Social Theory" and "leave alone the sex part" are not. *Let alone,* in these examples, means not to mention or never mind. SEE ALSO **leave**.

lense Misspelling of *lens.* • It's a quick step-by-step process to remove the cataract and insert a man-made *lense.* USE *lens.* • Administrators call this information another *lense* to view how schools are doing. USE *lens.* • A really good *lense* is a polarized *lense.* USE *lens.*

Lens, not *lense,* is the correct spelling. The plural of *lens* is *lenses.*

less Misused for *fewer*. • In a survey of 132 jumpers, *less* than half had complaints—all minor. USE *fewer*. • The number of car repossessions has doubled in just five years; home foreclosures have more than tripled in *less* than 25 years. USE *fewer*. • When we looked at that and the fact in this economy there are *less* investment bankers flying, *less* lawyers flying, we made the very difficult, but prudent decision to retire the Concorde. USE *fewer*. • There is a value to the audience they deliver but the value is becoming less and less as there are *less* and *less* of those people around. USE *fewer*.

And *fewer* is misused for *less*: • With the current number of members, even if *fewer* than 1 percent of the total membership post a link each day, it's far too many links to take in. USE *less*. • She noted that close to 200 U.S. students are enrolled in academic programs at Hebrew University this year, 40 percent *fewer* than before the violence. USE *less*.

The distinction between *fewer* and *less* (like that between *number* and *amount*) centers on what can be counted and what cannot. *Fewer* we use for numbers; *less* we use for quantities.

Even the confusion between these two words is being sanctioned by lexicographers, for many dictionaries now offer one word as the synonym of the other. In the end, lexicographers who suppress or discourage the distinctions between words reduce our ability to see clearly and reason convincingly. SEE ALSO **amount**; **much**.

less Misused for *lest*. • *Less* we forget, we won the national championship in football in 1998 and made it to the Final Four in basketball, holding the top rank for most of the season. USE *Lest*. • During the age of Ragnarok the gods would not be able to walk on the Earth *less* they should become mortal and lose all their powers. USE *lest*. • *Less* I be branded a hypocrite, it should almost go without saying that I am also writing this book for my own benefit. USE *Lest*. • In these days of great scientific advances, some people get scared, *less* we discover something that makes God redundant or irrelevant. USE *lest*.

Lest means for fear that. *Less* means not as great in amount or quantity; lower in importance. If people were to speak more clearly and enunciate their words, perhaps there would be slightly less confusion over words like *less* and *lest*.

lessor Misused for *lesser*. • So a nutrient that wasn't absorbed before may now be absorbed easily, resulting in a *lessor* amount being needed. Use *lesser*. • We will also be carrying the dyed lampshades in red and green in *lessor* quantities. Use *lesser*. • Buy one glass of wine, get one (of equal or *lessor* value) free. Use *lesser*.

Lessor, a person who leases something to another, is occasionally used where *lesser*—which denotes a smaller amount of significance or value or quantity—is required.

liable Misused for *libel.* • It's unfortunate, but in this country, if you're successful or famous, many courts will allow defamation, slander, and *liable* to go unpunished. Use *libel.* • Most clubs and officers do not know how vulnerable they are to *liable* suits. Use *libel.* • Right now, your only recourse is to sue for *liable* damages. Use *libel.* • If I maintain a fairly neutral description of a company and rely on others' writing, I suppose I am safe from any charge of *liable.* Use *libel.*

Libel (LIE-bel) is a noun that means a published or broadcast false and defamatory statement that damages a person's reputation. *Liable* (LIE-ah-bel) is an adjective that means legally bound or responsible; likely though undesirable. See also **slanderous**.

liable Misused for *likely.* • Because information is *liable* to change from time to time you should not rely on the information on this website but should check the accuracy of the information with the relevant supplier. Use *likely*. • There are a lot of kids, including my own, who are *liable* to start a grade proficient in standards at that grade level. Use *likely*. • These days, goods are just as *liable* to travel by air or truck as they are to travel by sea. Use *likely*.

Liable means undesirably likely; legally obligated ("Boeing is liable for all cost above the $4.9 billion contract ceiling"; "Fire is the basic motif at the center of the novel: natural fire, which is liable to destroy a forest; man-made fire, meaning military fire; and metaphorically speaking, internal fire, the electricity beating in the body").

liason Misspelling of *liaison.* • John Devine, aged 82, told BBC Radio he believed the bombers had targeted the home he shares with his wife, Eileen, in Strabane, in the west of the British-ruled province, because he is a member of a local police *liason* committee. USE *liaison.* • Drivers and *liason* officers had not been paid their allowances, and were only given limited money for petrol throughout the tour. USE *liaison.* • It also reports results to issuer and participating broker dealers and acts as a *liason* among trustees, issuers, broker dealers, and security depositories. USE *liaison.*

Remember, *liaison* is spelled *li, ai,* and then *son.*

library The pronunciation of *library* is (LI-brer-*ee*), not (LI-ber-*ee*).

licence Misspelling of *license.* • On Monday, the Health Department announced that Lott's *licence* to work as a nursing assistant had been summarily suspended. USE *license.* • Shop needs an experienced designer who can also perform landscaping tasks, provide good customer service, and possesses a valid Massachusetts driver's *licence.* USE *license.*

In the United States, *license* is the correct spelling; in England, Ireland, Canada, and elsewhere, *licence* is correct.

lie Misused for *lay.* • Many times I had to *lie* the book down and control my breathing as I found I would be holding my breath without realizing it! USE *lay.* • *Lie* him on his back on the floor with a play gym over his head; he will not only love watching the bright objects but will try and raise his hands to touch them. USE *Lay.* • The government wanted to attain revenue for *lying* pipeline from Turkmenistan, Iran, and India via Pakistan. USE *laying.* • He *lay* the bicycle down by the side of the road. USE *laid.* • They're all there among the 65,000 *lain* to rest over the generations beneath the baked, sandy surface of El Paso's Concordia Cemetery. USE *laid.*

And *lay* is, even more often, misused for *lie*: • We hear a big boom and turn and see a freshman *laying* on the field. USE *lying.* • She just *laid* down on the floor, alongside her cot, and we couldn't get her to respond. USE *lay.* • This reflects a throwback to the early days of the gathering, when a generation of flower children brought about the resurgence of handmade crafts—a specialty that had *laid* dormant through 1950s commercialism. Use *lain.*

And not uncommonly, the word *lied* is thought to be the past tense of *lie* or *lay*: • Zinka *lied* down on her bed and didn't go to lunch, drifting in and out of sleep until dinner. Use *lay.* • After his talk to all of the third and fourth graders, he *lied* down on the gym floor and arm-wrestled Alexandra Ritchie, 9. Use *lay.* • She *lied* it down on the coffee table and picked up her glass and walked into her bedroom. Use *laid.* • Would it damage a tower case PC if you *lied* it down flat? Use *laid.*

Present	Present Participle	Past	Past Participle
lie	lying	lay	lain
lay	laying	laid	laid

The verb to *lie* means to assume or be in a reclining position. The verb to *lay* means to put or place something. The verb to *lay* often takes an object; to *lie* does not.

lier Misspelling of *liar.* • Bustamente is a *lier* and a racist. Use *liar.* • How can you trust a *lier*? Use *liar.* • Most MT solvers had a two-step approach where they first ask a question to establish whether the person they are talking to is a *lier* or truth speaker. Use *liar.* • I want a man who shares the same interests; no cheaters or *liers*; he has to be mentally and physically attractive. Use *liar.*

Liar, not *lier,* is the correct spelling.

lightening Misused for *lightning.* • The pages loaded *lightening* fast. Use *lightning.* • Check-21 is a *lightening* rod for the banking industry, and smaller banks and credit unions are at the greatest risk of getting burned. Use *lightning.* • Those harsh conditions have included everything from major flooding, *lightening* storms, hail, 110-degree heat, forest fires, and an earthquake. Use *lightning.*

Though *lightening* once was the spelling to describe an electrical storm,

L

today the word is *lightning,* with no *e. Lightening* means becoming lighter in color; becoming less heavy or burdensome. *Lightening* also describes the fetal head beginning to descend into the mother's pelvis. SEE ALSO **lighting**.

lighting Misused for *lightning.* • After a couple of dry winters, Hawaii has become unaccustomed to the drenchings and the occasional thunder and *lighting* of the winter storms like the one that put a damper on the end of the Thanksgiving weekend across the state. USE *lightning.* • Strong winds and *lighting* storms are occurring around the Grassy Plains, the Puppy Field, and the Battle Field. USE *lightning.*

Lighting is a certain kind of light; the lights that produce illumination; illumination. *Lightning* is a flash of light in the sky caused by a discharge of atmospheric electricity; very fast and sudden. SEE ALSO **lightening**.

L

ligitimate Misspelling of *legitimate.* • Women are not the only group, or sex, for that matter, with a *ligitimate* grievance. USE *legitimate.* • And they wonder why *ligitimate* news stations don't consider them one. USE *legitimate.* • This is a *ligitimate* offer for a *ligitimate* car. USE *legitimate.*

Legitimate, not *ligitimate,* is the correct spelling. Suspect any offer that maintains it is *ligitimate.*

like An absurdity spoken by those who are dreadfully adolescent or fraudulently adult, *like* mars the meaning of every sentence in which it is used.

Often *like* is as meaningless as *umm* and *ahh* and *you know*: • Our family is *like* very open. DELETE *like.* • I should, *like,* get up and do something. DELETE *like.* • It's *like* just a habit. DELETE *like.* • *Like,* you can't really overuse words. DELETE *Like.*

Like is also meant to mean approximately or nearly: • They lived together for *like* twelve years. USE *some.* • He's *like* $10,000 in debt. USE *roughly.*

At other times, *like* is used to mean *say* or similar words: • *They're like,* "Yes." USE *They said.* • "When have you ever seen her leave?" and *he's like* "Never." USE *he says.* • *She's like,* "Don't you dare do that!" USE *She screams.* • When I saw the hot tub, I was *like* [*she claps*]. USE *delighted.*

The dehumanizing *like* also means whatever word or words its user does not know or cannot be bothered to think of: • I'm kind of *like* ooh, I want to eat here. • My mom said, "Why not circulate a petition and see what happens," which is what I did, but, *like,* I still can't believe it worked.

Like means everything and nothing at once. SEE ALSO **(he) goes**; **hey**; **OK (okay)**; **so**; **well**.

> I was like, "Why are they invited?"
>
> —Brook Baldwin, CNN anchor

like Misused for *as*. • The Vatican now says the marble shines *like* it did in the early part of the century. USE *as*. • It's going to revitalize the downtown—much *like* Quincy Market did for us. USE *as*. • *Like* I said, some men don't remember they put the mask on in the first place. USE *As*. • Other countries wouldn't be ripping us off *like* they're doing. USE *as*. • I don't know if we'll ever have people riding the trains *like* they do in Europe. USE *as*.

No solecism is as ubiquitous as this one. Though to the misguided masses, the cachet of using *like* instead of *as* may be appealing, to others it is nothing less than appalling. Knowing when to use *as* instead of *like* is the mark of conscientious people who still value one of the hallmarks of being human: using the language well.

• We appreciate the gravity of this situation and, *like any responsible company would,* are putting all necessary resources toward understanding the facts surrounding it as quickly as possible.

Like would be correct in this sentence if it were written thus:

• We appreciate the gravity of this situation and, *like any responsible company,* are putting all necessary resources toward understanding the facts surrounding it as quickly as possible.

As would be correct in this sentence if it were written thus:

• We appreciate the gravity of this situation and, *as any responsible company would,* are putting all necessary resources toward understanding the facts surrounding it as quickly as possible.

Like is a preposition; a noun or noun phrase (such as, in the preceding example, "any responsible company") must follow it. *As* is a conjunction; a clause must follow it (in the preceding example, "as any responsible company would"). Using *like* instead of *as* is considered incorrect and uneducated.

So if you feel passionate about "spider hole," I would suggest you vote early and vote often, like they do in Chicago.

—John Shibley, Lake Superior State University

Shibley, co-compiler of Lake Superior's Banished Words list, not only uses *like* instead of *as,* he uses the word in the sense he banished it in 1986. Shibley should know his shibboleths.

Our media has disgraced itself once again, like they did in Iraq and like they're doing in Iran and like they did in Vietnam and like they did in Panama.

—Oliver Stone, film director

And Oliver Stone rather disgraces himself, too—as do others:

Like I said, they are very popular, they're fun to talk about, and I do a lot of radio interviews about them.

—Steve Kleinedler, supervising editor, *American Heritage Dictionary*

Women don't really need men like they used to.

—Mark Regnerus, professor of sociology, University of Texas, Austin

> When we spend tens and tens of billions of dollars, hundreds of billions of dollars in adventurous wars like we did in Afghanistan—like we are in Afghanistan and like we did in Iraq, we are not investing in our economy.
>
> —David Sirota, syndicated columnist
>
> Does it help with bills like Aflac does?
>
> —Aflac TV commercial
>
> We can have a conversation just like you and I are.
>
> —Dr. Steve Perry, educator and consultant

like Misused for *as if* (or similar words). • I just remember feeling *like I was* on eggshells all the time. Use *as though I were.* • It's *like they're* taking out of your hand what you worked for the whole year. Use *as if they were.* • It's not *like we're* destroying their property or breaking out windows down here. Use *as if we were.* • She looked at me *like I was* insane. Use *as though I were.* • He would sing *like he was* praying. Use *as though he were.*

As if or *as though* is the proper expression to use when a verb in the conditional form follows (or should follow).

likely Misused for *apt. Apt* suggests a tendency or disposition to do something ("The Fed is more apt to raise rates if it believes that the economy is growing too quickly"), and *likely,* something expected or probable ("Most riders who use the Metro bus system within the city of Cincinnati likely won't have to pay a fare increase next year").

likewise Misused for *so do I* (or similar words).

• I cannot abide his behavior.

Likewise. Use *Nor can I.*

• It's nice to meet you.

Likewise. USE *As it is to meet you.*

• I love being with them.

Likewise. USE *So do I.*

In the sense of *similarly, in the same way,* or *in addition* ("I invite others to do likewise"; "Likewise, the nesting activities of house wrens, cardinals, chickadees, and other common birds can stimulate a lifelong interest in nature"), *likewise* is a perfectly good word. In the sense of *so do I* (or the juvenile *me too*) or *same to you,* it's ungrammatical.

lineage Misspelling of *linage.* • Dow Jones told investors at the UBS Warburg media conference that November ad *lineage* was down 12 percent, and that total ad *lineage* in December would be down about 30 percent from a year before. USE *linage.* • Increase your print *lineage* by running a directory ad that lists the businesses in town with websites. USE *linage.* • A hurricane howls between Havana and Miami, chewing up hundreds of hours of airtime and miles of newspaper *lineage,* all in the name of a six-year-old boy. USE *linage.*

Linage (LIE-nij) is the number of lines of printed, usually advertising, material. *Lineage* (LIN-ee-ij) is direct descent from an ancestor. Though some dictionaries offer the spelling *lineage* as a variant of *linage,* this practice is less than helpful, and doubtless little other than the result of people confusing one word for the other.

linguitics Misspelling of *linguistics.* • This book aims to provide such a broad perspective, based on expertise and experience of the contributors, who are specialists in *linguitics,* applied *linguitics,* phonetics, phonology, and ESL. USE *linguistics.* • Students can learn more about the minor in *linguitics* by contacting one of the three instructors of *linguitics* listed below. USE *linguistics.*

Linguists, perhaps more than others, incorrectly spell the word *linguitics.*

litany Misused for *list.* • Iverson listed a whole *litany* of reasons for a debacle that left the crowd booing the 76ers throughout the second half. Use *list.* • Zauzmer pointed to a mortgage of $227,000 that Commerce approved for Kemp despite a very low credit score and a *litany* of creditors seeking almost $40,000 from him. Use *list.* • In his annual State of the City address, Reed recited a *litany* of accomplishments that he said have taken place during those years. Use *list.*

A *litany* is a prayer consisting of a series of petitions recited by a leader alternating with fixed responses; a tedious recital or repetitive series. A *list* is a number of items, typically printed one below another.

literally Misuwsed for *figuratively* (or similar words). • I have been reading about indigenous tribes whose members have very few possessions and live very simple lives, yet they *literally* radiate happiness. Delete *literally.* • Ted Heller's diabolically witty debut novel, *Slab Rat,* is a *literally* bloody farce about life and death in a too-fancy New York magazine office housed in a slablike tower. Delete *literally.* • We are not only a society that is *literally* drowning in a sea of sexual evil, but we seem to be enjoying it. Delete *literally.*

The misuse of *literally,* which in these examples means actually or in fact, occasions more mirth than does the misuse of many other words.

> Characters from books literally leap off the page in this engrossing, action-packed fantasy by the author of *The Thief Lord.*
>
> —Sharon Rawlins, *School Library Journal*
>
> The characters, of course, do not *literally* leap off the page; since *literally* is the wrong word, we might easily wonder whether the book is indeed engrossing and action-packed or, more likely, tedious and unreadable.

literately Misused for *literally.* • The Fulton County Playhouse is a nonprofit theater located about a mile outside of Byrant, Illinois. It is *literately* in an old barn. Use *literally.* • Since *literately* anyone can stand up as representatives, there is room for entrepreneurs. Use *literally.*

• A properly crafted worm could *literately* hit millions or tens of millions of IM clients very quickly. USE *literally.*

Literately is the adverb of *literate,* able to read and write. *Literally* means in a literal or strict sense; word for word. SEE ALSO **alliterate**; **literally**.

literature The pronunciation of *literature* is (LIT-er-ah-*choor*), not (LIT-rah-*choor*).

loan Misused for *lend.* • The nation's largest union-owned life insurance company says it's willing to *loan* more than $110 million toward a new stadium for the Florida Marlins. USE *lend.* • The equipment is owned by the U.S. Forest Service, but can be *loaned* indefinitely to state forestry departments. USE *lent.* • We have money to *loan*. USE *lend.*

Loan is a noun. *Lend* is a verb. Today, *loan* is also much used as a verb because banks and mortgage companies are concerned with making loans, and the verb *loan,* better than the more casual *lend,* reminds people that they owe money. Use *lend*; usurers *loan*.

loathe Misused for *loath.* • In a culture based on a deep understanding of such interconnectedness, individuals would be as *loathe* to hurt their neighbor, or the ecosystem, as we are now *loathe* to stub our toe. USE *loath.* • New Zealand's wind power potential is vast, writes James Weir, but wind farms are something that many kiwis are *loathe* to have in their line of sight. USE *loath.* • I am breastfeeding her, and she seems *loathe* to give it up. USE *loath.* • Remembrances of you litter my apartment here and there, and so I am *loathe* to clean—and you linger still. USE *loath.* • Winter visitors have been *loathe* to leave this year. USE *loath.* • Americans value their malls, however, and would be *loathe* to see downtown derelict businesses, even the locally owned ones, rescued at the expense of mall-rat heavens. USE *loath.*

Loathe (LOATHE) a verb, means to dislike greatly, hate, or detest; *loath* (LOTH), an adjective, means disinclined, reluctant. If people could grasp the difference in pronunciation, perhaps they could grasp the difference in meaning. Here, too, dictionary makers do us a disservice by recommending the same pronunciation (and, some, even the same spelling) for both words.

long-lived Even though most people pronounce the word with a short *i* sound, the long *i* is correct. The *lived* of *long-lived* derives from the word *life,* not the word *live*. SEE ALSO **short-lived**.

lose Misused for *loose.* • The slogan "*lose* lips sink ships" was popularized during Word War II in Britain, when the entire country was mobilized, to increase security awareness in the population. USE *loose.* • She is a *lose* woman so any player who is able to role play it well enough could leave early. USE *loose.* • As the election saga in Florida winds up, the Bush and Gore legal teams tie up *lose* ends, including putting a stop to all legal initiatives. USE *loose.*

Lose (LOOZ) means to lack the possession of; to mislay. *Loose* (LOOS) means not fastened or restrained; not taut; not bound.

luxurious Misused for *luxuriant.* • Instead of keeping a *luxurious* growth of photosynthetic tissue from ground to crown, the typical palm sheds leaves as it grows, retaining only a tuft of greenery at the very top. USE *luxuriant.* • Such *luxurious* growth signals high productivity, and modern scientific measurements confirm this. USE *luxuriant.* • Its organic botanicals and minerals act like a conditioning tonic, insuring fuller, thicker, more *luxurious* hair. USE *luxuriant.* • We take you south of Puerto Vallarta, Mismaloya, into the beautiful, *luxurious* jungle where movies such as *Predator* were shot. USE *luxuriant.*

Luxurious means characterized by luxury; splendid, rich, or extremely comfortable. *Luxuriant,* characterized by a lush or abundant growth; excessively florid.

-ly An adverb (often ending in *-ly*), not an adjective, modifies a verb. Still, fewer and fewer people are bothering to pronounce (or spell) the *-ly* suffix. If it's laziness that accounts for this, then what is to deter people from one day also neglecting to pronounce other word elements, such as *-ic* and *-ed, -ing* and *-ous*? If it's ignorance, then what is to become of clarity, of understanding, of meaning itself? • Not only did the little boy get away *safe,* he also called the police. USE *safely.* • She learns very *quick.* USE *quickly.* • Women usually treat me *terrible.* USE *terribly.* • He is behaving very *irrational.* USE *irrationally.* • You're doing *fantastic.* USE *fantastically.*

• They showed us how to build the product as small and as *cheap* as possible. USE *cheaply.* • Your position on taxes is so *screaming* loud, we can't help but know it. USE *screamingly.* • Don't take this *personal.* USE *personally.* • Didn't they take you *serious*? USE *seriously.* • They never called in and said he was acting belligerent. USE *belligerently.* • I wondered what you meant by "sloppily written," since I do not write *sloppy*. USE *sloppily*.

Most adverbs end in the suffix *-ly,* but some, such as *seldom, often, very, quite, somewhat, rather,* and *altogether,* do not. An adverb modifies a verb; an adjective does not—except among the heathen. SEE ALSO **doubtlessly**.

We'd like high schools to take the twelfth grade serious.

—Bill Sederburg, Utah Commissioner of Higher Education

Live adventurous.

—Outback Steakhouse TV commercial

But you better move quick to your local Honda dealer.

—Honda TV commercial

Mm

machination The pronunciation of *machination* is (*mak*-ah-NAY-shen), not (*mash*-ah-NAY-shen).

manor Misused for *manner.* • It is perfectly possible to take the changes we are going to recommend in a revenue-neutral *manor.* USE *manner.* • His *manor* of deliverance was almost Shakespearian. USE *manner.* • Rape is a power-driven, violent assault that is acted out in a sexual *manor.* USE *manner.*

A *manor* is a mansion; the principal residence on an estate. *Manner* is a way of acting; a way in which something is done; kind or sort.

M

mantel Misused for *mantle.* • Our Lady was clad in a robe of dazzling whiteness, over which she wore a *mantel* of heavenly blue. USE *mantle.* • Johnson kept his illness out of public view and struggled to wear the mask and the *mantel* of the corporate executive. USE *mantle.* • Thus, when a strongman passes from the scene, there is often a dearth of qualified candidates to assume the *mantel* of leadership. USE *mantle.*

A *mantel* is a shelf above a fireplace. A *mantle* is a cloak or shawl; something that covers or conceals; an important role or responsibility that passes from one person to another.

Some dictionaries maintain that *mantel* is a variant spelling of *mantle,* and *mantle* of *mantel,* but this is hardly helpful. Let the distinct spelling of each word denote the distinct meaning of each word.

marrage Misspelling of *marriage.* • Janie's *marrage* to Logan Killicks is an unhappy one for her, as she loses many of her girlish fantasies about love and *marrage.* USE *marriage.* • A sham *marrage* is better than no *marrage* at all. USE *marriage.*

The word *marriage* contains *-iage,* "I age"—a suitable mnemonic. SEE ALSO **adultry**.

marshal Misused for *martial.* • Then-mayor Dewey Archambault declared *marshal* law and summoned National Guard troops and Works Progress Administration workers to help clear roads and maintain order. USE *martial.* • Once complete, the 36,000-square foot facility will offer a wide range of programs for children, including soccer, dance, basketball, *marshal* arts, cheerleading, climbing, and gymnastics. USE *martial.* • If charged, punishment will range from anything to no punishment at all to a court-*marshal,* which brings the case to trial in a military court. USE *martial.* • Rapier combat is a *marshal* activity enjoyed by many in the Society for Creative Anachronism, both as an exciting active pursuit and as a very entertaining spectator sport. USE *martial.*

The noun *marshal* means an officer; a military commander; an official in charge of ceremonies. The verb means to arrange in order; to array; to manage; to guide or usher someone ceremoniously. *Martial* means relating to war or military forces; warlike; characteristic of a warrior. SEE ALSO **marshall**.

M

marshall Misspelling of *marshal.* • Be discreet, be respectful at all times, be on time, dress appropriately, follow the directions of the parade *marshall* and you will be welcome next time. USE *marshal.* • Illustrious Master John D. Schaeffer served as *marshall* of ceremonies, Dorsey B. Reynolds was the toastmaster, and Joseph V. Gaddy delivered the after-dinner address. USE *marshal.* • The Alabama fire *marshall's* office, along with the ATF, are investigating the cause of the explosion, since no power or gas was hooked up to the house. USE *marshal's.*

The correct spelling of *marshal* has one *l,* not two. SEE ALSO **marshal**.

marshmellow Misspelling of *marshmallow.* • There will also be *marshmellow*-roasting, cookie-decorating, train rides, horse and buggy rides, and visits to Santa. USE *marshmallow.* • I tipped the *marshmellow*-shaped muscle into my mouth the same way you'd down an oyster, and I chewed. USE *marshmallow.*

Though pronounced (MARSH-mal-oh) or (MARSH-mel-oh), you spell the confection only *marshmallow.*

martial Misused for *marital.* • The purpose of the Women's Resource Center is to educate women on all pregnancy options, while promoting the values of the sanctity of human life, premarital abstinence, and *martial* fidelity in our community. Use *marital.* • Just ask for our wedding package and you'll be well on your way to *martial* bliss. Use *marital.* • If you had *premartial* sex during your engagement period is that still a sin? Use *premarital.*

And *marital* is occasionally misused for *martial*: • The Konasari Regulars represent the bulk of the Undercity's *marital* forces. Use *martial.*

Adjectives both, *marital* means of or relating to marriage or to a husband; whereas *martial* means of or relating to war or the armed forces.

masonary Misspelling of *masonry.* • She said 45 people were evacuated, but the station "stayed on the air" during the fire, which originated in an office in the middle of the one-story, *masonary* building. Use *masonry.* • We have been in the *masonary* business over 15 years and we have insurance. Use *masonry.*

A mason's trade, brickwork, or stonework, *masonry* (MAY-son-ree), not *masonary* (MAY-son-air-ee), is the correct spelling (and pronunciation).

masseur Misused for *masseuse.* • Being a qualified back *masseur,* she's bound to release all of your tensions! Use *masseuse.* • She is an excellent sports *masseur.* Use *masseuse.*

Masseurs are males who give massages; *masseuses* are females who give massages. Perhaps lexicographers will agree that this is a distinction that ought to be respected.

masterful Misused for *masterly.* • The world's most compromised human (see Michael Kelly's *masterful* 1993 *New York Times* magazine cover story "David Gergen: Master of the Game," if you don't believe me) was a terrific and evenhanded moderator for the only Coakley–Brown debate anyone bothered to watch. Use *masterly.* • Part of me hopes Barack Obama does not deliver yet another soaring, *masterful* speech for his maiden State of the Union address tomorrow. USE *masterly.*

These two sentences observe the distinction between the words: • Aren't women supposed to like domineering, *masterful* men like me? • He had an answer for Nadal's best tennis, playing with a stunning blend of power, *masterly* defense, and deft volleying.

The distinction between these two words is well worth preserving. *Masterful* means domineering or imperious, and *masterly* means expert or skillful.

masticate Misused for *masturbate.* • You can *masticate* at the beach, on a boat, in an airplane, or while talking on the phone. USE *masturbate.*

Old jokes are always new to some people. A person who doesn't smile or smirk on hearing this one may need to be told the punch line: *masticate* means to chew food; *masturbate* means to stimulate one's own or another's genitals for sexual pleasure.

mature The pronunciation of *mature* is (mah-CHOOR), not (mah-TYOOR).

maunder Confused with *meander. Maunder* (MON-der) means to talk incoherently; to move or act aimlessly ("Music makes me write this sort of maundering adolescent nonsense without embarrassment"; "This of course invokes the image of the maundering gypsy near an abyss with a sack tied to a staff hoisted over his shoulder"). *Meander* (mee-AN-der) means to follow a winding course; to wander leisurely ("If you were to explore almost any meandering river you would find the landforms that are shown in the diagram to the right"; "Included here is Doughty's meandering but strange hymn in praise of desert camels"). As you see, *maunder* and *meander* have similar meanings—to move about or express oneself aimlessly—but someone who *maunders* is being disparaged, whereas someone who *meanders* is not.

medias Misused for *media.* • When suicide bombers attack schools, bus stations, marketplaces, or other highly populated civilian areas, the biased liberal *medias* of the world all turn a blind eye. USE *media.* • Her art covers many aspects and *medias,* but today she is most widely noted for her sport action figures, portraits, and pet portraits, but also does seascapes, landscapes, or still life should a client request them. USE *media.* • I want extra batteries for the remotes, an extra bulb for the projector, two backup copies of the presentation (naturally, in two different *medias*). USE *media.*

As *data*—not *datas*—is the plural of *datum,* so *media*—not *medias*—is the plural of *medium.* Though *media* is sometimes used and allowed as a singular word, *medias* as a plural is insupportable.

mendicity Confused with *mendacity. Mendicity* (men-DIS-i-tee) means begging or beggary ("In 1814 an Institution for the Relief of the Poor of Douglas and the Suppression of Mendicity was established based on voluntary subscriptions whose aim was to help the needy poor"); *mendacity* (men-DAS-i-tee), untruthfulness, lying ("Bush's mendacity on economic matters was obvious even during the 2000 election, but lately it has reached almost pathological levels").

meretricious Misused for *meritorious.* • I informed her that that was a *meretricious* plan except for the fact that it involves lying. USE *meritorious.* • They serve the public interest by reminding readers not to believe a message simply because it is widely distributed, and carries the *meretricious* authority of the published word. USE *meritorious.* • If the Other Side is Wrong, their arguments, however *meretricious,* will not in the end survive exposure to ours. USE *meritorious.*

Meretricious means of or relating to a prostitute; falsely or vulgarly attractive; pretentious. It does not mean *meritorious,* having merit, deserving of honor.

meritous Misused for *meritorious.* • It is *meritous* to proceed to renew the ablution after having made an obligatory prayer or a supererogatory prayer and having gone round the Kaaba. USE *meritorious.* • The *Meritous* Circle of Honor is given to a member whose achievements in the field of battle, both in terms of leadership and servitude, are exemplary and unable to be fathomed. USE *meritorious.* • But for society to be able to reward a *meritous* person in right measure, society must first measure his merit.

Use *meritorious.* • In 1990, it received the ACS Award for Outstanding Performance by Divisions in recognition of its service to its members and its *meritous* contributions to the profession and the public understanding of chemistry. Use *meritorious.*

Meritous, at best, is but a mumbler's way of pronouncing *meritorious.* See also **superity**.

message Misused for *write* (or similar words). • "The third quarter is looking great," Lay *messaged* an Enron worker on September 26, three weeks before the company announced $638 million in third-quarter losses. Use *told.* • "Was your idea meant as tongue-in-cheek or are you serious?" *messaged* one reader. Use *wrote.* • Clyde went to check out the tractors the day before the sale and *messaged* John that both of them started easily, although it had been a couple of years since either had run. Use *emailed.*

In the sense of to send a message, the verb *message* is disagreeable; in the sense of to mail, email, write, or tell, it is abhorrent. In the sense of to instant message, it is conceivably useful, but most people today speak of texting rather than instant messaging.

metal Misused for *medal.* • I am the first male squash player from the United States to earn a *metal*! (Mark Talbott won a *metal* eight years ago, but he did not earn it, it was by default). Use *medal.* • Sara Gray and Sheena Bohn both *metaled* in the 800-meter run. Use *medaled.*

A *metal* (MET-el) is typically hard, shiny, malleable, and a good conductor of electricity and heat. A *medal* (MED-el) is often, though not always, made of *metal* and is given as an award or in recognition of some achievement or event. See also **mettle**.

metal Misused for *mettle.* • Trust me, I want to be pleased and surprised if both should not only prove their *metal* in supporting the progressive agenda. Use *mettle.* • Now Ring is given a chance to bring his undefeated record and show his *metal* against the biggest names in the sport. Use *mettle.*

Both *metal* and *mettle* are pronounced (MET-el). *Mettle* is the ability to cope with difficult situations; resilience; strength of spirit.

metric Misused for *measure* (or similar words). • Has TSA sought to develop a *metric* for the average time required to effectively and efficiently process passengers and baggage at each airport? USE *measure.* • Don't look at just one *metric,* such as the price-to-book value ratio, when researching a stock. USE *measure.* • Earnings are the single most important *metric* for a company. USE *measure.* • And what I would look at is not the *metric* of the bombings and the casualties, as tragic as they are, but some *metrics* which I would say would be a little bit more objective. USE *magnitude; measurements.*

Among the self-important and silly-headed, *metric* is displacing *measure* (or *measurement*). No highly regarded dictionary can claim that *metric* is a synonym for *measure,* but as people imitate the best of one another so they imitate the worst. Only the suffix *-metric* means relating to measurement.

This use of *metric* does not refer to metric weights and measures, not to the metric system, not to metric tons, not to metric miles. It is simply a scientific-sounding word that people, uneasy with their own understanding of words and numbers, use instead of a perfectly understandable word like *measure.*

> And then secondarily, what you see is there's obviously been a metric and a measurement of the Iraqi forces and their ability to take over, because I think most of the forces involved in Operation Thunder will be Iraqi forces.
>
> —Brigadier General James "Spider" Marks

mettle Misused for *meddle.* • As I *mettled* with the system I encountered a new firewall, which immediately locked the key functions. USE *meddled.* • I do not *mettle* in affairs of the heart. USE *meddle.*

And *meddle,* like *metal,* is misused for *mettle*: • He proved his *meddle* with a good qualifying effort at his home Grand Prix only to have the boat banged up in the second qualifying session after qualifying sixth and failing to start in Helsinki. USE *mettle.*

Mettle, a noun, is quality of character or temperament, especially, highly regarded qualities such as spirit and courage. *Meddle,* a verb, is to interfere in; to tamper with. SEE ALSO **metal**.

might Confused with *may*. *Might* is used to express a possibility that is less likely than that expressed by the word *may* ("The looming deficit might or might not be important, but it has no moral implications of any kind"; "A labor dispute will destroy any inroads the game has made into nontraditional hockey markets and it might just be the final straw for some of the loyal fans"). *Might* is also the past tense of *may.* SEE ALSO **can**.

milk toast Misused for *milquetoast.* • Common idea is that of being a spineless, cowardly, *milk-toast* creature—one who never gets angry, and who always compromises. USE *milquetoast.*

A *milquetoast* is a meek, submissive person (usually a man). The word was the creation of Harold Tucker Webster (1885–1952), an American cartoonist whose character Caspar Milquetoast was as bland as *milk toast,* buttered toast served in warm milk.

millenary Misused for *millinery.* • Karamu Performing Arts Theater seeks a *millenary* to make costume hats for its Black Nativity show. USE *millinery.* • In most cases *millenary* wire is sewn to the edges of buckram pieces to add extra stiffness and to be able to shape the final hat. USE *millinery.* They must have had a great *millenary* shop at the time. Not your basic hats! USE *millinery.*

Though pronounced alike (MIL-ah-*ner*-ee), *millenary* means of or relating to a thousand; a thousand years. *Millinery* means women's hats or the business of a milliner.

miniscule Misspelling of *minuscule.* • It should be noted that these three New York organizations are not small-time "mom & pop" groups that raise *miniscule* amounts at weekly church bake sales. USE *minuscule.* • Several *miniscule* but high-capacity drives from different manufacturers have been produced or are about to be, and some appeared at the recent Consumer Electronics Show (CES) in Las Vegas. USE *minuscule.*

Minuscule is so often misspelled *miniscule* that some dictionaries, bent as they certainly seem to be on promoting the dissolution of the language, allow the misspelling—which, of course, makes it more likely that people will continue to misspell the word—calling it a variant spelling when in fact it is altogether a misspelling. *Minuscule* derives not from "mini" (of small size, as in "miniskirt"); it derives from "minus" (less).

Aside from meaning very small, *minuscule* also refers to a lowercase letter; compare *majuscule* (a large letter, either capital or uncial). SEE ALSO **miniscule** in **appendix A**.

minutia Misused for *minute.* • Midway through his junior year, Rick switched majors ("I enjoy business," he said, "I didn't enjoy the sort of *minutia* study of it") and transferred to Calvin College, where he majors in mass media. USE *minute.* • A million-and-a-half dollars for a city is *minutia.* USE *minute.*

Minute (my-NOOT), an adjective, means exceptionally small; insignificant; extremely thorough and meticulous. *Minutia,* a noun, is a small, trivial detail. Perhaps more disturbing than the misuse of *minutia* for *minute* is the mispronunciation of it. *Minutia* is better pronounced (mi-NOO-shee-ah), not (mi-NOO-shah), as the lazy ones would have it. The plural of *minutia* is *minutiae,* whose only pronunciation is (mi-NOO-shee-ee). Though people may mean *minutiae* (mi-NOO-shee-ee), they invariably spell it *minutia* and pronounce it (mi-NOO-shah) or, occasionally, (mi-NOO-shy).

• It's the basic framework of government, not the day-to-day *minutia that is* involved in statutory law. USE *minutiae that are.* • They're all reminders—tangible or imagined—of the lives he touched, the people he knew and loved, the *minutia* that made up his life. USE *minutiae.* • Often in discussions like this people get bogged down in the *minutia* surrounding such attacks. USE *minutiae.*

mischievious Misspelling of *mischievous.* • They alleged that the construction of Kalabagh Dam was merely a *mischievious* act on part of the co-Musharraf ruling party to divert the attention of the public from the current national issues. USE *mischievous.* • The insinuation that three prostitutes were found in the rooms of our client and his colleague Garfield Smith is false, *mischievious,* and malicious. USE *mischievous.*

Two *i*'s, not three, are used to spell *mischievous.* At least one dictionary in the Fiske Ranking of College Dictionaries (see appendix B) does include the pronunciation (mis-CHEE-vee-es) as an alternative to the correct (MIS-chi-ves).

> It will be on ABC next weekend, a daunting job, keeping up with the mischievious little girl, who lives at New York's Plaza Hotel with her dog Weenie and her turtle Skipper B.
>
> —Daryn Kagan, former CNN anchor
>
> I think the stories that have been playing are just inaccurate and mischievious.
>
> —Former U.S. secretary of defense Donald Rumsfeld

misconfusion Misused for *confusion* (or similar words). • Sorry for the *misconfusion.* Use *confusion.* • And I don't like the *misconfusion* about our ethnicity and culture with the Arabs. Use *misunderstanding.* • My *misconfusion* again; I was thinking of William Macy who is in *Fargo.* Use *mistake.* • I bring this up because of the *misconfusion* here in the United States, and because of something I wrote earlier for a college personal statement. Use *confusion.* • Actually, to clear any *misconfusion* the refs use latex gloves as an extra precautionary measure. Use *confusion.*

Confusion, mistake, misunderstanding are all perfectly good words; *misconfusion* is a word only among those prone to confusion, mistakes, and misunderstanding.

misconscrew Misspelling of *misconstrue.* • You take a comment about the privacy of a family's pain and *misconscrew* it into something completely offtopic and wrong because you can't refute my original argument. Use *misconstrue.* • Why do you always *misconscrew* what I say? Use *misconstrue.* • If you are someone who may *misconscrew* it that way, then I suggest skipping this site and checking eBay for Lawrence Welk albums. Use *misconstrue.* • I think it is safe to say that my inner beauty outshines my outer beauty, but just so that you do not *misconscrew* that as meaning I must be a dog: I have pictures to exchange. Use *misconstrue.*

Misconstrue, to misinterpret or mistake the meaning of, is the true spelling.

mispell (misspel) Misspelling of *misspell.* • One common error in writing function is to *mispell* the function, in which case, either Excel effectuates an unwanted function or does not understand the function. USE *misspell.* • Proofread, proofread, proofread! I can't stress this enough. Especially when you are typing fast and not looking at the screen as you race to get your thoughts down, words get *mispelled* accidentally. USE *misspelled.* • Metabolife is sometimes *mispelled* as metabalife or metabalife 356. On occasion it has, also, been *mispelled* as metabilife or metabilife 356. USE *misspelled.*

Misspell is spelled correctly when it has two *s*'s and two *l*'s; all other spellings are misspellings.

mitigate Misused for *militate.* • But this is only one side of the story; inner cities are also rich in culture, institutions, and other resources that can *mitigate* against adversity and promote healthy development and learning. USE *militate.* • Nutri-Rice has been known to increase energy, improve general health, *mitigate* against numerous degenerative diseases, and slow the aging process. USE *militate.* • Other factors also *mitigate* in favor of appellant. USE *militate.* • Personality traits of activists *mitigate* in favor of and against archivists' adoption of marketing as a strategy for advancing the archival service to society, but the reference archivist must use character strengths to overcome the weaknesses. USE *militate.*

The phrase *against* or *for* or *in favor of* invariably follows *militate,* not *mitigate.* To *militate* is to work or fight against (or sometimes for), whereas to *mitigate* is to lessen or alleviate, to improve.

momentarily Confused with *momently. Momentarily* means for a moment ("Then came a play that momentarily disrupted the mood"). *Momently* means from moment to moment; at any moment ("We expect him to arrive momently").

mongerer Misspelling for *monger.* • George Bush is a war-*mongerer* in my opinion. USE *monger.* • I wonder how much of this climate of revenge against him he created by being a hate *mongerer* himself. USE *monger.*

• I'd heard about this from Carlo, who is a *mongerer* of conspiracy theories and other misinformation. USE *monger*. • Utah's second-leading scorer has noted *New York Post* rumor *mongerer* Peter Vecsey to thank for his heartburn. USE *monger*.

Monger, as either a verb or a noun, is the correct spelling; *mongerer* is incorrect.

monolog The spelling *monologue* is preferable to *monolog*. SEE ALSO **dialog**.

morale Misused for *moral*. • The *morale* of the story is to start celebrating backward decision making. USE *moral*. • They have no *morales* when it comes to customer satisfaction. USE *morals*. • So he chooses his own *morales*, his own beliefs, and among those *morales* and beliefs are he should help save humanity. USE *morals*.

A *moral* is a lesson or principle taught in a fable, story, or event; *morals* are standards, principles, or habits of right or wrong conduct. *Morale* is a state of mind or spirit with respect to courage, confidence, discipline, endurance, and the like ("The new rules don't keep the North Koreans from getting the military information they want, but it does hurt morale among South Korean troops"; "Killing Osama Bin Laden hasn't just been great for America's morale; it's also been great for Hollywood").

M

morays Misused for *mores*. • Finally, citing the existence of religious social *morays* has no bearing on the validity of atheism. USE *mores*. • In Amsterdam's Red Light District, social *morays* are cast aside. USE *mores*. • It is simply amazing that Ms. Whitney would find it amusing to denigrate the social *morays* of both the Valley and the University of Alabama in a single article, and that the editors considered and approved it as "newsworthy." USE *mores*.

The word for the customs, conventions, or traditions of a community or society is *mores*, not *morays*. People who misspell the word *morays* reveal they do not read, or if they read, they do not think.

Mores is pronounced (MOR-az), not (MOR), not (MORS), despite the second pronunciation that some dictionaries offer. The singular of *mores* is *mos*, pronounced (MO).

> In some issue areas where social morays are still being defined, such as the use of genetic engineering in food production, the Social Values funds take a precautionary approach by avoiding firms who expect to derive substantial revenues from products relying on acceptance of these technologies.
>
> —Acuityfunds.com
>
> Never do business with companies whose literature is badly written ("morays," "issue areas," "firms who"). If they take no time to prepare their literature, they take no time to please their clients.

more preferable Misused for *preferable.* • Like the gender approach, staff often regard participation as a more inclusive, and therefore *more preferable,* strategy for benefiting women. Use *preferable.* • It's possible to change the question to accommodate the answer, but in this case, it's much easier and *more preferable* to change the answer instead. Use *preferable.* • Why, you might even find some new ones *more preferable* to your own. Use *preferable.*

M

More preferable is redundant. *Preferable,* which means more desirable than an alternative, is all the comparison that is needed.

more . . . rather than Misused for *more . . . than.* • Many of the problems I present are more sociological and marketing-related *rather than* technical. Use *than.* • More office space was vacated *rather than* leased in 2001. Use *than.* • African-American teens also were more likely to identify figures known through the media *rather than* family or friends. Use *than.* • For Microsoft, the post release debate centered more on the product registration mechanisms of the new OS *rather than* on any of its other features. Use *than.* • Jill Kirschenbaum, the title's new honcho, emphasized her plan to give the magazine a facelift and focus more on women *rather than* the act of parenting. Use *than.*

After the word *more,* do not use *rather than* when *than* alone is required.

moreso Misused for *more so.* • While it may not be killing trees, it is alienating to be endlessly pitched to, even *moreso* when they have you figured out. USE *more so.* • We still get the best of the old standards—even *moreso* in some cases. USE *more so.* • We have now and will have even *moreso* in the future a unity that binds us all as one people, one family. USE *more so.* • It's partially because of the wacky plots and situations Mike Allred likes to put his characters into . . . but *moreso* because the book seems to vary in strength. USE *more so.*

Despite the frequency with which some people use *moreso,* it is necessarily two words, *more so,* meaning to an even greater degree or extent.

moresome Misused for *more* (or similar words). • The Couples Group is for couples and individuals who are part of a couple, triad, foursome, or *moresome.* USE *more.* • With one devilishly simple activity she manages to get them to delve way back into their pasts, open up, and get totally immersed in the activity, as well as potentially use every conceivable English tense and *moresome.* USE *more.* • Now Cockshutt, now Moline, now John Deere and Fordson! Then Oliver, Allis, Massey, and *moresome*! USE *others.* • Spanish style Hacienda home appr. 6,000 sq. ft. built with high quality construction large lot approximately 450' x 450' excellent landscaping, gazebo in rear and much much *moresome* furniture included. USE *more.*

Although meant to describe more than a two-, three-, or foursome—and often used by the sexually ever unsatisfied—*moresome* is finding its way into popular usage. Like the equally odious *moreso, moresome* is an abomination.

And then there are instances where the intended meaning of *moresome* is completely elusory: • Its extremely fruity bouquet, with that delicate touch of woodiness, makes it extraordinarily *moresome.* • In the case of *Satanic Verses* we had a book and an author. But the *moresome* Muslims hit that author the stronger that author became.

moribund Misused for *morbid.* • Park seamlessly sutures relentless violence, a *moribund* fascination with death, and the carnivalesque into shots bursting with perfection of color, angle, and composition. Use *morbid.* • HCPCS 43842, gastric restrictive procedure, without gastric bypass, is for *moribund* obesity. Use *morbid.* • A *moribund* curiosity has overtaken him recently, causing the unearthing of old notebooks, letters, photographs, and the usual detritus of existence. Use *morbid.* • My own favorite is Buster Keaton, whose visual gags and *moribund* humor are clear precedents. Use *morbid.*

Morbid means unhealthy or diseased; having an unhealthy interest in disturbing or gloomy subjects; gruesome or grisly; pathological. *Moribund* means dying; at the point of death; having little vitality.

much Misused for *many.* • The Dow Jones Industrials Average rose 57 points, or 0.6 percent, to 9,930 after being up as *much* as 53 points earlier in the session. Use *many.* • *Much* of these developments have their origins in the gradual developments in earlier prehistory within the region itself. Use *Many.* • Last time I checked, my rant about the *New York Times* had generated 85 comments, *much* of them splintering off into a discussion about which city has better cuisine: NYC or DC? Use *many.*

Like other words, *much* is used with amounts or quantities, and *many* with numbers or that which can be counted. See also **amount**; **less**.

muchly Misused for *very much* (or similar words). • Thank you *muchly.* Use *very much.* • I love you *muchly.* Use *very much.* • Thanks to the *muchly* revered Edward Norton and his performance in *Fight Club.* Use *much.* • She is annoying me *muchly.* Use *a good deal.* • Any help on this is *muchly* appreciated! Use *much.*

The correct adverb is *much* or *very much.* See also **thusly**.

mucus Misused for *mucous.* • The disease is spread through blood, *mucus* membrane contact, or breast milk—one of the main reasons African nations have been hit so hard. Use *mucous.*

Mucous, not *mucus, membrane* is correct. *Mucus* is a noun; *mucous,* an adjective. Both words are pronounced (MYOO-kes). Similarly, *fungus* is a noun, and *fungous* is an adjective. Both words are pronounced (FUN-ges).

musical Confused with *musicale.* A *musical* (MYOO-zi-kel) is a theatrical production featuring dialogue and a musical score. A *musicale* (*myoo*-zi-KAL) is a party or social gathering that features a musical program.

mute Misused for *moot.* • For the bolts there were a few good individual performances in Tempe but the subpar play of the team as a whole make it a *mute* point. USE *moot.* • This is the requisite "if I were stranded on a desert island I would take" list; of course, it's a *mute* discussion, since desert islands have no electricity. USE *moot.*

Mute (MYOOT) means unable to speak; not speaking or not spoken; a silent, or unpronounced, letter in a word. *Moot* (MOOT), as an adjective, means open to discussion; debatable; not worthy of discussion because the matter has been settled or no longer needs to be settled.

Nn

nauseous Misused for *nauseated.* • Why do I sometimes feel *nauseous* 15 minutes after a workout? USE *nauseated.* • Many women feel *nauseous* at some point in pregnancy, usually in the first trimester. USE *nauseated.* • Praying the rest of the drinks wouldn't make me *nauseous,* I took a right off of Huntington and walked to the Espresso Royal Caffe. USE *nauseated.*

Nauseous means causing nausea or stomach distress. *Nauseated* means suffering from nausea. In these examples, working out, being pregnant, and drinking cause nausea; they are nauseous. And the result is feeling nauseated. The word *feel* or *make me* often precedes *nauseated,* not *nauseous.*

nauty Misspelling of *naughty.* • Each time I upload my *nauty* party video clips they just disappear on me. USE *naughty.* • It was soon discovered that the Taliban were listed on the *nauty* list. USE *naughty.* • Santa Claus reads the list of who's been *nauty* or nice. USE *naughty.*

Spelling is best learned by memorization and reading. Eventually, you'll recognize that *accommodation* has two *m*'s; *accidentally,* two *l*'s; *aberration,* one *b,* two *r*'s; and *naughty,* a *gh.*

navel Misused for *naval.* • Israeli *navel* forces also kidnapped the fishermen Mahmoud Ahmed Hussein and Hussein Qaour. USE *naval.* • The Communists in Korea, he declared, can be stopped by air and *navel* forces instead of ground forces. USE *naval.*

Naval, an adjective, means relating to a navy. *Navel,* a noun, is the belly button, the depression in the middle of the abdomen that marks where the umbilical cord was attached to the fetus.

near Misused for *nearly*. • We can predict with *near* 100 percent certainty that at some point during the season Ben Bostrom will proclaim that his Suzuki GSX-R1000 is "the best bike in the world" or words to that effect. USE *nearly.* • Offering gear with *near-unheard-of* price/performance ratios was—and remains—an Alesis trademark. USE *nearly.*

In the sense of almost or just about or all but, the better word is *nearly,* not *near.*

necropsy The pronunciation of *necropsy*—an autopsy, especially one performed on animals—is (NEK-*rop*-see), not (NEE-*krop*-see).

niggardly *Niggardly* (used as an adjective or an adverb) means stingy; parsimonious; meager and inadequate. The noun (or adjective) *niggard,* a miser or stingy person, is seldom seen. Some dictionaries maintain that *niggardly* (and *niggard*) ought to be used very carefully, if used at all, because many people (no brighter than the average laxicographer) believe that the word means negro (or nigger) and that it is therefore offensive. SEE ALSO **racial**.

N

no Misused for *any.* • They wouldn't have *no* idea whatsoever unless they went up to the attic. USE *any*. • We don't have *no* money at all, 'cause I pay the rent, so right now, I don't have anything. USE *any*. • We don't need *no* chainsaws; we got explosives. DELETE *no.*

Although heard quite often in certain parts of the United States, *no* when used with *not* (or a contraction like *wouldn't*) is a double negative that grammatically undoes the intended meaning of any sentence in which it is used.

nohow Misused for *not at all* (or similar words). • I know what you're thinking about, but it isn't so, *nohow*. USE *not at all.* • Everyone from Krugman on down thinks that the best posture is not to flinch first—to say that none of the tax cuts will be renewed, *nohow,* as long as the Big Bucks Boys benefit from the bill. USE *none at all.*

Nohow is nonstandard for expressions such as *in no way, not at all, not in any way, not in the least.*

noisome Misused for *noisy* (or similar words). • Gaahl has a revolting screech, and somehow manages to be just as *noisome* when actually holding a note. USE *loud.* • Moreover, compared to cars, and also to buses and subways, bicycles are blessedly quiet. In crowded, *noisome* New York, the bicycle's economy of space and sound is a powerful advantage. USE *noisy.* • Produced to a metallic sheen by Deftones boardmaster Ulrich Wild, the group's debut album, Wisconsin Death Trip, is a pogo spectacular of the highest order, throbbing with industrial clangs, gritty electro beats, and *noisome* guitars. USE *raucous.*

Because one word resembles another is no reason to think that their meanings are similar. *Noisome* means offensive or foul, harmful or damaging; it does not mean *noisy.*

none The proper number of *none* has befuddled people for years, especially since there is some disagreement on the matter. Whether to use *none* as a singular or plural depends on how you use it in a sentence—that is, *none* may be singular or plural.

None might mean not one or no one, in which case it would likely be used as a singular word ("There hasn't been a major new refinery in the United States since 1976, and experts say none is on the horizon"; "Yet no recession has occurred—not even a deep slowdown—and the consensus among economists is that none is in the offing").

Or it might mean not any or no amount, in which case it would likely be used as a plural word ("None of the men who are behind the ad were actually on a swift boat with Kerry"; "None are of Ukrainian descent; all are of Jewish descent, which means they may have come from Ukraine").

nonplussed Misused for *undisturbed* (or similar words). • Media workers are *nonplussed* with their working lives, with 40% describing their jobs as "ordinary" and 30% going as far as saying they were "dispiriting." USE *unexcited.* • *Nonplussed,* the local Ipswich Thistle Pipe Band has decided to set up base camp outside Lang Park two hours before the evening kickoff and let rip. USE *Unperturbed.*

Nonplussed (not *nonplused)* means bewildered or confused; surprised so that one is unable to speak or act. It does not mean, as the *non-* may suggest to some, unruffled or calm.

> Although Clark appeared nonplussed by Gore's decision—"I don't pay attention to endorsements, unless they're for me," he said—political observers suggested that the former vice president's move may have altered the dynamic of the Democratic race.
>
> —Daniel J. Hemel, *The Harvard Crimson*
>
> If Clark had been, or even appeared, *nonplussed,* he may not have uttered an intelligent word. But since he was not *nonplussed,* it is Hemel himself who does not write an intelligent word.

no problem Instead of, for instance, *you're welcome* or *my pleasure* or *not at all,* the expression *no problem* is a graceless inanity. SEE ALSO **whatever**.

normalcy Misused for *normality.* • They really appreciate any semblance of *normalcy,* because they've been removed from it. USE *normality.* • The foes of the U.S.-led occupation want to slow down and stop the progress toward *normalcy* in Iraq. USE *normality.* • In exchange for America's admiration, the stars preach the importance of *normalcy,* gratitude, and above all hard work. USE *normality.*

Though both words are in common use, *normality* is considered preferable to *normalcy.*

north of Misused for *more than* (or similar words). • After *north of* 30,000 live performances, one tragic accident is an anomaly. USE *more than.* • These emerging applications, plus renewed growth in existing markets, will help propel the global GPS market *north of* $22 billion by 2008. USE *beyond.* • Such powerful branding is practically priceless, but, based on conversations with industry sources, we estimate that Google's brand alone is worth *north of* $2 billion. USE *upwards of.* • Right now, there are fifteen states that have unemployment rates *north of* 10 percent. USE *higher than.* • Jennifer Lopez is asking for *north of* $20 million. USE *more than.*

North of, an obtuse term for *more than, higher than, beyond,* and *upwards of,* is popular among directionless writers and dizzy speakers.

The heavyweight has gone north—as in, north of 250 pounds. A kid who's 250 pounds and reasonably coordinated is better off being a football player.

—Burt Sugar, boxing writer, as quoted in the *Los Angeles Times*

The United States has two commanders north of him on the organization chart.

—General Michael Hayden, former CIA director

no sooner . . . then (when) Misused for *no sooner . . . than.* • *No sooner* had the words left my mouth *then* the geometry of the circumstance sunk in. Use *No sooner . . . than.* • Because *no sooner* had we gotten General Motors, *then* I went to New York to talk to William Zeckendorf, who was their major moving force in a lot of their real estate endeavors. Use *no sooner . . . than.* • *No sooner* had Rahman landed on—and fallen off—a scorer's table *then* someone threw a chair into the ringside seats, triggering a ten-minute melee that involved dozens of spectators and security guards. Use *No sooner . . . than.* • Corporate Apple had *no sooner* popped the champagne cork at the Expo *when* the king of the clone makers Power Computing of Round Rock, Texas, took the wraps off their latest new bomber, the Power Tower G3/275. Use *no sooner . . . than.*

It used to be that critics carped about the expression *no sooner . . . when,* but today the expression *no sooner . . . then* (as well as, oddly, *no sooner . . . that*) seems the more popular. The only correct expression is *no sooner . . . than.* See also **hardly . . . than**.

notary republic Misspelling of *notary public.* • If you would like additional information on how to become a *notary republic* please contact the secretary of state at (916) 653-3595 or visit their website. Use *notary public.* • We do offer the services of a *notary republic* through our office. Use *notary public.*

The correct, and only, spelling is *notary public.*

N

not hardly (barely; scarcely) Misused for *hardly (scarcely).* • There is *not hardly* a point on the river, below Franklin, that the sound of the steam whistle of the furnace engine cannot be heard. DELETE *not.* • So, do we now have all of the answers so we know what to expect Thursday at Kobe Bryant's scheduled preliminary hearing? *Not hardly.* DELETE *Not.* • Now, this is an idea with merit, though *not scarcely* original. DELETE *not* or *scarcely.* • But *not scarcely* a minute later, as I looked out the front window, I noticed one of the crows with one of the larger pieces of bread. DELETE *not* or *scarcely.* • I *can't hardly* believe it. USE *can hardly.*

However, these sentences, in which *not* and *scarcely* and *not* and *hardly* are juxtaposed, are perfectly good: • Lemke infiltrates your brain whether you like it or not, and whether you think it is "good" or not scarcely matters. • Debt collection has become a very insidious task that is time-consuming and more often than not hardly cost-effective.

Hardly and *scarcely* are negative words. To use *not* with them means the opposite of what you intend. Not everyone who uses the phrase *not hardly* is illiterate; many people use *not hardly* (though not *not scarcely*) to emphasize, humorously, their distaste or disagreement for what is being discussed. But the unwitting misusage is never amusing.

Similarly, *without hardly* (like *without scarcely*) is incorrect for *with hardly* (*with scarcely*) or *without*: • My brother has never really grown up, and Mom has taken care of him *without hardly* a word. USE *with hardly* or *without.* • Diane has been seeing her boyfriend Anthony for about three years and yet *without scarcely* a second thought, she's willing to skip the country and wave good-bye to her "significant" other. USE *with scarcely* or *without.*

And *scarcely no* (like *hardly no*) is incorrect for *scarcely any* (*hardly any*) or *no*: • Except for a company logo there will be *scarcely no* mention of the company. USE *scarcely any* or *no.* • If we have a repeat of the premiere next week *scarcely no one* will be disappointed with the artistes or with the weather-gods. USE *scarcely anyone* or *no one.* SEE ALSO **hardly . . . than.**

> Texas doesn't hardly have any unions at all in it.
>
> —Harold Meyerson, editor, *The American Prospect*

N

> And second, hardly no one gives the Magic much of a chance to be the team that comes out of it.
>
> —Kyle Hightower, *The Canadian Press*

notoriety Misused for *fame* (or similar words). • The 46-year-old creator of hit TV show *The Office* insists he is "embarrassed" by his fame and feels guilty about the wealth such *notoriety* has brought him. USE *celebrity*. • Still, Washington State will get its share of *notoriety* if it can stay in the thick of the Pac-10 race. USE *recognition*. • Mattoon and Tuscola are competing with two towns in Texas for the *notoriety* and jobs that would come with hosting the prototype plant. USE *distinction*.

Notoriety means ill fame, infamy, public humiliation. As a synonym for fame, celebrity, or renown, it is widely misused, especially, it seems, among sportscasters, who may not always think about what they say.

nuclear The pronunciation of *nuclear* is (NOO-klee-er), not (NOO-kyah-ler).

Oo

obfusticate Misused for *obfuscate.* • It isn't true encryption, but a fast and easy online tool to *obfusticate* the source code of your own webpages, to prevent thieves from jacking your html. Use *obfuscate.* • Words like "nazi" and "monster" appeal to emotions and *obfusticate* the facts. Use *obfuscate.* • These terms *obfusticate* what is really happening, but it does not matter; they are both useful metaphors, and both valid but only to a point. Use *obfuscate.*

Some people would have you believe that *obfusticate* (a word doubtless born of mispronunciation) means to darken, becloud, make obscure, confuse, or make unintelligible. Other people know this is the definition of *obfuscate,* truly a word. Proclaiming the validity and usefulness of *obfusticate* is behavior worthy of a half-wit—or a laxicographer.

O

oblige Misused for *obligate.* • Failure to meet these conditions would *oblige* the IAEA to take the matter to the United Nations Security Council, where sanctions could be imposed. Use *obligate.* • Bern fears the article could be extended to cover tax evasion, which would *oblige* Switzerland to lift banking secrecy if it received a request for legal assistance from an EU country. Use *obligate.* • Unilever also said the ruling did not *oblige* retailers to stock their Unilever freezers with rivals' products. Use *obligate.* • We only heard about the allegations today and we are *obliged* to investigate. Use *obligated.*

Obligate means to bind or compel by duty or obligation. *Oblige* means to make grateful for a favor or kindness ("The center is much obliged to them for their support and advice"); to do a service or favor for ("Council members wanted county governments to play a bigger role in the new local transportation system, and the Senate obliged"). In decreeing that no distinction exists between these two words, lexlings would have us all wondering what sense is meant. To lose the distinctions between, the niceties of, words is to strip us of complexity and nuance, of understanding and clarity. Ultimately, any word will do; all words mean all things.

observation Misused for *observance* (or similar words). • Their careful writing and *observation* of standard English belies their linguistic views about language. USE *observance.* • The safety of every student depends upon the conscientious *observation* of rules that must be followed by all who work in the laboratory. USE *observance.*

And occasionally, *observance* is misused for *observation*: • Plus our *observance* of him on other forums and postings he's made there determine he is not exactly the kind of person we would want to allow to post on SG. USE *observation.*

The words have different meanings. *Observation* means watching something carefully; a comment or remark. *Observance* means complying with a law, rule, or tradition.

occasionly Misspelling of *occasionally.* • Here at KitGuru we don't often find the time to look at the latest software offerings on the market but *occasionly* we make an exception. USE *occasionally.* • I buy songs from iTunes from my iPod Touch *occasionly*. USE *occasionally.*

The word *occasion* is often misspelled with one *c* and two *s*'s or two *c*'s and two *s*'s: • I enjoy the simple things as well as an *occassional* splurge. And *occasionally* is misspelled—by those who mispronounce the word (ah-KAY-zhen-lee)—with an *-ly,* rather than an *-ally,* suffix.

Two of six dictionaries in the Fiske Ranking of College Dictionaries (see appendix B) allow the misspelling *accidently*; before long they will also likely allow the misspelling *occasionly*. SEE ALSO **accidently**.

occurence Misspelling of *occurrence.* • He also said it is a common *occurence* for politicians to test other options when the election season nears. USE *occurrence.* • The court has also appointed a lawyer to examine whether sexual harassment of women in state government offices was a common *occurence.* USE *occurrence.*

Occurrence is spelled with two *r*'s. SEE ALSO **reoccur**.

oculist Misused for *occultist.* • William Butler Yeats, a renowned Irish poet, used poetry as an outlet for his mystic and *oculist* beliefs. Use *occultist.*

An *oculist* (OK-yah-list) is an optometrist or an ophthalmologist. An *occultist* (ah-KUL-tist) is someone who believes in, studies, or practices magic or the supernatural.

odiferous Misused for *odoriferous.* • The reasons lay in the *odiferous* piles of moldering, rodent-infested clothing, furniture, books, expired coupons, bikes, and bike parts. Use *odoriferous.* • In reality, he is like the Roman toilet entrepreneur who famously remarked of his *odiferous* enterprise that "money doesn't smell." Use *odoriferous.*

Odiferous, called a variant spelling in some dictionaries, is actually a misspelling of, and incorrect for, *odoriferous.* Very likely, *odiferous* derived from, and endures because of, people's failure to pronounce all five syllables. See also **odoriferous**. See also **odiferous** in **appendix A**.

odoriferous Misused for *malodorous.* • Last fall, the city of Philadelphia put 11 tons of *odoriferous* garbage on a plane to Leibstadt, Switzerland. Use *malodorous.* • Skunks use a highly *odoriferous* secretion to deter predation: a yellow oil composed of thiols and thioacetate derivatives of these thiols. Use *malodorous.* • After ingestion, the *odoriferous* sulfur molecules circulate in the bloodstream and escape from your body through exhaled air and perspiration—as any nose will tell you. Use *malodorous.*

Odiferous, called a variant spelling in some dictionaries, is actually a misspelling of, and incorrect for, *odoriferous* (which, by the bye, is meant to refer to agreeable, not disagreeable, smells). *Odoriferous* means fragrant; aromatic; having an agreeable smell. *Odorous* also usually refers to a pleasant smell (though the noun *odor* usually refers to an unpleasant one). *Malodorous* means foul-smelling; disagreeably smelly. See also **odiferous**.

office Misused for *lease office space* (or similar words). • Our staff has been identified as the main reason companies select Front Office over our competitors and is always the factor when they continue to *office* with us year-after-year. Use *buy office services.* • Should you not need to *office* with us on a full-time basis, we can also offer you a DaySuite. Use *lease space.*

Office is a wholly loathsome verb. It may mean lease an office or hire secretarial staff. Is it that to *office* suggests an office and office services rather than the cost of them? Is it less objectionable than using the words *lease* or *hire, buy* or *rent*? No, it is not; it's an objectionable, even misleading, term.

> They may want to keep their businesses small, and stay with us a long time, or they may office with us until they get so big that they move on.
>
> —Abby Office Centers
>
> "Who offices with Abby?" their webpage further reads. Anyone who has little respect for, or interest in, the English language, that's who. Their secretarial and business services sound *abbysmal*.

officious Misused for *official.* • Welcome to the *officious* website of Hamilton, New Zealand, the soggy green heart of the Waikato. USE *official.* • The jeweler also gave Antonio a rather *officious*-looking document that indicated the diamond was worth $5,800. USE *official.* • Brazil's bestselling author, Amado began his career as a messenger of Nazism and continued as an agent of Stalinism and today is Roberto Marinho's (TV Globo network all-powerful owner) *officious* scriptwriter. USE *official.*

Officious means meddlesome; offering unwanted or unnecessary advice or services. *Official* means of or relating to an office or position of authority; authorized or authoritative; formally set or prescribed.

off the beat and path Misused for *off the beaten path.* • Listed below in no particular order are ten of the most interesting, *off the beat and path* heretofore unmentioned places we have visited on the net in 2002. USE *off the beaten path.* • The town the resort is located in is *off the beat and path,* so there is almost no shopping or activities nearby. USE *off the beaten path.* • Set *off the beat and path,* parking is never a problem, and our Main Street location offers plenty of convenient lunchtime eateries and shopping. USE *off the beaten path.*

The idiomatic phrase is *off the beaten path,* meaning in a little-known or isolated place; unusual or different.

oftenly Misused for *often.* • Parodies are criticisms and witticisms created by *oftenly* intelligent people, trying to change the world through exaggerating problems or faults of a certain subject. USE *often.* • The in-vitro cultivation is *oftenly* the only reasonable way to propagate big quantities of carnivorous plants in a relatively short time. USE *often.* • There are *oftenly* many concerts organized by FM Radio Rock n' Pop. USE *often.*

Though many adverbs do end in *-ly, often* never does. How unfamiliar with the English language some of us are is made alarmingly clear when people affix *-ly* to words that do not require it and fail to use *-ly* with words that do.

The preferred pronunciation of *often* is (OFF-en), not (OFF-ten), even though you may, as frequently, hear people pronouncing it (OFF-ten). (OFF-en), of course, requires less effort to articulate than does (OFF-ten). In a society that seems to value easiness (and entertainment) over all, it may be surprising that the t burst in (OFF-ten) finds such favor.

With the influence of phonetic spelling and speaking as you spell, some people began pronouncing the *t* in *often*—even though they never seemed to have thought to pronounce it in *soften* or *listen* or *hasten*. It is likely that people are less influenced by movements and teachings than they are by one another, by mimicry: people imitate what they hear. There is scant originality of thought, but there is a great deal of doing as others do. SEE ALSO **-ly**; **oftentimes (oftimes)**.

O

oftentimes (oftimes) Although less objectionable than *oftenly, oftentimes,* a wordy and unnecessary variant of *often* (and *oftimes,* an archaic and unnecessary variant), should be shunned: • *Oftentimes* teams with their "backs against the wall" will refer to a big game as a "must-win" game. USE *Often.* • There are innovative, disturbing, wacky, *oftentimes* surreal music videos out there. USE *often.* • We forget that poetry is *oftimes* meant for its own sake. USE *often.* SEE ALSO **oftenly**.

OK (okay) As an interjection announcing the end of one topic and the beginning of another, *okay* is unacceptable written, and prosaic spoken, English: • *OK,* I'm finally getting around to organizing this a bit. DELETE *OK.* • *Okay,* let's talk holiday parties. DELETE *Okay.* • *Okay,* now no one is more respectful than I am of newspaper editors; theirs is a hard and often thankless task, involving hundreds of small decisions every day. DELETE *Okay.* • *Okay,* so the badge-wearing grim reaper has been busy these days, and you've seen little about it at this news ranch. DELETE *Okay.*

> Okay, I go to see this *Last Samurai* movie with Tom Cruise over the weekend.
>
> —Bill O'Reilly, Fox News
>
> Not only, in this trebly embarrassing sentence, does O'Reilly begin his sentence with *Okay,* he uses the present tense to describe a past event ("I go to see"), and he leaves us wondering if he attended the movie with Cruise. Of course, it's quite possible that O'Reilly's audience thinks no better—and wonders no more—than he.

Equally maddening is the interrogative, the infantile, *OK?* as illustrated in these examples: • I have a master's degree, *O.K.?* but if I dress bad or speak bad, I'm treated bad, *O.K.?* • Once that sperm hits that egg, *OK?* you have no rights after that, *OK?* • What I did was wrong, *okay?* I shouldn't have done it, *okay?* I did my time for it, *okay?*

The people who use this device are either (1) unsure of their own words and of their being able to express themselves clearly, and so ask *okay?* or (2) like the people who repeatedly touch you when they are speaking, unsure of your interest in what they have to say, and so tap you with *okay?* to try to keep your attention or track your agreement. Annoying habits both. SEE ALSO **hey**; **I'll tell you**; **like**; **so**; **well**.

on behalf of Misused for *in behalf of.* • To correct this imbalance, Operation Sunbeam manipulates karma *on behalf of* all mankind by sending spiritual energy directly to Mother Earth. USE *in behalf of.* • Representatives of the North Metro Crossing Coalition, the League of Minnesota Cities, the North Metro Mayor's Association, and the Association of Metropolitan Municipalities explained to council members what they do *on behalf of* the city. USE *in behalf of.* • It takes an extraordinary person to speak *on behalf of* people who were once active members of our community and now need your help. USE *in behalf of.*

On behalf of means as the agent of; representing. *In behalf of* means in the interest of; for the benefit of. Because most dictionaries ignore the distinction between these two phrases (as they do so many others), people are increasingly ignorant of the distinction; and because people are ignorant of the distinction, ignominy is all. Dictionaries decline thus: ignore, ignorant, ignominy.

one in (of) (five) (are) Misused for *one in (of) (five) (is).* • One in three adults *have* arthritis. Use *has.* • One in three white teen girls *use* tanning booths. Use *uses.* • One in six adults *have* neurotic disorder. Use *has.* • One in five young Britons *suffer* mental health problems. Use *suffers.* • Nearly one in three companies (30 percent) *are* operating without a formal IT disaster recovery strategy in place. Use *is.* • One in ten long-haul travelers *risk* deep vein thrombosis. Use *risks.* • One in five Chinese entrepreneurs *are women.* Use *is a woman.* • One in four immigration "Diversity Lottery" winners *were from countries considered security risks.* Use *was from a country considered a security risk.*

The expression *one in (five)* takes a singular, not a plural, verb; the word *one* is the subject.

one of the only Misused for *one of the few.* • It is *one of the only* tools available to us where you can express a deeply personal, deeply moral opinion and be held accountable. Use *one of the few.* • Americana is *one of the only* radio formats that actually embrace the legends of country music. Use *one of the few.* • One of the men who got shot the night of the riot was Officer Isaiah McKinnon, *one of the only* black officers on the Detroit Police Force. Use *one of the few.*

Only does not mean two or more; it means one, sole, alone. *One of the only* then is altogether nonsensical—and further evidence that some people scarcely know what the words they use mean.

Of the six dictionaries I evaluated in the Fiske Ranking of College Dictionaries (see appendix B), *Merriam-Webster's Collegiate Dictionary,* alone, allows *only* to mean few. In fact, Merriam-Webster's clownlike editors use the expression *one of the only* as their justification for and example of *only* in the sense of few. See also **(very) unique**.

one of the . . . that (which; who) (has) Misused for *one of the . . . that (who) (have).* • Everyone knows that this was *one of the worst things that has* happened to America since Pearl Harbor. USE *one of the worst things that have.* • Carol is *one of the few people who gives* as good as she gets from Melvin. USE *one of the few people who give.* • She was *one of the women who was* charging ahead with the women's movement. USE *one of the women who were.* • Door-to-door service is *one of the benefits that sets* the Special Transportation Program apart from others. USE *one of the benefits that set.* • But it's *one of those words that has* radically altered its meaning down the centuries. USE *one of those words that have.* • *One of the actors who is* involved in the process will be speaking with us tonight. USE *One of the actors who are.* • *One of the people that falls* under the Scrooge's whip is Bob Cratchit. USE *One of the people that fall.* • Anticipating God in your future is *one of the qualities that separates* humans from the animals. USE *one of the qualities that separate.*

Do not use a singular verb after a phrase like *one of the . . . that (which; who).* The verb in this kind of sentence is not singular because the word *one* is not the subject; the verb is decided by the plural noun preceding the *that* (*which* or *who*).

one's The possessive of the indefinite pronoun *one* is *one's,* not *ones'* or *ones*: "One should mind one's own business." Better still is "A person should mind his own business" or "People should mind their own business" or "She should mind her own business" or "They should mind their own business" or "You should mind your own business." The impersonal *one* is rarely preferable to a personal pronoun or the word *person.*

only Be sure that *only* is properly placed, modifying the word or phrase it is meant to modify. • There was a time when you could *only eat tomatoes in summer,* peas in spring, oranges in winter, corn in summer. USE *eat tomatoes only in summer.* • Still others *only invest in* socially conscious companies, and some bill themselves as enhanced index funds, which are designed to outperform the benchmark. USE *invest only in.* • But given the level of consumer outrage, airlines should recognize that a failure to voluntarily cut back *may only be greeted with* the kind of takeoff and landing controls that Congress just lifted at several airports to boost competition. USE *may be* *greeted only with.* • A drug called finasteride can also restore hair but *is only approved by the Food and Drug Administration to treat men's hair loss.* USE *is approved by the Food and Drug Administration to treat only men's hair loss.*

Misplacing the word *only* results in your having written a sentence that does not mean what you intended.

on route Misused for *en route.* • According to police reports, the body was spotted about 9:30 A.M. by the driver of a church bus *on route* to pick up children. USE *en route.* • Slater weaved through a barrel *on route* to a round four win. USE *en route.* • Dr. Mark Pescovitz crashed his car because of severe weather conditions while *on route* to Indianapolis. USE *en route.*

The pronunciation of *en route* is (on-ROOT), which very likely accounts for some people spelling the expression *on route.* SEE ALSO **en route**.

on-slot Misused for *onslaught.* • Be ready for either an *on-slot* of films rushing through the door, or nearly none at all. USE *onslaught.* • There has been an *on slot* of new and upgraded tools flooding the adaptive technology market. USE *onslaught.* • I need a lot more information in order to be more accurate, so prepare yourself with an *on-slot* of questions. USE *onslaught.* • A quick search of web hosts will bring an *on slot* of unlimited bandwidth and transfer offers. USE *onslaught.*

O

This is what language has come to: meaninglessness. The fierceness of an *onslaught* is wholly lost in such absurd spellings as *on-slot* and *on slot.*

on tenderhooks Misused for *on tenterhooks.* • Everyone is *on tenderhooks* awaiting a Court of Appeal decision that may or may not resolve the matter. USE *on tenterhooks.* • At present our relations with the national bourgeoisie are very strained; they are *on tenderhooks* and are very disgruntled. USE *on tenterhooks.*

A *tenter* is a frame on which cloth is stretched for drying. *On tenterhooks,* not *on tenderhooks,* is an idiom that means to be uncertain, anxious, or in suspense about something.

opinionation Misused for *opinion.* • We started that trip as the usual collection of walking American egos and *opinionations,* and came back uniformly anti-Soviet, the liberals most of all. USE *opinions.* • The essay itself seems to establish pretty firmly, though rather against Hull's will, that the two writers are connected by very little more than Clarke's general knowledge of the world-field occupied by the *opinionations* of Shaw. USE *opinions.* • I thank all the readers who have borne with my Novial *opinionations,* especially those who have from time to time written letters of encouragement, and more especially those who have written to the editor. USE *opinions.*

Perhaps people who use the regal-sounding, polysyllabic *opinionation* feel as though it gives more weight to their views than does the plainer *opinion.* If laxicographers should ever add *opinionation* to their dictionaries, there will be no reason to consult them further.

There is also some use of the verb *opinionate*: • Gingrich spent a decade writing books and *opinionating* on Fox News. USE *opining.* • I met a teacher who explained that her job precluded the ability to attach her name to her online writing and *opinionating.* USE *opining.*

Opinionated—an adjective meaning having strong, even when unreasonable, opinions—is a perfectly useful word, but *opinionate*—a verb meaning to opine or express an opinion—is nothing of the sort.

No better is *opinioned*: • Circuit Judge Mary M. Schroeder *opinioned* that the Juneau Access Improvement Project failed to consider alternatives for improving the existing ferry service. USE *opined.*

opportunistic Misused for *opportune.* • After Medco made its offer in December, Dr. Williams said it was *opportunistic* coming so close to Christmas. USE *opportune.* • It's a very *opportunistic* time for these brands. USE *opportune.*

Opportunistic also is misused to mean seeking or welcoming opportunity: • Now, the Eagles must face an *opportunistic* Carolina team riding an emotional wave after dramatically snapping the Rams' 14-game home winning streak. • Be efficient throwing the football, *opportunistic* on defense, sound on special teams, and you can win without a running attack for the ages. • In the last three to six months, we've been more *opportunistic* than we ordinarily are; we've generated a lot of turnover.

Opportunistic means taking advantage, without regard to ethics or consequences, of a circumstance to further one's interests. *Opportune* means right for a particular purpose; occurring at an advantageous time.

> Strong goaltending from Pasi Nurminen, who has won both those games, and opportunistic scoring from Slava Kozlov, Patrik Stefan and J. P. Vigier were the recipe.
>
> —John Manasso, *The Atlanta Journal-Constitution*
>
> When did opportunism become a bad word?
>
> —Darva Conger, on the television program *48 Hours*
>
> These astonishing sentences reveal how little we know the meaning of the words we use or, even more disturbing, how little meaning matters.

ordnance Misused for *ordinance.* • Matewan is located at the end of Trail #10, where by means of a town *ordnance,* an ATV rider may turn left on Mate Street and enter the Town of Matewan and proceed to a designated free parking lot (located beside City Hall) and park his or her ATV in a safe parking lot next door to the police department. USE *ordinance.* • City *ordnance* was written in a manner to prevent the duty weapon from being seen. USE *ordinance.* • Since its inception in 1980, the program has released numerous municipal *ordnance* violators as well as persons arrested on state offenses. USE *ordinance.*

Ordinance is also misused for *ordnance*: • The purpose of the survey was to locate and document any military *ordinance* or other debris that may be deposited on the lake bottom. USE *ordnance.* • On the military side, among other uses GPR can be expected to help ferret out underground command and control bunkers, landmines, and unexploded *ordinance.* USE *ordnance.*

Ordnance is cannon and artillery; military weapons, including ammunition, combat vehicles, and other equipment. *Ordinance* is a governmental statute or regulation; an authoritative direction or command.

orgiastic Confused with *orgasmic. Orgiastic* means characteristic of an orgy; arousing unrestrained emotion; frenzied ("The yearly orgy of physical consumerism is over; all that's left is the equally orgiastic Cyber Monday"). *Orgasmic* means at the peak of sexual excitement, characterized by involuntary contractions of the muscles of the genitals ("Bubbly Palin, of course, can't get enough of all things outdoors, from guns—at one point in the show she reaches a near-orgasmic froth after shooting a picture of a bear—to camping").

orientate Misused for *orient.* • One objective of the project is to learn how herring-schools *orientate* under the changed environmental conditions of the Baltic. USE *orient.* • In creating a piece of documentation, we often find it necessary to *orientate* a user by using visuals. USE *orient.* • The meaning of practical training is to *orientate* students for future tasks and offer facilities for working life in general. USE *orient.* • Men tend to cite more *self-orientated* reasons, like improving their own fitness, whereas women are twice as likely as men to want to stop for the sake of their family and children or because of pregnancy. USE *self-oriented.* • The man was having trouble walking and appeared extremely intoxicated, confused, and *disorientated.* USE *disoriented.*

By careful writers, *orientate* and *disorientate* are eschewed. These words strike many as being more unwieldy and cacophonic than the less syllabic *orient* and *disorient.*

O

orphan An *orphan* is a child (a person between birth and about age fourteen), not a young adult or an adult whose parents have died.

or something Avoid ending sentences with *or something, or something like that, and everything, and everything like that, and like that,* and similar expressions: • To make a torch you twist a bunch of straw or sticks into a bundle and dip them in some flammable material like wax *or something.* • This is very upsetting news to United fans, and you have to end it with an insensitive comment just to make you look clever *or something.* • All he talks about now are video games, and *everything like that.* • Everybody has seen it before, and everybody knows the archetypes and *everything like that.* • You know it's amazing; soldiers can read *and everything.* • We talked about federal spending *and like that.*

These colloquial phrases ensure your sentence ends disappointingly and your thought incompletely. Take the time to think what you mean by these expressions, and use those words instead. SEE ALSO **all**; **out there**.

osculate Misused for *oscillate.* • Songs like *Stay Together* are reminiscent of Funkadelic songs with their *osculating* beat. Use *oscillating.* • If so you could try directing *osculating* fans toward the leaf zone. Use *oscillating.* • Sometimes a pump thrust with excessive axial clearance will allow the pump and motor shaft to move back and forth, endwise. This *osculating* motion will draw the oil out of an otherwise well-sealed motor bearing and deposit it on the windings. Use *oscillating.* • Similar to the vacuum fluctuations the book describes, Genz's prose and topic choice *osculate* between engrossing and dull, scientific, and philosophical. Use *oscillate.*

Oscillate means to swing back and forth with a regular rhythm; to be indecisive; to vacillate. *Osculate* means to kiss. Only rarely is *oscillate* used where *osculate* could be:

How do you titillate an ocelot?
You *oscillate* its tit a lot.

ostentatious Misused for *ostensible.* • Bangladesh was conspicuous by its absence and Dhaka has already expressed itself in favor of a new round of trade talks, though the *ostentatious* reason for its absence is cited to be the general election in the country. Use *ostensible.* • The *Independent* says the National Democratic Congress (NDC) made history on Tuesday when it lived up to the *ostentatious* meaning of the adage "Money Swine" by auctioning the first nine copies of its manifesto for a whopping 915 million cedis, with one of them going for 160 million cedis. Use *ostensible.* • The *ostentatious* reasons for branding women witches are infertility, menopause, matrimonial problems, property disputes, and other related socioeconomic problems. Use *ostensible.*

Ostentatious means showy or pretentious. *Ostensible* means apparent; professed; seeming.

otherwise Misused for *other.* • Spam—fraudulent and *otherwise*—continues to skyrocket, clogging overtaxed networks. Use *other.* • Future events and actual results, financial and *otherwise,* may differ from the results discussed in the forward-looking statements. Use *other.*

In the illustrations, *otherwise,* an adverb, is being used as an adjective; *other,* an adjective, is better suited to modify a noun. The word *other* is certainly correct; less so the word *otherwise*—even though few people today do not use *otherwise* in these constructions where *other* seems the better choice.

Only the punctilious use *other* instead of *otherwise,* and only the exacting can ever hope to say what they actually mean.

ought not Misused for *ought not to.* • I think Democrats *ought not* be afraid of their roots. USE *ought not to.* • We *ought not* be executing people who, legally, were children. USE *ought not to.* • If you shoot at a president, you *ought not* gripe when you lose your liberty—no matter the circumstances. USE *ought not to.* • If the Fabs are truly transcendent, *oughtn't they* light fires in listeners who are two, or twelve, or twenty-two, as well as those antique souls slouching toward their fifties, waiting to be reborn? USE *oughtn't they to.*

Ought not, as anyone knows who reads well, requires *to*: *ought not to.*

Similarly, though a less frequent mistake, *ought* alone requires *to*: • The motors and engines Americans rely on for transportation *ought* run only when there is good reason for them to be running. USE *ought to.* SEE ALSO **didn't (hadn't; shouldn't) ought to**.

out loud Whether to use *out loud* or *aloud* is largely a question of personal preference. *Out loud* is slightly less sonorous than *aloud,* but beyond that one expression is as good as the other.

In years past, *out loud* was discouraged by grammarians who maintained the phrase was colloquial, but today it does not seem to suffer from that stigma. SEE ALSO **done**.

outmost Misused for *utmost.* • The primary focus of the audit profession should be to faithfully use and enforce these auditing standards and accounting principles with the *outmost* diligence and integrity. USE *utmost.* • All information that you provide will be treated with *outmost* confidentiality. USE *utmost.* • The ANC is concerned about utterances of certain opposition parties, who in the recent past have been doing their *outmost* to undermine the voter registration and the entire election preparation process. USE *utmost.* • Since all books were highly prized during this period, protecting them was of *outmost* importance. USE *utmost.*

Although *utmost* may mean *outmost, outmost* does not now mean (though, some centuries ago, it may have meant) *utmost. Outmost* means outermost, farthest out; *utmost,* which in some contexts shares this meaning, more often means of the greatest degree, amount, or intensity.

out there Sometimes *out there* elliptically refers to a specific location such as a baseball field or the highway ("Be careful out there [on the snow-covered roads]"). Other times, *out there* is less specific, suggesting either society or the world at large: • There are a lot of apps *out there.* Use *available.* • I think it will definitely get my name *out there.* Use *before the public.* • We need to *get out there and make sure people know and understand* the importance of those controls. Use *promote.* • Is there a plan *out there* that I'm missing? Use *already devised.* • Most of you guys *out there* remember the drill quite well. Use *in the audience.* • He doesn't want to dwell on health care reform because that's still quite controversial *out there* with the American public. Delete *out there.* • But there aren't a lot of single moms *out there* who are making millions of dollars every year for being in a movie. Delete *out there.*

Out there is colloquial—even inarticulate when you consider the words that *out there* is meant to mean—and capable speakers will not use it. To written language, it is wholly inappropriate. There are many hundreds of colloquial words and expressions that capable writers know to shun; it is the inept and the false, the less readable writers, who pander to their audience by using informal expressions such as *out there* and *look-see* and *stuff* and *zone out* and *guys* and *ain't* and countless more. Clichés and colloquialisms effortlessly come to mind. Nothing is simpler to think of or write down, and little is more telling about an author's talent. Consider, for example, the everyday, even insulting to some, writing in *It Was the Best of Sentences, It Was the Worst of Sentences,* supposedly a book about how to write good sentences: • When I worked in that field, the Reader was always in my face. • The job of a subordinating conjunction is (drumroll, please) to subordinate. • There's no doubt you're in for a good read. • Some even say long sentences are an out-and-out no-no. • I write some major stinkers myself. • That just ain't so. • What's up with that? • I hate "in addition to." Don't get me wrong, I write it all the time. • The point is, either explain or don't. But don't half-ass it. • And pat yourself on the back for getting through this chapter. SEE ALSO **or something**; **removed from**; **(mad) skillz**.

overdue Misused for *overdo.* • The unit accommodates up to a 50-inch TV, with two shelves underneath for extras (just don't *overdue* it, Ikea states a maximum load of 66 pounds). USE *overdo.* • While you don't want to *overdue* exercise and injure yourself, 30 to 60 minutes of moderate daily exercise will help lower blood lipids. USE *overdo.*

Overdue means not paid when due; arriving after the expected time. *Overdo* means to do or say or use something too long or to excess.

oxymoron Misused for *contradiction.* • Let's face it, "dieting" during the holidays is an *oxymoron.* USE *contradiction.* • It's sometimes an *oxymoron* to have collaboration in a large organization because they often set up competition among groups in an effort to drive innovation. USE *contradiction.* • The idea may appear to be an *oxymoron* but it isn't. USE *contradiction.* • I've always thought of myself as a bit of an *oxymoron.* I'm not really super girly but I'm no tomboy. USE *contradiction* (or, perhaps, *moron*).

An *oxymoron* is not, simply, a contradiction. *Oxymoron* is a rhetorical term that means a juxtaposition of contradictory, or seemingly contradictory, words (such as small crowd, exact estimate, cruel kindness). Because some people use *oxymoron* loosely to mean a contradiction in ideas, the word has undergone pejoration (the process by which the meaning of a word becomes less respectable or less exacting over time).

> I know it's one of those oxymorons. You feel like you should be really angry about the outrage here. But on the other hand, we need the money.
>
> —Alexis Glick, Fox Business Network
>
> Alexis is indeed a-lexis.

Pp

palatable Misused for *palpable*. • If only we could capture that *palatable* feeling in a bottle so that it can touch us on a more regular basis, it would do so much good. USE *palpable*. • About six months later I remember thinking that we were headed for a full-fledged recession, there was an almost *palatable* uneasiness in the air. USE *palpable*. • The tension was *palatable* between the girls as breakup rumors started swirling in the British press. USE *palpable*.

And *palpable* is misused for *palatable*: • The curly fries were the only *palpable* food that we ordered. USE *palatable*. • I believe that there is only one *palpable* solution to how attendants of a church, whether long-standing members or first-time visitors, can freely attend a service that God has so decreed. USE *palatable*.

Palatable means agreeable to the palate or taste; acceptable to the mind or senses. *Palpable* means tangible or capable of being touched; easily perceived, noticeable.

P

This is just the sort of idiocy that laxicographers delight in. Within a few years, dictionaries will give *palpable* as a synonym for *palatable*, and *palatable* as a synonym for *palpable*.

palette Misused for *palate*. • A delightful wine, it excites the *palette* without being too sweet. USE *palate*. • Until he sought medical help, Boyle had no idea as he'd aged he had developed an enlarged *palette*, the hard and soft tissue making up the roof and sides of his mouth. USE *palate*. • Begin to focus on inhaling deeply through your nose, abdomen rising, and exhaling forcefully through your mouth, tongue resting gently at the top of your *palette*. USE *palate*.

Palette—a board used by artists for mixing colors; a range of colors used by an artist or in a painting; a range of qualities in other art forms such as music—does not mean *palate*—the roof of the mouth in some vertebrates; the sense of taste.

> The cardamom carrot syrup was an exotic complement to the dish, and the mildly bitter water crest salad revived and refreshed the palette.
>
> —Michael J. Reiss, FoodandWineAccess.com
>
> Michael J. Reiss's credentials as a food and restaurant critic might easily be questioned given that he does not know a *palate* from a *palette.* And like the *watercress,* his remarks leave a bitter aftertaste.

panoply The pronunciation of *panoply* is (PAN-ah-plee), not (PAN-ah-play).

parameter Misused for *perimeter.* • Firefighters have been having some success drawing a *parameter* around the flames. USE *perimeter.* • Our parliamentary committee refused to authorize SHS 400 million of public resources for Janet's UWESO office renovations and *parameter* wall. USE *perimeter.* • The fence now built along the western *parameter* of the city was begun a year ago. USE *perimeter.* • Two fire engines remained at the scene over the weekend to continue patrolling the *parameter* of the fire for "flare-ups" that might have surfaced. USE *perimeter.*

Parameter is also carelessly used to mean any number of other words: • Perhaps the most exciting *parameter* of success has been the extraordinarily high number of acquisitions that have taken place within the past year. USE *measure.* • The newspaper said Rashid-Merem acknowledged a supplier could lose its GM contract and not get reimbursed for money spent preparing for the contract, saying: "Yes, that's the case, but everyone will work *in that parameter.*" USE *under these terms.*

A *perimeter* is the outer boundary of a figure or area; the length of this boundary; circumference; the border of a military encampment or defended area. *Parameter,* a mathematical and statistical term, is a constant in an equation whose value varies in other equations; a quantity calculated from data that describes a population. *Parameter* ought not to be used to mean *perimeter.*

partially Misused for *partly.* • Andy Mullins, executive assistant to the chancellor, said he remembers one game where someone was parked *partially* on the grass and *partially* in a handicap spot next to the Lyceum. USE *partly.* • Terry A. King, 43, of 20206 Township 306, was driving his 2000 Jeep Wrangler on an unnamed haul road when he hit a *partially* opened gate. USE *partly.*

And *partly* is misused for *partially*: • The major sources of trans-fatty acids in the diet are from *partly* hydrogenated vegetable fat. USE *partially.* • Most academic information appears in print, so blind and *partly* sighted students rely on a support network for access. USE *partially.*

Much like the distinction between *number* and *amount, partly* is best used when a whole can be considered to have distinct parts, and *partially* is best used in the sense of to a degree.

Sometimes it is difficult to decide which would be the better word: • He was found by staff *partially* (or *partly*) clothed and attempting to sexually assault a male resident. • *Partly* (or *partially*) cloudy skies are expected, with a 30 percent chance of showers and thunderstorms. If both words work equally well, use *partly.*

P

passible Misused for *passable.* • They arrived at the Allegheny near Sharpsburg to find the river only partially frozen over and not *passible* on foot. USE *passable.* • Road "A," however, has fewer obstacles and is *passible*; road "B" has no obstacles and is *passible.* USE *passable.* • In junior high school my depression and anxiety were so great that my grades dropped from the high marks, to low, but *passible* grades. USE *passable.*

Passable means able to be passed or traveled on or over; adequate or satisfactory. *Passible,* a theological term, means able to feel or suffer. SEE ALSO **impassible**.

past Misused for *passed.* • Time *past* slowly as he sat waiting for her to acknowledge the discussion as far as he was concerned was over. USE *passed.* • He indicated that nearly eight to ten months *past* before the municipality objected to the hydronic system and the lack of insulation. USE *passed.* • Roman found Belle *past* out on the floor of the penthouse and gave her a shot to counteract the penicillin, for Belle was just as allergic as her mother. USE *passed.* • Richard *past* away in 2000 at age of 78. USE *passed.*

Passed is the past tense and past participle of the verb *pass. Past,* a noun, adjective, adverb, or preposition, is never a verb. If this confusion continues, lexicographers and linguists all will sanction it; usage, they maintain, not some notion of correctness or clarity, dictates what's effective.

patience Misused for *patients.* • Carleton Place Hospital selects Zycom to implement new mission critical server environment to run hospital *patience* records system. USE *patients.* • After you have become an established pediatrician, the number of *patience* who come to you depends on your reputation. USE *patients.*

Patience is calm self-control despite suffering, delay, boredom, or the like. *Patients* are people under a doctor's or other professional's care.

pawn off Misused for *palm off.* • People who bag animals in the wild undoubtedly get healthier meat than the plastic-wrapped flesh supermarkets *pawn off* on the paying public. USE *palm off.* • The leather store tried to *pawn off* a piece of cowhide that was too thick, saying it was the same thing as kangaroo. USE *palm off.*

To *palm off* is to pass off something inferior by fraud or deceit; to misrepresent. To *pawn off* is incorrect.

peaceful Misused for *peaceable.* • Unless irritated or attracted by blood, sharks are *peaceful* animals. USE *peaceable.* • I am concerned about increasing frustration among Iraqis and I am telling everyone that they are a *peaceful* people. USE *peaceable.*

And *peaceable* is misused for *peaceful:* Tens of thousands of protesters jammed central London on Thursday in a *peaceable* demonstration against President Bush. USE *peaceful.*

Peaceful means tranquil; undisturbed by strife or turbulence. *Peaceable* means inclined to peace.

peal Misused for *peel.* • *Peal* the rind off your orange and slice into 1-inch-thin slivers. USE *peel.* • This cute redhead loves to *peal* off her clothes and panties for the world to see. USE *peel.* • He said the entire dispute stemmed from some *pealing* paint on a third-floor window that his inspector failed to include in his paperwork. USE *peeling.*

And *peel* is misused for *peal*: • In the predawn light of April 19, the beating drums and *peeling* bells summoned between 50 and 70 militiamen to the town green at Lexington. USE *pealing.*

Though *peal* and *peel* sound alike, their meanings differ considerably. *Peal* means a loud ringing of bells; a set of tuned bells; a loud sound. As a verb, *peal* means to ring a bell loudly; to speak loudly. *Peel,* as a noun, means the skin or rind of some fruits and vegetables. As a verb, *peel* means to remove a layer of; to strip.

pedalogical (pedilogical) Misused for *pedagogical.* • The beauty of a Jewish school is that it wraps up all the values both *pedalogical* and religious that parents want for their children into one neat convenient package. USE *pedagogical.* • What is there can radically change the *pedalogical* approaches used by teachers to reach their learners. USE *pedagogical.* • I was not looking for psychological, *pedilogical,* nor philosophical discussions. USE *pedagogical.* • They do this by setting up institutes for professional training that teach both at the *pedilogical* level and at the content level for teachers. USE *pedagogical.*

P

Dictionaries have yet to list *pedalogical* (or *pedilogical*) as a "variant spelling" of *pedagogical,* but sham scientists (lexicographers, descriptive linguists, and others equally misguided) will likely soon begin excusing, justifying, and promoting these sham spellings.

peddle Misused for *pedal.* • This then poses the question: should we let our foot off the campaign *peddle*? USE *pedal.* • It seems like when this team smells a little blood we get going, and put the *peddle* to the floor. USE *pedal.*

And *pedal* is misused for *peddle*: • However, with this knowledge in hand, it's up to those *pedaling* goods and services to get through to the right person. USE *peddling.*

To *pedal* is to move or operate by the use of a pedal or pedals. As a noun, a *pedal* is a lever used to power a bicycle, car, drum, piano, or other mechanism. To *peddle* is to sell items from place to place; to hawk goods; to promote a view.

peek Misused for *peak.* • The clouds break apart and a mountain *peek* stares through. USE *peak.* • Recorded on July 13, 1991, this awesome display of pure rock emotion captures the band at the *peek* of their fame. USE *peak.*

And *peak* is misused for *peek*: • Take a few moments and sneak a *peak* at just some of CaterXpert's powerful features. USE *peek.* • I still could not control myself from stealing one last *peak* up her skirt. USE *peek.* • I took a *peak* at your Burchfield essay and do wonder about "The War of the Words." USE *peek.*

A *peak* is a summit of a mountain; the highest point of something; a pointed end. A *peek* is a furtive glance. Remember that *eye,* with which you take a peek, has two *e*'s, as does *peek.*

peek Misused for *pique.* • Paint Branch is presenting a few distinct courses that hopes to *peek* interest in the student body. USE *pique.* • I'm looking for someone who can stimulate my innermost thoughts and *peek* my curiosity. USE *pique.*

To *peek* is to glance at quickly and often secretively. To *pique* is to arouse; to cause to feel resentment.

Peak—which as a verb means to bring to a maximum of development or intensity or to form into a peak—is also misused for *pique*: • I saw you were reading it and it *peaked* my curiosity. USE *piqued.* • But once in a while, amid all the self-indulgent "persecution," a question or point is raised that *peaks* my interest. USE *piques.*

penultimate Misused for *last* (or similar words). • The *penultimate (last)* chapter is about the growing crisis of baroque armaments—their increasing cost, their declining effectiveness, and what this means for soldiers and defense workers. USE *last.* • The New Economy's successful leaders understand this permanence, too. Consider the *penultimate* computer lord, Bill Gates. USE *ultimate.* • Helena Bonham Carter has for most of her career been the *penultimate* corset girl. USE *ultimate.* • It was in these circumstances only that the *penultimate* rock star could be conceived: Ziggy Stardust. USE *quintessential.*

Penultimate (from Latin *paenultimus: paene,* almost, *ultimus,* last) means next to last, not, as some people assume, last, ultimate, best, definitive, or quintessential.

> The penultimate in performance and appearance, our Centaurus line of systems have no equal.
>
> —Directron.com
>
> The people at Directron.com might be mortified to learn they're boasting that their systems are second-rate, next to last in performance and appearance.

(as) per Misused for *as* (or similar words). • Write a rough draft for essay 1 *per* instructions in "Analyzing a magazine advertisement" and "Preparing a draft for peer conferences" in the class notes. USE *according to.* • *As per your request,* this cover letter keys the registrant's responses to the comments expressed in the above-referenced letter of comments and also provides any supplemental information requested by your staff. USE *As you requested.* • Each room at the Mark Twain Hotel is a classic accommodation featuring traditional cherry or pine furniture, oversized working desks, two-line telephones with conference capabilities, fax modems, and turn-down service *per your request.* USE *if you request it.* • *As per usual,* all the wallrats were out in force chalking up and taping various bodily parts. USE *As usual.* • Open your Word document *as per usual.* USE *as usual.* • *Per our discussion* in class on Thursday, below you will find two essays on racial profiling—the practice of using race as probable cause in policy work. USE *As we discussed.* • *As per our discussion* regarding tonsilar carcinoma, there is no way to make the diagnosis from the X-ray alone. USE *As we discussed.* • The LF147 opamp model Compensation Capacitance is set to 2e-12 F but it should be 1e-10F *as per* National Semiconductor specs. USE *according to.*

P

(As) per is commercialese—which is to say, an expression at once hideous and comical—and means nothing more than *as* or *according to.*

permanentized Misused for *make permanent* (or similar words). • Once the cognitive elements are manipulated in the desired direction, the programmed conditioning and behavior become *permanentized.* USE *permanent.* • Instead, I find myself repeatedly disappointed to meet women who insist they want the traditional vagaries, supposedly *permanentized* with a superstitious ceremony. USE *made permanent.* • Not once did the results come close to those three gentle and elegant arcs that he *permanentized* as the stoppages. USE *made permanent.* • That is why the half million people would come here; to rub some of the (muddy) fame off on themselves, participating as firsthand witnesses, *permanentized* in a moment of history. USE *immortalized.*

We know a concoction such as *permanentize* is objectionable when it's scarcely pronounceable. *Make permanent* or, perhaps, *immortalize* does nicely; the ungainly, needless *permanentize* does not.

permiscuous Misused for *promiscuous.* • We certainly haven't been as *permiscuous* in licensing our content as some other news and news wire providers, but it's actually a pretty decent revenue stream for us. USE *promiscuous.* • A fourteen-year-old school girl who had *permiscuous* sex is not a woman. USE *promiscuous.* • What was offensive in this movie was the continuous use of alcohol and *permiscuous* sex (some of which would be considered violent sex). USE *promiscuous.*

The people who misspell and mispronounce *promiscuous* seldom have liberal views and values. Descriptive linguists, who generally are liberal-thinking, would probably be mortified to mispronounce or misspell this word, but they allow, even encourage, others to do so. Only the small-minded embrace illiberal thoughts and actions, and only the dull-minded embrace ignorance and nonsense.

perpetrate Misused for *propagate.* • There are the ideas that get *perpetrated.* USE *propagated.* • You *perpetrate* views that are incredibly demeaning toward them, with statements that present them as passive and powerless. USE *propagate.*

To *perpetrate* is to commit or be responsible for something (usually something criminal or wrong). To *propagate* is to make widely known; to breed; to transmit or spread.

perpetuate Misused for *perpetrate.* • The third category is when a computer is used to *perpetuate* a crime, as in distributing child pornography. USE *perpetrate.*

And *perpetrate* is misused for *perpetuate*: • It confirms that the military is stage-managing elections announced for this year to *perpetrate* its rule with an ostensibly civilian parliament that is a front for continued military control. USE *perpetuate.*

To *perpetrate* is to commit or carry out. To *perpetuate* is to prolong the continuation of; to cause to last indefinitely.

perquisite Misused for *prerequisite.* • He said peace is a *perquisite* for development, adding that, until countries ensure equitable distribution of wealth they would continue to suffer from wars and host refugees. USE *prerequisite.* • Trust is a necessary *perquisite* for cooperative moral action. USE *prerequisite.* • Course 1 is a *perquisite* to course 2; course 2 is a *perquisite* to course 3. USE *prerequisite.* • A healthy economy is also a *perquisite* for a healthy financial sector. USE *prerequisite.*

Perquisite (commonly called a *perk* by the ever-monosyllabic, ever-hasty everyman) is something additional to regular pay; a privilege or benefit; a tip or gratuity. *Prerequisite* is something required beforehand; a requirement.

P

persay (per say) Misused for *per se.* • Students shouldn't be *persay* forced to learn. USE *per se.* • What I would say is that finance *per say* is not a constraint for infrastructure development today. USE *per se.* • Everett, while not an opponent of a gas tax *per say,* would have liked to see more money coming to municipalities where drilling occurs. USE *per se.*

Per se, not *persay* or *per say,* means in or by itself, as such. Only people who do not read could possibly spell *per se* incorrectly.

persecute Misused for *prosecute.* • When you remember that the court's mandate is to *persecute* crimes against humanity and genocide, it becomes much clearer why some countries have declared their acceptance of this international body while others have sought to reject it. USE *prosecute.* • Violation of this agreement will be *persecuted* in a court of law. USE *prosecuted.* • Forgery, other fraudulent acts, and any other dishonest use of any part or whole of this website are strictly prohibited and can be *persecuted* in a court of law. USE *prosecuted.*

And, as in this sentence where meaning matters mightily, *prosecute* is sometimes misused for *persecute*: • Why did Hitler *prosecute* the Jews? USE *persecute.*

To *persecute* is to harass or oppress continually; to annoy constantly. To *prosecute* is to institute legal or criminal proceedings against; to carry on or follow to the end.

personal friend A *personal friend* is but a friend, and a friend, more often than not, but an acquaintance. • I consider Wayne a *personal friend* and I don't think we've let the scores of the dual meets and our wins and losses ever get in the way. USE *friend.* • Gabby Giffords is a very close *personal friend* of mine, one of my best friends in Congress. USE *friend.*

personnel Misused for *personal.* • A complete exercise and fitness program will be designed and implemented by a certified *personnel* trainer. USE *personal.* • I know, however, from *personnel* experience, that it may not be the battle of choice in the war of issues our kids are facing. USE *personal.* • All of their equipment had to be destroyed, documents burned, and *personnel* belongings left behind. USE *personal.* • In his *personnel* life, Keith enjoys boating, water skiing, working on his home, and playing with his children. USE *personal.* • The DEA has been interested for some years in Pedro Juan Moreno Villa, one of the most important members of Uribe's campaign team and a *personnel* friend of the candidate. USE *personal.*

And *personal* is misused for *personnel*: • This site is aimed at human resources *personal* at major companies. USE *personnel.*

Personnel is a noun meaning the people employed by or associated with an organization or other group; people. *Personal* is an adjective meaning of or relating to a particular person; concerning a person's private relationships or concerns.

perspective Misused for *prospective.* • Personality profiles of *perspective* jurors and other courtroom players are prepared as part of the pretrial and jury selection process. USE *prospective.* • We are currently searching for a *perspective* leader. USE *prospective.* • Advertisements in newspapers or national publications may generate leads to *perspective* investors. USE *prospective.*

Perspective, a noun, is the viewing or drawing of objects or a scene in a particular way; a point of view; an objective judgment of something; a vista. *Prospective,* an adjective, means likely to happen or be; expected; relating to or effective in the future. SEE ALSO **perspectivize**.

> The best thing we can do is to send our counselors out and visit perspective students. . . . Students at Simpson have mixed feelings about commercials and how they impact perspective students. . . . Every step must be positive for perspective students to want to become a part of the Simpson community.
>
> —Shelly Zeller, *The Simpsonian*
>
> If Simpson College (an inauspicious though apparently apt name) finds its enrollment dwindling, we need not wonder why.

perspectivize Misused for *put into perspective* (or similar words). • The course intends to *perspectivize* some of the issues that have been at the center of the debates in pragmatics over the past few decades. USE *put into perspective.* • This atheist is simply saying that real faith would *perspectivize* one's life in terms of eternity; even grief, he says, "would occupy hardly a moment of my thoughts." USE *clarify.* • I mention these limitations without denying that potentials actually already exist, that *perspectivize* social development and thus act as immanent, critical correctives to the status quo. USE *focus.* • To *perspectivize* the gaping informational chasm into which Leigh Zermuhlen's naked corpse would nearly vanish, it should be pointed out that *Central Park West*—now so utterly forgotten—was one of the most media-hyped TV premieres in recent memory. USE *put into perspective.*

Even more benumbing than *finalize, prioritize,* and *incentivize, perspectivize* finds favor with academicians and others who think their intelligence is most accurately measured by how unintelligible their writing is—that is, the less intelligible their words, the more intelligent their thoughts. SEE ALSO **perspective**.

perspicuous Confused with *perspicacious*. *Perspicuous* means clear; easy to understand ("When thoughts are turned into words, even the most trying and apparently insurmountable problem becomes suddenly perspicuous"). *Perspicacious* means having acute discernment; insightful ("A wee while back, a few perspicacious Chilean winemakers bet on the country's so-cool-it's-cold coast as a promising place to grow sauvignon blanc").

peruse Misused for *skim* (or similar words). • My intention was to *peruse* the book quickly and then gossip with the good folks behind the bar. USE *skim.* • The Standard CV allows employers to *peruse* quickly and easily without having to turn a page for further information. USE *scan.* • Yet also portable enough to *peruse* easily on the bus, the book is, more significantly, a highly personal and readable overview that at times almost seems eccentric in its enthusiasms and grave judgments. USE *read.* • A quick *peruse* through the flashy liner notes gives a hint of what's in store for the poor listener. USE *look.*

Some people incorrectly maintain that *peruse* has two opposite meanings: to read thoroughly and to read hurriedly. *Peruse,* however, has but one meaning: to read with great care. It does not mean to glance over or to read quickly. Nor is it—no matter how grandiloquent someone wishes to appear—a synonym for the word *read.* SEE ALSO **peruse** in **appendix A**.

> The difference allows Williams to peruse works of art he doesn't own by visiting various museums around the country.
>
> —Eric R. Danton, *The Hartford Courant*
>
> A locker away, Hawkins would talk about the great Satchel Paige and peruse his collection of throwback jerseys.
>
> —Jim Souhan, *Minneapolis Star Tribune*

Though thousands head down U.S. Route 20 to Rockford this time of year to peruse Cherryvale Mall and the many chain stores lining East State Street, area residents don't have to travel at all to find unique and personal gifts.

—Gary Mays, *The Journal-Standard*

Danton, talking of artwork, Souhan, talking of pullovers, Mays, talking of a mall, all foolishly misuse the word *peruse. Peruse* does not mean to look at art or jerseys or malls; it means to read painstakingly, to read carefully, to read thoroughly.

phase Misused for *faze*. • Valencia, who were league leaders coming into this game, were not *phased* by the early setback and pushed hard for the equalizer. USE *fazed*. • Although Bracco had issues with the $26 million police station design that initially came to City Council, he is not *phased* by 80 percent of every tax dollar being spent on public safety. USE *fazed*.

And *faze* is sometimes misused for *phase*: • America is going through a bad *faze*, but like always we'll get out of it. USE *phase*. • Gibson has *fazed* in a new finish. USE *phased*.

Faze, a verb, means to embarrass or disconcert. *Phase,* as a noun, means a stage or period of something; an aspect or part. As a verb, *phase* means to do in stages; to synchronize.

P

phenomenon Misused for *phenomena*. • You write about three *phenomenon* that helped shape women's role in this country. USE *phenomena*.

Occasionally, *phenomena* is used instead of *phenomenon*: • Legs Diamond, Marcus Gorman, and Billy Phelan also figure in "Roscoe," a work that magnifies *this phenomena* yet further. USE *this phenomenon* (or *these phenomena*).

The plural of *phenomenon* is *phenomena* or, less often, *phenomenons*. SEE ALSO **criterion**.

picaresque Misused for *picturesque*. • Maybe it's the *picaresque* view, but the bridge is a popular end-of-the-line stop for the suicidal. USE *picturesque*. • In Michigan, the surprisingly *picaresque* town of Kalamazoo has a brewery making no fewer than half a dozen porter or stout variations. Use *picturesque.*

Picaresque describes a sort of literature involving the adventures of a *picaro,* or rogue; relating to a rogue or scoundrel. *Picturesque* describes something attractive enough to be a picture; vivid language.

plaintive Misused for *plaintiff.* • The judge's decision was against the *plaintive,* Seiko, who was suing Nu-kote, which had been marketing replacement cartridges at half the regular price. Use *plaintiff.* • Rep. Bob Barr (R-Ga.), another *plaintive* in a lawsuit seeking to overturn the law, said he was not surprised. Use *plaintiff.*

Plaintive (PLAN-tiv), an adjective, means expressing sorrow or melancholy; mournful. *Plaintiff* (PLAN-tif), a noun, is a person who brings a suit in a court of law.

plasticate Misused for *plasticize.* • If auto manufacturers would build rather than *plasticate* everything then we would be safer. Use *plasticize.* • He is wearing a plastic cover over his Kangol cap, much as people *plasticate* their three-piece suites or their car seats to keep them good as new. Use *plasticize.*

In the plastics industry, the verb *plasticate* means to make a plastic material malleable by heating or kneading: ("Use the entire cooling time to plasticate the next shot"; "A low-compression screw should be used with polycarbonate in general, but even more so with the metal fleck because it tends to plasticate more evenly").

Plasticate in the sense of to make, become, or cover with plastic is incorrect; that is the definition of *plasticize.* And even though plastic, factually and figuratively, overwhelms us, one word, *plasticize,* is quite enough to describe this unpleasantness.

playwrite Misspelling of *playwright.* • Besides being a novelist and a *playwrite,* Camus was an active journalist, writing hundreds of articles and editorials for newspapers. Use *playwright.* • I have worked as an actor, model, *playwrite,* director, and producer. Use *playwright.*

The *wright* of *playwright* means one who builds or makes something, not one who writes. Though archaic, the word *wright* means a person who makes or repairs something, often out of wood. *Wright* is also affixed to other words, such as *wheelwright* (a person who builds or repairs wheels) and *shipwright* (a person who builds or repairs ships). *Playwrite* is a common misspelling. SEE ALSO **writting**.

plus Misused for *and* (or similar words). • *Plus,* there are a ton of nighttime concerts that are happening around the city. USE *And.* • Those donating their hair will get a free styling, free round of golf, a rock sculpture, *plus* before and after photos. USE *as well as.* • *Plus,* I was curious to see how a guy would be struck by this explicitly women-focused network. USE *What's more.* • *Plus* we're deepening Cooking 101 with more guides and glossaries. USE *Moreover.* • *Plus,* why are senators and congressmen from other states suddenly authorities on the laws of California? USE *Besides.*

Disagreeable also is *and plus*: • You shouldn't be low-key *and plus,* you don't get that much respect in this game. USE *and.* • *And plus,* I'm not a scorer so that was big for me. USE *And.*

Though you may begin a sentence with *and,* with *but,* with *because,* you ought not to begin a sentence with *plus;* further, using *plus* midsentence is equally objectionable. Whether used as a conjunction (*and*) or an adverb (*besides*), *plus* is casual and hardly suitable for most published writing. Of course, most published writing is hardly suitable for publication.

poise Misused for *pose.* • Then, realizing each of these pamphlets was inaccessible, I *poised* a question still not adequately answered. USE *posed.* • He also very kindly *poised* for a photo with me. USE *posed.* • To many of us the mosquito is only a small insect that *poises* a danger to human beings because of its malaria virus. USE *poses.*

Pose, as a noun, is a bodily position, especially one held for an artist or photographer; a way of speaking or behaving. As a verb, *pose* means to adopt a posture; to pretend to be someone else; to be pretentious; to ask a question; to present, especially a problem, danger, or threat. *Poise* is ease and grace of manner; composure; self-assurance; a state of balance or equilibrium. As a verb, *poise* means to be balanced or perched.

It could very well be that if you lack grace and dignity, if you lack *poise* (POIZ), you spell it *p-o-s-e* and pronounce it (POZ).

politeful Misused for *polite.* • I did not find him *politeful* nor was he helpful. USE *polite.* • One of our goals (at least for me) is to have the kids grow up to be respectful, courteous, *politeful,* helpful, and loving. USE *polite.* • Is it in a *politeful* way or in a prideful way? USE *polite.* • I am certainly not asking for hand-holding, just a respectful and *politeful* response. USE *polite.* • But he's been very civil, very *politeful;* he's been very respectful of John McCain throughout this whole ordeal. USE *polite.*

If *politeful* were a word, it might mean fulsomely polite. As a synonym for *polite,* it is wholly unnecessary, utterly ridiculous.

populace Misused for *populous.* • They may not have the background and the time to do the necessary research, even if it involves the "biggest" running story of the second most *populace* country in Latin America. USE *populous.* • The strip is the most *populace* area in the world and it would have put up a fierce resistance, which would have caused a real massacre in case of an Israeli occupation. USE *populous.*

Populace means a population; the masses. *Populous* means crowded or thickly populated.

pour Misused for *pore.* • We *pour* over hundreds of books and book reviews to pick twelve of the most interesting titles we can find. USE *pore.* • It is remarkable that I still have a vivid memory of sitting at a little desk in the medical library, *pouring* over the book that first piqued my interest in PKU. USE *poring.* • And they evoke the most wonderful memories, of afternoons spent *pouring* over coloring books and pictures. USE *poring.* • Beads of sweat begin to flood from every *pour* in my body and I feel as if my temperature skyrockets to around 110 degrees! USE *pore.*

And *pore* is sometimes used for *pour.* • A true friend is a person to whom you can *pore* out your heart, grain and chaff together, into his/her patient hands and know that he/she will faithfully and gently blow the chaff away, then see clearly the essence of what you meant to say. USE *pour.*

Pour means to dispense from a container; to give full expression to. *Pore* means to read or study carefully; to reflect or meditate deeply; or, as a noun, a minute opening in tissue.

practicable Misused for *practical.* • It is full of old-fashioned *practicable* advice and is equipped with easy-to-use indexes to help find answers to questions. USE *practical.* • It has proved to be the most wholesome, the most comprehensive, and the most *practicable* guide for all sectors of human life. USE *practical.*

Practicable, a word that cannot be applied to people, means capable of being done or put into practice; feasible ("Pakistan can take action against the JuD chief if India provides practicable evidence against him"; "Vested shares will be delivered to the reporting person as soon as practicable following the applicable vesting date"). *Practical* means useful; capable of being put to use. The difference, though slight, is important, for from such distinctions we know subtlety of thought. And without subtlety there can be little society.

precedents Misspelling of *precedence.* • Any announcements made at the lake take *precedents* over written rules. USE *precedence.* • This chapter shall take *precedents* over and supersede any other provisions of this title which appear to regulate charitable solicitations. USE *precedence.*

Precedence is the condition of being more important than something else; priority; the order of importance of people having different rank. *Precedents* is the plural of *precedent,* an act or statement that serves as an example or justification in a legal case; an earlier instance or occurrence of something regarded as a guide for later events.

> Keep in mind that scholarly activities take precedents over all other activities for which we use the computers.
>
> —Salem Academy
>
> Although we are told that "Academic achievement is at the center of" Salem Academy, this sentence from one of Salem's webpages may make us question their activities and academics.

preceed Misspelling of *precede.* • For Canadian symbols, *preceed* the symbol with the letters CAN. USE *precede.* • When addressing mail to an assemblyman, the title *Honorable* should *preceed* his full name, i.e.,

"The Honorable firstname lastname." Use *precede.* • A special pre-concert "informance" will *preceed* this entertaining and educational concert experience. Use *precede.* • Take a look at these definitions and then choose the appropriate word for the sentences that *preceed* them. Use *precede.* • The epithelium may become dysplastic—a change that may *preceed* the development of gastric carcinoma. Use *precede.*

In confusion with *proceed,* the word *precede* is sometimes—actually, quite regularly—misspelled *preceed.*

preceed Misspelling of *proceed.* • At this point you can verify the quantity and costs of your order and either modify, delete, or *preceed* with your purchase. Use *proceed.* • Without writing a thick volume on angels, demons, and Satan, let's *preceed* with some answers from the only reliable source that God has given mankind—the Bible. Use *proceed.* • Click the Enter button if you are at least 18 years of age and do not object to adult subject matter and wish to *preceed.* Use *proceed.*

And a little less understandable, the word *proceed* is sometimes misspelled *preceed.*

precip An increasingly popular abbreviation for *precipitation* (or rain or snow or sleet), *precip* will soon be entered into increasingly appalling dictionaries. By including the abbreviation *precip,* and then, as they surely will, calling it a back formation, as though doing so gives this abomination (which even sounds illicit) some standing, lexlings further the simplification, the mono- and disyllabification (respelling or abbreviating polysyllabic words so that they are only one or two syllables—and more telling terms than the footballesque "back formation"), of the English language and, as troubling, the thoughts we have: • At this point, Acadiana appears to be divided right down the middle between liquid and frozen *precip.* • Was it supposed to get cold this quickly, or will temperatures rise at the onset of *precip*? • Right now it looks like Tuesday could begin with mixed *precip,* possibly rain-snow mix or freezing rain, transitioning to snow by mid-day. See also **a.k.a.**; **enthuse**; **invite**; **def** in **appendix A**.

precipitous Misused for *precipitate.* • In what Johns Hopkins believes to be an unwarranted, unnecessary, paralyzing, and *precipitous* action, the Office of Human Research Protection (OHRP) has today suspended all federally supported medical research projects involving human subjects at almost all of our institutions. USE *precipitate.* • In the absence of *precipitous* behavior on the part of the subject, negotiators should initiate dialogue in English, working on the assumption that the subject might take the opportunity to talk. USE *precipitate.* • Obama assured 10th Mountain Division soldiers today that the drawdown in Afghanistan is not *precipitous,* and that gains made there will be sustained. USE *precipitate.* • There is no need for *precipitous* action now before all pertinent factors are carefully considered. USE *precipitate.*

Precipitate, as an adjective, means moving rapidly; done abruptly or rashly; occurring suddenly. *Precipitous,* like a precipice; very steep. There are *precipitous* declines, falls, and drops, and *precipitate* actions, behaviors, and drawdowns.

predominate Misused for *predominant.* • But of course, the magnificent flag of the USA flies in the *predominate* position on the Giant Stride. USE *predominant.* • While this pattern conforms to that predicted based on known changes in diving physiology and metabolic control, the overriding influence of age on the diving behavior of pups younger than three months contrasts with the *predominate* influence of size and condition observed in yearling seals. USE *predominant.* • While central station power will continue to be the *predominate* delivery system for our industry for years to come, Consumers Energy is exploring the use of on-site generation often times referred to as distributed generation. USE *predominant.* • Her workshop on Feminist Perspectives on Masculinity will examine the *predominate* view of what it means to be a "real man" in society and explore more life-affirming options for male development. USE *predominant.*

The adjective is *predominant,* not—despite what some dictionaries now suggest—*predominate. Predominate* is a verb meaning to prevail or dominate. That this word is now sometimes used to mean the adjective *predominant* (having superior strength, authority, influence, or force; most common or conspicuous) is due to people's confusing the words and, what's worse, to laxicographers endorsing people's ignorance. SEE ALSO **dominate**.

Among Middle East experts, it has become the predominate wisdom that real progress toward peace can only be achieved if not just Palestinian Leader Yasser Arafat, but also Sharon, step down as leaders of their nations.

—Richard Gwyn, *Toronto Star*

Wolfson also seems to buy into "personhood theory," the predominate view in bioethics that people with severe cognitive impairments are less than fully equal persons, and hence, have fewer rights.

—Wesley J. Smith, *The Weekly Standard*

The adjective is *predominant*. These writers—all writers—ought to know that dictionaries chronicle the dissolution of the language; they *are* the new doomsday books. Without sensible words, dependable meanings, there can be no sane world.

preferable The pronunciation of *preferable* is (PREF-er-ah-ble), not (pri-FER-ah-ble).

prejudice Misused for *prejudiced.* • I think the main reason why some people dislike other people is because they are *prejudice.* USE *prejudiced.* • Since *prejudice* people cannot deal with their inner frustrations, they stereotype, blame, and attack less powerful groups. USE *prejudiced.* • I walked with him for a moment not saying anything, then I asked if he was *prejudice* against Starbucks. USE *prejudiced.*

Prejudice is a noun or verb. The adjectival form of *prejudice* is *prejudiced;* the past participle is also *prejudiced.* SEE ALSO **cliché**.

premier Misused for *premiere.* • The *premier* airs at 7:30 P.M. The hour-long *premier,* cosponsored by NASA Langley, will feature highlights of the 12-part series produced by Tom Hanks and is scheduled to run on Cox Cable in April and May. USE *premiere.* • Paceline Systems co-sponsors the *premier* of the InfiniBand Association's *IT Roadshow.* USE *premiere.* • A world *premier* of the play *Nobody Knows You're a Dog,* will take place on the WPI campus on November 16-18. USE *premiere.*

And *premiere* is sometimes misused for *premier*: • One of those was the *premiere* of the Soviet Union, who extended an invitation to the artist to visit Moscow as a guest of the Union of Artists of the USSR. Use *premier.* • Paul Okalik, the *premiere* of Canada's Nunavut Province, has his finger directly on the denial button. Use *premier.*

Premier, the noun, means a prime minister or a chief administrative officer. *Premiere* is the first public performance, as of a movie or play.

prescribe Misused for *subscribe* • How do we *prescribe* to the magazine and what is the cost? Use *subscribe.* • Further, we do not *prescribe* to the theory that increased regulation will lead to an appreciation of the local currency, hence currency hedge pays and exporters are still very much favored stocks in our opinion. Use *subscribe.* • No longer will students feel shut out or underrepresented just because they *prescribe* to a certain philosophy. Use *subscribe.* • On the website of IRC Western and Southern Sweden, you can *prescribe* to our newservice "Technologies on-line" and get access to all offers and requests. Use *subscribe.* • Whoever would like to have information about sporting and cultural events and what's on here on a regular basis, should *prescribe* to our free newsletter. Use *subscribe.*

Prescribe means to lay down as a rule or direction; to recommend; to issue as a medicine. *Subscribe* means to contribute a sum of money; to sign one's name to a document; to authorize someone to receive access to a publication or service; to express approval or assent to. See also **ascribe**; **proscribe**.

P

> The purpose of language is to communicate, rather than prescribe to rules and standards.
>
> —Scott Kapel, *Solecisms of Mechanics and Grammar*
>
> The correct word is *subscribe,* not *prescribe,* though the author of this sentence, an English teacher and a so-called descriptive grammarian—who further writes "rules were either created or sternly upheld by those insecure, upper-class intellectuals who insisted upon them to prove their education over that of the lower elements"—might try to rebut this.

presently Misused for *currently* (or similar words). • Is lava *presently* flowing out of Mauna Loa? USE *now.* • I am *presently* an undergraduate student at Northern Arizona University. DELETE *presently.* • John Jeter is *presently* in his seventh season as the music director and conductor of the Fort Smith Symphony. DELETE *presently.* • Our site is *presently* under reconstruction and some links or shopping cart functions may not be working. USE *currently.*

Presently is best used to mean soon or in a short time ("Tell her we will be there presently"; "A good, offensive joke may smell for a while, but the odor will leave presently and you will be none the worse for wear"). In the sense of now or currently, it is less defensible.

presumptious Misspelling of *presumptuous.* • It would be *presumptious* of me to consider my life to be significant enough to warrant an autobiography, and I am not a *presumptious* person. USE *presumptuous.* • Isn't it a little *presumptious* of us humans to think we can be the arbiters of design everywhere in the universe? USE *presumptuous.* • How *presumptious* of the perennial white-shirted World Cup chokers. USE *presumptuous.*

If we pronounced *presumptuous* (pri-ZUMP-choo-es) correctly, we would be more likely to spell it correctly. SEE ALSO **assumptious**.

P

presumptive Misused for *presumptuous.* • It's also quite *presumptive* of him to assume that all 25,000 of those students have never heard of Christianity. USE *presumptuous.* • If God does have a predetermined time for the earth's Judgment, it is *presumptive* and arrogant for humans to think that they can foresee that which only God can know. USE *presumptuous.* • I was taught that addressing a stranger by his first name was *presumptive* and rude and too personal, that a stranger should always be addressed formally as Mr. or Mrs. or Miss if and until a friendship is established. USE *presumptuous.*

Presumptive—which often refers to heirs, political nominees, and criminal sentences—means giving grounds for belief; based on probability ("The former North Carolina State quarterback will arrive on campus as the presumptive starter this season"; "In Louisiana, the presumptive heir is he who is the nearest relation of the deceased"; "The presumptive sentence in the murder charge ranges from 22 to just more than 30 years"). *Presumptuous* means presuming, excessively forward, arrogant, or bold.

prevaricate Misused for *procrastinate.* • Iraq, the U.S. believes, wants inspectors who have as little knowledge as possible of the weapons they are looking for, wants a list of inspection sites so that it can clean them up well in advance, and wants a time limit so that it can *prevaricate* and eventually call a halt if the inspectors ever get close to finding something incriminating. USE *procrastinate.* • But if you continue to *prevaricate,* your window of opportunity will close, consigning you to the ranks of nonentities who have governed Japan for too many years. USE *procrastinate.* • In the prevailing climate, President Habyarimana and the extremists who surrounded him hoped that if they could *prevaricate* until UNAMIR's mandate expired on April 5, 1994, the Security Council would lose patience and withdraw the force. USE *procrastinate.*

To *prevaricate* is to stray from the truth; to equivocate; to lie. To *procrastinate* is to put off; to postpone or defer.

preventative Misused for *preventive.* • The PCMHs are expected to improve health care delivery while moderating costs by emphasizing *preventative* and coordinated care. USE *preventive.* • Michelle Obama announced Wednesday a plan for free *preventative* health care services, a part of the Affordable Care Act. USE *preventive.*

Preventive is preferable to *preventative* because it has one fewer syllable. What's more, it very well may be that the origin of *preventative* (ca. 1676) was simply people mispronouncing *preventive* (ca. 1639).

prevert Misspelling of *pervert.* • I think you're some kind of deviated *prevert.* USE *pervert.* • Why am I not surprised that a NAMBLA *prevert* like you is defending a child molester like Jackson. USE *pervert.* • But you clicked on the link, so obviously you are a filthy *prevert* and only found DrF because you were searching for free porn, weren't you? USE *pervert.*

And *preversion* is a misspelling of *perversion.* It may be that *prevert* is sometimes used to add a sense of perversion to the noun *pervert,* to emphasize the perversion, but all the usage typically unveils is a stupid, often repugnant, person.

Pervert is a perfectly good verb, the meanings of which are not often heard: to lead away from what is right, correct, moral, or good; to debase;

to misconstrue or distort ("Google is not going to pervert its search results, regardless of any contract language"; "A second count alleged that he conspired to pervert the course of justice by providing false evidence about the allegations").

prey Misused for *pray*. • *Prey* for help from whatever power is greater than you. USE *Pray*. • *Prey* to god for mercy because you will find none from us. USE *Pray*. • We all hope and *prey* for his return to good health. USE *pray*.

To *pray* is to hope for; to make supplication; to recite a prayer; to worship God or other deity. To *prey* is to hunt or kill other animals; to rob or plunder; to swindle or exploit someone; to weigh heavily on.

principle Misused for *principal*. • We are delighted to have the generous support and assistance of our *principle* sponsors. USE *principal*. • Today, the Russians are our *principle* partner in space exploration, a fact inconceivable in 1957. USE *principal*. • Students also must complete the highest level of math offered at their high school before taking a college math class unless an exception is made by the high school *principle*. USE *principal*.

A *principle* (always only a noun) is a truth, law, standard, or rule. *Principal*, as an adjective, means chief or highest in importance. As a noun, it means a person who holds a high position or has a main role; a sum of money that is owed and on which interest is charged.

> Then there's the Muslim practice of not charging explicit interest: that opens the door to having creditors write off interest but not principle.
>
> —*The Wall Street Journal*
>
> If the *Wall Street Journal*—three times in one editorial—does not know the difference between *principle* and *principal*, we might mistrust their figures as much as we must their words.

privlege (privledge) Misspellings of *privilege*. • Authentication does not give you any *privlege*, it only provides a basis for deciding *privlege*. USE *privilege*. • For tax purposes, income is defined by the Supreme Court as a gain or profit earned by *privlege.* USE *privilege.* • To earn a Fun Friday, the children must earn the *privledge* to participate. USE *privilege.* • Is Bush about to withhold information, by invoking executive *privledge,* from the 9-11 investigation? USE *privilege.*

Privilege (PRIV-i-lij) or (PRIV-lij), neither *privlege* (PRIV-lej) nor *privledge,* is the correct spelling. The *d* that people so often want to include in *privilege* is found in the adjectival form: *privileged.*

problemsome Misused for *problematic* (or similar words). • These nonunique solutions are *problemsome* and we appeal to additional considerations to find the one(s) that actually will appear in nature. USE *problematic.* • Even with this joint underlying mission, the relationship between these two agencies has often been *problemsome* and on some past occasions the size and scope of the altercations were legendary, such that stories still circulate. USE *problematic.* • The current version of Cisco IOS has been a little *problemsome* and another version has come out that should address some of the minor issues we have been seeing. USE *problematic.*

Despite the existence of *worrisome, troublesome,* and *fearsome, problemsome* is not in the English lexicon. *Problematic* (as well as *problematical*) is.

P

prone Misused for *supine.* • This involves placing the child in the *prone* or faceup position, since in this position children have the greatest access to their hands. USE *supine.* • One interesting note: cockroaches affected by this product will die *prone (faceup)* rather than on their backs as is the norm for other control products. USE *prone (facedown).*

Prone means facedown; *supine,* faceup.

pronounciation Misspelling of *pronunciation.* • With the landslide selection of Arnold Schwarzenegger as the state's newest governor, local politicians had more to mull Wednesday than the *pronounciation* of "Kawleefornia." USE *pronunciation.* • Also, not that you asked but now that I'm offering *pronounciation* guidelines, Warre is pronounced "war." USE *pronunciation.*

People who spell the word incorrectly may also pronounce it incorrectly: (pro-*nun*-see-AY-shen), not (pro-NUN-see-*ay*-shen).

proofreading Misused for *copyediting. Proofreading* means only one thing: comparing one document (an edited manuscript or galley) to another (a typeset galley or page proof) to ensure all changes have been correctly made. *Copyediting* means reviewing a manuscript for grammatical errors, spelling, punctuation, and the like. Proofreaders are not copy editors.

> Pity the poor proofreader. Imagine wading through the thicket of contemporary written English, uprooting such verbal weeds as misplaced *who*s and *whom*s, hopeless *hopefully*s, singular *data, whatever*.
>
> —Robert Siegel, *All Things Considered*
>
> Mr. Siegel nicely illustrates the incorrect, the common, use of *proofreading*.

prophesy Misused for *prophecy.* • Gaze into our crystal ball for the predictions and *prophesy* made by ancient millennium prophets and modern experts concerning the fate of our planet and the future of mankind. Use *prophecy.* • The Birthday *Prophesy* makes a great gift for that someone special. Use *Prophecy.* • Some churches try to use the successes of futuristic *prophesy* to justify faith, particularly faith in the infallibility of Scripture. Use *prophecy.* • The upshot was a situation with many of the features of a bank run, in which the fear that even fundamentally sound institutions might fail, can become a self-fulfilling *prophesy.* Use *prophecy.*

Prophesy (PROF-i-*sigh*) is the verb, *prophecy* (PROF-i-see), the noun; not misspellings, they are different parts of speech.

proportion Misused for *portion.* • Don't get me wrong, I'm not anorexic, I just eat small *proportions.* Use *portions.* • In general, Thai eat several small meals throughout the day and evening and nowhere near the large *proportions* of food that farang (i.e., Westerners) eat. Use *portions.* • If you think you are hungry enough to eat a large *proportion,* put a medium *proportion* on your plate. Use *portion.*

Proportion refers to a part considered in relation to a whole or a comparative relationship between things or parts of things with respect to size, amount, or degree. *Portion,* in the sense discussed here, refers to a helping of food.

> So what are the best ways of staying healthy? Eat small proportions.
> —Dr. Mallika Marshall, WBZ-TV

proscribe Misused for *prescribe.* • We are on record to abide by the 1949 Geneva Conventions and their relevant sections that *proscribe* the rules of war. USE *prescribe.* • They often *proscribe* rules of behavior that we must follow to attain rewards or avoid punishment in this or the after world. USE *prescribe.*

To *proscribe* is to prohibit, forbid, or disallow; to *prescribe* is to set down, order, or recommend. SEE ALSO **prescribe**.

prostrate Misused for *prostate.* • BioSafe PSA4 *Prostrate* Cancer Screening Test provides the same clinical results that can be obtained from a local laboratory, but without the inconvenience of keeping an appointment and the need to draw blood from the arm. USE *Prostate.* • Eating tomatoes, ketchup, tomato sauce, and tomato paste-topped pizza more than two times a week can reduce the risk of *prostrate* cancer by 21 to 43 percent according to Dr. Edward Giovannucci of the Harvard University School of Public Health. USE *prostate.* • Preventing *prostrate* cancer is easier than fighting *prostrate* cancer. USE *prostate.*

Prostate means of or relating to the prostate gland. *Prostrate* means lying facedown; overcome.

proven Misused for *proved.* • Has the existence of extraterrestrial life finally been *proven*? USE *proved.* • SalesLink has *proven* our success with hundreds of satisfied customers. USE *proved.* • Chairman of the Forum for Unity, Cohesion, and Justice in East Timor, Domingos MD Soares, has maintained that the partisanship of the UN Assessment Mission in East Timor (UNAMET) with the anti-integration camp has been *proven* beyond doubt. USE *proved.*

Past participles both, *proved* and *proven* may be used in the examples shown. *Proved,* however, is best used as a verb (had been *proved*; was *proved*), and *proven* as an adjective (*proven* ability; *proven* technology).

psuedo- Misspelling of *pseudo-*. • The transsexual in question, whose *psuedonym* is Eri, worked at the same cabaret club as Aki (also a *psuedonym*). USE *pseudonym.* • Nine-year-old Matiesse Reid has been in Pittsburgh with her family for almost four years, after suffering from chronic *psuedo* intestinal obstruction. USE *pseudo.* • Because even if it is a *psuedo-study* designed solely as a PR boost, it's tough to ignore this claim. USE *pseudo-study.* • It may have been the closest race in this writer's tenure of producing these *psuedo-columns* in the wake of essentially every WVU football and men's basketball game. USE *pseudo-columns.*

Pseudo- is the correct spelling, not *psuedo-*, even though the prefix is pronounced (SOO-doh).

publically Misspelling of *publicly.* • The university's chapter of NAACP held a rally Tuesday during lunch to *publically* show its support of the decision to change the on-the-field mascot. USE *publicly.* • Even on the U.S. Supreme Court there are several who have *publically* stated that we must look to foreign legal systems for our legal precedents and ignore our own Constitution. USE *publicly.*

At least one dictionary maintains that *publically* is an acceptable spelling of *publicly,* and that is the dictionary you should not buy or refer to. SEE ALSO **accidently**; **publicly** in **appendix A**.

pundant (pundent) Misspelling of *pundit.* • Tonight, Jerry Springer had the best explanation of the election I have heard from any *pundant.* USE *pundit.* • However, because of our winner-take-all electoral system, *pundants* like to talk about states being either red or blue. USE *pundits.* • A *pundent* seems to be someone who has enough knowledge and experience with politics to be able to not only analyze but also predict and advise. USE *pundit.* • He is a nice guy with a dazzling smile but (as one *pundent* put it) "has never had an unspoken thought." USE *pundit.*

The correct spelling is *pundit* (PUN-dit): a critic; a person knowledgeable about a particular topic.

pundify Misused for *pontificate* (or similar words). • My thought is to touch security only with respect to the primitives in OGSI/OGSA and also describe only actual use cases and working grids than *pundify* on various mechanisms. USE *opine*. • But there are some people saying today—some people do the same things you all do which is *pundify*—are saying this is really good, this is really good for Kerry. USE *pontificate*.

To speak learnedly or critically, to teach, or, maybe, to pontificate or opine would likely be the definition of *pundify*, were there such a word.

But in other instances, *pundify* means nothing more than *speak* or *write*: • I think our current situation is pretty far from any "sacred institution" I keep hearing the pundits *pundify* about. USE *speak*. • Odd (but sad) that, as usual, as in yet another *New York Times* piece, pundits *pundify* on language with no reference to scientific work. USE *write*.

(is) purported Misused for *purports*. • I've seen what *is purported* to be the preliminary report on the autopsy. USE *purports*. • Even China *is purported* to be headed down the flat-tax road. USE *purports*. • It is tough to vote against anything that *is purported* to be property tax relief. USE *purports*.

The verb *purport* should not be used in the passive; it is regarded as passive, and means is supposed or is represented. *Purports*, not *is purported*, is correct.

What's more, the subject of *purport* ought not to be a person: • Will Martin write this book, revealing to the world the "monstrous, appalling things" his great-grandfather *is purported to have* done? USE *is accused of having*. • It is also clear that as brilliant a man as Clark *is purported* to be, running for president requires its own special set of skills. USE *is said*. • The Iraq War was initially justified because Hussein *was purported* to have weapons of mass destruction and ties to Al-Qaeda. USE *was thought*.

purposefully Misused for *purposely*. • None of these worthies could give any explanation as to why they, in collusion with the corrupt officers of the KDA and KBCA, had *purposefully*, deliberately, and grossly violated the building code, building in some cases as much as 200,000 sq. ft. in excess of what is permissible. USE *purposely*. • While you are waiting to register the name, it is often worthwhile to temporarily reserve the name with a name reservation form so that it is not accidentally or *purposefully* obtained by a competitor or unwitting third party. USE *purposely.*

Purposely means on purpose or deliberately. *Purposefully* means with a specific purpose in mind ("He had a relatively quiet first half, but played more purposefully in the second and scored Bayern's first goal"; "She'll soon start a residency program in emergency medicine, a field she purposefully chose because it offers more structured hours, allowing her to continue to race professionally").

Qq

quadricep Misused for *quadriceps*. • Michael Vick is listed as probable with a *quadricep* injury, but says he's feeling 100 percent. USE *quadriceps*. • Margie Weiss gives you safety tips for a *quadricep* workout in this video. USE *quadriceps*.

The singular of *quadriceps,* the four-part muscle at the front of the thigh, is *quadriceps*. The plural is *quadricepses,* and the adjective is *quadricipital.* SEE ALSO **bicep**; **tricep**.

quandry Misspelling of *quandary*. • Lost in all the nonsense about the Steelers' quarterback *quandry* is that the defense was downright horrendous against the Oilers. USE *quandary*. • Singapore's *quandry*: Use the Internet, but only use it responsibly. USE *quandary*. • With the acquisition of Skype, Microsoft faces the familiar tech *quandry*. USE *quandary*.

The spelling *quandry* has no etymological basis and no justification.

quite Misused for *quiet*. • We are onstage, in costume. The audience has *quitened.* USE *quietened.* • The genius within is waiting *quite* and still for an opportunity to guide our path. USE *quiet*. • How come Microsoft, Cisco, and Lucent were all deadly *quite* last week? USE *quiet*.

Quite is an adverb meaning to the fullest extent, completely; actually, really; to a degree, rather. *Quiet* is an adjective meaning silent; calm or peaceful; untroubled; not showy; understated.

quotation Misused for *quotient*. • Cognitive testing and neurobehavioral measures can also be used, although caution is in order with full-scale intelligence *quotation* (IQ) scores because they can mask subtle neuropsychologic patterns of abnormality. USE *quotient*. • We pay particular attention to stimulating the intellectual curiosity and increasing the emotional *quotation* of the child. USE *quotient*.

Quotation (which is preferable to the noun *quote*) refers to words repeated or reproduced by another; the estimated price of a job or service. *Quotient* refers to the result obtained when one number is divided by another; the amount of a specific quality or characteristic.

And unsurprisingly, some people misuse *quotient* for *quotation*: • Try a Google search with "Fiber Edge+garden" without the *quotient* marks. USE *quotation*. • *Quotient* marks " " are used to phrase a sentence whether whole or partial when showing someone speaking. USE *Quotation.*

Rr

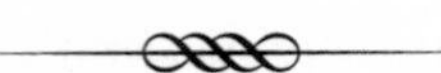

racial Misused for *racist.* • The suspect, who is white, made a derogatory *racial* comment against Watson, who is black. USE *racist.* • A city police officer is under internal investigation after being accused of making an inappropriate *racial* comment. USE *racist.* • Limbaugh quits ESPN after making a *racial* comment. USE *racist.* • Mr. Howard's resignation was prompted by reports that he made an inappropriate *racial* comment. USE *racist.* • As appalling as his *racial* remark was, it is not enough of a reason to destroy a man who has contributed so much to the black community, this university, and this state. USE *racist.*

People once were accused of making *racist* comments; today, they are as likely, or more than likely, to be accused of *racial* ones. A *racial* comment is not necessarily discriminatory or reprehensible; a *racist* one is. A "derogatory" racial comment might more accurately be called a racist comment; an "inappropriate" racial comment, a racist one; an "appalling" racial remark, a racist one. *Racial* is for people who are afraid to use *racist.* SEE ALSO **niggardly**.

racquet Misused for *racket.* • Why don't you make a loud *racquet* and embarrass them? USE *racket.* • And to get you geared up for an energetic day, the Pro AM crew, PJ and Spanky, from local radio station Lantern FM will be on site making a *racquet* with sounds of the latest moves and grooves. USE *racket.*

Racket means, as *racquet* does, a light bat or paddle used in a game; a game. But only *racket* is an uproar; loud or noisy confusion; a means of obtaining money illegally; a livelihood of some sort.

rational Misused for *rationale.* • What is the *rational* for having many secondary schools when the existing National High Schools have served that purpose well? Use *rationale.* • Our *rational* is if you don't use a dictionary you only use the words you already know. Use *rationale.* • The board's mission is to provide Chamber members with a clear indication of the business *rational* for funding or failing to fund charitable requests. Use *rationale.*

Rational (RASH-ah-nel) means having the ability to reason; reasonable or logical. *Rationale* (*rash*-ah-NAL) means the rational basis for a course of action or belief.

ravage Misused for *ravish.* • The first scene involves a homeless Vietnam Veteran and three red, white, and blue painted figures who *ravage* a woman painted with symbols and messages wearing a Native American headdress while a man in "black-face" sings the National Anthem. Use *ravish.*

And *ravish* is misused for *ravage*: • In addition, the incursion of illegal Israeli settlements that displace Palestinians and *ravish* the landscape must be prohibited. Use *ravage.*

Ravage means to destroy; to plunder and sack. *Ravish* is to seize and carry away; to rape; to enrapture.

realator Misspelling of *Realtor.* • Because it has been so slow, a serious seller would have been very foolish to give one *realator* an exclusive on his property. Use *Realtor.* • Whether you are a *realator,* travel agent, tour guide, contractor, or wedding coordinator, immersive imaging can help your business. Use *Realtor.*

R

The correct spelling is *Realtor,* not *realator*; thus, the correct pronunciation is (REAL-ter), not (REEL-ah-ter). Although *Realtor* is a trademark, it often is spelled with a lowercase *r.* See also **abilify**.

re- back Misused for *re-.* • Under the lease agreement, if LRMC did not use the building for that purpose, ownership would *revert back* to the city. Delete *back.* • Next, the officers are heading to Long Island to visit another base and will *return back* to South Africa on Saturday. Delete *back.* • The results are saved so that patients and doctors can *refer back* to them at a later date. Delete *back.* • This is a day we can *reflect back* on the long and rugged journey from where we came. DELETE *back.* • After receiving the message you will have to *reply back* to confirm your subscription to the list. DELETE *back.*

Revert back, return back, refer back, reflect back, reply back, and similar expressions are all redundant. SEE ALSO **convey back.**

> It looks like they're having a big reverting back to prefreedom times.
>
> —Martha Zoller, radio talk show host
>
> That this unexceptional woman has an audience is disquieting: it must be that her listeners are no brighter, and speak no better, than the host herself.

rebound Misused for *redound.* • Another obstacle dream, but this one pertains to personal behavior and is a warning that you should try to avoid giving false impressions that could *rebound* to your discredit. USE *redound.* • Our Christian young men, having broken away from fear of evil spirits and their animistic practices, are rejoicing that they can see ways of cooperating with the progressive party, which will evidently *rebound* to the praise and glory of the Lord Jesus Christ. USE *redound.* • No good deed goes unrewarded. If you help someone, it will somehow *rebound* to your credit. USE *redound.* • But the exposure of Danish artists to New York City's own historically vibrant culture will also *rebound* to their benefit and therefore to their audiences on both sides of the Atlantic. USE *redound.* • In addition, the Howes were opposition Whigs and reluctant to win a victory that would *rebound* to the credit of the Tory government. USE *redound.* • Morgan Stanley, eager to ensure the highly profitable BGI relationship stayed in place, was all too happy to join in any conversations that might *rebound* to their advantage. USE *redound.*

Redound means to have an effect or consequence; to contribute or lead to. *Rebound* means to spring or bounce back after hitting or striking something; to recover as from a setback or illness.

Laxicographers, further disaffecting careful writers and speakers, assign the meaning *rebound* to the definition of *redound.*

recall (recollect) Confused with *remember.* To *remember* something is to do so effortlessly, or without much difficulty. To *recall* or *recollect* suggests a harder time of remembering. That said, the word *cannot* is best used with *recall* and *recollect*; the words *do not* with *remember.*

recieve Misspelling of *receive.* • Welcome to rock-web and rock365.com free subscriptions, keep in touch with us and *recieve* a regular newsletter about our latest features and free services. USE *receive.* • For more info on diving in southern Maine and to *recieve* our Northeast Dive Resort Video contact York Beach Scuba. USE *receive.* • The Center for Literacy is to *recieve* a grant from the proceeds of Export "A" Skins Golf Tournament. USE *receive.*

Some people seem unable to remember the spelling of *receive.* You can therefore be sure that some dictionaries will, one day, list *recieve* as a variant spelling of *receive.*

recognization Misused for *recognition.* • Honestly, the *recognization* of my work, sale of the painting to him, and the offer to get my work seen in New York is really just being done out of the kindness of his heart. USE *recognition.* • Other patriotic events for the week include American Red Cross blood donations, a public naturalization ceremony, and a veterans *recognization* ceremony. USE *recognition.* • As we know, the cell *recognization* mechanism exists in animals, such as the immunization mechanism. USE *recognition.*

Rather than *recognition,* some people manage to mouth—as well as to write—*recognization.* Though used in the nineteenth and early twentieth centuries, *recognization* is, or ought to be, obsolete; the word has no usefulness today.

> His daughter, Chris Thomas of Cherryville, was in attendance for his special recognization.
>
> —*Lincoln Tribune*

> It's a pleasure for the entire team to see their work receive global recognization for not only one, but two significant events.
>
> —Ed Burke, CEO, The Look Company

reëlection The dieresis, which is rarely used today (though occasionally in *naïve*), is placed atop the second of two juxtaposed vowels to indicate two separate sounds are to be pronounced. And though two sounds are found at the beginning of *reelection,* no one (except perhaps the lexicographers at Merriam-Webster) is likely to pronounce the word (ree-LEK-shen).

Today, the hyphen, far more often than the dieresis, is used in this country to indicate two sounds (*coöperate* was later spelled *co-operate,* for instance, and today it is usually spelled *cooperate*) but more often still to separate a prefix from a word stem or to distinguish one word from another (*re-create* from *recreate,* for instance).

refer Confused with *allude.* To *refer* is to mention something or someone directly ("They refer to all other women as 'boy-women,' implying they are dense and oafish like little boys, woefully short on their own fabulous womanliness"; "These bands are technically referred to as drum and bugle corps, not marching bands"). To *allude* is to mention something or someone indirectly without naming it or him; to suggest or hint at ("Reports of the time allude to the fact that, with the help of prominent business families, Methodism was established here"; "He also talked of expanding access to health care and alluded to his proposal to add personal investment accounts to Social Security"). The same distinction applies to the nouns *allusion* and *reference.* SEE ALSO **allude**.

refudiate Misused for *refute* (or *repudiate*). • It only takes a casual "stroll" through the iambic forums to completely *refudiate* this egregious claim. USE *refute.* • If she does have documentation he can *refudiate* the errors either using the CCC or the Bible. USE *refute.* • Note I highlight your words, so as to *refudiate* them. USE *repudiate.* SEE ALSO **refute.**

> They could refudiate what it is that this group is saying.
> —Sarah Palin, former governor of Alaska

To *repudiate* is to reject as untrue or unjust; to reject the validity or authority of. To *refute* is to prove to be false; to deny the truth or accuracy of. A mix of *refute* and *repudiate, refudiate* means nothing whatever.

refute Misused for *rebut* (or similar words). • The Red Sox have said they will not confirm or *refute* trade rumors. USE *deny.* • Few *refute* that purposeful exercise-walking is beneficial, and golf is yet another opportunity for low-impact, recreational fitness. USE *disagree.* • The panel is expected to *refute* the school board's request at the next state board of education meeting this month. USE *rebuff.* • Because Ashcroft has not attempted to *refute* the racist inclinations and pronouncements of such Christian evangelists as Franklin Graham, Jerry Falwell, and Pat Robertson, American Muslims are deeply frightened by these born-again, mostly Republican right-wing fundamentalists. USE *rebut.* • Amid the mounting suggestions on the market bubbles, the Bank of Korea has doggedly *refuted* the proposal to raise the interest rate. USE *rejected.*

Refute means to prove to be wrong; confute; disprove. It does not mean to rebut, deny, contradict, rebuff, disagree, dispute, repudiate, or reject. *Rebut* means to contradict, counter, or argue against. *Rebuff* means to reject an offer; to repel an attack. *Reject* means to dismiss; to refuse to agree with; to rebuff. SEE ALSO **refudiate**.

regime Misused for *regimen.* • Subjectivity requires intersubjective relationships mediated through a *regime* of possessing, enjoying, and exchanging an object of desire. USE *regimen.* • With a regular *regime* of exercise, the aches and pains will be minimized or even disappear. USE *regimen.* • Metformin works much better if combined with a strict *regime* of diet and exercise. USE *regimen.*

A *regime* (ri-ZHEM) is an authoritarian government; a way of doing something ("President Bashir knows very well that the survival of his regime depends on oil, and the oil is going to be lost"; "The President cited ECOWAS five percent tax regime on goods coming into ECOWAS countries from outside the subregion"; "Their increasingly turbulent resistance to prolonging the harsh austerity regime is likely to strengthen calls for cutting the country loose from the monetary union"). A *regimen* (REG-i-men) is a program of exercise, medical treatment, or other activity to achieve a benefit.

regiment Misused for *regimen.* • Shay plans to take some time away from education by traveling to Europe, visiting family, and starting up an exercise *regiment.* USE *regimen.* • It is any impatient treatment or any medical condition that incapacitates them for more than three days provided that they have seen a doctor and they are under a continuing *regiment* of medical care. USE *regimen.* • Paroxysmal supraventricular tachycardia (SVT) was considered acceptable if well controlled with any acceptable medical *regiment.* USE *regimen.*

A *regiment* is a unit of an army; a large number of things or people. A *regimen* is a course of medical treatment, exercise, or other activity.

regimentate Misused for *regiment.* • We must pre-arrange our material control and *regimentate* our production lines in such a manner that we may fulfill your requests as soon as possible. USE *regiment.* • It is important to *regimentate* strong efforts in the region by promoting the cooperation among the public and private sectors. USE *regiment.* • Policy and polity refer to attempts to *regimentate* or to regulate politics as an action and motion. USE *regiment.*

R

To *regiment* means to systematize; to subject to uniformity and order. *Regimentate* is misspelled, mispronounced, misused—just the sort of word that lexlings long for.

registrar Misused for *register.* • To *registrar* call Dee Morton, the center market manager, at 794-2011. USE *register.* • I would like to *registrar* as a certificate student. USE *register.*

A *registrar* (REJ-i-*strar*) is a person responsible for keeping a *register* (REJ-is-ter), an official list of names or other data. To *register* is to enter a name or other data into an official list.

regretful Misused for *regrettable.* • She said FIDA in its 25 years of operations in Ghana has been consistent and unrelenting in its gender empowerment endeavors but it was *regretful* that its operation essentially remained an urban phenomenon. USE *regrettable.* • At the same time, he said it was *regretful* that there appeared to be so much racial tension on today's school campuses. USE *regrettable.* • When asked about casualties in Iraq, Mr. Cheney responded that though human loss is always *regretful,* figures are extremely low in comparison to other warfield scenarios in the defense of freedom. USE *regrettable.*

Regretful means feeling or showing regret; sorry or sorrowful. *Regrettable* means giving rise to or deserving regret; undesirable. People are *regretful*; events, *regrettable.*

rein Misused for *reign.* • I'd like to find the place where happiness *reins,* where life is free and there are not restraints. USE *reigns.* • Darkness *reined* and many evil things happened led by her wicked brother. USE *reigned.* • The extent of Iranian arms production includes a small arms and ammunition plant at Parchin, which has been in operation for over 50 years, and some aircraft and air-to-air missile service and repair facilities established during the shah's *rein* through his arms supply relationship with the United States. USE *reign.* • Though fear *reined,* Jesus perceived everything through the eyes of love. USE *reigned.*

And *reign* is sometimes misused for *rein,* especially in the expression *free reign* (or *full reign*). *Reins* are the straps that control a horse; someone or something given *free rein* is freed of restraint and has, at least, some measure of control. *Free reign* is thus quite senseless, for *reign,* as a noun, means rule or dominance; as a verb, it means to rule or to be predominant.

R

reiterate Misused for *iterate*. Strictly, *iterate* means to say or do a second time; *reiterate* means to say or do a third or subsequent time.

relanguage Misused for *reword* (or similar words). • It's probably better to *relanguage* things for yourself than to try to accommodate a nomenclature that isn't working for you. USE *rewrite.* • The Israelis said that they asked you to give them reformulation of the language, too, and that both you *relanguage* and discuss it this week. USE *rephrase.*

Relanguage, some would have us believe, means to rephrase, reword, rewrite, or even translate. Others, it seems, believe *relanguage* also means to redefine: • We must *relanguage* powerlessness to refer to the addiction and create other kinds of empowerment that do not include "power over" but liberate us to find "power to." USE *redefine.* • In my view these endless subtle mutations are the fruit of pride; they demonstrate a resistance and violence toward the truth by attempting to *relanguage* it in terms acceptable to the individual but incomprehensible to anyone else. USE *redefine.* SEE ALSO **languaging**.

relive Misused for *relieve.* • Understanding the range of choices that are available to *relive* anxiety and discomfort makes you a well-informed dental consumer. USE *relieve.* • Opiates help to *relive* pain by acting in both the spinal cord and brain. USE *relieve.*

Relive means to experience a past event again. *Relieve* means to ease, lighten, or reduce. SEE ALSO **alleve**.

> Our mission is to provide individuals and families with assistance to lighten the load and relive the stress caused by financial burdens.
>
> —Christian Debt Management
>
> CDM means what it writes. Those who have the misfortune of somehow being on their spam list do indeed relive the stress.

removed from Instead of *since* or *after,* some people, sportswriters more than others, use *removed from* following the word *hours* or *days, weeks,* or *years.* • One year and nine weeks *removed from* playing arena football, Will Pettis made a surprising decision to return to arena football. USE *since.* • Less than 24 hours *removed from* the greatest victory in the history of its program, the Flintridge Prep boys' basketball team was assured its finest season wouldn't be coming to a close. USE *after.* • Here we are several days *removed from* the Brawl on Long Island and the backlash is still being felt. USE *since.*

This unpleasant expression, a favorite among sportswriters and other hacks, indicates how any mix of words can be used to mean all manner of things. There is no charm in fabricated expressions such as these, no elegance, no sense. SEE ALSO **out there**.

renumeration Misspelling of *remuneration.* • The prime minister said he was not against doctors getting decent *renumeration,* which they well deserved, but there had to be a limit in a poor country to one's ambition and greed. USE *remuneration.* • Wolper Jewish Hospital offers *renumeration* packaging, free food, and parking for staff as well as the opportunity to work in a friendly and supportive environment. USE *remuneration.* • Any person who in good faith renders emergency care, without *renumeration* or expectation of *renumeration,* at the scene of an accident or emergency to a victim of the accident or emergency shall not be liable for any civil damages resulting from the person's acts or omissions, except for such damages as may result from the person's gross negligence or wanton acts or omissions. USE *remuneration.*

The word is *remuneration* (ri-*myoo*-nah-RAY-shen), not *renumeration. Remuneration* means pay or compensation. *Renumeration* is *remuneration* with the *m* and the *n* transposed—that is, it is nothing much at all.

> MedWorld is currently recruiting editors, writers, and contributors from medical schools and hospitals across the world. All positions on MedWorld are volunteer-based, without renumeration or compensation.
>
> —MedWorld
>
> Stanford University's MedWorld clearly does need editors and writers though perhaps not from this group:
>
> Article 3—Renumeration and Rewrites. There shall be no minimum Script Fee. All Script Fees are negotiable.
>
> —Writers Guild of Canada

reoccur Misused for *recur.* • Reading your August 27 front-page article "Tending to Teens' Need to Sleep" irritated a *reoccurring* wound. USE *recurring*. • Jason Kauppi, Swift's spokesman, said yesterday that the initial treatment has been successful and that doctors wanted to keep the girls an extra day to make sure the problem did not *reoccur.* USE *recur.* • If you want the appointment or meeting to *reoccur* on a daily basis then tap on the Daily tab. USE *recur.* • The Top Ten Periodic Frequency graph displays the top ten numbers that are due to come up because of their tendency to *reoccur* in a periodic manner. USE *recur.* • If a problem did *reoccur,* however, I was puzzled as to why, for the basis of his work is that the problem should be fixed and not recur unless there is new trauma. USE *recur.*

Reoccur and *reoccurrence* are errors for *recur* and *recurrence.* Some critics and dictionary makers maintain that *recur* means to happen repeatedly, and *reoccur* to happen, merely, again, but this is a specious explanation for what was at first, and will be to the last, nothing but a blunder.

And then there are those who use *reoccurrence* instead of *recurrence*: • Basically, what this study is doing is looking at state-of-the-art treatments for depression and looking at how well they work in the short term, but also how well they prevent *reoccurrence.* USE *recurrence.* • Gross margins for the three months ended October 31, 1999 increased to 35 percent from (5 percent) in the prior year, primarily due to the *non-reoccurrence* of inventory-related charges that resulted in the negative margin for the second quarter of last year. USE *non-recurrence.*

Neither *reoccur* nor *reoccurrence* should exist in any reputable English-language lexicon. The use of *reoccur* has nothing to do with nicety, everything to do with nescience. SEE ALSO **occurence**.

R

repartee Misused for *joke* (or similar words). • Phong quickly *repartees*: "Happiness is like an ostrich, for the longer you bury your head the more happy you will be." USE *returns.* • Sir Martin *repartees* with a wicked smile: "I think Tony should worry about his own group." USE *retorts.* • The four men behind us flirt pointedly with the waiter, who good-naturedly *repartees* back. USE *jokes.* • Hughes, in fact, scared the crap out of me by just how sharp she was and how she very skillfully *reparteed* Jon's barbs. USE *replied to.*

Repartee, conversation characterized by witty comments, is a noun; it is not a verb even though it derives from the French *repartir,* to retort.

repel Misused for *rappel.* • You must *repel* down the side of the building in the midst of explosions and flames until you get to a lower rooftop, a few hundred feet down. Use *rappel.* • Homicide detectives spent several hours at the scene before an emergency rescue crew was allowed to *repel* down the shaft to remove the boy's body. Use *rappel.* • For ice rescue, we use the same half-inch line we use *repelling* off a building. Use *rappelling.* • From 1,000 applicants he was among the 50 selected to compete in the challenge of mountain biking, running, swimming, orienteering, *repelling,* and rock climbing. Use *rappelling.*

To *rappel* (rah-PEL) means to descend a mountain, building, wall, or other vertical surface by rope. To *repel* (ri-PEL) is to reject; spurn; turn or drive away.

> Although upon reaching the top of the wall, many climbers choose to repel down, park officials said.
>
> —*The Kentucky Post*
>
> This writer is best left unacknowledged, as the *Post,* for its own reasons, itself decided. Until misused words are no longer to be found, we all might prefer being no-name writers.

replete Misused for *complete.* • Steve Jobs, Apple's interim chief executive, unveiled on Wednesday the company's new low-cost computer: the iMac, a translucent teal and white plastic box, *replete* with monitor, keyboard, and mouse, that sells for $1,299. Use *complete.* • Finding himself the only Scot in Cannes without a kilt last year, former pop idol Rod Stewart had one—*replete* with family tartan and sporran—flown all the way from his favorite kilt maker in Glasgow for an evening concert. Use *complete.* • Gonzalez said the performance is "in a sense like a Broadway show," where you are entertained throughout by dancing, huge sets, costumes, and an original musical score *replete* with violin accompaniment. Use *complete.*

Ludicrous are the laxicographers who promote *replete* (which means abundantly full) as a synonym for *complete.* Dictionary makers, we must remember, simply document how the language is used; they are not keen thinkers; they do only as they are told. See also **replete** in **appendix A.**

report out Misused for *report.* • They report this information to private parties; for them to say it's burdensome to *report* it *out* flies in the face of reality. USE *report.* • And then we kind of go back home and *report* it *out* to our membership. USE *report.* • They'll ask readers to comb through databases and documents, emailing their tips, findings, original research, leaks, and personal expertise to Westervelt, who will *report* them *out.* USE *report.* • My job is to find interesting stories and *report* them *out.* USE *report.*

Report out instead of *report,* as used in these examples, is nonsense. It's as though the verb *report* does not effectively define itself. Not every verb needs a phrasal preposition following it to be meaningful. The expression *report out* means nothing much to most people—and nothing at all to others. SEE ALSO **separate out**.

representated Misused for *represented.* • If the student is represented by an attorney, UCSD may be *representated* by the Office of the General Counsel, or other appropriate representative. USE *represented.* • For all of the schematics below, the phosphorylated FixJ is *representated* by the green wireframe and the unphosphorylated FixJ is *representated* by the white wireframe. USE *represented.* • Swanwick helped pioneer the League of Nations Society, *representated* Great Britain at the International Conference of Women, and was appointed by Ramsey MacDonald to be a member of the British government delegation to the League of Nations Assembly in Geneva in 1924 and in 1929. USE *represented.*

R

The past tense of *represent* is *represented,* not *representated.*

repress Confused with *oppress. Oppress* means to subjugate; to tyrannize; to worry or trouble ("Establishing democracy in Iraq will deprive terrorists of their main theme of propaganda—that Western powers want to oppress the Middle East"; "Unfortunately, it does not provide clearly for the human rights of Afghan women or mandate a change in laws used to oppress women in the past"). *Repress* means to restrain; to subdue ("By all means, don't try to repress your feelings of anger, guilt, or sorrow"; "There are governments that still fear and repress independent thought and creativity in private enterprise").

respectful Misused for *respectable.* • Ms. Patterson said that was a *respectful* number, considering attendance was based on word of mouth. USE *respectable.* • Students and parents share the responsibility for making sure that students dress cleanly and neatly at all times and for making sure that students maintain a healthy and *respectful* appearance while attending school and school activities. USE *respectable.* • I think they've offered him a *respectful* amount of money. USE *respectable.* • Like most beginnings, we had to operate from a smaller locale in hopes of building a solid and *respectful* reputation. USE *respectable.*

Respectful has but one definition: showing proper regard or deference ("I want to explain to the police that they need to make changes and be more respectful"; "We encourage respectful debate"). *Respectable* has several definitions: worthy of esteem; having a good social standing or reputation; of good or suitable quality; considerable in size or number; presentable. One word does not mean the other.

respectively Misused for *respectfully.* • Choose complimentary close according to formality required: Use Sincerely for most business letters. Use *Respectively* yours when writing to the president of the United States. USE *Respectfully.* • Graduates of St. Clare School will act *respectively* toward self and others. USE *respectfully.* • Behave *respectively* to adults and each other. USE *respectfully.* • I urge you to consider them carefully and I think you will agree that they meet the objectives of the Commission without the negative implications of the proposed wording. *Respectively* yours, Jeffrey W. Pruett CPA. USE *Respectfully.*

Respectively means in the order designated or mentioned ("Women's soccer players Paula McGinn of Lynn and Caitlin D'Amario of East Longmeadow were named to the NSCAA second and third teams, respectively"; "Tracks by the Who and the O'Jays, used in the opening credits of CBS's *CSI: Crime Scene Investigation* and NBC's *The Apprentice,* respectively, generate six-figure deals annually"). *Respectfully* means characterized by or showing respect or deference. Even though, in Shakespeare's day, *respectively* apparently meant *respectfully,* the word in that sense has long been obsolete.

Despite the rather widespread misuse, no present-day dictionary has yet suggested that *respectively,* once again, also means *respectfully.*

restless Misused for *restive.* • Now there is talk of intervening in the turmoil afflicting Serbia's *restless* province of Kosovo. USE *restive.*

More disheartening still is the use of *restive* to mean the near opposite of what it does mean, to mean restful: • I hope to have a *restive* Saturday . . . and tomorrow should be leisurely productive. USE *restful.* • Set atop elevated ground, SouthLinks has tall, balmy trees, luxuriant shrubs, and tropical plants which create a *restive* and relaxing environment. USE *restful.* • Now situated on 14 acres of the original property, the Stone Mansion offers an elegant and refreshing alternative for a secluded office retreat, a relaxing picnic, or a *restive* holiday party. USE *restful.*

Restless means uneasy or unquiet; unable to rest or relax. *Restive* means impatient or fidgety under pressure, restraint, or opposition.

If people continue to watch television more than they read, and listen to music more than they think, descriptive dictionaries, which feed on foolishness, will surely claim that *restive* does mean *restful.*

restrospect Misused for *retrospect.* • This, in *restrospect,* was a foolish argument for picking a captain, and in some sense I bought it. USE *retrospect.* • In *restrospect,* I look at the Indians of the late '90s as a collection of great players. USE *retrospect.* • That hardness made her comment about the influx of Africans and Arabs seem, in *restrospect,* ominous. USE *retrospect.* • *The Color Purple* in *restrospect*: twenty years after the debut, the film's beauty never fades. USE *retrospect.* • It's extremely diluted and bland music designed for an audience that, in *restrospect,* must have been from another planet: Planet Lame. USE *retrospect.*

No misspelling, *restrospect,* instead of *retrospect,* is bare stupidity. Do the people who use *restrospect* also use *restro* instead of *retro*?

retch Misused for *wretch.* • He's a *retch* and needs a primitive education that can only be conducted out behind a barn or a woodpile. USE *wretch.* • I believe that Ragamuffin Soul is the story of a man, a *retched* man, but that god still loves him, him and his *retched* soul. USE *wretched.*

And *wretch* is sometimes misused for *retch*: • I have horrid memories of this bar, not because of the bar itself but because the last time I went I got so drunk I *wretched* all over the house. USE *retched.*

Wretch (RECH) is a miserable or unfortunate person; a despicable or base person. *Retch* (RECH) means to vomit.

reticent Misused for *reluctant* (or similar words). • Despite the seemingly endless challenges, Gallup appears *reticent* to give up either of his jobs. Use *reluctant.* • Without this information, leaders are unclear about where to invest resources and thus are *reticent* to do so. Use *reluctant.* • Open Port may still be *reticent* about going public, but the company has moved intrepidly into the Dark Continent. Use *disinclined.* • In the modern church we have educated pastors who will not take a stand on any biblical issue while they are not *reticent* to take a stand on a political issue. Use *reluctant.* • More enterprises have been less *reticent* to gamble on Linux during the last 18 months. Use *disinclined.*

Reticent means disinclined to speak; taciturn; quiet. *Reluctant* means disinclined to do something; unwilling; loath. Because some people mistakenly use *reticent* to mean *reluctant,* dictionaries now maintain *reticent* means *reluctant.* Dictionaries promote the misuse of the English language; dictionaries endorse illiteracies.

> He's been raised in a culture reticent to talk about social and moral conduct.
>
> —David Brooks, *The New York Times*

R

rifle Misused for *riffle.* • We *rifled* through the book for recipes and found one called Roast Pork Tenderloin with Leeks and Whole Grain Mustard Sauce. Use *riffled.* • And having *rifled* through all the cards in our warehouse, I can understand why the price point for the Ultimate Memorabilia sits where it does, especially when compared to other products featuring a memorabilia card in every pack. Use *riffled.*

To *rifle* (RI-fel) means to ransack or pillage; to steal; to cut spiral grooves on the inside of; to hurl with great speed. To *riffle* (RIF-el) means to leaf through a book; to shuffle cards.

rightfully Misused for *rightly.* • A lot has been *rightfully* made out of Matt Dodge's inability to kick the ball out of bounds. USE *rightly.* • The school-board model is being *rightfully* placed under a microscope. USE *rightly.* • These dealers are nervous about their future, and *rightfully* so. USE *rightly.*

Rightly means properly or correctly. *Rightfully* means having a just or legal claim or right to something; equitably, fairly ("He claims the camera is rightfully his, and is part of his personal collection of memorabilia"; "Marsha Tickler is suing her next-door neighbors over a three-foot strip of land between their houses that she says is rightfully hers").

ripe with Misused for *rife with.* • Pivotal scenes between Tony Soprano and his lady "shrink" are *ripe with* moral ambiguities. USE *rife with.* • Nastier-than-thou tracks "P-Poppin'" and "Blow It Out" are *ripe with* adult content that would make Howard Stern blush. USE *rife with.* • What the show inadvertently says is that in the Bay Area, artists are creating chairs, tables, and lighting *ripe with* symbolism and metaphor. USE *rife with.* • It never took long to find company at places like this, and the Dragon's Inn in particular was *ripe with* men looking for companions. USE *rife with.*

Ripe means ready to be harvested; mature; fully grown or developed; pungent or foul-smelling. *Rife* means widespread; plentiful; numerous. *Rife with* means full of. Infuriatingly, some dictionaries—the worst of them—claim that *ripe with* also means full of. Once we confuse the meanings of words, little is left for us to depend on.

R

> The debate, ripe with accusations, interruptions, barbs and knee-slapping ripostes, was more entertaining than any game show.
>
> —Karen Breslau, *Newsweek*
>
> Ms. Breslau apparently does not know the difference between the words *ripe* and *rife*. If her dictionary says *ripe* means the same as *rife,* she's as much of a fool for believing it as the dictionary's editors are for writing it.

rise Misused for *raise.*

Present	Present Participle	Past	Past Participle
rise	rising	rose	risen
raise	raising	raised	raised

The verb to *rise* means to assume a standing position or to move to a higher position. The verb to *raise* means to move something to a higher position. To *raise* often takes an object; to *rise* does not. SEE ALSO **sit**.

role Misused for *roll.* • The Band Blast featuring five rock and *role* and blues bands will take place tonight in the back lot of Roberta's Catering. USE *roll.* • Sausages, cheese and biscuits, and *roles* will be available. USE *rolls.*

And *roll* is misused for *role*: • If you have sent me an e-mail with the character you are going to play, you can just jump right in now and *roll*-play. USE *role.* • Lou Piniella will have played a monumental *roll* in the outcome. USE *role.*

A *role* is a part played by an actor; the required or expected social behavior of an individual; a specific function. *Roll* has many meanings; none of them these three that *role* has.

S s

-'s Misused for *-s.* • In the *1870's,* the Japanese emperor wanted to move away from that traditional approach and make Japan a secular nation, which it is today. USE *1870s.* • Plump *banana's* on sale. USE *bananas.* • So we muddled through the purchase by the seat of our *pant's.* USE *pants.* • We provide free *gift's* to all our riders and if there is something we can do for you, please don't hesitate to ask. USE *gifts.* • Where wood is likely to come into direct contact with fish, it is essential that the preservative used does not taint *foodstuff's* and is nontoxic to humans. USE *foodstuffs.* • If you have any questions or comments about our *chat's* then please contact us. USE *chats.* • When putting mustard on your *hotdog's* use American mustard and not hot English mustard. USE *hotdogs.*

Use an apostrophe to show possession, not to show plurality (except in a few specific instances such as with numbers, 1's, 2's, and letters, *a*'s, *b*'s).

sacreligious Misspelling of *sacrilegious.* • It almost felt *sacreligious* that my first gondola ride was not with someone that I was actually in love with. USE *sacrilegious.* • The one scene that I could really do without would be, of course, the extremely *sacreligious* scene in the middle of the show. USE *sacrilegious.*

The adjectival form of *sacrilege* is spelled *sacrilegious,* not *sacreligious.* The words *sacrilegious* and *religious* are etymologically unrelated: the first is from the Latin *sacrilegus,* one who steals sacred property.

saloon Misused for *salon.* • At a grocery store he was approached by a woman who owns a hair *saloon.* USE *salon.* • The inauguration of a beauty *saloon* and spa center was in the spotlight on Friday afternoon as models walked the ramp and showed everyone how to keep it stylish. USE *salon.*

A *salon* is a business establishment, for instance, a hairdresser's or beautician's; a reception room used for greeting guests; a gathering of intellectuals or artists. A *saloon* is a bar or restaurant where alcoholic drinks are sold; a tavern.

salubrious Misused for *salacious.* • Grab yourself a nice stiff drink, preferably a martini, and check out the *salubrious* sounds of Sexy Diablo. Use *salacious.* • He also appears to feel warranted in partaking in the *salubrious* joys of a swinging single life. Use *salacious.* • An absolute must for the girl on the move, this excellent love shortie is in the style of the one worn by the *salubrious* Jennifer Lopez. Use *salacious.* • It was a long, *salubrious* kiss with twisting exploring tongues darting in and out. Use *salacious.*

Salacious means lustful or lecherous; obscene. *Salubrious,* though it sounds rather sexy (compare *lubricious*), means something quite different: conducive or favorable to health or well-being; wholesome.

British actor Hugh Grant's hopes of buying a luxury retreat off France's Cote d'Azur could be scuppered by locals who disapprove of his salubrious past.

—Contactmusic.com

sanction Confused with *sanction. Sanction* has nearly opposite meanings: either to authorize or approve ("Since receiving that prize, Arafat has continued to sanction and even order terrorist attacks against Israeli Jews") or to penalize or punish ("A judge's decision to sanction one of Denver's premier law firms last week could lead to stern discipline for some of its lawyers but is unlikely to damage the firm's reputation or bottom line").

S

sanguine Misused for *sanguinary.* • A monastic life was utterly incompatible with the intensely worldly activity of the warrior, nor could the promised peace of mind in secular life be attained, even with the purest faith in his capacity, amid the *sanguine* warfare that was his vocation. Use *sanguinary.* • The proliferation of light weapons in the country was an enabling factor in prolonging a particularly *sanguine* war. Use *sanguinary.*

Sanguine means cheerful and optimistic; ruddy; of the color of blood. *Sanguinary* means accompanied by bloodshed and carnage; bloodthirsty.

Being sanguine, I've been lucky in having had a steady donor, who is my husband.

—Barbie Cantu, Vampire Church

Barbie, managing director of the Texas Vampire Association, is hardly sanguine; she is *sanguinary.* By confusing the words, she gives vampires a very bad name indeed.

sans There is no need to use the Gallicism *sans* instead of *without*: • And most of that air is getting pulled right through your mouth—*sans* filtering—into your lungs. USE *without.* • Walter Cronkite was once named the most trusted man in America because he could be relied on to report the facts fairly and *sans* bias. USE *without.* • The event takes place at the Agenda restaurant, and tickets are $150 ($75 for show and party, *sans* dinner). USE *without.* • He's a man *sans* a plan. USE *without.*

No piquancy, no zing or kick, is to be had by adding the French *sans* to otherwise English-language sentences. This is falsely clever, truly common.

sarcasm Confused with *satire. Sarcasm* is a mocking or caustic remark used to express contempt. *Satire,* often a literary or artistic genre, is the use of sarcasm, ridicule, irony, and so on to expose or criticize stupidity.

S

scantly Misused for *scantily. Scant* is an adjective meaning barely adequate. Its adverbial form is *scantly* (SKANT-lee). *Scanty* is an adjective meaning meager or meager in quantity; revealing or skimpy. Its adverbial form is *scantily* (SKANT-ah-lee). These are two words with two meanings, two spellings, two pronunciations. *Scant* and *scanty* are sometimes synonyms, but in the adverbial sense of revealingly or skimpily, only *scantily* is correct.

Thus "In the Great Depression, cash was *scantly* available" shows the correct use of *scantly,* but "The business' website, which included photos of *scantly* clad women in provocative poses, was down for maintenance Wednesday afternoon" shows the incorrect use.

scurrilous Misused for *scandalous* (or similar words). • But given the *scurrilous* campaign of radical feminists to undermine the constitutionally protected right of due process, perhaps it is they who owe a letter of apology to Mr. Bryant. Use *scandalous.* • The NAACP's move to condemn the Tea Party movement as racist is a *scurrilous* attack by a group that itself is unambiguously guilty of same. Use *scandalous.* • Meanwhile, Fox goes on blithely packaging things they know are *scurrilous* lies and pretending they are truth. Use *scandalous.*

Scurrilous (SKUR-ah-les) means expressed in, or given to, coarse or vulgar language; foulmouthed. But *scurrilous,* which originally meant speaking the language of a buffoon, has taken on still another meaning: making defamatory claims about someone. This usage may be the result of people confusing *scurrilous* with *scandalous.* Lexicographers are as easily duped, for many of them, too, now, maintain that *scurrilous* is a synonym for making defamatory remarks.

There is no need for *scurrilous* to mean scandalous or defamatory since we have those words and others, but to lose, or be about to lose, *scurrilous* in the sense of expressing coarse or abusive language is a shame, for with the loss of that meaning there is increasing, if unspoken, permission to use foul language—about which we should complain not for senseless moral reasons but for sound linguistic ones.

seasonable Misused for *seasonal.* • As firms disaggregate, there is a growing need for part-time labor, *seasonable* labor, consultants, and other non-traditional modes of employment that facilitate the outsourcing of non-core functions. Use *seasonal.*

And *seasonal* is misused for *seasonable*: • Its weather is *seasonal,* without ever getting too hot or too cold, its climate tempered by its coastal location. Use *seasonable.*

Seasonable means suitable to the season; opportune, appropriate, or timely. *Seasonal* means relating to the seasons of the year or what applies to the season of the year.

seguay Misspelling of *segue.* • I think many people are looking to *seguay* from 9 to 5, time constraints and traffic, into being able to develop an income-producing situation that mirrors their values and beliefs. USE *segue.* • That story is only useful as a *seguay* to one of my favorite geek poems, "Abort, Retry, Ignore" (with all the appropriate apologies to Edgar Allan Poe). USE *segue.* • Marshall Field's and Mervyn's came along as a *seguay* to bridge the gap between the upscale and the working class—appealing to the economic group in between. USE *segue.*

Whether noun or verb, *segue,* not *seguay,* not *segway,* means a transition, or to transition, from one part to another; a continuance, or to continue, without pause from one musical theme to another.

seize Misused for *cease.* • Farming the way we know it has changed dramatically, but it will *seize* to exist if we don't do something to increase our income without government help. USE *cease.* • Yes, the search engine tags probably said we had *Futurama* episodes, however, everything regarding *Futurama* has been taken down due to a nice *seize* and desist from Twentieth-Century Fox. USE *cease.* • It does not *seize* to be barbaric, horrifying, and wicked because of this! USE *cease.* • I never *seize* to be amazed by the sheer hugeness of biological complexity and the beauty and elegance of biological design. USE *cease.*

And *cease* is misused for *seize*: • Ian tries to combine that idea with "carpe diem" or "*cease* the day." USE *seize.*

To *seize* means take hold of suddenly and forcibly; capture using force; confiscate; take eagerly and decisively; to fuse with another part as a result of high pressure or heat. To *cease* means put an end to; discontinue.

S

seldomly Misused for *seldom.* • We held this local rally for those who can't go to a large city protest, and to gather members of the community we see so *seldomly.* USE *seldom.* • Kerry is seen as a loner in Washington, *seldomly* socializing out on the town and keeping most acquaintances as just that. USE *seldom.* • Bartow left the press podium with a *seldomly* seen smile. USE *seldom.* • If you are going to eat sweet foods, try to eat them *seldomly* and in small amounts, then have them with a high-fiber meal rather than alone. USE *seldom.*

The adjective (meaning rare or infrequent), though archaic, is *seldom,* and the adverb (meaning rarely or infrequently) is *seldom,* not *seldomly.*

-self (-selves) Misused for *me* (or similar words). • Richard and *myself* are going to lunch. Use *I.* • Very large people like *yourself* can eat tiny amounts of food and not lose an ounce. Use *you.* • Let's hope someone comes along, like *myself,* to take his place. Use *me.* • We feel Mr. Roedler's comments do an injustice to collectors like *ourselves* who currently pay $1,500 to $2,000 for radios of this type. Use *us.* • Neither the mayor nor *myself* desires to comment on the status of the matter. Use *I.* • In the course of the discussions that President Bush and *myself* had, we of course discussed many other issues. Use *I.*

Some people, uncertain of which pronoun (*I* or *me, he* or *him, she* or *her, we* or *us*) to use, depend on *-self* pronouns; others, still less deliberate, apparently have no idea that these reflexive pronouns are improperly used in the contexts shown here. A reflexive pronoun is a personal pronoun having *-self* or *-selves* as a suffix to show that an action affects the subject itself.

> But while I confided in Sally a lot about the distress between my mother and myself, she never did the same with me.
>
> —Susie Bright, Salon.com
>
> A heartrending story, from which this sentence comes, is made less moving when bad grammar encumbers the telling of it.

self-deprecate Misused for *self-depreciate.* • In almost every role he takes on, Stiller is the poster boy for *self-deprecation* and disaster. Use *self-depreciation.* • First baseman Jason Giambi was absent for the spots because of personal business—and if you know the hilarious Giambi, that is truly a missed Hollywood moment—and joshed his teammates about the *self-deprecating* ads. Use *self-depreciating.* • In this way his *self-deprecation* and modesty are strikingly English, but not at all affected. Use *self-depreciation.* • That wry, *self-deprecating* humor is one of the pleasant surprises of *Unvanquished,* an otherwise bitter account of the United Nations' struggles with a hostile United States. Use *self-depreciating.*

The distinction between *self-deprecate* and *self-depreciate* has been almost wholly eroded by careless writers and speakers—and, of course, the dictionaries that record their errors so that others may make them as well. *Deprecate* means to disapprove of, whereas *depreciate* means to belittle. The confusion is most often found when *self-deprecating* is used instead of *self-depreciating.*

sensual Misused for *sensuous.* • Heads turn and diners salivate as the waiter at New York's Zenith restaurant brings a sizzling plate of mushroom steak, steaming with the lusty scent of garlic and *sensual* Asian spices. USE *sensuous.* • The Eid, which occurs this year on or about December 27, ends the month when Muslims abstain from food, drink, and other *sensual* pleasures from daybreak to sunset and concentrate on God's commandments. USE *sensuous.* • We all live in a *sensual* world, but often we are too busy to realize the joy in life. USE *sensuous.* • It would appear that the ascetic and the *sensual* are incongruous and diametrically opposite concepts, but in this complex art the two concepts are juxtaposed in a variety of ways. USE *sensuous.*

And *sensuous* is sometimes misused for *sensual:* • How long have you been searching for erotic sex with stimulating babes, seductive girls, and *sensuous* women? USE *sensual.*

The word *sensuous* is used in reference to the senses, especially those concerned with aesthetic pleasures such as art or food; *sensual* is properly restricted to the physical senses, especially sexual pleasure.

separate out Misused for *separate* (or similar words). • We're trying to *separate out* what happened with the helicopter from what happened to our people out there. DELETE *out.* • The oak on the Chardonnay seems to *separate out* into a resinous slick, while the fruit tastes fat, almost rancid, instead of buttery. DELETE *out.* • UPS will *separate out* the packages that are to be delivered to the rural areas and turn them over to the local post office for final delivery. DELETE *out.* • We define "play in Peoria," but don't *separate* it *out* from the rest of the entry, so we didn't specifically look for the earliest example of this phrase. DELETE *out.*

We don't need the *out* in *separate out* any more than we do in *stress out* or *print out. Separate, stress, print,* alone, all express the meaning fully. SEE ALSO **report out**.

seperate Misspelling of *separate.* • There might be a chapter for each class and a *seperate* section for each method. USE *separate.* • Hotel Vianen A2 has 222 hotel rooms, all with bath, *seperate* shower and toilet. USE *separate.* • The game pops up in a *seperate* window and certain areas of the page are reserved for your logo and even your advertising banner. USE *separate.*

People who do not read or, much the same thing, who read only to be told a story, are likely to spell *separate* as *seperate.* These people do not attend to words or sentences, how they are spelled or fashioned. The tale interests them, not the telling.

serial Misused for *cereal.* • My host family always eat *serial* or toast for breakfast, but on Saturday and Sunday they always eat a hotcake for breakfast. USE *cereal.* • Eat this brand of soda, or this burger, or this breakfast *serial* and you too could turn out just like me, naively, selfishly, greedily, and arrogantly flogging a dangerous product to kids. USE *cereal.*

Though this misusage is well known among punsters and clowns—"Could crop circles be the work of a cereal killer?"—others, less clever, do indeed confuse the words.

shaked Misused for *shook.* • In the capital of Tokyo, buildings *shaked* violently. USE *shook.* • She went and totally redeemed herself with a skimpy outfit that she shimmied and *shaked* all over in. USE *shook.*

The past tense of *shake* is *shook,* not *shaken.*

The past participle is *shaken,* not *shaked* or *shook*: • They have *shaked* hands. USE *shaken.* • I have *shook* hands with Allison and Torry. USE *shaken.* • Chanel handbags is known to have *shook* the fashion world. USE *shaken.*

Present	Present Participle	Past	Past Participle
shake	shaking	shook	shaken

shamen The plural of *shaman*—a priest who has the power to cure illnesses and control events—is *shamans,* not *shamen.* • Our pick, though, is a week-long journey across Mongolia, traveling deep into the Altai Mountains, meeting local *shamen* and learning eagle hunting. USE *shamans.* • *Shamen* trying to perform an exorcism in eastern Russia allegedly suffocated the four-year-old boy they were trying to save. USE *Shamans.*

sherbert Misspelling of *sherbet.* • Pat beeng-soo (*sherbert* dish) is a kind of Korean sundae with ice, fruit, and syrup. USE *sherbet.* • *Sherbert* Orange Freeze. 4 cups orange *sherbert* 2 cups orange juice 1/4 cup Sue Bee Honey 1/2 cup milk. USE *sherbet.*

Even though some dictionaries maintain that *sherbert* (SHUR-bert) is acceptable, *sherbet* (SHUR-bit) is the only correct spelling (and pronunciation). This is still another illustration of how lexicographers embrace people's ignorance. Dictionaries have virtually no standards, offer scant guidance, and advance only misunderstanding. SEE ALSO **sherbet** in **appendix A**.

shibboleth Misused for *truism* (or similar words). A dictionary or two holds that *shibboleth* (SHIB-ah-lith) means a truism; a commonplace saying. But this is simply what people have mistakenly come to believe *shibboleth* means. And dictionaries, ignominiously pandering to the public, record the definition. A *shibboleth* is an identifying word, phrase, custom, or belief that distinguishes a sect, group, or class; a password or watchword.

shoe-in Misused for *shoo-in.* • People with degrees in acting are not *shoe-ins* for Broadway or motion picture roles or even a speaking part in a community theater production. USE *shoo-ins.* • Even though she was the number two player in the league and would have been a *shoe-in* for all-league, she chose to play in the Connecticut Women's Open. USE *shoo-in.*

This idiom, spelled *shoo-in* (not *shoe-in* or *shew-in*), was originally used to designate the winner of a rigged horse race. Today it means a person or thing sure to succeed.

shop (it) against Misused for *compare (it) to (with).* • Most will *shop it against* the Contour, Malibu, and Altima, which are really small cars positioned between those segments. Use *compare it with.* • *Shop it against* the Audi A4 or BMW 325i and it seems like a bargain. Use *Compare it to.* • And by all means, *shop one against* the other. Use *compare one to.*

Apparently created by salespeople, *shop against* is an ugly phrase. Though using *against* instead of *with* or *to* in the phrase *compare against* is common (and quite wrong), using *shop* instead of *compare* is contemptible for it insinuates—certainly more than *compare*—that you should buy. See also **gift . . . (with)**.

short-lived Since the *lived* of *short-lived* derives from the word *life,* not the word *live, short-lived* is correctly pronounced with a long *i* sound. See also **long-lived**.

shutter Misused for *shudder.* • I hope to have another baby in a few years, but the thought of going through this again makes me *shutter* with fear. Use *shudder.* • Just the name of Jesus caused the demons to *shutter* and tremble and run and flee in a hundred other directions. Use *shudder.* • Knowing this, we *shutter* to realize that surely this is not the last of their diabolical deeds. Use *shudder.* • Can we distort what God designed with His own hands anymore than this? I *shutter* to think about it. Use *shudder.*

A *shutter* is anything used to cover a window or other opening. To *shudder* means to tremble or quiver.

sight Misused for *site.* • It does not do any good to advertise on our web *sight* if no one knows about it, so our web *sight* is advertised locally through business cards, signs, brochures, and other means. Use *site.* • We were also impressed with the fact that you were on the building *sight* a great amount of time during the construction. Use *site.*

Sight is the ability to see; seeing; something seen; the foreseeable future; mental perception. *Site* is a place or location; a website. See also **site**.

silicon Misused for *silicone.* • Now the stuffing is put directly inside the flesh, in the form of *silicon* implants. USE *silicone.*

And *silicone* is misused for *silicon*: • Man knows how to use these changes technologically, e.g., the different role of *silicone* in sand and in computer chips. USE *silicon.* • The *silicone* in semiconductors is used as a insulator for the copper/aluminum interconnects that carry the electrical signals. USE *silicon.*

Silicon (SIL-i-*kon*), a chemical element, is found in sand and elsewhere and used in glass, semiconductors, and other products. Silicone (SIL-i-*kone*), a synthetic substance, is used in some breast implants, lubricants, adhesives, and so on.

> Instead Hulu nurtured a corporate culture you'd see in a Silicone Valley startup—with shoestring budget to match.
>
> —Wayde Robson, *Audioholics*

since *Since* may be used either in the temporal sense ("Ford stock closed down $2.52 to $16.27, its worst one-day percentage decline since the spring of 2009, when it dropped 17.6 percent"; "James Kendrick has been using mobile devices since they weighed 30 pounds") or as a synonym for *because* ("Of course, none of us know the Wilpon's personal finances since they are not a publicly traded entity"; "Since I am now 80 years old, my wife advises me not to go out in my kayak"). SEE ALSO **as.**

sit Misused for *set.*

Present	Present Participle	Past	Past Participle
sit	sitting	sat	sat
set	setting	set	set

The verb to *sit* means to assume or be in a sitting position. The verb to *set* means to put or place something. To *set* often takes an object; to *sit* seldom does. SEE ALSO **rise.**

site Misused for *cite.* • Pedestrians, bicyclists, and any other highway user can be *sited* for failing to comply with these signals. Use *cited.* • The night Norman Wickes and his son were *sited* with the ticket that landed them in court, it was 28 degrees outside and all the shelters were full. Use *cited.* • All information *sited* and given on this site is copyright its original owner and author in full. Use *cited.* • Students are to follow the policy regarding the duties and responsibilities of school van passengers as *sited* below. Use *cited.* • Carvis has been *sited* for bravery five times. Use *cited.*

The verb *cite* means to quote or refer to; to commend for meritorious action; to enumerate; to call before a court of law. The verb *site* means to locate, and the noun means a location. See also **sight**.

(mad) skillz Jargon and junk (sometimes called slang) are written by people who feel as though they write well but who are, in truth, unaccomplished writers. Naive and impressionable, these writers may be trying to sound knowledgeable or insightful, cool or clever, but they actually sound senseless. One of their dreadful terms, *(mad) skillz,* is illustrative: • Adam Sandler took home two comedy awards, one for his acting *skillz* and one for his movie *Grown Ups.* • But hear me out, folks—I've got *mad skillz* in the cooking department, and I'm also a pretty snappy writer. • In 2008 it was nearly 16,000 according to Smith and her nifty Google map *skillz.* • So as you are positioning your young ones to be a future leader, in addition to Mandarin lessons and public speaking, make sure they've got *mad* shoveling *skillz.* • To lighten the mood, here's Murky showing off her *mad* write-in educational *skillz.*

As the popularity of a person is no measure of his intelligence or kindness or even likability, so the popularity of a word is no measure of its ability to convey meaning. Slang may be fun to say once or twice, but never, if you aspire to write well, is it appropriate in your writing. It is not hip, it is not cool, and the only people who think it is are no better at writing than the people whose writing they emulate, the jargon and junk users.

These sentences are as forgettable as the slang used to compose them: • At any other school, his Johnny Depp good looks and *Aberzombie* style would secure him a place among high school royalty. • If it is utterly *fantasmarific,* I'd probably order from them again. • "Sceotical" sounds like a highly *majuberous* term to me. • Liberace would have *ralphed,* and so would Rachmaninoff. • Since i frequently do not capitalize i's when i'm just typing that could certainly have been *my bad,* but really, it should be capitalized. • We scour the internet looking for epic *fails* and post only the best quality *fail* pictures and videos.

Slangy words (slapdash ideas and other incompetencies) are forever trying to take the place of literate words (thoughtfulness and care). SEE ALSO **out there**.

slackard Misused for *slacker*. • I cannot empathize with a *slackard,* a shirker, and a coward. USE *slacker.* • I challenge anyone to observe one of my lessons and call me a *slackard;* I am a professional—not a *slackard.* USE *slacker*. • It makes no distinction between young and old, good or evil, *slackard* or enthusiast, phylum, species, or subspecies. USE *slacker.*

Though *laggard* and *sluggard, drunkard* and *dullard* are words, *slackard* is not; it is inadmissible.

slanderous Misused for *libelous.* • He has routinely abused his position by writing *slanderous* statements and in some cases, blatant lies about me. USE *libelous.* • *Fortune* magazine has launched an invective, vitriolic, *slanderous* campaign against the Vatican by committing the major sin of journalism—assuming facts that aren't there and condemning with no proof in regard to a scam manipulated by a priest singlehandedly. USE *libelous.*

S

The difference between *slander* and *libel* (at least in the United States) is the difference between spoken and written (or recorded) calumny. SEE ALSO **liable**.

slash Avoid using the slash or virgule (/) in place of words: • The Quigley Corporation makes no representation that the U.S. Food and Drug Administration or any other regulatory agency will allow the aforementioned compounds to be tested *and/or* marketed in humans *and/or* animals. • An epigraph or footnote could be included so that readers who *didn't remember/didn't know* the myth would be satisfied with some degree of clarity after *reading/hearing* the poem. • In some situations, a businessperson may be evasive. One way *he/she* can do this is by changing the subject. • The Council has 25 members, including trustees, *alumnae/i,* businesspeople, and citizens interested in international education. • I love the company of *friends/family/partner*. • *S/he* will also have a record of encouraging and nurturing collaboration by example and deed. • My *killer/burglar/monster* was a fireworks display at a distant fair. • What collaborative spirit is imagined, created, or assumed when we choose to identify ourselves *w/others*?

This is slipshod writing. The inadvisability of using the slash is apparent if you try reading these sentences aloud: they are scarcely readable. The word *or* or *and* can most often be used in place of the slash. Worse still is the word *slash*: • Brody's first step toward stardom started with enlisting the help of Spencer Pratt, Jenner's "Hills" co-star and so-called manager-*slash*-publicist-*slash*-agent-*slash*-stylist. See also **back slash**.

slayed Misused for *slew.* • The procedural rebuke effectively *slayed* repeal of the "Don't Ask, Don't Tell" policy at the time, and also killed an immigration reform initiative known as the DREAM Act. Use *slew.* • A highlight in today's vampire-obsessed age might be the grave of Durynk, who *slayed* young Zdislav in an effort to be king. Use *slew.*

The past tense of the verb *slay* is *slew*. The slangy *slay,* for overwhelm or impress, is often used in the past tense: *slayed.*

The past participle is *slain,* not *slayed*: • We begin with a selection of the games that have entered FA Cup lore as those days when a giant was *slayed* by a lower-league David. Use *slain.* • Harley Davidson riders escort the corpses of the *slayed* soldiers in the Iraq War. Use *slain.*

S

Present	Present Participle	Past	Past Participle
slay	slaying	slew	slain

slight of hand Misspelling of *sleight of hand.* • But despite a little late-game *slight of hand* that led to the Patriots tying the score with only 1:16 to play, it was the Cougars who pulled a rabbit out of the hat along with a 2-1 win in overtime. USE *sleight of hand.* • WorldCom used a basic accounting *slight-of-hand* to inflate profits. USE *sleight of hand.*

Sleight of hand is the skillful use of one's hands to perform tricks or magic; legerdemain; the trick or tricks performed; skillful deception or trickery.

> The leaked letter brought to light a host of touchy subjects for the administration, necessitating yet more feats of rhetorical slight-of-hand.
>
> —*Mother Jones*
>
> Rhetorical *sleight-of-hand* is nothing we could charge this clumsy "mishandler" with.

sluff Misspelling of *slough.* • He will *sluff* off any questions about whether it actually works. USE *slough.* • These diseased cells inside the gut *sluff* off, are excreted, and can infect other pigs. USE *slough.* • They can't *sluff* off responsibility by blaming God or the Devil. USE *slough.*

To *slough* means to cast off or shed. *Sluff* (SLUF) is the pronunciation of *slough,* nothing more.

Sluff off is also sometimes used to mean goof off, be idle, or malinger. • You can use the weight room at St. Ben's all you want, but there are times when it's easy to *sluff off.* • He did his work and didn't *sluff off.*

And to some school administrators and their students, the word means tardy: • Unexcused absences are considered a *sluff.* • Students who are more than 20 minutes late to class will be marked as a *sluff.*

so At the beginning of a sentence, *so* means as much as *umm* and *ahh* and *well* and *like* do—that is, it means nothing at all and suggests only that the people who depend on this expression, and the others, need a few more seconds to articulate a response or a remark. This *so* does not mean thus or therefore; nor is it the intensive *so* meaning very ("She is so pretty"; "That is so not true"); nor is it the transitional *so* that people often use to introduce a new topic or change from one topic to another. This is the stalling, the shilly-shallying, *so.* SEE ALSO **hey**; **like**; **OK (okay)**; **well.**

so Misused for *so that.* • The guitar can be color-coded *so* students can learn to play different chords with a visual support system. USE *so that.* • I structured my life *so* I wouldn't need to own a car. USE *so that.* • What is taking in fluids *so* the body functions properly called? USE *so that.*

So (instead of *so that*) in the sense of in order that or with the result that is casual English. Use it in your texting and talking if you wish, but not in your writing.

so don't I Misused for *so do I.* • The crowd liked that number and *so don't I.* USE *so do I.* • You live in Vermont, don't you? *So don't I.* USE *So do I.* • I know you hate me. *So don't I.* USE *So do I.*

By *so don't I* (or, say, *so doesn't he*), people mean *so do I* (or *so does he*). If you do not use the contraction (if you use *do not* instead of *don't*), you quickly see how silly the expression can be.

solution Misused for *solve* (or similar words). • They talk about the events that are important to them: love, financial situation, brainstorming about *solutioning* problems, etc. USE *solving.* • MKSG is glad to offer service in our three core business areas: lifestyle, electronic/computers, and software *solutioning.* USE *problem-solving.* • I explain my problem because if it isn't possible maybe there is a workaround or another way to *solution* the problem. USE *solve.* • When I have an idea to *solution* the problem I will tell you. USE *fix.*

Solution is a noun, not (though many businesspeople and others equally ill-advised may demur) a verb. It makes a very bad verb indeed.

some Misused for *somewhat.* • Fishing has slowed *some* but there are still some good fish to be caught. USE *somewhat.* • I still think these are great magazines, though CGW has fallen off *some* in the past few years. USE *somewhat.* • I woke up at 12:30 and felt *some* better, but I must complete this journal. USE *somewhat.* • It rained *some* this morning. USE *somewhat.* • While they might respect and even love her *some,* they had no regard for her quest. USE *somewhat.* • This felt really great but also frightened me *some.* USE *somewhat.*

In sentences such as these, use *somewhat,* not *some,* as an adverb. *Some* is informal for *somewhat.*

somewhat of a Misused for *something of a* or *somewhat -ing.* • One wonders why a film with such high-quality production values, a solid young cast, and such timeless themes can prove *somewhat of a bore.* USE *something of a bore.* • Getting there was *somewhat of a challenge,* but Tammara Cole, Mike Doosey, David Mathis, and Trey Cavin all agreed that the view was spectacular. USE *somewhat challenging.* • Streambank, lakeshore, or land erosion was seen as *somewhat of a problem* by 135 of the 290 respondents. USE *something of a problem.* • Her extremely sexy voice has become *somewhat of a trademark* that she exploits very well. USE *something of a trademark.* • It is *somewhat of a surprise* that this works. USE *somewhat surprising.*

Somewhat is an adverb (meaning rather; to some extent or degree); do not use *somewhat* as a pronoun (meaning something).

somulent Misused for *somnolent.* • Managers have very different ways of managing portfolios—from fast and loose to slow and *somulent.* USE *somnolent.* • Rather than still and *somulent,* these guys are bright-eyed and bushy-tailed—so to speak. USE *somnolent.* • Approximately seven hours postoperatively, the patient became significantly *somulent,* and was not responsive to verbal stimuli. USE *somnolent.*

Somnolent (SOM-nah-lent)—meaning sleepy; inducing sleep; soporific—is the word, not *somulent.*

sorted Misspelling of *sordid.* • Tasteless paintings of nudes engaged in all sorts of *sorted* behavior adorn the walls. USE *sordid.* • Now, with this *sorted* story coming to light, it only serves to call Allstate's motives and methods further into question. USE *sordid.* • Not at anytime in my life did I ever think that the God of Heaven was behind the *sorted* behavior exhibited to me throughout my stay in the Church of Jesus Christ of Latter-Day Saints. USE *sordid.*

Sordid means base or ignoble; squalid or filthy. *Sorted* is the past tense and past participle of *sort.*

spade Misused for *spayed.* • The adoption fee for a neutered and *spade* dog is $200.00, and $175.00 for a non-neutered and *spade* dog. USE *spayed.*

Spade is a tool to dig with; one of the four suits in a deck of cards. *Spay* is to remove surgically an animal's ovaries.

spend Misused for *expense* (or similar words). • Compared to figures for the first quarter of 2007, the *spend* marks an increase of 50.5 percent. USE *cost.* • Since the *spend* is expected to increase so dramatically, while display advertising is expected to decline, then something must be working in this arena. USE *expense.* • The notion essentially provides more options for holidaymakers, and by bringing it to Jamaica, the minister said that it will increase both visitor arrivals and the *spend* of the tourists. USE *spending.* • Today 80 percent of the *spend* is with 200 suppliers. USE *expense.* • The article also cites third-party sources to say that Google dominates the U.K. paid search market with about an 80 percent share of the *spend.* USE *expenditure.*

Cost or *expense, expenditure* or *disbursement* are all infinitely better than the asinine *spend.* When there is no need to turn a verb into a noun, there can be no patience for it.

spiritual Confused with *religious. Spiritual* means relating to the soul or spirit; relating to religion or the sacred. *Religious* means relating to religion, the church, and worship; pious. A *spiritual* person is not necessarily *religious* any more than a *religious* person is necessarily *spiritual.* SEE ALSO **spirituel; spirituous.**

S

spirituel Misused for *spiritual.* • In this album you can hear both little-known old spiritual songs of the 16th and 17th centuries and traditional and authors *spirituel* hymns of liturgies of the 18th to the beginning of the 20th centuries. USE *spiritual.* • Helena Tornberg Malpana offers you services in mental and *spirituel* well-being and health care. USE *spiritual.* • I am able to relate through the *spirituel* world the path you need to be on and the direction you need to take to achieve happiness, prosperity, and success. USE *spiritual.*

Spiritual (SPIR-i-choo-el) means relating to the spirit or sacred world rather than the physical world. *Spirituel* (*spir*-i-choo-EL), in English, means having a refined intellect. *Spiritual* people (or people who contend they are) are mundane, in abundance, whereas *spirituel* ones scarcely exist; for that reason, the use of *spirituel* is most often a mistake for *spiritual.* SEE ALSO **spiritual**.

spirituous Confused with *spiritual. Spirituous* means alcoholic or distilled ("You don't need to go see half-naked ladies or indulge in spirituous liquor on the weekends to have a good time"). *Spiritual* means relating to the human spirit or soul rather than to material or physical concerns; relating to religion. SEE ALSO **spiritual**.

splitting image Misspelling of *spitting image.* • My daughter is the *splitting image* of my mother. USE *spitting image.* • I found a website of a different actress named Katie Stuart, who is also a young teen girl and just happens to be the *splitting image* of Kitty Pryde. USE *spitting image.* • A revamped 2005 Nissan Frontier is the *splitting image* of the company's Mississippi-made truck. USE *spitting image.*

Spitting image, meaning a perfect likeness, not *splitting image,* is the correct expression.

stalactite Confused with *stalagmite.* Both words refer to icicle-shaped calcium deposits that form inside caves. The difference is that a *stalactite* is a column of deposits that hangs from the roof, whereas a *stalagmite* rises from the floor.

S

start off (out) Misused for *start.* • Many people *start off* with good intentions, but the resolve for the resolution soon fades. DELETE *off.* • Here are some of the millionaire's tactics to *start off* the New Year in a great new way. DELETE *off.* • His plan is to *start out* slowly and be inconspicuous for a while. DELETE *out.* • But the year certainly did not *start out* well, dominated as it was by the war in Iraq. DELETE *out.*

Neither *start off* nor *start out* says anything more than *start* itself does. SEE ALSO **first off**.

stationary Misused for *stationery.* • Shop for your favorite greeting cards and *stationary* in the comfort of your own home. USE *stationery.* • Digital 2000 is the leading supplier of office consumables and *stationary* to businesses throughout the U.K. USE *stationery.*

Stationary, an adjective, means not moving; the noun *stationery* means writing paper.

What's more, *stationery* is also misused for *stationary.* • With Ballard focusing on PEM units for *stationery* power plants and transportation applications, and Plug Power focusing on homes and small businesses, we expect DCH Technology to be the leader in the portable power application. USE *stationary.* • If the treadmill, stairmaster, rowing machine, or *stationery* cycle doesn't excite you, sample some group activities that strike your fancy. USE *stationary.*

statue Misused for *statute.* • AAUW will support efforts to extend the legal *statue* of limitations in cases of gender discrimination, harassment, and retaliation. USE *statute.* • Students attending the Nevada campus are required by Nevada Regulatory *Statue* to complete course work in the essentials of the Constitution of the United States and the Constitution of the State of Nevada. USE *Statute.*

A *statue* (STACH-oo) is a figure of a person, animal, or abstract design made of wood, clay, bronze, or other material. A *statute* (STACH-oot) is an established regulation; a law passed by a legislative body. SEE ALSO **stature**.

stature Misused for *statue.* • My love of New York City inspired me to create replicas of the Empire State Building, the *Stature* of Liberty, and the World Trade Center. USE *Statue.* • It is the only *stature* erected to honor the memory of Tennessee's famous hunter, frontiersman, soldier, legislator, statesman, patriot, and Hero of the Alamo, Colonel David Crockett. USE *statue.*

Stature (STACH-er) is the height of a person or animal; a person's status or level of success. *Statue,* a sculpted, carved, molded, or cast figure. SEE ALSO **statue**.

staunch Misused for *stanch.* • Soldiers wore rubies to *staunch* the blood of wounds received in battle and as a talisman against getting shot by arrows. USE *stanch.* • Local children vow to *staunch* the flow of drugs and alcohol. USE *stanch.* • As carriers take desperate measures to *staunch* their losses, cargo initiatives are in danger of dying because of lack of commitment and resources. USE *stanch.*

Stanch, a verb, means to stop the flow of blood or other liquid. *Staunch,* an adjective, means firm, faithful, loyal, steadfast; strong or solidly made; substantial. Since so many people confuse one word, or spelling, with the other, dictionaries offer one word as the variant of the other.

step foot in Misused for *set foot in.* • The only problem is that Kiffin probably never plans to *step foot in* Knoxville again. USE *set foot in.* • How much did she spend on her apartment in New York that she will probably never *step foot in*? USE *set foot in.* • How often do we hear now of children who are truly literate before they *step foot in* a classroom? USE *set foot in.*

The correct, well-established idiom is *set foot in* (meaning go into). *Step foot in* is a bastardization born of mishearing and nurtured by imitation. Those who embrace a descriptive approach toward language will certainly maintain that—since this expression is indeed found in our speech and, even, writing—it is an acceptable usage. These are the same people who are disinclined to reject *for all intensive purposes, beckon call,* and other monstrosities.

S

stigmatism Misused for *astigmatism.* • Soft lens to correct *stigmatism* was a big breakthrough in the eighties. USE *astigmatism.* • I went to an eye exam yesterday to find out that my *stigmatism* has gotten worse yet again. USE *astigmatism.*

Stigmatism is normal vision; *astigmatism* is a visual defect.

straight-laced Misspelling of *strait-laced.* • He's as healthy and *straight-laced* a guy as you'll meet, and in today's society, that is amazing. USE *strait-laced.* • Anyone who's worked in advertising knows it's not exactly a *straight-laced* environment. USE *strait-laced.* • There were those in the media who, *straight-laced* and rigid in their ways, objected strongly and publicly to the use of a 17-year-old as a sex symbol. USE *strait-laced.*

Strait-laced means having strict or severe moral views. (*Strait* is from the Latin *strictus,* strict.) The variant spelling, as descriptive dictionaries label *straight-laced,* is, in truth, a misspelling. The responsibility they had as arbiters of language, dictionaries long ago abnegated. And since they no longer espouse correctness or clarity in language, we obviously can no longer regard them as having much authority in these matters.

strait Confused with *straight. Straight* means having no curves or angles; not crooked; upright; undeviating; honest; in a row; and several other meanings ("The Bengals came in looking to enhance their turnaround season with a fifth straight win"; "This site provides some straight talk about developmental verbal dyspraxia"; "The Y intercept of a straight line is simply where the line crosses the Y axis"). *Strait,* as a noun, means a narrow waterway connecting two bodies of water; (usually plural) distress or difficulty. As an adjective, it means narrow or confined ("The U.S. has repeated a call for both sides to back off from their rhetoric to assure stability in the Taiwan Strait"; "The bridge district has been in such severe financial straits that it slashed bus service by a third last month").

strided (stridded) Misused for *strode.* • Donna said she didn't run that fast, but as we *strided* up Old Reservation for the second time that day, it didn't seem slow! Use *strode.* • At 9:11 A.M., we *strided* into the room taking pictures left and right. Use *strode.* • They *strided* out into the rain only to find that their opponents were back in the bar nursing pink drinks and waxing lyrically about Ricky. Use *strode.*

Strode, not *strided* (or *stridded*) is the past tense of *stride.*

The past participle is *stridden,* not *strided*: • As the end of the school year comes around the bend, I have watched with pride how far my little men have *strided* and grown, learning from their own failures. Use *stridden.* • Ford had a rough 90s, but has *strided* and drastically improved because they need to. Use *stridden.*

Present	**Present Participle**	**Past**	**Past Participle**
stride	striding	strode	stridden

S

strived Misused for *strove.* • Andy Warhol star Candy Darling loved movies so much that she *strived* to live in that projected flicker between illusion and reality. USE *strove.* • But beyond that, he was an individual that we all *strived* to be, and had a personality we all envied. USE *strove.*

Strove, not *strived,* is the past tense of *strive.*

The past participle is *striven,* not *strived*: • At Psychic Stars we have *strived* to make our service as easy to use as possible. USE *striven.* • For a combined 32 seasons, they had *strived* in vain to call themselves champions until Celtics mastermind Danny Ainge, channeling the late, great Red Auerbach, gave them a chance to do it together. USE *striven.*

Present	Present Participle	Past	Past Participle
strive	striving	strove	striven

subliminal The pronunciation of *subliminal* is (sub-LIM-ah-nel), not (sub-LIM-in-ah-ble).

supercede Misspelling of *supersede.* • It also determines that basic laws *supercede* regular laws. USE *supersede.* • All amendments *supercede* the initial bylaws and all later (more recent) amendments *supercede* earlier amendments. USE *supersede.*

Supersede is the correct spelling; *supercede,* whatever your dictionary may suggest, is not an acceptable spelling. SEE ALSO **supersede**.

S

To be fair, the future that the robot symbolizes hasn't arrived because it has been superceded by an alternate future: the age of soft machines.

—*Red Herring*

This is only one of (at least) three instances in one issue of *Red Herring* magazine where *supercede* is used instead of *supersede.*

superity Misused for *superiority* (or *superior*). • Since then, Chinese movies have had a total *superity* over the western. USE *superiority.*

• This market *superity* has placed Nasdaq ahead in name recognition even though ECNs execute roughly 30% of all Nasdaq stock trades. USE *superiority.* • With Viper II's air *superity,* and Fei's advantage speed on land, the result is we can't hit each other. USE *superiority.* • We must help one another not for personal gain or *superity* but, because race problems will never go away, because we can't live in isolation of one another or hate. USE *superiority.*

To Eeyores, *superity* is a gloomy collection of letters, too few to mean anything. "Nobody minds. Nobody cares. Pathetic, that's what it is." SEE ALSO **meritous**.

supernumery Misspelling of *supernumerary.* • A *supernumery* tooth is simply an extra tooth. USE *supernumerary.* • Black or black Caribbean *supernumeries* (extras) needed. USE *supernumeraries.*

Some people misspell *supernumerary;* others, leaving out, or perhaps slurring, the penultimate syllable, mispronounce it.

supersede Misused for *exceed.* • The *National Weekly* found that at most schools where the vaccine is being administered, demand *supersedes* supply. USE *exceeds.* • Kathy's professionalism and willingness to help you *supersedes* expectations. USE *exceeds.* • The system meets or *supersedes* all requirements for a modern, towed artillery system, which is made possible through a number of improvements. USE *exceeds.* • Amazon's price *superceded* all others. USE *exceeded.*

Using *supersede* (or the misspelling *supercede*) instead of *exceed* is altogether witless and further evidence that people neither read nor read well. SEE ALSO **supercede; exceed**.

S

supposably Misused for *supposedly.* • Everything God has ever *supposably* said is in the Bible. USE *supposedly.* • *Supposably* people can't figure this out for themselves. USE *Supposedly.* • The vet gave him an injection of antibiotics or some such thing *supposably* to help the tendons and bones form together better. USE *supposedly.* • He was killed in action, but he *supposably* saved his whole platoon. USE *supposedly.*

Supposably means capable of being thought or supposed. *Supposedly* means presumably or seemingly. *Supposably* is not a synonym for *supposedly*; indeed, it exists as such only in the minds of muddled speakers and failed writers. SEE ALSO **supposingly**.

suppose to Misused for *supposed to*. • Midland was *suppose to* play Calamus-Wheatland Friday night in basketball. USE *supposed to.* • They should have salt down there now because it's *suppose to* warm up today. USE *supposed to.* • As long as these Marines keep doing their jobs the way they are *suppose to,* HMH-363 should be celebrating 40,000 and even 60,000 mishap-free hours in the years to come. USE *supposed to.*

Supposed to, not *suppose to,* is the correct expression. SEE ALSO **use to**.

supposingly Misused for *supposedly.* • Hazel had a brother named James McCoy who died in Redford, Michigan, and a sister, Pearl, who *supposingly* is still living, *supposingly* in Texas. USE *supposedly*. • Come experience a self-guided tour of a *supposingly* abandoned corporate facility where a strange unearthly discovery slaughtered everyone who was in contact with it. USE *supposedly*. • *Supposingly,* there are also add-on programs that allow you to enter those characters. USE *Supposedly*.

Like *supposably, supposingly* is incorrect for *supposedly*. SEE ALSO **supposably**.

sure and Misused for *sure to.* • Be *sure and* translate the META tags and title too. USE *sure to.* • As you browse, be *sure and* visit the Useful Links page for resources and reviews on computers and technology. USE *sure to.* • Hey parents, make *sure and* visit the Magazine Rack for magazines just for parents! USE *sure to.* • Be *sure and* check out these other sites to find more women looking for relationships. USE *sure to.*

Like *try and, sure and* is ungrammatical, and more evidence (along with, for instance, *congradulate*) that how people speak is not necessarily how they should write. SEE ALSO **try and**.

sympathy Confused with *empathy. Sympathy* is compassion or pity for another person ("Today is World Aids Day. The members of the public will offer some sympathy. But everything will be forgotten tomorrow"; "U.S. Secretary of State Colin Powell has telephoned Japan's foreign minister to express his sympathy for the killings of two Japanese diplomats in Iraq"); *empathy,* the ability to imagine how another person feels ("Studies show that around 2 years of age, children start to show genuine empathy, understanding how other people feel even when they don't feel the same way"; "Let's face it, they personify every ugly suspicion you've ever had about the very rich: the overwhelming arrogance, the shocking ignorance, the absence of empathy for anyone whose background differs from theirs").

syrup The pronunciation of *syrup,* which has two syllables, is (SIR-up), not (SURP).

Tt

taunt Misused for *taut.* • He watched her walk toward the bathroom, her *taunt* belly bouncing with the movement. Use *taut.* • Using a very complex system of weights and counterweights forces the hammer to strike a stiff, *taunt* string. Use *taut.* • When a patient develops a distended and *taunt* abdomen, the measurement of abdominal compartment pressure can help with early recognition of organ dysfunction. Use *taut.* • Still, a movie that offers such beautiful acting, such well-considered direction, and such *taunt* writing is a movie simply asking to be considered on its own terms. Use *taut.*

To *taunt* means to mock or insult in a contemptuous manner; to ridicule. *Taut,* an adjective, means pulled or stretched tight, not slack; tense, not relaxed; concise and controlled.

team Misused for *teem.* • This weekend saw a whole host of events take place in the city—with the city center *teaming* with people on Saturday night following Armed Forces Day. Use *teeming.* • Tourist center of the city, Fisherman's Wharf, and adjacent Pier 39 *team* with activity, including scores of restaurants, shops, street performers, and tourist attractions. Use *teem.* • Spring through fall, the rivers of Montana *team* with fish, and anglers come from all over to catch them. Use *teem.*

And *teem* is occasionally misused for *team*: • The Braves are, without a doubt, Strasburg's biggest *teem* yet he has faced. Use *team.*

Team, a noun, means two or more people or animals that work together; as a verb, *team* means to form a team. *Teem,* a verb, means to be full of or abound with.

temperment Misspelling of *temperament.* • Hicks said Denley has the even *temperment,* sense of humor, and ethics needed to be a high school principal. Use *temperament.* • I believe I have both the *temperment* and experience to help meet these challenges and to ensure that our children get the best education possible. USE *temperament.*

Though the correct pronunciation is (TEM-per-ment), the correct spelling is *temperament.*

temperture Misspelling of *temperature.* • The *temperture* will rise slightly on Monday with a low of 0°C and a high of 2°C and periods of rain or snow. USE *temperature.* • The average *temperture* in the classrooms is between 55 and 57 degrees. USE *temperature.* • She told me she was sick and had a fever, so I got her some ginger ale and took her *temperture* but she was fine. USE *temperature.*

Everyone has a *temperature,* no one has a *temperture,* and only those with a *temperature* above 100 (or so) degrees Fahrenheit have a fever—even though many dictionaries today claim that one definition of the word *temperature* is fever.

tenant Misused for *tenet.* • These *tenants* of faith are the basic foundation for Word of Life Center, as well as for all Christianity. USE *tenets.* • These religious *tenants* are legitimate for the good Father and for those members of his church who choose to accept them. USE *tenets.* • On the whole it will adhere to the time-honored Republican *tenants* of limited government, limited taxes, and freedom as defined by the Constitution and the Bill of Rights. USE *tenets.*

A *tenant* (TEN-ent) is a person who holds a lease or rents land or property. A *tenet* (TEN-it) is a belief or principle held to be true. What accounts for the now common use of *tenant* in place of *tenet*? It's careless pronunciation, careless spelling, careless reading, careless thinking, all of them the ingredients of and the truth behind modern-day dictionary making. No dictionary now holds that *tenant* means *tenet,* but every one of them soon will if people do not use the language carefully. As democracy falters when we neglect it, so does language fail.

> More recently the concept of humanism has been incorporated into the tenants of Unitarian Universalism, which is practiced by over 160,000 people in the U.S. alone, and many more globally.
>
> —Cynthia D. Trombley, *Observer-Tribune*

Neither Trombley nor her editor seems to know the meaning of *tenant*. What other words do they not know? What other words do they confuse the meanings of? What thoughts do they not think because they do not know the words to think them with? And of the thoughts they can think, how many are muddled or mistaken because they confuse the words they use to think them?

tenor Misused for *tenure.* • Gus is a college English professor who has just been granted *tenor.* USE *tenure.* • It is really a shame that he has *tenor* in MU, and that he is the only person who teaches this course. USE *tenure.* • Navajo should be the centerpiece of a strong Native American program with *tenor*-track professors. USE *tenure.*

And *tenure* is sometimes misused for *tenor*: • In an Op-Ed, he argued that the *tenure* of the debate has shifted away from free trade policies unconnected to labor or the environment. USE *tenor.* • Our minds, our thinking, govern the *tenure* of our lives. USE *tenor.*

Tenor has several meanings, including a singing voice between baritone and alto; a singer with such a voice; an instrument such as a saxophone; the general sense or meaning of something; the course of something, such as a person's life. *Tenure* is the conditions under which real estate is held; the time during which something is held; the holding of an office; guaranteed permanent employment.

thankfully Misused for *I am thankful* (or similar words). • These folks spent more time on Japanese beetles, a pest that *thankfully* hasn't yet moved into our region. USE *we are thankful.* • *Thankfully,* this didn't keep him from composing some of the greatest music ever written. USE *Let us be thankful that.* • You're unlikely to see a relative of the latter, an otter, although *thankfully* they are returning to the upper reaches of the Thames. USE *we are grateful.*

Thankfully means in a thankful manner; it does not mean, as in all these examples, I am thankful or let us be thankful or we feel grateful. The incorrect usage of *thankfully* (like *hopefully*) is virtually all we encounter today. To see either word properly placed in a sentence would be no less than startling, nothing other than joyful ("The producers, Chris Moore and actor Matt Damon, spoke thankfully about HP's generosity in providing equipment and tech help"). SEE ALSO **hopefully**.

that there Misused for *that* • I believe that every living word in *that there* book is as true as gospel. DELETE *there.* • Boy, those girls are sure having a good time washing *that there* car. DELETE *there.* • Can you cite some code for *that there* law? DELETE *there.*

Though *that book there* is perfectly good English, *that there book* is not. SEE ALSO **this here**.

that (this) would be *That would be* is a mindless excrescence.

• So, how much carbon does a typical car add to the atmosphere each year, anyway?

That would be about 30 pounds. DELETE *That would be.*

• Who is the tour guide?

That would be me. DELETE *That would be.*

• Do you recognize the handwriting and initials?

That would be my handwriting. *That would be* my initials. USE *That is; These are.*

• What is the first storm of the season?

That would be Arthur. DELETE *That would be.*

• Who's that in the background?

That would be my offspring. DELETE *That would be.*

Only people who ape others—people who neither think about nor listen to what they say—could possibly utter the nonsensical, the comical *that (this) would be.*

> CNN's Charles Lavadera is in one of the hardest hit communities—that would be Port Charlotte.
>
> —Wolf Blitzer, CNN anchor

theirself (themself) Misused for *himself* (or similar words). • I am also looking for someone that likes *theirself* and can like others. USE *herself* or *himself.* • How can you respect someone who doesn't respect *themselves*? USE *herself* or *himself.* • Love does not stand by idly and watch while a person destroys *themself.* USE *herself* or *himself.* • Each potential contestant needs to bring a nonreturnable photo of *themself.* USE *herself.* • West of Baghdad, one bomber killed 43 people after blowing *themself* up. USE *himself.*

This is the sort of nonsense we can expect from creative writing teachers and others who are too timid to use either *himself* or *herself.* When referring to a person whose gender is unknown, use *himself* or *herself* or recast your sentence. SEE ALSO **themselves**; **they (them**; **their)**.

themselfs Misspelling of *themselves.* • They will never experience it for *themselfs* and will never fully inderstand it like those who go through it. USE *themselves.* • I'm sorry but it is time for people to step up and account for *themselfs.* USE *themselves.*

Themselves, never *themselfs,* is the correct word.

themselves Misused for *himself* (or similar words). People commonly, when they do not know a person's gender, use the reflexive personal pronoun *themselves*: • A person's home is a reflection of *themselves.* USE *himself; herself; himself or herself.* • Everybody's patting *themselves* on the back because Auburn and Oregon—it worked out good this time. USE *himself; herself; himself or herself.* • She received harassing text messages by someone identifying *themselves* as a family acquaintance. USE *himself; herself; himself or herself.*

But people are also using *themselves* when there is no reason at all to do so: • A good match for me would be a man who can laugh at *themselves,* loves life and all its ups and downs. USE *himself.* • I am looking for a woman who likes *themselves,* is comfortable with their body, and is not a head case.

USE *herself.* • Can a man use a dildo on *themselves*? USE *himself.* • TV stars campaign to help every busy mother find some time for *themselves*. USE *herself.*

Themselves is not just a convenient word to use if you do not know a person's gender; it also has come to take the place of *himself* and *herself* in all instances, even when a person's gender is known. What's more, using *themselves* is rarely a deliberate decision; it's simply, for too many people, the accepted pronoun to use. Like other disreputable forces in the world today, lexlings who encourage people to use *themselves* in this way conspire to reduce nuance to nonsense, meaning to idiocy. SEE ALSO **theirself (themself)**; **they (them; their)**.

then Misused for *than.* • There is no science or anything that proves that men are smarter *then* women or women are smarter *then* men. USE *than.* • A good idea lost is no better *then* not having an idea in the first place. USE *than.* • But if you want to guarantee that your parcel packages arrive to their destinations on time, you need to have them in the post office no later *then* Thursday. USE *than.*

And *than* for *then*: • *Than* we will drive to Bursa, which was the first capital of the Ottoman Empire. USE *Then.* • But desperate times call for desperate measures, and if the Packers are going to be down three wide receivers this Sunday against the Lions, as it appears they will, *than* somebody has got to budge. USE *then.*

Than is used in comparative statements; *then,* which means at that time or next in time or at another time, in temporal ones. *Then* also means besides or moreover; therefore or consequently.

there Misused for *their* (or *they're*). • Tell them you're not *there* friend anymore. USE *their.* • They are already calling for a White Homeland, and have shown *there* willingness to use terror tactics against blacks, with recent bombings in Johannesburg. USE *their.* • They did a few of *there* well-known songs, a couple old ones, and a couple new ones. USE *their.*

There is also misused for *they're:* • I think *there* made out of marble. USE *they're.* • Don't turn your back on them, *there* smarter than they look. USE *they're.*

Though pronounced alike, *there, their,* and *they're* have distinct meanings and uses. *There,* as an adverb, means at, in, or toward that place or point; as a noun, that place or point. *Their,* the possessive of *they,* is a word that shows ownership or possession. *They're* is a contraction of *they are.*

therefor Misused for *therefore.* • We disagree with both courts and *therefor* reverse and remand the case to the trial court for further proceedings. Use *therefore.* • Responsive tumors are generally fast-growing but have normal cell-death mechanisms and *therefor* are susceptible to cancer therapy. Use *therefore.*

Therefor (thar-FOR), a legal term, means for that; *therefore* (THAR-for) means hence or consequently.

there is (there's) Misused for *there are.* • Where we are located *there's* a million people within reach who probably will never get downtown. Use *there are.* • I could write a book about it, but *there's* no hard feelings. Use *there are.* • We're still looking for identity this year, because *there's* so many young guys. Use *there are.* • *There's* just no goals. Use *There are.* • *There's* many, many people who are homeless. Use *There are.*

The plural *are* is necessary when the subject of the sentence is plural. You can often avoid this solecism altogether by not using the word *there*: • Where we are located *there's a million people* within reach who probably will never get downtown. Use *a million people are.* • *There's many, many people who* are homeless. Use *Many, many people.*

This caution also pertains to *there appears* and *there seems:* • In terms of the information you've got, though, *there seems* to be some inaccuracies. Use *there seem.* • Overall, *there appears* to be more ducks in the west Tennessee area than last year, and hunting has been good in several areas. Use *there appear.*

T

> Don't play politics. There's too many people's lives at stake.
>
> —Bono, musician
>
> We're in the airport and there's these two women.
>
> —U.S. Representative Dick Gephardt

Many people apparently do not understand that the verb to use in constructions like these is decided by the words that follow the verb. That is, neither musician Bono nor Congressman Gephardt thought before he spoke.

these (those) kind Misused for *these* (*those*) *kinds* (or similar words). • These aren't the *kind* of negotiations where you can predict when the ending will be. USE *kinds.* • These are the *type* of results you can expect when you have the whole team playing well. USE *types.* • They're easy to sell because they're the *sort* of products every household wants and needs, and they're reasonably priced. USE *sorts.* • They understand it is in their interest to have these *type* of security measures in place. USE *types.*

Kind (*sort* and *type*) are singular, and should not be used with the word *these, those,* or *they.*

they (them; their) Misused for *he* or *she* (or similar words). • This user has chosen to not list *their* email publicly. USE *his* or *her* or *his or her.* • If you let a student post *their* personal webpage, you need to post all students' personal webpages. USE *his* or *her* or *his or her.* • An informed consumer needs to know what *their* choices are for local service and long-distance and bundled service. USE *his* or *her* or *his or her,* or *Informed consumers need.* • As a courtesy to the deaf-blind person let *them* know immediately when you arrive and what you or others may be doing. USE *him* or *her* or *him or her,* or *deaf-blind people.* • If you see your child does have those symptoms, keep *them* home. USE *him* or *her* or *him or her,* or *children do.*

They, them, and *their* are plural pronouns; they should not be used as singular pronouns. Only imprudent people who cannot be bothered to think about what they say (or impudent feminists consumed with resentment over what others say) use these pronouns as though they were singular.

He/she and similarly intolerable eyesores are never acceptable. As some of the preceding examples show, rewriting a sentence with a plural, rather than a singular, subject is often a good way of avoiding this pronominal unpleasantness.

That the English language has no pronoun that neatly includes both genders is a shame, but so it is. A generic or epicene *they* or *them* or *their* is not the word to use; *he or she, his or her, him or her,* cumbersome though they are in many instances, are better. Of course, it is well established that the masculine form alone applies to both sexes.

> So I now have the liver of a mid-twenties person who died in a car crash and was generous enough to donate their organs.
>
> —Steve Jobs, Apple CEO
>
> You can take a Russian teenager and say recite some poetry, and they will give you strophes of Pushkin.
>
> —John McWhorter, in *The New York Times*
>
> If your child won't wake up or they won't drink enough fluids; if your child seems to be so irritable, they don't want to be held or touched; or if your child gets sick, gets better, and they get sick again, that's a sign that a bacterial infection may have set in.
>
> —Holly Firfer, CNN reporter
>
> Then the murderer turned their attention to Heyward Brown.
>
> —ABC News correspondent

• Each of the women during this eight-week program developed *their* body as well as *their* mind and emotions. USE *her; her.* • Everyone has *their* own story. USE *his* or *her* or *his or her.* • No one wants *their* name and information given to anyone and we at Elante Luggage hold this to be paramount to good business. USE *his* or *her* or *his or her.* • A quick email to thank somebody for *their* time goes a long way. USE *his* or *her* or *his or her.* • Every international student when *they* first came to Toorak College must have felt a bit nervous and homesick. USE *he* or *she* or *he or she.* • If you want to see what someone truly feels *they deserve,* just look at what *they have.* USE *he deserves* or *she deserves* or *he or she deserves; he has* or *she has* or *he or she has.* • Every one of the contestants wore a patch on *their vests.* USE *his vest* or *her vest* or *his or her vest.* • How do you tell someone that you love *them*? USE *him* or *her* or *him or her.* • It's time for anyone who still thinks that singular "their" is so-called bad grammar to get rid of *their* prejudices and pedantry! USE *his* or *her* or *his or her.* • When you love somebody, you have to marry *them* and make a family. USE *him* or *her* or *him or her.*

Also avoid using the plural pronoun *they, them,* or *their* following words such as *each* and *one, every* and *any, everyone* and *everybody, anyone* and *anybody, someone* and *somebody,* and *no one* and *nobody*: • This was a particularly brutal incident about whipping somebody, and beating *them.* USE *him.* • No one has said *they* can't handle it. USE *he* or *she* or *he or she.* • I learn continuously from my patients, each of whom brings a new story of *their* own into my office. USE *his* or *her.* • Everybody has a right to write a book about *their lives.* USE *his life* or *her life* or *his or her life.* • These two men really need each other to become the visionary and businessman extraordinaire that each wishes *they were* individually. USE *he were.* • Shelia's big Irish family never let anyone take *themselves* seriously. USE *himself* or *herself.* • To each *their* own, but what really gets me is that he is adjusting his primary chain once a week. USE *his.*

All these words—*each* and *every, everyone* and *everybody, anyone* and *anybody, someone* and *somebody, no one* and *nobody*—are singular in number. They therefore require singular, not plural, pronouns. If you must use the plural *they, them,* or *their,* change the antecedent to a plural expression such as *all of them* or *people* or *my clients.* SEE ALSO **theirself (themself)**; **themselves**.

T

It is clear there is someone among us who we cannot trust—that one coward, that one sniveling, spineless, gutless coward, that one person who doesn't have the courage to say that they went to the press.

—James H. Fagan, Massachusetts state representative

After all those *ones,* however can *they* be allowed to follow?

thing Avoid the phrase *(a; an; the) . . . thing* when you are able to. • The mind is *an amazing thing*. Use *amazing*. • It's *a very important thing*. Use *very important*. • We have won the battle, but the war is *an ongoing thing*. Use *ongoing*. • You do this by comparing something your listeners know a lot about with something they know little or nothing about in order to make *the unfamiliar thing clear*. Use *the unfamiliar clear*. • She is an adamant reader and prolific writer with a list of accolades under her belt, but *the most astonishing thing about her* is that she is only 18! Use *most astonishing*.

The following sentences also should be rewritten to avoid the word *thing*: • Here's the *thing*: at these levels, executive compensation is not about performance. • Though I once heard him read from *The Anxiety of Influence,* I've never read the *thing* myself. • The judge is doing the prejudicial *thing*.

The amorphous *thing* means almost anything you might imagine, which is why it is a poor word to use. You may need to use *thing* to refer to something you *cannot* identify or describe; otherwise, take the time to think of a more precise word.

thingify Misused for *objectify* (or similar words). • Anytime we *thingify* another person instead of valuing and honoring the whole individual, that's wrong. Use *dehumanize*. • Lots of us love to *thingify*, just like all of us love generalizing. Use *hypostatize*. • Regardless of the social spin-offs here, legalizing prostitution would inevitably *thingify* women. Use *objectify*. • The image, be it of electrons, or plants, or animals, or man, is not that of a pack of cards being shuffled. In thinking that way, we too readily *thingify* the universe. Use *secularize*. • Where this most democratic form of government known to man, died out almost completely in Europe, it survived even the slave trade in Africa—the worst testament of man's inhumanity to man, the *thingification* of African women and men. Use *commodification*. • I do not believe our understanding is enhanced through the *thingification* of dynamic, meaning seeking processes as if they are static and definitive. Use *reification*.

As piteous as the word *thing* usually is, it's not nearly so distasteful as *thingify* (and *thingification*). Though the concept is, in many contexts, repugnant, so, too, is this word used to describe it.

this (these) A superfluous, ill-placed *this* or *these* will discourage anyone who reads your writing from continuing to do so. • I have *this* interest in administration and informatics and was hoping to set up a short elective. USE *an.* • Late at night, when the children are in bed, she has *these* thoughts of revenge. DELETE *these.* • He has *this* friend whose name sounds very similar to mine. USE *a.*

this here Misused for *this* • *This here* lady says a victory is more than possible. DELETE *here.* • I thought my candidate would do a better job as governor of *this here* state. DELETE *here.* • It's been a long time since I've written one of those *The Greatest . . . of All Time* columns, and a topic came up a while back that I couldn't refuse mentioning in *this here* little column. DELETE *here.*

This lady here is standard English, but *this here lady* is nonstandard. SEE ALSO **that there**.

tho Misused for *although* (or similar words). • Online is fine, *tho* I hope you grow large enough and rich enough to offer a mail subscription version, too. USE *although.* • Chrome's music score *tho* should really get some kind of an official award. USE *though.* • On the other hand *tho,* I've never actually seen one in that condition. USE *though.*

The people who use *tho*—an entry in many dictionaries—are the same people who use *um* and *ah* and *er;* the same people who use *you know* and *I mean* and *whatever*; the same people who use *if you get my meaning* and *let me tell you something* and *can I ask you a question?*; the same people who use *trepidacious* for *fearful* and *alot* for *a lot* and *inimical* for *inimitable.* SEE ALSO **altho**; **although**; **thru**.

T

threw Misused for *through.* • She came *threw* with flying colors. USE *through.* • You were one of the best people I ever knew, I will always remember you *threw* and *threw.* USE *through.* • The festival will begin with camp set up and continue *threw* the weekend, finally ending on Sunday night. USE *through.* • If you want to compare digital camcorders *threw* the eyes of other consumers, then you should read some digital camcorder reviews. USE *through.*

And even *threwout* is used instead of *throughout*: • Brad and Mike both were friends *threwout* junior high and high school. Use *throughout.* • The plot is thick and keeps you guessing as to what's going to happen *threwout* the whole book. Use *throughout.*

Threw is the past tense of *throw.* It does not mean *through.* See also **through**.

throngs Misused for *throes.* • When the movie opened, the shot of Will Smith in a tub with a woman, obviously in the *throngs* of passion, should have been my first clue this was not going to be appropriate for my 9-year-old. Use *throes.* • The animations of the characters and the monsters are quite realistic; the death *throngs* of many creatures will force a smile on your face, trust me. Use *throes.* • This book reads like a call to arms that must have had quite an effect on a regional community that was already in the *throngs* of economic devastation after the war. Use *throes.*

And from a University of Michigan webpage on the nineteenth-century English novel: • From the slaughterhouse, Pip immediately is thrown into the *throngs* of death at Newgate Prison, which was rebuilt between 1780 and 1783.

Throngs, large crowds of people or animals, and *throes,* severe pain or agonizing struggle, have neither sense nor spelling nor sound in common. See also **throws**.

through Confused with *thorough. Through* (THROO) means from end to end; among; during; around; by means of; because of. *Thorough* (THUR-oh) means complete; painstaking; absolute. See also **threw**; **thru**.

throughfare Misused for *thoroughfare.* • Hicks Avenue is a *throughfare* with a posted speed limit of 30 mph, not 25 mph, like a residential street. Use *thoroughfare.* • This creates a traffic problem, which is compounded by the fact that there is only one major *throughfare* passing through town. Use *thoroughfare.*

A *thoroughfare* is a main road or highway; a *throughfare* is a dead end, the result of people confusing *thoroughfare* and *throughway.* See also **throughway**; **thru**.

throughway Both *throughway* and *thruway*—also called a highway, a superhighway, and an expressway—are used, but the latter, the shorter, is more commonly used. SEE ALSO **throughfare**; **thru**.

throws Misused for *throes.* • Design software specialist Macromedia is in the final *throws* of appointing a select band of resellers for the Australian market. USE *throes.* • When it comes to the instrumental equivalent of an atrocity or the sound of a menacing machine's death *throws,* industrial delights in the terrifying sounds of technology. USE *throes.* • As it turns out I wasn't in the *throws* of a serious heart attack; rather, I was experiencing a severe muscle pull and the inflammation was causing chest pains. USE *throes.* • They slumped there together with Saskia listing the things she has to do in preparation for Friday night, sounding more like a retired couple than lovers in the *throws* of passion. USE *throes.*

Throws is the plural of *throw. Throes,* also a plural, is a violent struggle or severe pain, such as often accompanies death or birth or other agonizing experience. *In the throes of* means in the middle of a difficult or painful event. SEE ALSO **throngs**.

> Rattoon is in the throws of settling a deal for the sale of 3 million Tattersall's shares for which it will pay $10 million.
>
> —Helen Matterson, *The Australian*
>
> This kind of coordination in the throws of the act itself astounds you and you get on your knees and bow to him and his composure as he swings above you, soon dead.
>
> —Greg Sanders, *Mississippi Review*
>
> Ms. Helen and Mr. Greg both—
> She scarcely reads, he seldom hears
> (Some say they pronounce Goethe Goth
> Like many of their toss-pot peers)—
> Are graceless writers clearly loath
> To learn what wrong writing rears.

thru Misused for *through.* • During the time period from 1961 *thru* 1969, the standard error of the OECD coefficient was 1.301. USE *through.* • You'll tan right *thru* the medium-level sunscreen fabric in cool comfort. USE *through.* • I know the heartache and torture that families and loved ones go *thru* when dealing with this hideous disease. USE *through.* • Herein are listed the E *thru* I holdings of our library. USE *through.* • Epson C80 printers go *thru* ink cartridges like a hot knife *thru* butter. USE *through.*

Thru appeals to people who are fond of abbreviations and acronyms, people who prefer scribbling a note to composing a sentence. And if they abbreviate their words, so they abbreviate their thoughts. SEE ALSO **tho**; **through**.

thusly Misused for *thus.* • Because this was described as school shootings and *thusly* presented as gender neutral, the gendered nature of the killing and shooting was ignored. USE *thus.* • *Thusly* the Pagans treat their Idols, and *thusly* the Orthodox Christians treat their Icons, and *thusly* most Christians treat their Bible. USE *thus.* • Questions numbered *thusly*: 1) are in their final form. Questions numbered *thusly*: 1] remain unrevised. USE *thus.* • It is impossible not to like a movie in which Elizabeth Hurley is cast as Satan, and she is *thusly* cast in *Bedazzled,* about which there is considerable buzz, as they say. USE *thus.* • So, if we were being as literal as it is possible to be, we would construe Mr. Davies's passage *thusly*. USE *thus.*

Thusly, like the equally silly *muchly,* is a substandard word. *Thus* is the adverb. SEE ALSO **muchly**.

tie (me) over Misused for *tide (me) over.* • If only I had the *Glee* DVD box set to *tie me over.* USE *tide me over.* • We arrived so late in the afternoon that I decided to skip a proper lunch and only have sweets to *tie me over* until dinnertime. USE *tide me over.*

To *tide over* is to support or help to survive during a difficult time.

together When preceded by *assemble* or *blend* or *bond* or *cohabit* or *connect* or *gather* or *join* or *merge,* or similar words, *together* is unnecessary.

too (as well) Misused for *moreover* (or similar words). • *Too,* it's a lot of sewing machine for the money! Use *What's more.* • *As well* we offer globes, calling cards, birthstones, and plaques. Use *Moreover.* • *As well,* Already Gone came in at #25, Good Day Ray at #68, and Passenger at #100. Use *Further.* • *As well this is* a place for you to make specific comments and requests. Use *This is also.* • *As well,* I will publish selected questions with my responses from e-mail communications with students of all ages and all levels. Use *Furthermore.* • *Too,* he was that rare politician who never spoke unkindly of his rivals. Use *Moreover.*

Do not begin a sentence with *too* or *as well* in the sense of also, moreover, or furthermore.

tortuous Misused for *torturous.* • Only water can correct this acid imbalance and relieve the *tortuous* pain it causes. Use *torturous.* • His middle childhood years, to be sure, were filled with *tortuous* pain and agony beyond imagination for most of us. Use *torturous.* • Dying of starvation and experiencing *tortuous* suffering, he writes how he knows that within a couple of hours the fires raging about him will end his life. Use *torturous.* • Yet they are still forced to live *tortuous,* short lives; denied access to their young, deprived of basic freedoms, fed on unnatural diets and chemicals, kept in cramped conditions where they frequently develop physical and psychological abnormalities. Use *torturous.* • It was one of the most horrific, slow, *tortuous* deaths ever invented. Use *torturous.*

Tortuous means marked by repeated twists and turns, winding; complex; circuitous; devious. *Torturous* means pertaining to or causing torture; strained.

towards The American preferred spelling is *toward* (TORD); the British preferred spelling, *towards* (TORDZ). See also **afterwards**; **backwards**; **forwards**.

tow the line Misused for *toe the line.* • The ripple effect of this decision has now been felt in other metros, which will also have to *tow the line* and shut counters early. Use *toe the line.* • The expert books may give you stern advice to follow to make your child *tow the line,* and it may be good advice for the multitude of children. Use *toe the line.*

The idiom is *toe the line* (not *tow the line*) or *toe the mark* or *toe the scratch,* and it means to do as you are told or what is expected of you, to conform to rules or obey orders.

tradegy Misspelling of *tragedy.* • This same route was followed for a candlelight procession on the first anniversary of the September 11 *tradegy.* Use *tragedy.* • Add also Graham Crowden's Player King who is the one other character in the play with whom these two shadowy, Pirandellian onlookers are liable to get their best chance of being importantly involved in the *tradegy* of Hamlet, prince of Denmark. Use *tragedy.*

The misspelling *tradegy* is nothing other than pitiable. *Tragedy* surrounds us even though social, political, and religious influences try, for their own self-interest, not for our sake, to shelter us from much of it. If we can no longer spell the word, it may, in part, be because we scarcely recognize the concept.

trama Misspelling of *trauma.* • Can head *trama* make you lose your voice? Use *trauma.* • I am an adult and recently I was *tramatized* by a verbally abusive dentist. Use *traumatized.* • She also recounted a *tramatic* experience where she felt threatened by the victim's friend. Use *traumatic.*

The noun is spelled *trauma*; the verb, *traumatize*; the adjective, *traumatic.*

transpire Misused for *occur* (or similar words). • After years of research of the Pierce County elections, these skills were necessary to capture an incident that took only a few minutes to *transpire.* Use *happen.* • Publishing is in an intense state of flux—which means no one has a clear handle on how to best publish books, what distribution will be like in two years, or what unexpected corporate shifts and mergers will *transpire.* Use *occur.* • The communications activities *transpire* within the Communication and Signal Processing Laboratory. Use *take place.*

Transpire means to pass through a surface; to leak out; to come to light; to become known. Unfortunately, its better-known meaning—to come about, happen, or occur—is also its worse one, for no other word means quite what the word's less common usage does. The fewer words we know, the fewer thoughts we have.

Transpire has also come to mean, to a wayward few, to unfold or to pass: • The light-welter unification match between Zab Judah and Kostya Tszyu is all set for November, but the champs' recent shared doubleheader provided little insight into how their eventual meeting might *transpire.* USE *unfold.* • How many minutes *transpired* there? USE *passed.*

trepidacious (trepidatious) Misused for *fearful* (or similar words). • Together, they decide to write a biography of France and arrive in Galen on a slow, summer day; expectant, delighted, and a little *trepidacious* of what they might find. USE *fearful.* • As we introduced ourselves, the common strand which emerged was of a group of people all wanting to improve what they were doing, either unhappy with what had been done or *trepidacious* of their tasks ahead. USE *apprehensive.* • In these *trepidacious* times for investors, we at Vanguard believe that discipline and patience are more relevant now than ever. USE *anxious.*

Trepidation, meaning fear or apprehension, is a word. But *trepidacious* (*trepidatious*), except among those who flout understanding and forge meaning, is not a word.

Much like the silly and informal *braggadocious, trepidacious* (*trepidatious*) is a formation suited only to comical use. SEE ALSO **braggadocious.**

> Howe laughed off a suggestion that homeland security officials were trepidacious about venturing into northern climes during snow season.
>
> —Steve Orr, *Democrat and Chronicle*
>
> Meanwhile, the Elgar estate, which controlled the copyright to the sketches, became trepidacious about anyone continuing work on them, and thus violating their great uncle's deathbed wish.
>
> —Jonathan Yungkans, writer, editor, former English teacher
>
> Even though people use it (horrible to hear, ridiculous to read though it is), only the *New Oxford American Dictionary* (3rd edition, 2010) has included *trepidatious* in its listing.

tricep Misused for *triceps.* • In trying to achieve slender and toned arms, the biggest issue is that the *tricep* is one of the most underused muscles of the body. USE *triceps.* • Busto hasn't played a game for the Dogs this year because of a torn *tricep*. USE *triceps.*

Triceps, a large three-headed muscle, is the correct singular form. *Tricep* is incorrect; it is nonstandard. The plural of *triceps* is *triceps* or *tricepses.* SEE ALSO **bicep**; **quadricep**.

triumphant Misused for *triumphal.* • Lawyers are often like the workers who clean the streets when the elephants and horses have left after the *triumphant* procession. USE *triumphal.* • This massive, beguiling, sorrowful, *triumphant* poem is about the idea of Homer and the idea of poetry written on a homeric scale. USE *triumphal.* • For many, this beautiful *triumphant* arch is the single most important symbol of Greenwich Village. USE *triumphal.*

Triumphal means relating to a triumph; celebrating or commemorating a triumph or victory. *Triumphant* means victorious; rejoicing in victory or success. Most often, people are *triumphant,* events, *triumphal.*

troop Misused for *troupe.* • Because of his mainstream success, Waters has the money and the clout to get a great *troop* of actors who play his characters truly. USE *troupe.* • They've been coming to Cherry Valley and performing with Studio B dance *troop* for the past for years. USE *troupe.* • Standing in the line for boarding passes in front of me were a *troop* of circus clowns in full costume and makeup. USE *troupe.*

Troop means a group of people, animals, or soldiers; a great many. *Troupe* means a group of performers such as actors, dancers, or singers.

try and Misused for *try to.* • Experts say *try and* manage your time. USE *try to.* • I would like to *try and* get a summary of the questions and the points that are made, and then at the next meeting to *try and* see if we can't incorporate some of those suggestions in the premium support model. USE *try to.* • It is interesting to *try and* understand which way the encapsulation is running. USE *try to.* • But the important thing, as they said, is to get it right, not necessarily to *try and* do it fast. USE *try to.*

Though *try and* is probably more often heard than *try to,* it is nonetheless incorrect. Public figures and spokespeople who use the unassuming, easy-to-ignore *try and* will never be considered eloquent. Some people even maintain that *try and* has a meaning different from *try to*. It does not. SEE ALSO **sure and**.

turgid Misused for *turbid.* • The range-gated LASER Imager can improve vision in *turgid* water. USE *turbid.* • As is fitting, the boys make their way due east into a *turgid,* turbulent beachfront, not the placid harbor stockpiled with schools of fish they had expected. USE *turbid.* • The end result is five ounces of a liquid that looks like *turgid* urine and smells exactly like the musk from a dragon in heat, only amplified a hundredfold. USE *turbid.*

Turgid means swollen or distended; bombastic or grandiloquent. *Turbid* means muddy or cloudy; thick or dark; confused or muddled.

Uu

ubiquitous Misused for *numerous* (or similar words). • The Pentagon persuaded Congress to spend $8.7 billion on 2,096 Strykers because of their ability to be loaded into the *ubiquitous* C-130 cargo planes. USE *numerous.* • "The whole album has been like a road map for me," says Clark, her *ubiquitous* cowboy hat on the table beside her. USE *inseparable.* • The *ubiquitous* struggle in Iraq is not nearing a conclusion. USE *continuing.* • When you have a product as *ubiquitous* as Google has become, everyone is going to have an opinion about its every move. USE *popular.* • Want evidence that the *ubiquitous* claim that Minnesota is a battleground state in the presidential election is not just a bunch of hot air? DELETE *ubiquitous.*

Now and then, people are especially attracted to using a particular word—perhaps because they have heard a celebrity or other well-known person use it, or perhaps because the sound of it appeals to them as much as or more than the meaning—which soon seems everywhere heard and read. At about this same time, the definition of the word becomes less exact or incorrect. If *ubiquitous* is today much or more used, you can be sure some people are not using the word well.

Ubiquitous means omnipresent, found everywhere. It does not mean popular, numerous, continuing, inseparable, or other words. When a word is thought to have so many meanings, we can hardly be surprised that it is often misused.

U

unanimity The pronunciation of *unanimity* is (*yoo*-nah-NIM-i-tee), not (yoo-NAN-i-mi-tee).

unaware Misused for *unawares.* • Set up a process to handle late requests to take an examination at an alternate time so that you are not taken *unaware* by these requests. USE *unawares.* • Pedestrians are caught *unaware* as a giant wave lashes a popular promenade in Bombay, India. Use *unawares.* • Floodwaves more than 30 feet high have occurred many miles from the rainfall area, catching people *unaware.* Use *unawares.* • Come to Me when the Hour has not yet come—do not wait for My Justice to arrive, do not let My Justice take you by surprise and *unaware.* Use *unawares.*

Though *anyways, anywheres, nowheres,* and *somewheres* are incorrect, *unawares* is sometimes correct. *Unaware,* an adjective, means not aware, unconscious. *Unawares,* an adverb, means by surprise, unexpectedly.

unbeknown (unbeknownst) Misused for *unknown.* • *Unbeknownst* to the neighbors, hidden beneath this home is a vast secret hideout. Use *Unknown.* • The operation, *unbeknown* to the American authorities, flouted U.S. sanctions against Sudan. Use *unknown.*

Unknown is preferable to both *unbeknown* and *unbeknownst.* See also **amongst**.

unbridaled Misspelling of *unbridled.* • Only a vengeful soul like you can have such *unbridaled* anger. Use *unbridled.* • Dr. Dan Yachter brings an *unbridaled* passion to his seminars. Use *unbridled.*

The word *unbridled* means unrestrained, uncontrolled, as in *unbridled passion.* See also **bridal**.

unctuous The pronunciation of *unctuous* is (UNGK-choo-es), not (UNGK-ches).

under the auspicious of Misused for *under the auspices of.* • The accountants from Australia *under the auspicious of* the CPAA were active on many fronts. Use *under the auspices of.* • The Grand Assembly (Loya Jirga) should take place *under the auspicious of* the United Nations. Use *under the auspices of.* • The undersigned further agrees to participate in all functions and promotional activities conducted by and managed *under the auspicious of* the Pageant Committee and Chinese American Civic Council (CACC). Use *under the auspices of.*

Auspicious, an adjective, means marked by a good omen; conducive or favorable to success; propitious. *Auspice,* a noun, means a promising sign for the future. The correct idiom, *under the auspices of,* means with the help or support of; under the protection or backing of.

> The Office on Aging, which falls under the auspicious of the Department of Human Services, seeks to help improve the quality of lives of our senior citizen population.
>
> —Department of Human Services, Perth Amboy, New Jersey
>
> On the other hand, it could be that the Office on Aging encourages the mental deterioration of its elderly population by confusing them with expressions such as *under the auspicious of.*

undoubtably Misused for *undoubtedly.* • You will *undoubtably* be thinking for much less time, so you cannot expect to find all the best moves. USE *undoubtedly.* • I will *undoubtably* seek to speak at such a meeting and put the party line across. USE *undoubtedly.* • For door-to-door service this is *undoubtably* the way to go. USE *undoubtedly.*

Undoubtably is incorrect for *undoubtedly*.

unindate Misused for *inundate.* • I am now *unindated* with these little tiny dimples, which was very disturbing to me. USE *inundated.* • Meanwhile, I have truly watched the field of exercise become *unindated* with terrible and misleading myths and false hopes. USE *inundated.* • Many of my clients are getting *unindated* with too much spam. USE *inundated.*

The word meaning to deluge or overwhelm with something is *inundate* (IN-un-*date*), not *unindate* (UN-in-*date*).

U

> We can no longer quote fares or respond by email; our posted addresses are being unindated by spam, viruses, worms, and forwarding via address spoofs.
>
> —Los Angeles Yellow Cab
>
> We sympathize with Yellow Cab's plight, but not with its inuntelligent use of *unindated.*

(very) unique Misused for *unique.* • Willkie is *somewhat unique* in that its partnership is diverse. DELETE *somewhat.* • This is a *rather unique* look at Europe that traces the history of ethnic groups, their affinities, and languages. DELETE *rather.* • In terms of songwriting, the song is very interesting, not just because of the *sort of unique* lyrics, but also because of the *sort of unique* chord progression. DELETE *sort of.* • Due to its isolation in the Bay, Alcatraz has developed a *very unique* flora and fauna. DELETE *very.* • They have cards for special occasions like birthdays, holidays, graduation, and *more unique* ones like crossword puzzles, word searches, and more. DELETE *more.* • Our range of pewter-based motorcycle sculptures are *quite unique,* and have proved to be our most popular line. DELETE *quite.*

Unique, it has long been said, ought not to be modified with *very* or *truly* or *more* or *most* or *quite* or *somewhat,* or any other qualifier. In a society, however, where imitation is supreme and cliché crowned, it's hard to claim anything or anyone is *unique.* SEE ALSO **one of the only**.

unjustice Misused for *injustice.* The word *unjust* does indeed exist, but *unjustice* has not been much used since the early twentieth century. The word used today is *injustice* or *unjustness*: • This type of *unjustice* literally turns my stomach. USE *injustice.* • Finally Arabs demonstrate against *unjustice*! USE *injustice.* • Too frequently have people been a victim of *unjustice* by those who were chosen to enforce these laws and to protect. USE *injustice.*

unkept Misused for *unkempt.* • You'll want to make a good impression, and showing up to an interview in wrinkly, *unkept* clothing will make you look unprofessional. USE *unkempt.* • The male suspect is described as: Caucasian, 6 feet tall, very skinny, *unkept,* having a big bulbous nose, black greasy, curly hair, a long face with pockmarks. USE *unkempt.*

Unkept means not kept, disregarded, or not honored; *unkempt* means untidy, not cared for. A few dictionaries offer *unkept* as a synonym for *unkempt.* This is wholly idiotic. Some people, not knowing that *unkept* has a meaning different from *unkempt,* have, over the years, used *unkept* to mean *unkempt.* Lexicographers record the misusage, enter it into their dictionaries, and then even more people use *unkept* to mean *unkempt.*

Consider the consequences if this practice continues unabated; consider the consequences if words mean whatever we want them to mean; consider the consequences if we do not loudly complain.

Yes, *unkept* (un-KEPT) sounds slightly similar to *unkempt* (un-KEMPT), and not kept bears some slight similarity in meaning with *unkempt,* but being able to distinguish between similarities in sound and meaning is integral to being human.

-up The need to add *up,* as a sort of suffix, to certain words is another sign of the weakening of our words. More that that, it's a sign that we are increasingly inarticulate and unfamiliar with more suitable words. It could be that people invent expressions like *flavored-up* or *amped-up* more easily than they remember words like *flavorful* or *amplified.* But more disturbing still is that *-up* is a monosyllabic, two-letter word, an intensive, that has come to mean all manner of things: • Probably one of the most *flavored-up* products today is spit tobacco. USE *flavorful.* • We take make salads and we *herb them up*. USE *add herbs.* • Sources said Holcombe *lawyered up* and struck back at the board. USE *hired a lawyer.* • I've been more *amped up* in my few relief appearances than I have in any start. USE *determined.* • Now he needs to *man up* and face the consequences. USE *be a man.*

Of course, *-up* is well known in expressions like *break up, pull up, screw up, make up,* and hundreds more, but in these instances the terms are established phrasal verbs. These newer *-up* usages may signify an unraveling of reason, a diminution of memory.

U

upliftment Misused for *betterment* (or similar words). • The annual report also detailed the company's involvement in social *upliftment* and community development. USE *improvement.* • So I ask that any organization that can provide some form of *upliftment,* please come to Galveston. USE *betterment.* • Hence, let your presidency be a beginning of renewed spirit for the *upliftment* and progress of all the subjugated people around the world. USE *advancement.*

To *uplift* is to raise the spirits of; to raise to a higher social, moral, or intellectual state. *Upliftment* means nothing.

upmost Misused for *utmost.* • Humor is of the *upmost* importance to me. Use *utmost.* • Even if I don't like everything that I'm hearing I still have the *upmost* respect for every artist putting their heart into what they are doing. Use *utmost.* • It makes buying a book a sin of *upmost* stupidity; however, it makes remaining illiterate in college an even greater offense. Use *utmost.* • I am a Christian woman, and my walk with God is of *upmost* importance to me. Use *utmost.*

The word *utmost* exists; the word *upmost* does not. Descriptive linguists and lexicographers welcome the use of *upmost* instead of *utmost.* To them, it's just another example of the evolution of language. Confusion and imitation, of course, more than anything else, drive the so-called evolution of language.

use to Misused for *used to* (or similar words). • When my older brother and I were young, we *use to* go back in the woods and check out our "muscadine tree" in early spring. Use *used to.* • I *use to* work in a big German company, but now I am a housewife, cooking for my husband. Use *used to.* • They were not the kids we were *use to* meeting; they had the look of battle experience. Use *used to.*

The correct phrase is *used to,* since *used* is the past tense of, as well as the adjectival form of, *use.*

> Have you ever moved into a new apartment or home that use to be inhabited by a smoker?
>
> —Dave Thomas, *San Diego News Examiner*

Didn't use to (and *did . . . use to?*) are cumbersome phrases best avoided: • People *didn't use to* think of butterflies as wildlife. Use *never used to.* • He *didn't use to be* like that. Use *was never.* • What sort of clothes *did* they *use to* wear? Use *once.*

Illiterate are *used to could* and *used to would*: • I *used to would* do it with the bike unloaded but not on the centerstand. Delete *would.* • We *used to could* do anything, not even lock our doors, but people will steal anything now. Delete *could.* See also **suppose to**.

usuage Misspelling of *usage.* • The subscription fees, *usuage* charges, and other fees for the service will be as stated in Brain NET Price List. Use *usage.* • William Strunk's 1918 guide to English language *usuage* and composition has been published electronically by the Bartleby Project. Use *usage.*

Usuage, like *mispell* and *grammer,* is a misspelling that no respectable writer would ever wish to make.

Vv

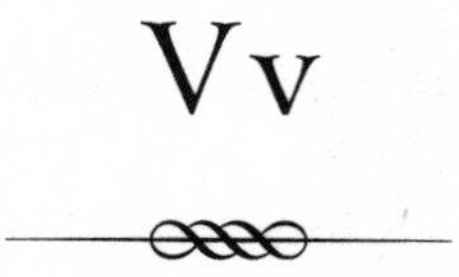

vehement The pronunciation of *vehement* is (VEE-ah-ment), not (vi-HEE-ment).

venal Misused for *venial.* • During that talk show, Jakes said he asked the cardinal whether police brutality is a sin, and if it is, whether it's a mortal or *venal* sin? Use *venial.* • A mortal sin, which is more serious than a *venal* sin, that has not been absolved in confession prior to one's death condemns one's soul to hell. Use *venial.* • Of course, this is all a merely *venal* offense in comparison to reporter Gail Plewacki's pointlessly cruel, three-part hidden camera account of alcohol and pot use by assembly line workers at the Highland Park Ford plant. Use *venial.*

And, of course, *venial* is misused for *venal*: • The London premiere had Denis Quilley as the sinister Todd, the legendary barber and serial murderer (our doctors were formerly barber-surgeons!) not to be deflected from the pursuit of vengeance for wrongful suffering at the hands of a corrupt and *venial* judge. Use *venal.*

Venal means characterized by, or open to, bribery or corruption; marked by corrupt dealings. *Venial* means pardonable or easily forgiven; pertaining to a minor offense that can be overlooked or pardoned.

venerable Misused for *vulnerable.* • All are *venerable* to atmospheric corrosion when used in the unprotected state and therefore must be protected. Use *vulnerable.* • Children are not simply small adults; for a variety of reasons they are more *venerable* to threats from environmental contaminants than are adults. Use *vulnerable.* • This site describes about how Windows XP is more *venerable* to DOS attacks. Use *vulnerable.*

Venerable means worthy of reverence; accorded a great deal of respect. *Vulnerable* means susceptible to attack or injury.

veracious Misused for *voracious.* • Though many major-league sports sought to appease the *veracious* appetite of the Superfan, it was NFL Apparel that really took hold first and helped make sports apparel big business. USE *voracious.* • She is a *veracious* reader who "consumes" books as if her life depended on it. USE *voracious.* • When this happens there is a limitless and *veracious* desire to meet the needs and desires of one's partner. USE *voracious.*

Veracious (vah-RAY-shes) means honest; truthful. V*oracious* (voh-RAY-shes) means consuming or craving large quantities of food; having an avid interest in something.

verbal Misused for *oral.* • A *verbal* contract is legally valid—but as Sam Goldwyn once stated, a *verbal* contract isn't worth the paper it's written on, because it's hard to prove a *verbal* contract. USE *oral.* • Remember, your *verbal* agreement to buy may become an immediate legal contract in some states. USE *oral.* • However, many magazine subscription companies do not honor *verbal* cancellations; to make sure your cancellation notice is honored, it's best to submit it in writing and within a certain time period. USE *oral.*

Oral means by mouth; *verbal* means, simply, in words—whether by mouth or by hand, spoken or written. Choose between *oral* and *written,* not between *verbal* and *written.* SEE ALSO **aural**.

verbal Misused for *commit* (or *verbally commit* or similar words). • He *verbaled* to us after *verbaling* to UH, then visited UH once again. USE *committed; committing.* • The 6-foot-4, 300-pounder committed to the Badgers back in July and these exclusive clips are the first seen on this site since he *verbaled.* USE *committed.* • A defensive lineman, Johnson *verbaled* to Michigan State but de-committed after the coaching change. USE *committed.*

To *verbal* is nothing but nauseating. A favorite among sportswriters and players, this hideous expression is now also being used by others equally inarticulate: • The server *verbaled* the desserts: chocolate mousse, peach crumble, baked "Alaskan." USE *mentioned.*

verbiage Misused for *words* (or similar words). • Children don't lie about these things; they don't have the knowledge or the *verbiage* about that sort of thing. Use *words.* • Continuing their meeting from Tuesday night, the CCU met Wednesday afternoon to put the finishing touches on *verbiage* that will constitute a recommendation to the governor, requesting he declare a state of emergency for the southern drinking water system. Use *wording.* • But then in Mr. Bush's interview with Fox News anchorman Brit Hume, the president did give his reaction to Kennedy's *verbiage.* Use *words.*

Verbiage means excessive use of words, wordiness, not—except among the hopelessly impressionable—words or wording, diction or the way in which words are expressed. What's more, people who don't know its proper meaning also do not know its proper pronunciation (VUR-bee-ij), not (VUR-bij) and may not know its proper spelling (*verbiage*), not (*verbage*).

Along with being misused, *verbiage* is also misspelled *verbage*: • It was a fundamental attack on the *verbage* that Senator McCain chose. Use *verbiage.* • The change to the policy is deletion of some *verbage* regarding scooters. Use *verbiage.* • The *verbage* "In God We Trust" appears on license plates all over the nation, but some find it controversial. Use *verbiage.*

versing Misused for *playing against* (or similar words). • The first was a game of pairs between Pole Cole and Pam Lucas *versing* Betty Carroll and Jean Gill. Use *playing against.* • It doesn't matter who I'm *versing,* I want to win. Use *competing against.* • The funniest episodes were Garth Brooks *versing* Maralyn Manson, the Knight Rider guy *versing* John Tesh, and Arnold Schwarzenegger *versing* Sylvester Stallone. Use *fighting against.*

As a verb form of the preposition *versus*—which we know means against or in contrast with—*versing* is popular among schoolchildren and other intellectual tyros, such as descriptive linguists who feel that any word used in any way is a further marvel of language.

very Do not use *very*—one of the least useful yet most used words—to modify words that clearly do not need to be so modified: • Palmer was *very* fascinated with Innate Intelligence and its relationship to the nervous system. Delete *very.* • Whether it is someone who uses C-SPAN with students every week or just once a year—but in a *very* unique way—these selected teachers share their expertise with C-SPAN in the classroom and with members and staff. Delete *very.* • They should be sprinkled with cinnamon sugar or dipped in cinnamon sugar for a *very* exquisite North African taste. Delete *very.* • I was able to watch more of the cast this time, and they were all *very* terrific. Delete *very.* • The great cutting of the Glenbrook deviation is a *very* stupendous engineering work. Delete *very.* • The trout caught in the Zap Stream are *very* delicious. Delete *very.* • This board is *very, very* dead. Delete *very, very.* See also **all**.

vigorous Misused for *rigorous.* • Iceland has a very *vigorous* climate, which has a negative effect on the habitat. Use *rigorous.* • Each day at noon David Faber, top money manager Gary Kaminsky, and the Strategy Session team convene for *vigorous* analysis, discussion, and debate. Use *rigorous.*

Vigorous means robust; strong and energetic. *Rigorous* means harsh or severe; thorough or precise.

viligent Misused for *vigilant.* • News Channel 19's Dan Satterfield, the area's most *viligent* and trusted meteorologist, is also a part of our morning team. Use *vigilant.* • Ever *viligent* of art, record company executives fruitlessly scavenge around looking for the next "Seattle"—an area providing a gold mine of marketable bands. Use *vigilant.* • Aside from abortion, which women's issues do you think will require the most *viligent* protection given the administration for the next four years? Use *vigilant.* • The arching steel beams vault, as *viligent* protectors, toward a central gate composed of panels to honor those who lost their lives in the September 11 disaster. Use *vigilant.*

Vigilant means watchful, alert, attentive. *Viligent* is a solecism, a misspelling. Lexicographers give credibility to solecisms like this by citing misusages; that is, if dictionary makers cared to, they likely could find many instances of *viligent* in writing over the last several centuries. Use alone is often enough for these blackguards to admit a word to their increasingly useless dictionaries.

> I asked a question from the floor as to whether we boxed ourselves in to this point by not being viligent enough in denouncing some of the lyrics.
>
> —Curtis Harris, LiterateNubian.com

villian Misspelling of *villain.* • We can now crack straight into setting up the narrative tension of ROTK, which features Sauron as the *villian.* USE *villain.* • I have maintained that the principal *villian* in the failure to see news accounts of war dead is the media. USE *villain.* • Where cinematic productions constantly contort Christian themes with some deranged persona, such as the movie *Seven,* where the *villian* embarks on a murderous, judgmental rampage against victims who epitomize the seven deadly sins. USE *villain.*

Villain, not *villian* (Ian is not the villain), is the only correct spelling.

vitamen Misspelling of *vitamin.* • For decades, we've known that *vitamen* D helps preserve bone strength. USE *vitamin.* • Brewer's yeast (a supplement) has traces of *vitamen* B1. USE *vitamin.* • Gerber makes *vitamen* drops that are supposed to be apple-flavored. USE *vitamin.*

Vitamin is so spelled because it derives from the Latin *vita* (life) and the word *amine* (vitamins were once thought to be amines), an organic compound derived from ammonia.

vivid Misused for *livid.* • But the old man was so *vivid* with rage that he just shoved the money away. USE *livid.* • We were appalled to see Gretchen *vivid* with anger. USE *livid.*

Livid means enraged or furious; ashen or pale, grayish-blue; discolored as if from a bruise. *Vivid* means lively; bright and intense; strikingly clear. Only the unread would confuse *livid* with *vivid.*

vociferous Misused for *voracious.* • He was a *vociferous* reader, a superb writer—and was able to make a distinctive contribution to American sociological theory especially in the areas of class, power, and social structure. USE *voracious.* • At the age of 18 she opened her own studio and began to teach; a *vociferous* reader, she read everything she could about dance and took master classes from all the recognized leaders. USE *voracious.* • The birds are *vociferous* eaters, each gobbling up about one pound of fish daily. USE *voracious.*

Vociferous means characterized by vehement outcry; clamorous. *Voracious,* greedy in eating; gluttonous; insatiable. Neither homonyms nor synonyms, these words are being used by people who only think they know their meanings. Once we confuse the meanings of words, little is left for us to depend on.

vociferous Misused for *ferocious* (or similar words). • That's why they're fighting so *vociferously.* USE *ferociously.* • Why do you think the Musharraf regime has been so *vociferous* in fighting the Da'wah carriers there, why do they arrest, kidnap, and beat those who carry the Da'wah for Islam? USE *fierce.*

Though *vociferous* has long been confused with *voracious* ("Having become a vociferous reader in Grade 4, he became a vociferous reader of religious materials in Grade 8"), it is now, it appears, being misused for *ferocious* or, perhaps, *vicious. Vociferous* means noisy or boisterous. *Ferocious* means savagely fierce or violent, and *vicious,* savage or characterized by violence.

volumptuous Misused for *voluptuous.* • Our glamor sets are for the woman who wants to create a *volumptuous* lip. USE *voluptuous.* • On October 8, 1997, an astonishingly large, *volumptuous* pumpkin appeared nestled atop Cornell's McGraw Tower. USE *voluptuous.* • Sensual, *volumptuous* actress Gina Lollobrigida (born Luigina Lollobrigida) was a sex symbol in her native Italy before becoming a Hollywood star. USE *voluptuous.* • I'm 5 feet tall, blue green eyes, long brown hair, and *volumptuous.* USE *voluptuous.*

Voluptuous means full of, characterized by, or producing delight or pleasure to the senses; suggesting sensual pleasure by fullness and beauty of form; fond of or directed toward the enjoyments of luxury, pleasure, or sensual gratifications. *Volumptuous,* except among lumpen lexicographers, means nothing.

Ww

w00t Merriam-Webster, which apparently likes the idea of being mocked, announced in December 2009 that its Word of the Year is *w00t*—that's *w,* zero, zero, *t.* It's an alphabetic–numeric word that online gamers use to express their pleasure or approval, their happiness or triumph at, say, having defeated an online enemy. Some people exclaim *yay*; others, *w00t.*

Yes, numbers have come to words, owing largely to video games and text messaging, and the dupes at Merriam-Webster who celebrate and promote this idiocy.

Online gamers sometimes substitute numbers for letters to form *l33t*—that's *l,* 3, 3, *t*—or *leet* speak. *Leet,* short for "elite"—consider the irony—apparently has no more than a handful of words at its disposal, which must be all these "leetle" people need to express their few elementary thoughts.

Merriam-Webster president John Morse, clearly a good boy who does as he is told, said, "It shows a really interesting thing that's going on in language. It's a term that's arrived only because we're now communicating electronically with each other. . . . This is simply a different and more efficient way of representing the alphabetical character."

Mock *Merriam.*

walkage Misused for *walking* (or similar words). • She only goes a few feet at a time, but it is definite *walkage.* Use *walk.* • There's this one pretty long street from my mom's house to a stop sign; in two weeks I'd like to be able to run to the stop sign and back without any *walkage.* Use *walking.* • My dog is annoyed that it's too cold for more *walkage.* Use *walks.*

Walkage will appeal to the least articulate, the most foolish among us.

-ware Misspelling of *-where.* • I like dining out, long rides to *noware* with good conversition, seeing a good movie, clubing, walking with a friend, reading a book, watching TV with my puppy in my lap. Use *nowhere.*

• A large human edited directory is not going to just pop up out of *noware,* it's going to be constructed from over a year of research and development. USE *nowhere.* • Is there a step-by-step set of instructions *someware* on this site, or could someone give me one? USE *somewhere.* • It was ruled a suicide even though there were several packed suitcases, as if she was going *someware.* USE *somewhere.* • Clients can make payment by using net banking money transfer or depositing cash/check in our HDFC Bank account through any of the HDFC Bank branches *anyware* in India. USE *anywhere.* • Forced Witness features the most shocking content available *anyware* on the web. USE *anywhere.*

Some people misspell *where, ware;* others misspell *wear, ware*: • Last week, similar restrictions were imposed by the United States on cotton trousers, knit shirts, and *underware.*

warrantee Misused for *warranty.* Toyota's hybrid battery has a seven-year or 100,000-mile *warrantee.* USE *warranty.* • But the money still doesn't get you a guarantee, a *warrantee,* or a buyer's protection plan. USE *warranty.*

Warrantee, a legal term, means the person to whom a warrant is given. *Warranty* means official authorization; justification for an action; a guarantee.

wary Confused with *weary. Wary* (WARE-ee) means cautious, circumspect; watchful ("Based on the tone of those questions and the reaction to several of them, the audience appeared wary and unconvinced"). *Weary* (WEIR-ee) means fatigued, worn-out; tiresome ("The crowd broke into applause when a weary-looking John Paul was wheeled out to the altar in his throne-like chair, dressed in golden vestments and a bejeweled miter").

W

wave Misused for *waive.* • They have special deals with some of the airlines to *wave* the fee for changing return flights at the last minute. USE *waive.* • The "to be" new registered agent promised the client the registrar would be persuaded to *wave* the requirement for Certificates of Good Standing. USE *waive.* • The suspicion of cheating does not *wave* the obligation to confirm a battle. USE *waive.*

To *waive* is to give up or forgo; to refrain from insisting on; to postpone. To *wave* is to move up and down or back and forth in an undulating motion; to signal with a movement of the hand.

waver Misspelling of *waiver.* • Those families that accepted the purifiers were asked to sign a *waver* denying them any future compensation from Enbridge for medical issues. USE *waiver.* • An AD noted that the conference simply could go to the NCAA and ask for a *waver* or a rule change. USE *waiver.*

To *waver* is to vacillate or to be uncertain; to sway unsteadily or falter. A *waiver* is relinquishment of a right or claim.

way Misused for *much* (or similar words). • It's *way* too early to tell what this means for Apple, but a lot will depend on when the new company is spun off and how it fares. USE *much.* • The City Council is *way* too involved in the details and nit-picking versus providing leadership for long-term issues. USE *far.* • There's no question that what we're doing is *way* better than all the schools around here. USE *a good deal.* • We obviously export *way* more movies than we import. USE *many.*

But it gets worse: • It's joining the superior original and *way* awful sequel on DVD on December 11. USE *especially.* • The food was *way* good. USE *very.*

The widespread, if witless, use of *way* to mean *much* or *far, very* or *especially* reveals how people favor simplicity over precision, easiness over elegance, popularity over individuality. It's unacceptable to use this sense of *way* in your writing, and it's unbecoming in your speaking. SEE ALSO **ways**.

> I've been here way early in the morning and then very late at night.
>
> —Thelma Gutierrez, CNN reporter
>
> Now our Internet's way faster.
>
> —Comcast TV ad

ways Misused for *way*. • We've got a long *ways* to go; we are not a great team, and we have to build in certain areas. USE *way*. • Regulators still have a *ways* to go to map out plans for private equity fund registration. USE *way*. • By now I feel as if I've already traveled quite a *ways* and I haven't even gotten on the plane yet. USE *way*. • Eventually he caught up with a couple in overcoats walking their dog, which he raced for a *ways*. USE *way*.

As the puerile *way* is inferior to *much,* so the popular *ways* is inferior to *way*. The puerile and the popular overwhelm our speech and undermine our writing. SEE ALSO **anyways**; **way**.

wearas Misused for *whereas*. • Original toys have "Takara Japan" stamped on them, *wearas* the reissues have "China" stamped on them. USE *whereas*. • Even though he missed a lot of the third and fourth quarters he still had a chance to get a vote, *wearas* Hird didn't. USE *whereas*. • So if you're wearing plate boots and walking on a flagstone road, it would make metallic clinks, *wearas* if you were wearing leather, you wouldn't hear it as much. USE *whereas*.

Wearas is solecistic for *whereas*. SEE ALSO **assume**.

weather Confused with *whether*. *Weather* is the atmospheric conditions regarding temperature, cloudiness, sunshine, rain, wind, and so on. *Whether* is a conjunction meaning if, either, or in case.

well Like *umm* and *ahh* and *so* and *like, well* serves to delay our listeners while we try to fashion a sentence that might conceivably be understood. People confident in themselves and in what they want to say, who do not need to rely on grammatical gimmicks like *well,* are a pleasure to listen to; others less so. SEE ALSO **hey**; **like**; **OK (okay)**; **so**.

wet Misused for *whet*. • You played in the Seve Trophy and the World Cup—how much did this *wet* your appetite for team golf and next year's Ryder Cup? USE *whet*. • The food displays will not only *wet* your appetite but will soak you with the idea of wanting one of everything. USE *whet*. • We asked Rain Station to give us a little information about the creation of this song and both Mark Harvey and Jay Moores sent us a couple paragraphs to *wet* our interest. USE *whet.*

Whet means to sharpen or hone; to stimulate. *Wet,* as a verb, means to dampen or drench; to urinate.

whatever *Whatever* is a dismissive response made by ill-mannered people who, in using the expression, admit they have nothing intelligent to offer. SEE ALSO **no problem**.

where Misused for *in which.* • We have a situation *where* there were opportunities, apparently, to be able to ward off this terrible blow. USE *in which.* • The games weren't tightly scripted Homeric epics *where* warriors dropped their weapons every four years to honor the twin virtues of amateur sport and brotherhood. USE *in which.*

The word *where* is permissible, though not always desirable, in place of the phrase *in which.* In these sentences, and in most careful or deliberate writing, the formal *in which* sounds better than the casual *where.*

where Misused for *that.* • I read *where* Clinton, before he left office, signed another 29,000 pages of executive orders. USE *that.* • He read *where* the commissioner of the NBA said to stay in school. USE *that.* • Unless the Yoda leaped forward and bit you, unless the blindfold burned your cornea, unless your photo and name appeared in the Hooter's employee newsletter under the headline "Gullible Girl with Silly Name Really Believed Oldest Pimp Joke in the World," I don't really see *where* you have a case. USE *that.* • It is wonderful, although I can see *where* they might have thought it went on too long. USE *that.*

Where instead of *that* is nonstandard English usage. SEE ALSO **where** in **appendix A.**

where Misused for *whereas.* • It's the Libra in this coupling that desires to express and create many social outing and friends, *where* on the other hand the Capricorn desires a quiet evening at home. USE *whereas.* • Thus, *where* on the one hand it portrays grandeur, on the other hand, an eagle tearing out the meat of its prey can present a gory sight. USE *whereas.* • It has been forecasted for Portsmouth that there will be a significant decrease of jobs demanded in the manufacturing sector, *where* on the other side of the coin, the number of residents within the labor workforce will increase. USE *whereas.* • *Where* some people consider risk a problem, others see it as an opportunity. USE *Whereas.*

Whatever a dictionary may say, the word *where* is incorrect for *whereas. Where* refers to a place or situation. *Whereas* means in contrast or comparison to or, in an opening remark, inasmuch as or since.

where . . . at (to) Misused for *where.* • So, the question is, *where* are they *at* so there will be the motivation to improve? DELETE *at.* • It took a while to remember *where* the car was *at.* DELETE *at.* • Dante is at a certain place in his life when he has this vision of hell, explain *where* he is *at* and why he must make this journey. DELETE *at.* • *Where* have they gone *to*? DELETE *to.* • And *where* have you been *to* in England? DELETE *to.*

Neither *at* nor *to* is necessary after *where* in the preceding examples. Avoid *at* when *where* refers to a location; avoid *to* when *where* refers to a destination.

wherefore Misused for *where.* • Sony 24x firmware: *wherefore* art thou? USE *where.* • You want me to believe that blocking access to my kitchen phone is a blow against the First Amendment? *Wherefore* art thou, Thomas Jefferson? USE *Where.* • Before Bears fans fall in love with Romeo, they would want to know *wherefore* art thou, offensive genius? USE *where.* • A scheduling change has Butte residents asking, "*Wherefore* art thou, Shakespeare in the Parks?" Officials couldn't find a local sponsor for the popular event. USE *Where.*

Properly used, *wherefore* asks an existential why or for what reason. It does not mean a mundane where.

W

whether or not *Whether or not* often says nothing more than *whether* does alone. When *or not* is unnecessary to write, it is also unpleasant to read: • *Whether or not* we get to fifty dollars will probably depend on *whether or not* anything else goes wrong.

In other sentences, *whether* alone does not work: • Kerry basically supports Bush's war to overthrow Saddam—*whether or not* the facts and arguments employed by Bush to persuade the Congress and nation to go to war were at all truthful or made any sense. • We're therefore encouraging all the Arab states, *whether or not* they're official participants.

In the largely British *whether or no,* the *or no* is often just as superfluous. If, however, you want to emphasize both possibilities, the *whether* and the *not* (or *no*), use the full expression.

which Misused for *and* (or similar words). • The transfer could take years because both state governments and Congress must approve. *Which they should, says a Utah state senator.* Use *The transfer could take years because both state governments and Congress must approve, and, says a Utah state senator, they should.* • Gambling indirectly hurts children, they argue. *Which is true.* Use *Gambling indirectly hurts children, they correctly argue.* • His vision, his integrity, his strength, his dignity, his honor will be the standard by which American presidents are measured for decades to come. *Which is as it should be.* Use *His vision, his integrity, his strength, his dignity, his honor will be the standard by which American presidents are measured for decades to come, which is as it should be.* • But there are those who believe that the doctrine of Original Intent has the capability to solve all present-day problems. *Which is nonsense.* Use *But there are those who believe that the doctrine of Original Intent has the capability to solve all present-day problems, which is nonsense.* • It has handed us a wave of wealth so broad and deep that it would be almost disorienting if we thought about it a lot. *Which we don't.* Use *It has handed us a wave of wealth so broad and deep that it would be almost disorienting if we thought about it a lot—we don't, of course.*

Separating a subordinate clause that begins with the word *which* from the sentence in which it belongs is the writing style of juveniles—and, of course, journalists.

which Misused for *that.* • A massive double car bomb *which* devastated a Riyadh compound of Arab expatriates, killing at least thirteen people, struck close to homes of Saudi royals. Use *that.* • Actually, the bill undermines the entire Medicare program, pushing people into the very HMOs *which* contribute heavily to Republican lawmakers and barring the government from negotiating for lower drug prices. Use *that.* • Our service is for the person or family that has become overextended due to high interest rates, medical expenses, job loss, and other factors *which* result in high credit card or other unsecured debt. Use *that.* • It is merely an ample illustration of the kind of structures in place *which* organizes, limits, and controls American cultural output. USE *that.* • Studies have shown that activities *which* exploit a person's natural abilities, be it dribbling a basketball or making good conversation, generate more satisfaction than pricier yet mindless endeavors such as lounging on a yacht. USE *that.* • Parody is not the only thing *which* is confused with satire—sarcasm is another relative of satire *which* can be. USE *that.*

In the United States, by careful writers, the restrictive, or defining, *that* is used when the clause it begins is necessary to the meaning of a sentence; the nonrestrictive, or nondefining, *which* is used when the clause is not necessary, when it is parenthetical, to the sentence. *Which* clauses are generally separated by commas (or preceded by a comma) or dashes; *that* clauses are not. Observing the distinction between these two words and their clauses is indispensable to understanding clearly and effortlessly the sentences in which they appear.

> "Friday" is a banal pop song which counts down the days of the school week until Friday which, of course, anticipates the weekend.
>
> —Philip Terzian, *The Weekly Standard*
>
> Terzian uses the word *which* twice but in neither instance does he use it correctly. The first *which* should be *that,* and the second *which* should be preceded by a comma.

while Although many people use the conjunction *while* in the sense of although, even though, or though ("While an ugly split within the Tea Party might leave a bruise, it won't be fatal to the movement"; "Now, while a number of factors led to such a severe recession, the primary cause was a breakdown in our financial system"), *while* is best used, and least often misunderstood, in the sense of during the time ("While traveling today we will get a chance to visit several interesting historical locations"; "We caught up with Gary while he was waiting in line for his new iPhone").

Using *while* in both senses in a single sentence is especially inadvisable ("While some competitors may have hair that is graying while trying to find five capable starters for their rotation, Cincinnati has the so-called embarrassment of rotation riches"). SEE ALSO **although**.

who Misused for *that* or *which.* • The fund will be administered by individuals and organizations *who* are not connected to Siemens. USE *that.* • She became an activist after a 1986 conference revealed the perilous future of the animals, *who* are hunted (for food and as pets) and are ill-treated in medical research. USE *which.* • But spokesman Bob Carolla acknowledges that the group receives substantial funding from drug firms, *who* provide most if not all of the anti-discrimination campaign's $4 million annual budget. USE *which.* • A Gaussian surface surrounds an elephant, *who* resides on an insulating platform. USE *which.* • He leaned down to pat the dog, *who* wiggled gleefully and then dashed off in pursuit of some small creature that darted before him. USE *which.* • Animals *who* have been orphaned or otherwise directly affected by the terrorist attacks can receive aid under the guidelines of the program as listed below. USE *that.* • In many parts of Europe and in the United States, however, it is the black cat *who* is ill-omened. USE *that.* • Animal shelters across the country are full of companion animals *whom* their guardians couldn't keep, and many of these animals are killed. USE *that.* • The car *who* Ford introduced was a modern follow-up to the Le Mans winner, the Ford GT40. USE *that.*

In standard, nonsolecistic English, *who* is used to refer to people, *that* to both people and things, and *which* to things alone. Further, *which* is the preferred word to begin nonrestrictive (or nondefining) clauses (those that use a comma or dash before the word *which*), and *that* to begin restrictive (or defining) ones.

> For now it's the Ericsson T28 World cell phone (the cost, depending on the service provider: from nothing to $199; www.ericsson.com) with VoiceStream Wireless or Cingular Wireless, who include international service.
>
> —*Real Simple* magazine
>
> This magazine is true to its name, for it doesn't let the apparent complexity of using correct grammar (*which includes* instead of *who include*) interfere with its mission.

who Misused for *whom.* • You all know exactly *who* I am talking about—which is odd considering that we don't have princes. Use *whom.* • This is a man *who* even Republican cohorts sometimes find disturbing, for the way he uses almost anything to his advantage. Use *whom.* • APT's members are public interest groups and individuals, some of *who* historically have been left out of the Information Age. Use *whom.*

And *whom* is misused for *who*: • If I did it again, maybe I'd be a little fairer with regard to *whom* the real villains were. Use *who.* • I am a strong-willed lady, *whom* supports herself. Use *who.*

Who is used where a nominative pronoun could also be used; if you can substitute *I, we, he, she, you,* or *they, who* is correct. *Whom* is used where an objective pronoun could be; if you can substitute *me, us, him, her,* or *them, whom* is correct. If "I am talking about she" is egregiously bad English, so is "You know exactly who I am talking about."

Knowing when to use *whom,* however, is more than most people can manage. And if people rarely use *whom* in spoken English, they quickly become disinclined to use it in written English. Clumsy speech influences us more than careful writing does.

If *whom* sounds "stilted" in spoken English, it's surely because we seldom hear it used. People have been prognosticating about the disappearance, the death of the word *whom* for some years, but it endures, here and there, among those who still value elegance in language.

> I just try to work with people who I admire or whom I think has got it.
>
> —Kanye West, singer

whoa Misspelling of *woe.* • This isn't a *"whoa* is me" plea; I am blessed beyond measure in countless ways, and God is indeed good. Use *woe.* • You might share about broken relationships, not to wallow in the mutual *whoa*-is-me of it all, but to be released from pain and anger and move into love. Use *woe.* • This whole *whoa*-is-me, Gen-X attitude is getting a little tired. Use *woe.*

W

Whoa is a pathetic (and apathetic) misspelling of *woe.* Few who use the absurdity *whoa* can have much heartfelt sense of what is meant by *woe*: deep distress, grief, or misery; calamity or affliction. What's more, the correct expression is "woe is I" (misery is I; calamity is I), not "woe is me."

who's Misused for *whose.* • It has brought wonder to the thousands of people who have flocked to see the car *who's* trunk was caved in by a visitor from outer space. USE *whose.* • The person *who's* idea we use will receive a free set of Kirlian postcards. USE *whose.* • The grandkids argue over *who's* turn it is to use it. USE *whose.* • Happy birthday to my dad, too, *who's* birthday was a day before mine. USE *whose.* • All systems were go and it looked like this was an idea *who's* time had come. USE *whose.* • Palo cortado is a rare Oloroso sherry *who's* style is between a normal Oloroso and an Amontillado. USE *whose.*

And *whose* is misused for *who's*: • He was the creator of some of the greatest of the modern blues bands, and a list of the various members of his bands, reads like a *whose* who of modern blues. USE *who's.*

Do not confuse *who's* (that is, *who is*) with *whose,* the possessive form of *who* or *which.*

wierd Misspelling of *weird.* • Wallace overtook teammate Jeremy Mayfield over the last 100 laps and weathered a couple more *wierd* adventures. USE *weird.* • New science aims to explore systems as wholes and the *wierd* new properties which can emerge as things "switch states" and only apparently go "out of control." USE *weird.*

Despite the popularity (and sham purposefulness) of *wierd* on the web, the only correct spelling is *weird.*

wildflower Misused for *wildfire.* • Urban legends grow and spread like *wildflower* because it gives people something fun to talk about. USE *wildfire.* • In the last three years Spragga's singles released in Jamaica have burned up the place and spread like *wildflower* into the dancehalls abroad in the States, Canada, the United Kingdom, and Japan. USE *wildfire.*

Wildflowers do indeed spread, but the correct idiom is *like wildfire,* that is, intensely; quickly.

-wise Misused for *in* (or similar words). • It was a step up *careerwise.* USE *in her career.* • If you want to save regularly but aren't yet in the *big* *leagues moneywise,* bonds can be a good starting point. USE *big financial leagues.* • In Germany, where almost anything goes *TV-wise,* the program is being aired on the struggling private network RTL II, which generally reruns U.S. shows such as *Home Improvement* and soft-core porn. USE *for TV.* • I'm alone for the first time in my life, *relationshipwise.* USE *For the first time in my life, I'm not in a relationship* or DELETE *relationshipwise.* • Hopefully he will be back in plenty of time as he is *close enough fitness-wise* to start the game. USE *fit enough.* • *What do you think is driving, issuewise,* college students? USE *What issues do you think are driving.*

This suffix is a device that people rely on when they cannot easily think of how to express themselves better. We fasten the suffix *-wise* to words when we have not sufficiently thought about what we want to say or, even more so, how we want to say it. With *-wise,* though there may be some substance to our thought, there is scant style.

witch Misspelling of *which.* • When booting the PC, I see fast track stating a Striping Raid configuration (*witch* is correct). USE *which.* • The movie also had points of comedy in it *witch* is strange, but good for war era movies. USE *which.* • Guess *witch* monster survived the biggest building. USE *which.*

Before long, considering the disrespect and indifference that many people feel for the English language, we may find *witch* in our dictionaries as a variant spelling of *which.*

with regards to Misused for *with regard to.* • The former *Friends* actress says her *Scream* costar—who she married in 1999—opened her eyes *with regards to* relationships as he had been through far more women than she had men. USE *with regard to.* • That is the situation in which the region finds itself *with regards to* the quality of air service at Pittsburgh International Airport. USE *with regard to.* • I've seen some good arguments, pro and con, especially *with regards to* his defense. USE *with regard to.*

With regard to is correct, standard English. *With regards to* is incorrect; it is illiterate. No politician who uses *with regards to* (or *in regards to*) should ever be elected to office; no businessperson should ever be hired; no college student should ever be graduated. SEE ALSO **in regards to.**

> With regards to partial birth abortion, I think you have an overwhelming consensus in this country that it's wrong, that it should be banned, and for that reason, I would ban it nationally.
>
> —Mitt Romney, sometime presidential candidate
>
> Greetings from Dell. This is with regards to the recent onsite service performed on your Dell Inspiron 580 desktop.
>
> —Dell Computer

wont Misspelling of *won't.* • We hope it will stop some of the pockets of resistance out there and that it *wont* be quite as deadly. USE *won't.* • Walsh has to get better or the NBA *wont* even give him a second look. USE *won't.* • Doctors are being very selective and *wont* give just anyone a flu shot. USE *won't.*

Won't (WONT), of course, is the contraction of *will not. Wont* is a misspelling. Another word, *wont* (WANT), is an adjective meaning accustomed to or in the habit of, or a noun meaning custom, practice, habit ("But Miller, as he is wont, made a 3-pointer to thwart the run"; "As is her wont each December, Whitfield is ensconced in the Plush Room of the York Hotel, one of the last truly great cabaret spaces in the country").

world-renown Misused for *world-renowned.* • In Chor Boogie's *world-renown* signature style, begins the reimagining of a world undivided by walls, channeled straight from his heart and mind's eye. USE *world-renowned.* • Sir Gilbert Levine "never set out to become friends with a pope," said the *world-renown* conductor, a Jew originally from Flatbush. USE *world-renowned.*

The correct adjectival form is *world-renowned.*

world wind Misused for *whirlwind.* • Join writer A. J. Ensor on a trip through the Great Hole in the Wall, into the Griffin Valley and on a *world wind* voyage as Luke Carter comes of age. USE *whirlwind.* • It was love at first sight and the pair married after a *world wind* romance, before settling down in Mrs. Leij's hometown of Newport. USE *whirlwind.*

Whirl, not *world,* is the correct term in this expression. *Whirlwind* means tumultuous, rapid; a confused rush.

worser Misused for *worse.* • Is it getting *worser* or is it getting better? USE *worse.* • The war, barely began, is all but finished and grows *worser* than ever. USE *worse.* • Disc number two in Retromedia's optimistically named "Italian Science Fiction Collection" is clearly the *worser* of the two. USE *worse.*

Some people apparently feel that since the comparative of *good* is *better,* the comparative of *bad* must be *worser.* They are mistaken.

Equally mistaken, to put it charitably, are the people who add the word *more* to *-er* (or *most* to *-est*) terms, such as *more better, more worse* (*most simplest, most happiest*).

worth wild Misused for *worthwhile.* • What are the most *worth wild* water excursions to do at St. Thomas? USE *worthwhile.* • Are there any *worth wild* cold air intake upgrades? USE *worthwhile.*

Worthwhile is an adjective that means worth your while (or time and effort). *Worth wild* is what some people, nonreaders all, think they are hearing.

would Misused for *were (to)* or *should.* • What do you think we should do if something like this *would* happen? USE *were to.* • If this *would* take place you would be without sin, for evil is sin. USE *were to.* • He promises to limit himself to two terms if he *would* win. USE *should.*

In conditional sentences that are contrary to fact, the clause introduced by *if* must contain a subjunctive verb ("if I *were* going" or "if I *were to* go" or "if I *should* go"), not the word *would.* SEE ALSO **would have**.

> What would you do if the world would end?
>
> —Suzanne Malveaux, CNN anchor

would have Misused for *had.* • I think I would have gotten nervous if I *would have* looked at her. USE *had.* • What would have been the harm if he *would have* published the article without using her name? Use *had.* • None of this would have gone on if the husband *would have* let the parents care for their daughter. Use *had.* • If you *would have* read the story, you would have seen it had to do with lawnmower pollution. Use *had.* • If she ever *would have* hit her, I would have fired her. Use *had.* • I wish I *would have* known. Use *had.*

Would have is incorrect for *had* in a sentence that states or implies a condition. This solecism is increasingly widespread and is commonly used even among otherwise bright and articulate people. Using *would have* instead of *had* strips your sentence, and whatever meaning it was meant to express, of grace and style.

Doubly annoying is that if you ask some of the people who say *would have* instead of *had* to write the sentence in which they use the expression, they will spell it *would of*: • If I *would of* been there she *would of* been okay. Use *had*; *would have.* See also **could of**; **would**.

> If I would have been a publishing house, I would've eagerly taken David's book.
>
> —Rich Lowry, editor, *National Review*
>
> Mr. Lowry's use of *would have* exposes an inability to reason well—as does his imagining he might conceivably have been a publishing house.
>
> I wish I would have said something else.
>
> —James Carville, political consultant
>
> Would that you had said something else, yes.

wrack Misused for *rack.* • *Wracked* with pain from his advanced form of cancer, Jimmy V courageously reminded us all to cherish every moment of every day. Use *Racked.* • Those who did work were *wracked* with guilt, with 92 percent wishing they were at home with their child. Use *racked.* • There was a large TV set in one corner, a magazine *wrack* propped against a wall, and several sofas arranged around the room. Use *rack.*

To *rack* means to trouble or afflict; to torture; to strain mightily. As a noun, a *rack* is an instrument of torture; a shelf or structure for storing items. To *wrack* means to wreck or, as a noun, wreckage; it does not mean to trouble or torture.

wreathe Misused for *writhe.* • For all we know that child is consciously with the One, even as we see the body moan and *wreathe* in pain. USE *writhe.* • The word had spread among all 4000 of them that a top-track honor student, and one with a reputation (to the extent they had heard of him at all) of being a bit of a wimp, had attacked Big Bill Hall . . . and left him *wreathing* in agony on the cafeteria floor. USE *writhing.*

To *writhe* (RITHE) is to make twisting movements; to squirm, especially in pain; to suffer emotional distress. To *wreathe* (RETHE) is to coil, twist, or entwine around something; to decorate with wreaths; to cover or surround.

wreck Misused for *wreak.* • Yet with TSC continuing to *wreck* havoc on people's lives, more than 1,500 families in the United Kingdom now rely on its services. USE *wreak.* • After destroying a liberal weekly modeled on the *New Republic* and making an enemy of its literary editor Lionel Heftihed, he goes on to *wreck* havoc elsewhere. USE *wreak.* • Partly to save herself from the trouble of explaining the games, and partly to *wreck* revenge upon John Proctor, Williams leads the local girls in a complicated charade of "confessing" to their "witchcraft." USE *wreak.* • Lesson IV: How to *Wreck* Vengeance on Anyone Who Has Ever Done You Wrong. . . . and Get PAID FOR IT! USE *Wreak.*

To *wreak* (REEK) is to inflict upon a person; to vent; to bring about or cause. To *wreck* (REK) is to destroy or tear down.

wreckless Misspelling of *reckless.* • Sixteen-year-old Cordara "Cory" Lewis is charged with *wreckless* use of a firearm and involuntary manslaughter. USE *reckless.* • Prosecutors on Friday charged the child's mother, Amy Detlor, 19, with four felony counts in connection with the baby boy's death, including *wreckless* homicide. USE *reckless.*

Though *reckless* is a word (without heed to consequences; careless), *reck* is an archaism (meaning to pay heed or be of concern). And though *wreck* is a word (a shipwreck or the remains of one; the remains of anything badly damaged; destruction or ruin; a person physically or emotionally in poor health), *wreckless* is a misspelling.

> Roy Jester Vowell, 31, of 88 Old Homestead Rd in Big Sandy was also charged with criminal attempt to manufacture meth along with wreckless endangerment, three counts, because of the three children in the house.
>
> —Robert Cobb, *The Camden Chronicle*
>
> In a separate but related incident, Robert Cobb and *Camden Chronicle* have been charged with *reckless* endangerment of the English language.

writting Misspelling of *writing.* • Unfortunately, poor grammar used in the *writting* of the character descriptions completely ruins the value of this extra. USE *writing.* • Todd Alsop said the problem was that McCorkle never followed their warranty claim procedure, which requires all homeowners to put all requests in *writting.* USE *writing.*

The noun of *write* is *writing.* SEE ALSO **playwrite**.

Xx

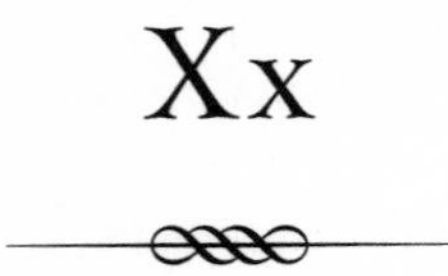

Xmas The *X* stands for Christ and derives from the Greek *Christos,* which begins with the letter *chi* (*X*). *Xmas* is not a derogatory term; it is merely an abbreviated one. The word *Xmas* may be pronounced (KRIS-mes) or (EKS-mes). The spelling *exmas* is disallowable: • I recommend you enjoy the *exmas* party, eat and eat as much as you can. USE *Xmas.* • After the closing of the feast, the *Exmas* celebration officially begins. USE *Xmas.*

x-ray As a noun, *x-ray* may be spelled *X ray* or *x ray, X-ray* or *x-ray*. As an adjective, it may be spelled *X-ray* or *x-ray*. The preferred spelling, for both noun and adjective, is *x-ray*.

X

Yy

yolk Misused for *yoke.* • October 24, 1964, signified the breaking of the *yolk* of colonialism and foreign domination, yet 39 years later, we are not any better. Use *yoke.* • The day featured some of the region's finest fiddle groups, sheep dogs at work, *yolk*-oxen, horse-drawn rides, arts, crafts, a farmer's market, and a traditional banquet feast. Use *yoke.*

Yolk is the yellow substance of an egg. *Yoke* is a frame that harnesses two oxen together; a pair of harnessed animals; something that binds or bonds; something that oppresses.

your Misused for *you're.* • However, if you've done the research and feel good about the area, then *your* likely to make the right choice. Use *you're.* • If *your* not a member, consider joining now! Use *you're.* • *Your* with us or against us. Use *You're.* • *Your* not my type. Use *You're.*

And *you're* is sometimes misused for *your*: • Now, do what *you're* gut tells you not to do. Use *your.* • It's not *you're* fault, so stop blaming yourself. Use *your.*

The misuse of *your* for *you're* (and *you're* for *your*) suggests a certain contempt for the careful use of language; it's one of the countless mistakes that descriptive linguists and other language liberals wouldn't think of censuring but also wouldn't think of making.

your's Misused for *yours.* • Find out how it can be *your's* here! Use *yours.* • Mine is bigger than *your's.* Use *yours.* • Sincerely *your's.* Use *yours.* • Do you want to share your views and ideas? Post *your's* here. Use *yours.* • If you don't see *your's* listed, ask us if it is compatible. Use *yours.* • Do respect the rights and opinions of others, and expect them to respect *your's.* Use *yours.* • If *your's* is over this size, additional fees may apply. Use *yours.* • In the boxes below, please enter the recipient's name and e-mail addresses and *your's.* Use *yours.*

The possessive pronoun *yours* is never spelled *your's* (or *yours'*). Equally incorrect are *her's* (instead of *hers*), *it's* (instead of *its*), *our's* (instead of *ours*), and *their's* (instead of *theirs*).

youthinize Misused for *euthanize.* • If I take it in to the Humane Society they will put it to sleep (*youthinize* it). Use *euthanize.* • I can't rid the world of dumbasses, I wish I could though. I would *youthinize* them all. Use *euthanize.*

Euthanize (YOO-thah-*nize*) means to kill a person or animal so as to relieve pain or suffering. Though *youthinize* is sometimes used to mean to make young or youthful; to revitalize ("Cooper was the major plank in the effort to youthanize the news at CNN, which was perceived as the old fart news network"), it nevers means *euthanize.*

Zz

zenophobia Misspelling of *xenophobia.* • Frankly, if you knew the extent and severity of *zenophobia* in SA you may rethink that statement. USE *xenophobia.* • The International Coalition Against Chattel Slavery, Racism, and *Zenophobia* is working to build a better world, free of racism and slavery and related intolerance. USE *Xenophobia.* • He has hijacked his city to pursue his *zenophobic* agenda at this city's expense. USE *xenophobic.* • Just in case you thought that the disturbing speech that's come to define John McCain's rallies of late has been limited to vaguely racist diatribes and the fear mongery of *zenophobes,* you can now add religious divisiveness as well. USE *xenophobes.*

The prefix *xeno*—meaning foreign, strange, or different—derives from the Greek *xenos,* stranger. *Xenophilia,* the opposite of *xenophobia,* is also sometimes misspelled.

zerox (copy) Misspelling of *Xerox.* • Our crime is that our democracy is not a replica, it is not a *zerox* copy of Western democracy. USE *Xerox.* • In addition, they will arrange to hang a copy at the offices and will preserve another one for producing a *zerox* if asked by anyone. USE *Xerox.*

Xerox, not *Zerox,* is the correct spelling; what's more, *Xerox,* a trademark, ought not to be used as a synonym for photocopy. *Xerography* (zi-ROG-rah-fee) is a photocopying process and the origin of the Xerox Corporation's name.

zoology The pronunciation of *zoology* is (zoh-OL-ah-jee), not (zoo-OL-ah-jee).

Epilogue

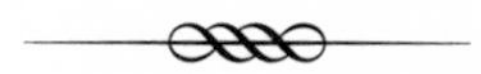

Language Craven: A Definition

On August 23, 2007, the *Wall Street Journal* published "What Did U $@y? Online Language Finds Its Voice," an article in which I was quoted.

Soon afterward, lexicographer Grant Barrett—whose specialty is slang and "new usages" (though he was interviewed for the *WSJ* piece, his words were not used)—wrote, rather bitterly, on his blog:

> Robert Hartwell Fiske isn't a linguist. He's a self-involved curmudgeon—that's not a compliment, but a criticism of his intellectual limitations—who is the go-to guy for the same kind of dismissive claptrap you'll hear from anybody who's speaking on language outside their area of expertise.

In response to this, I commented, also on Barrett's blog:

> Grant Barrett sounds terribly upset, but perhaps I would be, too, if I were not quoted in the *Wall Street Journal.*
>
> You need not have a Ph.D. to have some knowledge of or views on the English language, and the notion, as Barrett suggests, that you need an advanced degree to have a sense of how the language is, or ought to be, used I am sure is abhorrent to a great many people, virtually all of whom have views about how the English language is used.

Barrett, ever clever, replied:

> Please quit, Robert. You've got a third-rate act playing for smarm circles in the few minutes after the Kool-aid is served and just before everyone starts reaching for their throats.

"Please quit," he pleaded. Barrett apparently would have me abandon my prescriptive views (or at least stop talking about them). Better still, I suppose, would be if I spinelessly acquiesced to his exhortation and embraced his own descriptive views.

"Language cravens,"[1] like Barrett and his sort, can be identified by several common characteristics:

- Language cravens, as Barrett nicely illustrates, are intolerant of anyone, who does not have a degree in linguistics,[2] commenting or offering views about the language. If language cravens were less fearful and insecure—less craven—they might more graciously accept, or at least tolerate, views that differ from their own.

Of course, it is the people least knowledgeable about standard English usage and grammar—the people who use slang and new usages, the people who know little, and care less, about grammar—whom LCs both pay the most attention to and give the most credence to.

- Language cravens—impressionable and whiny, as many of them seem to be—celebrate slang, encourage ever-changing usages, and welcome the simplification of grammar. Nothing could be easier, nothing more popular: ease and popularity, of course, being high on the list of what language cravens value.

The less well we use the language, the less thoughtful, cogent, and communicative we likely are. If people continue to heed lexicographers and descriptive linguists and other language cravens, the words will not matter: "Any spelling, any usage, any meaning" . . . the motto of all LCs.

- Language cravens think alike; they are, indeed, lemminglike. They find whatever scraps of intellectual courage they may claim in knowing that other linguists (of whom there are a fair number) think as they do. Rarely do language cravens disagree, which, quite clearly, is the mark of people who think badly. So cowardly are LCs that they support one another in their inability to think for themselves.

However would these LCs manage if the country were overcome by terrorists or North Koreans or evangelical conservatives? Would they tergiversate? Would they become quislings?

- Language cravens, though they welcome all manner of language change (semantic shifts and blends and variant spellings, all of these terms argot for what other people, we non-Ph.D.s, know as errors in grammar and usage), on the whole, try to observe the rules of grammar and avoid making egregious mistakes in usage.

That is, their typically careful writing and observance of standard English belie their linguistic views about language. This is decidedly craven of them.

Barrett and other LCs may one day realize that most people value clear writing and speaking: they want rules of grammar and usage observed; they want distinctions between words maintained. Barrett and the language cravens may one day realize that by promoting the dissolution of standard English, their work has been but folly.

RHF

Acknowledgments

Jan Kardys, my enthusiastic literary agent, within a week or so of sending my proposal to publishers, had an offer from Simon & Schuster. Thank you, enthusiastic Jan.

Colin Harrison, my editor at S&S, told me his having received my manuscript was "propitious," for he, too, values clarity and correctness in language. Rather than simply give the manuscript to a copy editor, Colin read the manuscript and let me know what he thought needed more attention or different wording. Thank you, propitious Colin.

David Russinoff and John Kilgore and Mark Halpern, fine writers and regular contributors to *The Vocabula Review,* reviewed all or part of the manuscript for errors and oversights. Thank you, fine David, fine John, fine Mark.

Appendix A

Mock *Merriam*

Consider the following ten entries from the eleventh edition of *Merriam-Webster's Collegiate Dictionary,* and perhaps you, too, will mock *Merriam*:

1. peruse
Pronunciation: \pə-'rüz\
Function: transitive verb
Inflected Form(s): **pe·rused; pe·rus·ing**
Etymology: Middle English, to use up, deal with in sequence, from Latin *per-* thoroughly + Middle English *usen* to use
Date: 1532
1 a: to examine or consider with attention and in detail: study **b:** to look over or through in a casual or cursory manner
2: READ; *especially*: to read over in an attentive or leisurely manner
—**pe·rus·al** \-'rü-zəl\ noun
—**pe·rus·er** noun

Merriam-Webster's definitions of *peruse* nicely illustrate how useless this book has become. *Peruse* does, indeed, mean to read or examine thoroughly (note the etymology: *per-* means thoroughly) or carefully; to study. Only people who consult valueless dictionaries like *Merriam-Webster's* would believe that *peruse* also means to read or to read casually or hastily.

Merriam-Webster's includes *peruse,* in the sense of "to read cursorily or casually," but it does not include the far more interesting and useful *cuckquean.*

2. def
Pronunciation: \'def\
Function: adjective
Inflected Form(s): **def·fer; def·fest**
Etymology: probably alteration of death (from the phrase to death excessively)
Date: 1979
slang: **cool**

Merriam-Webster has the temerity, the gall to include this absurd, useless word in its dictionary. The eleventh edition was first published in 2003; then, as now, *def,* in the sense of "cool," is seldom heard, rarely read. Most often *def* is used as an abbreviation for "defeated" or "definition" (as in "high-def") or "definitely."

Merriam-Webster's promotes the slang term *def,* but it does not include the far more interesting and useful *solonist.*

3. sherbet
Pronunciation: \'shər-bət\
Variant(s): *also* **sher·bert** \-bərt\
Function: noun
Etymology: Turkish & Persian; Turkish *şerbet,* from Persian *sharbat,* from Arabic *sharba* drink
Date: 1603
1: a cold drink of sweetened and diluted fruit juice
2: an ice with milk, egg white, or gelatin added

As you see, *Merriam-Webster's* offers *sherbert* as a variant spelling of *sherbet. Merriam-Webster's* adds to its compilation the mispronunciations and misspellings that careless people make. The dictionary is not meant to be a record of people's idiocy; it's meant to be a definitive guide on how to spell, pronounce, and define words.

Merriam-Webster's promotes the misspelling, the misuse of *sherbet,* but it does not include the far more interesting and useful *mentulate.*

4. bemuse
Pronunciation: \bi-'myüz, bē-\
Function: transitive verb
Date: 1735
1: to make confused: puzzle, bewilder
2: to occupy the attention of: distract, absorb
3: to cause to have feelings of wry or tolerant amusement <seems truly *bemused* that people beyond his circle in Seattle would be interested in his ruminations—Ruth B. Smith>

Merriam-Webster's maintains that *bemuse* also means amuse (though in Ruth B. Smith's sentence, *bemused* might as easily mean bewildered). In what the clowns at Merriam-Webster would have us believe, we can have little faith indeed.

Merriam-Webster's promotes the misuse of *bemuse,* but it does not include the far more interesting and useful *philogeant.*

5. replete
Pronunciation: \ri-'plēt\
Function: adjective
Etymology: Middle English, from Middle French & Latin; Middle French *replet,* from Latin *repletus,* past participle of *replēre* to fill up, from *re-* + *plēre* to fill
Date: 14th century
1: fully or abundantly provided or filled <a book *replete* with . . . delicious details—William Safire>
2 a: abundantly fed **b:** FAT, STOUT
3: COMPLETE

Replete, which has long meant "abundantly provided or filled, abounding, filled to satiation," now, according to the laxicographers at Merriam-Webster, also means *complete.* It may mean *complete* to people who know little, to people who feel that *replete,* perhaps because it rhymes with *complete,* is simply a synonym for *complete,* but that is no reason for Merriam-Webster to offer this definition in its odious dictionary.

Merriam-Webster's promotes the misuse of *replete,* but it does not include the far more interesting and useful *misosophist.*

6. ginormous

> We are gigantic, enormous idiots. And *don't* you say ginormous because that's not a word. —Emerson on *Pushing Daisies*

Merriam-Webster has added nearly one hundred new words to the 2007 update of the eleventh edition of its *Collegiate Dictionary.* Among them is the word *ginormous,* a synonym of the equally loathsome, equally silly *humongous.*

Combining "gigantic" and "enormous," *ginormous* is a word for which we already have a great many synonyms. It's easy to create synonyms of readily understandable concepts like largeness.

Better than new, ill-defined words for simple concepts like largeness would be new words for less easily understood or less often encountered concepts like bravery or justice or truth. Having more synonyms of words such as these may, over time, affect people's behavior and increase the occurrence of bravery, the spread of justice, or the value of truth.

Ginormous is a silly slang term that does nothing to improve our understanding of ourselves or our world.

The 2007 update of the eleventh edition of *Merriam-Webster's* includes the inanity *ginormous,* but it does not include the far more interesting *alethiology.*

7. odiferous

Pronunciation: \o-'di-f(ə-)rəs\
Function: adjective
Etymology: by contraction
Date: 15th century ODORIFEROUS

Odiferous, called a variant spelling in some dictionaries, and not an entry in others, is actually a misspelling of, and incorrect for, *odoriferous.*

Very likely, *odiferous* derived from, and endures because of, people's failure to pronounce all five syllables.

Merriam-Webster's promotes the misspelling *odiferous,* but it does not include the far more interesting and useful *philodox.*

8. where
Function: conjunction
Date: 12th century
1 a: at, in, or to what place <knows *where* the house is> **b:** at, in, or to what situation, position, direction, circumstances, or respect <shows *where* the plan leads> **c:** the place or point at, in, or to which <couldn't see from *where* he was sitting> <kept that horse and gentled him to *where* I finally rode him—William Faulkner>
2: WHEREVER <goes *where* she likes>
3 a: at, in, or to which place <the town *where* she lives> **b:** at or in which <has reached the size *where* traffic is a problem> <two fireplaces *where* you can bake bread in the ovens—Randall Jarrell>
4 a: at, in, or to the place at, in, or to which <stay *where* you are> <send him away *where* he'll forget> **b:** in a case, situation, or respect in which <outstanding *where* endurance is called for>
5: THAT <I've read *where* they do it that way in some Middle Eastern countries —Andy Rooney>

Though *Merriam-Webster's* fifth definition (meaning its most recent definition), *where* in the sense of "that" is insupportable—at least among those who understand that how they speak and write is a reflection of who they are and how they are regarded. The laxicographers at Merriam-Webster support the insupportable.

Merriam-Webster's promotes the misuse of *where,* but it does not include the far more interesting and useful *cyanope.*

9. publicly
Pronunciation: \'pə-bli-klē\
Variant(s): also **pub·li·cal·ly** \-li-k(ə-)lē\
Function: adverb
Date: 1563

1: in a manner observable by or in a place accessible to the public: OPENLY **2 a:** by the people generally **b:** by a government

The online version of *Merriam-Webster's* calls *publically* a "variant" spelling of *publicly*. The eleventh edition itself, shows:

publicly \'pə-bli-klē\ *also* **pub·li·cal·ly** \-li-k(ə-)lē\

The eleventh edition offers this pronouncement:

> When another spelling is joined to the main entry by the word *also,* the spelling after *also* occurs appreciably less often and thus is considered a secondary variant. . . . Secondary variants belong to standard usage and may be used according to personal inclination.

Merriam-Webster, in stating that a secondary variant both "occurs appreciably less often" and "belongs to standard usage and may be used according to personal inclination" promotes irregular spellings. Merriam-Webster promotes misunderstanding and applauds illiteracy.

Merriam-Webster's includes *publically* and would have us believe it's an acceptable spelling of *publicly,* but it does not include the far more interesting and useful *scleragogy*.

10. miniscule
variant of MINUSCULE

supercede
variant of SUPERSEDE

tho
variant of THOUGH

Among the variant spellings that Merriam-Webster includes in its *Collegiate Dictionary* are *miniscule* and *supercede* and *tho*. Including these words is tantamount to endorsing them. A dictionary lists and defines words available for people to write and speak. If the editors at Merriam-Webster wanted to discourage people from using these spellings, they would not have included them in their compilation. As it is, the editors promote the use of misspelled words and nourish an analphabetic readership.

Merriam-Webster's includes *miniscule* and *supercede* and *tho* as variant spellings of *minuscule* and *supersede* and *though,* but it does not include the far more interesting and useful *moirologist.*

Merriam-Webster's: no longer "your assurance of quality and authority."

Mock *Merriam.*

Appendix B

The Fiske Ranking of College Dictionaries

The Fiske Ranking of College Dictionaries (FRCD) ranks the following six college dictionaries, based on their handling of twenty-five words and phrases:

• *American Heritage Dictionary* (4th ed., 2002)	AH
• *Webster's New World College Dictionary* (4th ed., 2002)	NW
• *Microsoft Encarta College Dictionary* (1st ed., 2001)	ME
• *Random House Webster's College Dictionary* (2nd ed., 2001)	RH
• *New Oxford American Dictionary* (3rd ed., 2010)	OA
• *Merriam-Webster's Collegiate Dictionary* (11th ed., 2003)	MW

This ranking does not consider the number of entries or quality of definitions in each dictionary, nor does it consider etymologies or usage notes, the opacity of the paper or clarity of the typeface, or other features. The FRCD is concerned solely with how these six dictionaries treat the words and phrases listed in the table that follows, for how they treat them provides insight into how they regard the language.

The inclusion in a dictionary of a nonstandard word—even though a usage note may accompany it—is reason enough for its being listed in the FRCD. Its inclusion, whatever a usage note might say, is an implicit sanction, an authorization to use the word, not an injunction against using it. Lexicographers understand this perfectly well, as do the people who consult these books, all of whom pay far more attention to definitions and spellings than they do to remarks about usage.

A check mark (√) signifies that the nonstandard word or usage in the leftmost column is included in the dictionary named at the head of the column. The higher the total number of check marks for a particular dictionary, the more descriptive,[1] that is, the worse the dictionary.

Some of the words designated nonstandard (those not enclosed in parentheses) are not, in themselves, incorrect (*enormity* is a perfectly good word, for instance). These nonstandard words are incorrect only when they are used to mean the standard word—when *enormity* is used to mean *enormousness*—which is how they are being evaluated here. For example, consider terms 1–4: two of the dictionaries offer the spelling *accidently* as an alternative to the spelling *accidentally*; all six dictionaries include entries for *alright* and *anyways*; and two of the dictionaries maintain that *cliché* is a perfectly good adjective.

Nonstandard (Standard)	**AH**	**NW**	**ME**	**RH**	**OA**	**MW**
1. accidently (accidentally)	✓					✓
2. alright (all right)	✓	✓	✓	✓	✓	✓
3. anyways (anyway)	✓	✓	✓	✓	✓	✓
4. cliché (clichéd)				✓		✓
5. disconnect (miscommunication)	✓	✓	✓	✓	✓	✓
6. enormity (enormousness)	✓	✓		✓	✓	✓
7. fatal (fateful)	✓	✓	✓	✓		✓
8. fearful (fearsome)	✓[a]	✓	✓	✓	✓	✓
9. flaunt (flout)	✓	✓		✓		✓
10. get (get)[b]		✓				✓
11. historic (historical)	✓	✓	✓	✓		✓
12. hone in (home in)	✓					✓
13. in behalf of (on behalf of)		✓	✓	✓	✓	✓
14. infer (imply)	✓	✓	✓	✓		✓
15. less (fewer)	✓	✓		✓		✓
16. peruse (read casually)		✓	✓[c]	✓		✓

Nonstandard (Standard)	AH	NW	ME	RH	OA	MW
17. precipitate (precipitous)		✓				✓
18. predominate (predominant)		✓				✓
19. publically (publicly)						✓
20. reoccur (recur)		✓	✓	✓	✓	✓
21. reticent (reluctant)	✓		✓			✓
22. sherbert (sherbet)	✓		✓	✓		✓
23. supercede (supersede)		✓			✓	✓
24. where (that)		✓		✓	✓	✓
25. zoology (zoology)[d]	✓	✓			✓	
Total	**15**	**19**	**12**	**16**	**10**	**24**

a *American Heritage* makes no effort to distinguish these two words. The first meaning of both entries is: "causing or capable of causing fear."

b This entry deals with the pronunciation of *get*: the nonstandard *GIT* versus the standard *GET*.

c Some of these definitions are too entertaining: "to read or examine something in a leisurely or careful way."

d This entry deals with the pronunciation of *zoology*: the nonstandard zoo-OL-ah-jee versus the standard zoh-OL-ah-jee.

As you see, based on these twenty-five words, *Merriam-Webster's Collegiate Dictionary* (11th edition, 2003) has the highest total score—24 of 25. It is, therefore, the most descriptive, the least useful of the six dictionaries.

Two of the newest dictionaries are also two of the best: the *New Oxford American Dictionary* (3rd edition, 2010)—10 of 25—and *Microsoft Encarta College Dictionary* (1st edition, 2001)—12 of 25.[2]

Dictionary publishers might do their readers (and even themselves) a considerable service by labeling their products. As recordings, films, and video games are rated, so let our dictionaries be ranked. Based on the FRCD, *Merriam-Webster's Collegiate Dictionary*'s label would read

"Ranked 24 of 25 in the FRCD" (which would clearly please Merriam-Webster), whereas the *New Oxford American Dictionary*'s would read "Ranked 10 of 25 in the FRCD" (which may or may not please Oxford's editors). This essay, or other explanatory notes, could be printed on the dust jacket flap of each dictionary.

Appendix C

Write to a Laxicographer

Robert Hartwell Fiske encourages you to send the following letter to the editors of descriptive dictionaries. Cut out, copy, or revise the following letter and mail it to:

Executive Editor
American Heritage Dictionary
Houghton Mifflin Company
22 Berkeley Street
Boston, MA 02116

Editor in Chief
Merriam-Webster's Collegiate Dictionary
47 Federal Street
P.O. Box 281
Springfield, MA 01102

Project Manager
New Oxford American Dictionary
Oxford University Press
198 Madison Avenue
New York, NY 10016

Editor in Chief
Microsoft Encarta College Dictionary
St. Martin's Press
175 Fifth Avenue
New York, NY 10010

Editor in Chief
Webster's New World College Dictionary
John Wiley & Sons, Inc.
111 River Street
Hoboken, NJ 07030

Editorial Director
Random House Webster's College Dictionary
Random House Reference
1745 Broadway, 15-3
New York, NY 10019

Dear Sir:

I am appalled by the descriptive posture you take in

____.

I want a dictionary that helps me write and speak clearly and persuasively, not one that promotes any meaning, any spelling, any usage whatever.

Do be sensible.

[Add your own indignation here:]

Regards,

Notes

Prologue

1. From the Merriam-Webster website: "Passing Fancies." (http://www.m-w.com/service/realwords.htm). This webpage, I discovered recently, has been removed from the Merriam-Webster website—perhaps in response to this article, an earlier version of which first appeared in *The Weekly Standard* and *The Vocabula Review* in August 2003.
2. Merriam-Webster does publish a number of "specialty dictionaries," including *Merriam-Webster's Biographical Dictionary, Merriam-Webster's Geographical Dictionary, Merriam-Webster's Dictionary of English Usage, Merriam-Webster's Dictionary of Synonyms,* and *The Merriam-Webster Dictionary of Quotations,* but it has not published a dictionary of slang. Since the editors at Merriam-Webster are so enamored of slang, let them publish a specialty dictionary of it.
3. Lexicographers often try to justify the inclusion of a solecism, such as *disinterested* in the sense of *uninterested,* in their dictionaries by citing examples from authors who have used the word incorrectly. The obvious response to this is that authors—well known or not—are not immune from misusing and misspelling words and have forever done so. In the seventeenth century, *disinterested* did have the meaning "without interest or concern," but for the past three hundred years, the word has meant "impartial or without bias."
4. Though *Merriam-Webster's* is very likely the most descriptive dictionary on the market today (see appendix B), many of my criticisms of it are also applicable to other popular college dictionaries. The *American Heritage Dictionary,* the *New Oxford American Dictionary, Webster's New World College Dictionary, Microsoft Encarta College Dictionary,* and *Random House Webster's College Dictionary,* for instance, all include, and thereby endorse, the solecism *alright.*

5. *Boeotian*: of or like Boeotia or its people, who were reputed to be dull and stupid; *diaskeuast*: someone who makes revisions; *logogogue*: one who legislates over the use of words; *nyctophobia*: an abnormal fear of darkness or nighttime; *myriadigamous*: pertaining to someone who marries all kinds; *ubiety*: the condition of being in a particular place; *womanfully*: with the characteristic grace, strength, or purposefulness of a woman.
6. Of course, it's in the financial interest of dictionary makers to record the least defensible of usages in the English language, for without ever-changing definitions—or as they would say, an evolving language—there would be less need for people to buy later editions of their product.
7. Merriam-Webster boasts that their eleventh edition contains "4,000 usage notes," though they may have miscounted. The book itself has 1,623 pages, so we might expect an average of two or three usage notes a page, but this is hardly what we find. Perhaps, by "usage notes," Merriam-Webster also means synonyms (or "syn," as they abbreviate the word). The editors at the *American Heritage Dictionary* may count more carefully—or better know the meaning of the word *usage*—for they speak of their 300 usage notes, and the *Microsoft Encarta College Dictionary* advertises its 600 usage notes.
8. *New Oxford American Dictionary,* 3rd edition, New York: Oxford University Press, 2010.
9. I've not included the five usage notes that the editors use to illustrate some of their remarks.
10. This is not to say that English, whether spoken or written, always needs to be standard or elegant. That's a burden most people would not want to bear. There are times when informal speech or writing is appropriate and, indeed, welcome. Still, using the English language carefully and correctly is often advisable and necessary.
11. Of course, it could be that I have some small talent in this area.

Epilogue

1. Steven Pinker usurped the term *language maven* (*maven* is from the Yiddish word meaning "expert") from William Safire, who referred to himself as one. But in *The Language Instinct,* Pinker describes language

mavens as self-appointed authorities on the language, prescriptive grammarians who do not have a degree or training in linguistics.

2. By "linguists" I mean, in particular, descriptive linguists. It's they who often become lexicographers.

Appendix B

1. A battle rages between descriptivists and prescriptivists. As I write in the prologue:

> Lexicographers are descriptivists, language liberals. The use of *disinterested* to mean *uninterested* does not displease a descriptivist. A prescriptivist, by contrast, is a language conservative, a person interested in maintaining standards and correctness in language use. To prescriptivists, *disinterested* in the sense of *uninterested* is the mark of people who do not know the distinction between the two words. And if there are enough people saying *disinterested* (and I'm afraid there are) when they mean *uninterested* or *indifferent,* lexicographers enter the definition into their dictionaries. Indeed, the distinction between these words has all but vanished owing largely to irresponsible writers, incompetent teachers, and boneless lexicographers.

2. Had I chosen a different twenty-five words, the scores also would have been different, but I dare say *Merriam-Webster's* still would have ranked highest, that is, worst (most descriptive), and *New Oxford American* and *Microsoft Encarta* still would have ranked lowest, that is, best (least descriptive). Of course, had I chosen twenty-five words and phrases that were once controversial but are now largely accepted, the ones many prescriptivists have lost hope of reclaiming—*transpire (occur), careen (career), disinterest (uninterest), decimate (destroy), enthuse (excite), fortuitous (fortunate),* and so on—it's likely that all six dictionaries would have scored very high (that is, very badly) indeed.

About the Author

Robert Hartwell Fiske is the editor and publisher of *The Vocabula Review* (http://www.vocabula.com), a monthly online journal about the English language. He is also the author of *The Dictionary of Concise Writing*; *The Dimwit's Dictionary*; *101 Elegant Paragraphs*; and *The Best Words*. He is the editor of *Vocabula Bound 1: Outbursts, Insights, Explanations, and Oddities,* and *Vocabula Bound 2: Our Wresting, Writhing Tongue.*

If you would like to comment on *Robert Hartwell Fiske's Dictionary of Unendurable English,* please visit http://www.UnendurableEnglish.com.